Sport and Society

Series Editors

Benjamin G. Rader
Randy Roberts

D1572303

A list of books in the series appears
at the end of this book.

Stagg's University

ATHLETICS

Stagg's University

The Rise, Decline, and Fall of Big-Time Football at Chicago

Robin Lester

University of Illinois Press   Urbana and Chicago

Illini Books edition, 1999
© 1995 by the Board of Trustees of the University of Illinois
Manufactured in the United States of America
1 2 3 4 5 C P 6 5 4 3 2

This book is printed on acid-free paper.

A portion of chapter 1 appeared in an earlier form in *The New
    York Times.* Copyright © 1980 by The New York Times
    Company. Reprinted by permission.
A portion of chapter 3 appeared in an earlier form in the
    Journal of Sport History.
A portion of chapter 4 appeared in an earlier form in the
    Chicago Sun-Times. Reprinted with permission, *Chicago Sun-
    Times* © 1994.

Library of Congress Cataloging-in-Publication Data
Lester, Robin, 1939–
    Stagg's university : the rise, decline, and fall of big-time
football at Chicago / Robin Lester.
        p.   cm. — (Sport and society)
    Includes index.
    ISBN 978-0-252-02128-2 (cloth : acid-free paper)
    ISBN 978-0-252-06791-4 (pbk. : acid-free paper)
    1. University of Chicago—Football—History. 2. Stagg, Amos
Alonzo, 1862–1965. I. Title. II. Series.
GV958.U519L47   1995
796.332'09773'11—dc20   94-34018
                                                               CIP

To Helen,
for the best of reasons

So this story is a test of its own belief—that in this cock-eyed world there are shapes and designs, if only we have some curiosity, training, and compassion and take care not to lie or be sentimental.

—Norman Maclean, *Young Men and Fire*

Contents

Photographs follow pages 98 and 174.

Acknowledgments

This book had its origins in my early love for football when I was a boy growing up on Willa Cather's prairie. That background later combined with the fortunate circumstance of my being asked, as a doctoral student, to unpack and sort the newly arrived Stagg Papers at the University of Chicago in the 1960s—the result being the first intercollegiate football case study in any department of history.

My subsequent teaching and administrative work at Columbia College and four independent schools—Collegiate School and Trinity School in New York City, University High School in San Francisco, and the Latin School of Chicago—deferred this book but made me a better historian. My work as headmaster with the various constituencies of the last three schools named, especially their boards of trustees, helped me understand the quite remarkable pressures that were present in the lives of the trustees, administrators, and coaches in this book. I appreciate that the visionary reach toward greatness of any of these institutional players was often limited by the others and by the realities of mission and budget. It is also wise to remind ourselves that if the actions of our leading historical actors seem at times to be devoid of social or ethical merit, the problem may be in ourselves—our own lack of historical information and life experience and not merely the actors' abysmal sensibilities. And my judgments have also been tempered by the memory of how enormously important athletics were in my young life, even to the despair of my parents. I thank my former coaches and Archie Strachan, emeritus athletic director of the University of St. Andrews in Scotland, who taught the beauty of the dedicated effort rather than the importance of the final score.

It was Robert Rosenthal, curator of Special Collections at the University of Chicago Library, who asked me to unpack the papers of Amos Alonzo Stagg and who then joined Arthur Mann in encouraging me to undertake this unusual cultural history. I remain deeply indebted to both these exemplary scholars and gentlemen—they are deeply missed.

Richard J. Storr and William H. McNeill were leaders of my early seminars at the University of Chicago. They created, in turn, *Harper's University* and *Hutchins' University*. Now, Amos Alonzo Stagg has *his* university and, in the process, links the two presidents. Additional encouragement from the dean of American historians of higher education, Frederick Rudolph, and from one of the keenest early students of football, David Riesman, and subsequent work with Daniel J. Boorstin made the study possible.

I have been helped by those who studied and/or taught in the College of the University of Chicago in the 1930s. From Norman Maclean's delightful instruction on the use of the semicolon through Jimmy Cate's orders to dig up the football skeletons, and from Bernie Weinberg's inspiration to Ned Rosenheim's and Robert Streeter's recent wisdom and wit, the story has taken almost as long in the retelling as it did in the making.

After a score of oral interviews and correspondence with the veterans of 1930s Maroon football, I can only say that these doctors, lawyers, merchants, and chiefs are as impressive a group as any university in creation could wish. I thank them for their time and pains and their life-long demonstration of what student athleticism should be all about.

This book's copious citations—which are included in the indexed material—are only possible where archivists have been so accommodating. Librarians and archivists at the Chicago Historical Society and the New York Public Library and from the universities of Illinois, Iowa, Michigan, Minnesota, Wisconsin, and from Columbia, Indiana, Ohio State, Northwestern, Notre Dame, Princeton, Purdue, and Yale universities have proved responsive and interested in the project. The custodians of the Stagg Collection at the Amos Alonzo Stagg High School in Palos Hills, Illinois, Ann Fleming and Dominic Bertinetti, Jr., were generous with their time and advice. I thank most profoundly the superb University of Chicago Special Collections staff that has worked with me over the past twenty-five years—from the 1960s staff including Al Tannler and Sid Huttner to the present group of Daniel Meyer, Richard L. Popp, Stephen Duffy, and Debora Levine led by Curator Alice D. Schreyer. Stephen Longmire has done a fine job preparing photographs that were faint and seemingly inaccessible.

Members of the North American Society for Sport History have been enormously helpful. I have never been part of a more inclusive, selfless

group of educators. It was at an annual meeting of the group that I met
University of Illinois Press Director Richard L. Wentworth, who early
encouraged me to write this book. Steven A. Riess has been a friend
since the 1960s, and he has also been a major influence in my decision to bring this research to life. He has read the entire manuscript
and done his best to make it worthwhile. William J. Baker, Donald
Mrozek, and Ronald A. Smith provided insightful criticism at important points.

I thank the University of Illinois Press series editors Benjamin G.
Rader and Randy Roberts for their keen sense of substance and style
and the anonymous readers for their criticisms and editing suggestions.
Copy editor Mary Giles has done a fine job with the material I provided. Bob Herguth of the *Chicago Sun-Times* helped me slay the academic
"propensity for pretension." Shirley Schnetzer and Audree Pospisil of
New York and Tracy Franklin-Smith of Chicago were long-time collab-
orators and typists. Of course, it remains my book, and I shall fight to
the death for full credit and criticism!

Finally, I acknowledge the crucial help of my wife Helen Sargent
Doughty-Lester, a many-times-published author whose life and editing are marked by intelligence, humanity, and constancy.

Introduction

When scholars from abroad visit most major American universities they are certain to note the football stadiums. And as the visitors get better acquainted with American higher education, they are prone to ask leading questions about the presence of the football program in academic institutions. Questions regarding the origins, rationale, and effect of football are asked—and although intercollegiate sport continues to be one of the most difficult issues on the modern campus with its congeries of disputes over academic purpose, accessibility, gender, and scale—the host American scholars have little recourse but to admit that the American academy has done remarkably little investigation of the origins and course of this historical phenomenon. College football is now such a part of the American landscape that campus insiders have seldom marked and examined its cultural accretions, and the attentions of the outsider have been sporadic and incomplete. Indeed, football has been one of the totems of national college life that Americans not only wanted but also felt they needed.

The historian's challenge is to place American higher education and its quintessential extracurricular activity—football—within the larger American context and also view it as a cultural organism growing within the university and sometimes dominating individual institutions. This book constitutes the first scholarly case study of the full course of intercollegiate football at an American university. Chicago provides a narrative that has an unusual beginning, a significant middle, and a unique end. And the Chicago case prefigures today's gridiron glory and scandal because Stagg's university pioneered in making football a mass entertainment industry on the American campus.[1]

This book is the story primarily of three men: William Rainey Harper, Amos Alonzo Stagg, and Robert Maynard Hutchins—they are also the major real and mythological figures in the history of the University of

Chicago. The narrative follows Harper and Stagg and their development of intercollegiate football to its death at the hands of Hutchins. Harper was endlessly creative and generous, and he never lived to have to meet the consequences; Stagg, although short, was a man of large presence and attendant fallibilities; Hutchins, although tall, could seem even taller but at times could prove to be very small. None of the three was always heroic, but they were all credible men who made considerable contributions to American life, and they can inform us greatly about our world.

This book is also the story of a modern American university; it is not, however, a chronological register of its presidents and their limestone monuments. I will consider the nature and compass of the generic American university and how it has determined to communicate its mission and life to the larger republic. My book is a history of football, but it is not a game by game record of team and player glory. It is a record, mostly from silence, of an activity that had no place for women, except on the supportive sidelines, and which thus effectively barred them from one of the surest means to personal reward and social acceptance on the American campus. Finally, the story is about American society at work and play and the difficulty we sometimes have determining the difference.

Frederick Rudolph stated that "no episode was more important in shaping the outlook and the expectations of American higher education . . . than the founding of the University of Chicago, one of those events in American history that brought into focus the spirit of an age." John D. Rockefeller's new Baptist university on the prairie opened in 1892 with Thorstein Veblen's original "captain of erudition," William Rainey Harper, at the helm, nine former college or seminary presidents on staff, and ten "authentic leaders of the several disciplines." The new university of John Dewey, Veblen, and Albert Michelson also opened complete with Associate Professor Amos Alonzo Stagg, appointed by his former Yale professor Harper to lead the football team and the Department of Physical Culture (with the largest graduation requirement of any department). Stagg, an all-American football player, was also the first coach to take over much of what college chaplains had done before the abolition of compulsory chapel and the onset of the elective curriculum.[2]

Harper and Stagg were exemplars of the self-made man, and their views on education were characterized by nonelitism and accessibility. Neither man seemed to need, or have time for, a philosophy of education. One looks in vain for any philosophical considerations among the many innovative and precedential football activities that

Harper and Stagg planned and carried out; rather, there are considerations of budget and an acceptance of the football team as a "traveling advertising organization of the University." The Chicago president and his coach were among the first to apply these American approaches to this gentleman's leisure-time activity, just as Harper had been among the first to apply marketplace principles to the genteel traditions of academia.

Harper was perhaps the first American university administrator to grasp fully the educational and philanthropic possibilities of physical education and intercollegiate football. He seized upon those activities as indicative of the kind of academic center he wished to create: one in which few new approaches would be rejected and one in which his uncanny sense of publicity would cut a wide swath. Harper saw football as an important means to elbow his way into the select circle of higher education, and his initiative was successful. Football by itself did not place Harper's university in the first rank of American universities by the time of his death in 1906, but it did take its own proud place as an index of Chicago's ranking at that time. Quite likely, Harper's run would have suffered considerably had he survived his cancer—his obsessive encouragement of people and programs regardless of funding and future would have spelled doom. But Harper did live just long enough to save Stagg and football at Chicago from a university senate with blood in its eye—without his overwhelming presence and memory through the winter of 1905–6 a majority of the senior faculty were prepared to live without the game and its confident little coach, at least for a time, perhaps forever.

If Harper was the "P. T. Barnum of education" running "The Greatest Show on Earth" (in a favored professor's phrase), Stagg served as one of his brilliant ringmasters, and the activity they presented to the public became an important symbol of the university. In fact, Coach Stagg later became so important to the public image of the university and so powerful within that the institution could be properly styled "Stagg's university." Harper and Stagg planted purposefully and cultivated carefully, and yet this football seedling was so perfectly adapted to the American soil that they reaped a harvest their institution couldn't control or house. Finally, even the signal university that had given academic tenure to its football coach and made physical education a part of the curriculum found itself powerless in the face of alumni and general public pressure to produce winning teams; and this occurred where the institution was comparatively new, alumni numbers were sparse, and the values and structure of intercollegiate football seemingly invulnerable.

By 1905, President Harper and his single-minded coach had used the spectator and player reservoir provided by America's second city to make their football team an acknowledged national power. If John D. Rockefeller could repeat Herbert Spencer's social Darwinian principles to his Sunday school class, William Rainey Harper could preside over his university's focused application of the same principles to gain the ascendancy in intercollegiate relationships. It was, indeed, Harper's and Stagg's potent understanding of the human and institutional needs of the late-nineteenth-century university and their own artful athletics of Darwinism that were particularly significant and successful. They employed their dominant demographic position in Chicago and gave no quarter; they bent their public principles and offered no apology. The result of all this furious energy expended on the urban prairie seems to have been a peculiarly American creation: the new model research university that could be a world leader in the production of Nobel prizes and schools of thought *and* a major American intercollegiate athletic power at the same time.[3]

Football at Chicago after the mid-1920s did not follow its own logical development. The logical commercial trail set by Harper and Stagg led to an unalloyed mass entertainment industry. Although Chicago was a national football leader from 1905 to 1925, it finally joined the early eastern leaders in a permanent state of comparative ineptitude. Chicago's last Intercollegiate Conference championship was won in 1924, and the years 1925–39 constituted the decline and fall of Chicago football. Institutions elsewhere, including the other members of the premier Intercollegiate Conference (which came to be known as the "Western Conference" and the "Big Ten"), did follow the logic of Stagg's university, building giant stadiums and employing the new media—radio and newsreels—in order to lodge the entertainment industry on campus. Ironically, Chicago had been a pioneer in creating the attitudes and forces in American intercollegiate athletics that would swiftly erode the university's own position; moreover, the coming of President Hutchins and the forced retirement of Stagg would prompt a unique conclusion to the Chicago story.

The transmogrification of the student-athlete into the athlete-student had gone virtually unrepented and unwept on most American campuses; the iconoclastic Hutchins took notice, and action over the change. But even at Chicago it required an extraordinary combination of factors to abolish the sport. It took an unusual president with attendant administrators and faculty, a series of disastrous seasons, and a mythic view of Chicago's pure athletic past under the sainted Stagg to carry a sufficient number of university constituencies along with the decision. Other institutions dealt with different histories and constituencies from Chicago's and would never be afforded the luxury of such a decision.

And yet an important question about the nature of the American university remained: How could an institution communicate with the larger public after it had disposed of a prime portion of the American college vulgate, the football vocabulary? Most academicians have not dealt with this problem; usually only those who have the task of interpreting and selling the academy to the larger tax-paying or philanthropic public are even aware of the issue. As at least a partial response to the question, we do know that, for whatever the complex reasons, the University of Chicago lost its place as an endowment leader in American higher education during the twenty-one-year Hutchins administration and that the institution's educational ranking was also eroded.

Hutchins's university did not inspire any other major university to emulate its abolition of football. In fact, the twentieth-century intercollegiate football industry has shown a remarkable ability to survive each rare reform binge and to emerge with a firmer hold on institutions and market. It was not until the 1980s that significant reform proved most likely to enter the football arena—and that was not through the traditional and sporadic handwringing of the critics of American higher education but because of the new goals and sensibilities of feminism in American life. The courts' application (due to Congress's Civil Rights Restoration Act of 1988) of the long-deferred requirements of the 1972 Title IX, which prohibited sexual discrimination in the nation's schools and colleges, began to put vital reform pressure on intercollegiate athletics budgets; and this, ironically, reached the prime sport and one considered a male-only preserve: football.

The Knight Commission (1991–93) asked that campus presidents take complete control of college sports and called for measures that would "place the well-being of the student-athlete at the forefront of our concerns." The history of such intentions does not suggest an easy road or a beneficent conclusion because football is so attuned to the American soul as not likely to admit to character defects short of long-term national therapy. The direct challenge of university presidential reformers and the indirect challenge of feminist egalitarians of the 1980s and 1990s have resulted in some traditional business-as-usual models and, most significantly, in bringing the federal legislature and courts into the field of inquiry. This suggests the possibility of a distinctly different outcome through the candid redefinition of the American universities' mission.

If the foreign scholars who visit the University of Chicago ask the location of the football stadium, they will be shown the impressive Joseph Regenstein Library. But before that building existed there was a decaying hulk of a structure alive with vegetation and angular vents within which humankind's first self-sustaining atomic reaction occurred in 1942. And for fifty years before Enrico Fermi's experiments with the Manhattan Project there was the grey, mock-medieval heart of the place—the football stadium of Stagg's university.

Stagg's University

Prologue: William Rainey Harper and Amos Alonzo Stagg

Two men, as different as the deciphering of ancient Semitic texts is from the coaching of young athletes, came together and created in the 1890s a part of a new university that proved so significant in the life of the institution as virtually to define it in the minds of many Americans for more than four decades. They each left the university separately by death and age, only to have the part of the university they created together disposed of as an excrescence.

Soon after the brilliant young Yale Professor Harper had been offered the presidency of the new university on Lake Michigan by its patron, John D. Rockefeller, he wrote to his former student Stagg. Rockefeller's trustees had granted Harper six months at their September 1890 meeting in which to decide, and his contact of Stagg was probably his first recruitment foray to test the waters of the Chicago enterprise. Harper wished to arrange a meeting on "a matter of great importance" that "deserves careful consideration." The breakfast meeting took place at the Murray Hill Hotel in Manhattan in the early autumn of 1890. Within days Stagg wrote his acceptance of Harper's offer of the precedential tenured academic position in physical culture and football in the clear hand and fervent spirit so much his own: "After much thought and prayer I feel decided that my life can be best used for my Master's service in the position which you have offered."[1]

The World of Harper

"I attended store and we had a babe born about 11½ o'clock A.M.," recorded Ohio village storekeeper Samuel Harper in 1856. The babe was named William Rainey, and he would become one of the best-known educators of his time. We know little of the family's life, but the toddler looks out directly from an early portrait, with set jaw and piercing eyes, as if he cannot wait to go to work.[2]

Such an address of the world led to the claim by his major biographer, Thomas Goodspeed, that "the boy made such phenomenal progress" that he entered Muskingum College in his home town of New Concord when he was only ten. The course of study at Presbyterian Muskingum was relatively austere, and Harper made rapid work of the curriculum, especially in languages. When the schoolboy graduated from college at fourteen he was selected to give a lecture in Hebrew that accompanied the usual commencement addresses in English, Latin, and Greek.[3]

Harper was a linguistic prodigy, yet he was considered too young for graduate studies and spent this awkward period helping his father in the family store. Muskingum College's president, Dr. David Paul, whose daughter Harper later married, became the boy's mentor and led Harper to Yale University. Harper was seventeen when he began his graduate studies at Yale in 1873, and if he was remembered as a "somewhat unsophisticated country lad," he hit his stride during his second year and completed his doctoral thesis, "A Comparative Study of the Prepositions in Latin, Greek, Sanskrit, and Gothic," while he was still eighteen.[4]

William Rainey Harper's first full-time jobs in education were teaching schoolboys in Tennessee and serving as principal of the Preparatory Department at Denison University in Granville, Ohio, where he was barely older than his students. Dr. E. Benjamin Andrews, Denison's young president, soon "divined that he had, in this young doctor, acquired a genius." In one revealing episode, when some of Harper's students began to frequent a local saloon he briskly routed them and lectured the proprietor on the proprieties.[5]

Harper also attended to the personal matter of his faith and church affiliation while at Denison. Although he had been surrounded by the Presbyterianism of his family and Muskingum College and had been baptized, Harper had never formally committed himself to the creed or joined a church. He chose to become a Baptist at a prayer meeting in 1876. That freely arrived at denominational affiliation would later prove crucial to his work with John D. Rockefeller and their founding of the University of Chicago.[6]

In 1878, Harper became a Hebrew instructor at the Baptist Union Theological Seminary of Chicago. That seminary was among the top Baptist institutions, and the secretary of the seminary, Thomas W. Goodspeed, described the twenty-two-year-old: "I met him in Presi-

dent Northrup's study. . . . I found a young man, black-haired, stocki-
ly built, 5'7" tall smooth-faced, spectacled, youthful in looks, but so
astonishingly mature in mind that I immediately forgot he was not of
my own age. He had a singularly winning personality. We both yielded to its charm and from that day forward were his devoted friends
and admirers."[7]

After he took up his position, the young Professor Harper could not
understand why colleges and seminaries took the summer off. So he
didn't. He conceived and established a school of Hebrew in the summer of 1881 and soon expanded to include other ancient languages and
campuses; during the 1880s, his summer schools grew to more than
thirty nationwide. When Harper discovered that many Americans who
wished to study the ancient languages could not afford the time or
money for the summer work, he created an extensive correspondence
school. His schools, combined with his instructional books and popu-
larized scholarly work, made the entrepreneurial Harper a national
figure.[8]

Yale took proper note and invited him in 1886 to accept a Semitic
languages chair created expressly for him. John D. Rockefeller was a
leading Chicago seminary trustee, and he pled in vain for Harper to
remain there. The wise Thomas Goodspeed salvaged what he could—
he presciently wrote Harper that summer, "Hold yourself ready to return here sometime as President of a new University."[9]

Collaterally, William Rainey Harper became the chief educational
administrator at New York's Chautauqua Assembly as he moved to Yale.
Perhaps no other job could have provided him with such exposure. Most
important, the Chautauqua experience solidified Harper's administrative
training. Without it he might have struggled for years trying to prove
that his abilities went beyond those of being a kind of ringmaster of linguistic popular culture. He had to hire a faculty of a hundred for the
sixty-day Chautauqua summer session enrolling two thousand students,
and he arranged some three hundred special lectures by eminent educational, literary, and political leaders. This gave Harper an unparalleled
opportunity to scout the land and to hone his emerging capacities for
talent recruitment. He was also witness to the beginnings of the transformation of Yale from college to university under the leadership of Tim-
othy Dwight. All in all, Harper, at thirty, was in the proper position to
prepare for his errand into the wilderness.[10]

The glow of one idea had proved lasting for Harper, and it had been
kindled in 1887 by John D. Rockefeller's reappearance in his life. The
two men contrasted strikingly: Rockefeller, spare and contained, a util-
itarian who was abstemious with food, drink, and expression, while

Harper, short, thick, bouncy, and ebullient, had seldom met an idea he wouldn't try—and yet both possessed Baptist credentials that brought them together and kept them together. The philanthropic Baptist talked with Harper about Rockefeller's desire to found an ambitious new university in New York City. Harper leaped at the concept and joined his old Chicago colleagues in diverting Rockefeller's attention and riches westward. Soon, Rockefeller was in deeply, as Harper led him toward the founding of a major American university.[11]

Perhaps George E. Vincent, who worked with Harper in the early university and then worked with the Rockefellers when he headed their foundation, put the persistent rumor of Harper's unrestrained use of the oilman's purse in the proper wry perspective when he stated, "This is a far too simple and romantic notion. If it had been true, and Dr. Harper had lived, it is a question whether even the Rockefeller fortune could have survived."[12]

Many contemporaries saw the University of Chicago in its first decades as "Harper's university," a concept that Richard J. Storr, a historian of the institution's early years, formalizes in *Harper's University: The Beginnings.* Storr does not see Harper's early university plans as following some theoretical new model university; rather, "As a university president he did not deduce the elements of the institution placed under his care from an idea or formal theory about the universe and the ways men must seek to understand it. Rather, his manner of working was inductive, a word which he used constantly. His plan was a mosaic, the bits of which were cemented into a pattern by a generalization derived from a single case, his own life as an investigator and teacher of the Bible."[13]

Perhaps Harper's method was never better illustrated than by his proud institution of a Latin American course. A young history graduate fellow, Elizabeth Wallace, who wished to study that subject found no encouragement from Head Professor Hermann von Holst, just arrived from the University of Freiburg: "'Vy did you come to me? I know notings von tose countries. For me tey do not exist. Tey are tead!'" "I carried my problem to Dr. Harper," Wallace recalled, "and he was delighted. He liked nothing better than to find an unexplored field. This was an auspicious year to further the study of Latin America. . . . It was a new world opening up. He would make an appropriation for books, they should be ordered immediately. I should give a course on Latin American history and institutions in the spring quarter, and we should be the first institution in the country to initiate such studies."[14] Wallace taught the course the following spring.

President Harper was also in the vanguard of nineteenth-century educational leaders who sensed that the future of American higher education belonged to the specialists—and no one encouraged specialization more thoroughly. One of the young graduates he had recruited from a women's college arrived on campus mere days before the university opened. She inquired of a woman who was on her hands and knees scrubbing the floor of Cobb Hall, "President Harper?" and received the response, "I don't know." "Dr. Goodspeed?"—"I don't know. I don't know nothin' but just scrubbin'." When Myra Reynolds related her story to Harper, he was delighted and claimed it proved Chicago would be great because, "We've already begun to specialize!"[15]

William Rainey Harper viewed simply as a giant of American higher education or the Colossus of the Midway blurs him as Christian and teacher, a not inconsiderable part of the man.[16] Later University of Chicago generations have created a Harper in their own image, one that can be taken proudly into their rational, secular, and specialized world. The prevailing image of the founding president is difficult to reconcile with a good deal of what Harper felt and wrote. And to understand the peculiar place of intercollegiate football in Harper's university, and the special relationship Amos Alonzo Stagg enjoyed with Harper, it is necessary to meet the religious Harper.

Perhaps Harper's most revealing expression regarding what he thought important in life and learning appeared in *Religion and the Higher Life: Talks to Students,* which contained the addresses he had given to students at the University of Chicago and elsewhere. Harper dedicated the book "to my father and mother in honor of the fiftieth anniversary of their marriage" and felt that the collection of his thoughts "which it has been my privilege to address in these last years to companies of young men and women . . . discharged in a measure a responsibility which has weighed upon me more heavily than any other connected with the office which I have been called to administer." That "responsibility" was the place of religious faith in the university. In this volume Harper, one of the most important founders of the modern research university in America, addressed "whether, as a matter of fact, it was growing more and more difficult to deal with subjects of this kind in a university atmosphere."[17]

Harper's most pointed discussion of the connection between Christian faith and the purpose of the university occurs in his chapter "Religious Belief among College Students." Here, he dealt with his unease about the modern university's influence on religious belief: "It would be curious, and something very sad, if the institutions founded by our fathers as training schools for Christian service should come to be centers of influence destructive to that same Christianity." Harper's concern was addressed to all of American society: "There has been a peculiar and a fatal lack of proper religious instruction for the young during the past twenty years, and we are just beginning to feel its terrible effects." Then the sturdy and optimistic Chatauquan rallied with the question and answer, "Does college education lead men into infidelity? No. . . . I maintain that infidelity, so far from increasing, is rapidly decreasing."[18]

President Harper's volume concluded with his hortatory prediction and encouragement to nation and scholar: "America, then, is to be the leader of the world's influence and thought during the next twenty centuries, just as Babylonia, Syria, and England, each in turn, has been leader during the past centuries. . . . Centuries will pass; and gradually humanity will come to recognize the significance of love; gradually Jesus the Christ will come to reign in the hearts of men. In this work of educating humanity to understand God and itself, America is the training-school for teachers."[19] Storr observes, somewhat diplomatically after quoting from Harper's chapter on Christian apologetics in the same volume, "These were the words of an earnest man, who practiced inquiry, loved God, and sought to prepare the young, both in mind and soul, for life in the family embracing mankind."[20]

Physical culture in the curriculum and intercollegiate football in the extracurriculum were part of President-elect Harper's mosaic. Like so much else that developed at Chicago in the first decade, the sound body ideal had an autonomy and integrity all its own in the person and vision of Harper's appointee to lead it. But in this area Harper got considerably more than he may have planned for: Amos Alonzo Stagg was the youngest, least experienced, and yet the most publicly celebrated of all Harper's department leaders. Moreover, Stagg's department was to prove one of the most seminal of all in Harper's university, whether or not that was precisely intended. In fact, Hutchins's university forty years later found itself faced with personnel and programmatic challenges from within (Stagg's overdue retirement) and without (a disastrous intercollegiate football situation) that had their genesis at the hotel breakfast where Harper pressed a tenured academic appointment upon the callow Yale all-American. Certainly, the way that Robert Maynard Hutchins chose to deal with the oldest tenured veteran of the Harper years and with the most visible residue of that entrepreneur's labors—football—would provide the greatest notoriety of Hutchins's university.[21]

The World of Stagg

President Harper's student and colleague Amos Alonzo Stagg was born in August 1862, the fifth of eight children, in a workman's cottage in West Orange, New Jersey. His father had been bound out at age seven as an apprentice to a shoemaker, had run away at sixteen, and taught himself to read and write by age twenty. He supported his family by cobbling and by working as a general laborer. Alonzo remembered his father as poor but "superbly honest and just." He also remembered his father in another, unusual way: In a rough neighborhood known for its public drunkenness, including many of his friends' parents, Stagg's father was temperate. The son responded in a characteristic manner— he became a teetotaler and never touched either tobacco or coffee.[22]

Young Stagg attended the local public school in West Orange. His circle of friends began dropping out of school after three or four grades; at best, they were satisfied with a grade school education. But Lonny was different, and his desire to continue his education probably came from his desire to excel at sport. The boy was a gifted natural athlete, and his dearest childhood and adolescent memories were of his experiences as a pitcher. There was no local secondary school so he had to pay nonresident tuition at nearby Orange High School. He entered ninth grade at eighteen, his grade school progress having been slowed by his heavy work schedule with his father. He remembered working his way through high school in three years by "tending furnaces, lawns and gardens, cutting wood, beating carpets and other boys jobs when my father did not need me." His father did need him frequently, especially in the Jersey meadowlands harvesting grain by hand, and Stagg was proud of his skill with the scythe. The young athlete concluded matter-of-factly, "By inheritance I had a stocky, sturdy body, and work and play developed it."[23]

The assistant principal at Orange High School, a Yale graduate, was the first to suggest college work to Stagg, who remembered, "When I objected that I had no money he told me of several of his college mates who had worked their way. The suggestion fell on fertile soil, for I was restless with an ambition I saw no way of realizing. When nearly seventeen, I joined the First Presbyterian Church of Orange." The church introduced him to a different social stratum, one that would understand and give substance to his dreams and rising ambition. Indeed, he related that "a devout earnest girl" from the church "urged on a half-formed aspiration I had for the ministry, and properly to fit myself I should go to college."[24]

Stagg discovered at graduation in 1883 that he could not pass the Yale entrance examinations based upon his high school work. An Orange High School classmate and friend, George Gill, son of the mayor of Orange, went on to Phillips-Exeter Academy in New Hampshire as a "post-graduate" to make up the same entrance deficiency. Young Gill wrote enthusiastically to Stagg that fall and informed him of the possibility of financial aid. "When he came home for the Christmas holidays," Stagg remembered, "he was so persuasive that I decided to return with him." It was a big step for young Stagg—he had been sixteen before he first journeyed the sixteen miles into New York City, and he had never slept away from home. His mother "wept at every meal from the day I decided to go back with Gill until I went. My father's backing, however, kept my spine erect." George Gill gave him one of his own suits, and Stagg determined not to accept any more "favors" from anyone else. It was an important point of pride, and when his Presbyterian minister seemed to reach out in a farewell handshake with money, Stagg shook his other hand.[25]

Stagg was twenty-one when he arrived on the Exeter, New Hampshire, train platform, clad only in Gill's suit and no underwear to commence "three months of the bitterest winter I ever spent." He lived in an unheated garret room and subsisted on soda crackers, stale bread, and milk for 16 cents a day. He worked as a "PG" (postgraduate) on Latin, Greek, and mathematics and pitched for the Exeter baseball team that spring.[26]

Dartmouth attempted to recruit Stagg when they heard of his superb play at Exeter. The president of the Dartmouth Athletic Association wrote Stagg that he could be certain of a place on the team, adding, "There is no first class college in New England where a man can get along on less money. A large number of the fellows pay their own way, receiving, of course, considerable aid in the way of scholarships, and so on." But Dartmouth did not have a divinity school, and Stagg had already written regarding admission to President Noah Porter of Yale. Porter replied in his own hand: "To good scholars the college has given from the Ellsworth Fund $175 a year. Beyond this the college, as such, can do little or nothing; but opportunities for self help present themselves and are soon discovered by those who keep their eyes open to discern them."[27]

Stagg sat the Yale entrance examinations in June and passed. He took some pains in his autobiography to establish his impressive state of mind and morals at the time: "A boy sitting alongside me asked me to whisper the answer to some question. I looked at him in shocked amazement. As a younger boy, in playing raggedy mole, in which we raced around several blocks, other boys cut the corners when out of sight, but I scrupulously ran the full course always."[28] Stagg matriculated at Yale in September 1884, and remained until 1890. His Yale career included four years as an undergraduate, one year as a part-time student (1888–89), and one year as a Yale Divinity School student (1889–90).

When Stagg arrived at Yale he was a twenty-two-year-old would-be divine with $32 to his name. Tuition was $50 each term less his abatement of $20.20 as a future divinity student. Once again, Stagg found a drafty garret room, for which he paid $1 a week. He allowed himself 5 cents for breakfast, 10 cents for the noon meal, and 5 cents for dinner, a diet that led to the first illness of his sturdy young life. When a doctor recognized the undergraduate's malnourishment and ordered an adequate diet, Stagg found a job waiting table for his board in a student dining club peopled by the well-born and by future national leaders (e.g., Henry Stimson). Within three years, the waiter had been elected to Yale's most elite company, Skull and Bones.[29]

Stagg was an active undergraduate if a mediocre scholar; he sang with the Yale Glee Club (first tenor) and served as the financial manager of the *Yale News*. He failed to make the football team in 1884 and did not play regularly until 1888. Instead, he concentrated on the baseball team, and it did not take him long to become the ace Yale pitcher. He then led the team for six years, compiling a 42 and 8 record against Harvard and Princeton. He had many impressive performances on the mound. His finest was against Princeton in 1888, when he struck out twenty Tiger batters and allowed two hits.

But all was not perfect. The unsparing *New York Sun* reported a rare Yale loss to Harvard, 9-8, and explained, "Stagg didn't pitch in his usual good form. He attended a reception at Wellesley last night, and didn't return until the small hours of the morning. Perhaps that dissipation accounts for the loss of today's game." The *Boston Herald* commented, "The perennial Stagg was in the box for Yale, but he was not the Stagg of old. The same broad smile was there; the same easy, courteous manner; the same peculiar style of delivery" and yet the reporter was baffled by the unusual loss. Perhaps the play of Stagg's teammates provided the best explanation—fully eight of the Harvard runs were unearned, and only one Yale teammate joined Stagg as an error-free player that day. He completed his baseball playing career at Yale as a graduate student in 1890, when he was nearly twenty-eight.[30]

Baseball made Amos Alonzo Stagg a collegiate hero well beyond New Haven. As *The Young Men's Journal* stated in 1890, "Of America's distinguished young men none perhaps are more widely known than

A. Alonzo Stagg, the robust Christian athlete of Yale College." He was known not only as a collegiate hurler, but also as a committed amateur who refused many a major league offer to become a professional player. Stagg recalled the time in 1887 when his college team played the Boston Nationals and defeated them: "In the ninth inning I struck out Ten-Thousand-Dollar Kelly, the Babe Ruth of his time, and became a baseball celebrity. As Kelly reached the bench where his team mates were, he is reported to have said in a tone of mingled surprise and disgust, 'Think of a son of a gun who can pitch like that going to be a minister.'"[31]

Stagg claimed in his autobiography, written during the 1920s, that he refused all the baseball contracts for two reasons: his "loyalty to Yale" and what he termed "the character of professional baseball." He described the latter as a game played by "a hard-bitten lot" surrounded by shady hangers-on and ready sex and alcohol; indeed, "the whole tone of the game was smelly." Stagg's antipathy toward professional sports continued throughout his life. He believed that graduated players should go to work, because if they played professionally they became used to "earning large sums of money, with comparatively little exertion," and "there is a tendency to lead a young man to become a 'sporting loafer.'"[32]

Stagg remained at Yale after his graduation in 1888 because he wished to study divinity. He was then elected to the prestigious position of student secretary of the Yale YMCA, the most active and best known of the local chapters among American colleges. He led the group impressively but soon found that the job was so demanding that he had no time for full enrollment in the Divinity School. He enrolled instead for a few courses, including a biblical literature course taught by Professor William Rainey Harper. The thirty-two-year-old instructor was only four years older than Stagg; Harper later remembered Stagg as a student "when he was at the height of his student athletic career at Yale" and recalled that "an attachment was formed between us that, so far as I am concerned, has grown closer every year since that time."[33]

Stagg also determined in the fall of 1888 to go out for football in earnest. The Yale football program had been assisted by Walter Camp for years and was the strongest in the country. Stagg must have felt comfortable with this football community because a captain of the period attributed Yale's success to "so many praying men" on the teams. Camp's squads during Stagg's undergraduate years had included George W. Woodruff (later to become attorney general of Pennsylvania and the University of Pennsylvania's seminal football coach) and the artist Frederick Remington. The group Stagg joined included Woodruff, William "Pudge" Heffelfinger, Gifford Pinchot, and Lee McClung. Heffelfinger was considered the first "big man" to make the all-American team, Pinchot became a national conservation leader and governor of Pennsylvania, and McClung later served as treasurer of the United States. Stagg won a starting position at right end on the 1888 Yale unit that set an all-time major college record by scoring 698 points to none for their opponents.[34]

Stagg made many appearances throughout the East for the YMCA. The *Brooklyn Eagle*'s October 1888 headline "He Fires Hot Balls of Truth over the Home Plate" heralded an enthusiastic report of a Stagg YMCA sermon. His face bruised and an eye blackened by a recent football scrimmage, he drew a large audience. Many were young men who came because they were curious "to see the great pitcher who had refused a big salary for the sake of studying for Christian work." The reporter continued:

> Mr. Stagg chose no text but went right into the subject, which was largely personal. He spoke of his own faith in Christ and love for his work, and urged others to follow his example in serving God. . . . He believed a man was better every way for being a Christian, and thought it a duty that young men owed to their country as to themselves. . . . To young men, he said, he looked for the future of the country and to young men he appealed. He knew that they would feel better satisfied with themselves and the world and have a broader view of life if they became Christians. He did not close with a set peroration. When he got through he just stopped and walked back to his seat.[35]

The large group of young men who attended to see the well-known Yale athlete left immediately when Stagg sat down. They didn't want to chance having to undergo the evangelistic mop-up work of the YMCA professionals who followed him.

In fall 1889 Stagg was reelected YMCA secretary, and this time he ensured that he had time to enroll in the Yale Divinity School as a full-time student. He played football again, and the successful Yale season was followed by his selection to Walter Camp's first all-American team at left end. However, Stagg left divinity school after one year, never to return. It must have been a wrenching decision, because he had planned on entering the ministry virtually since joining the Presbyterian church as a seventeen-year-old. In his autobiography, Stagg stated, "An inability to talk easily on my feet led me to put aside the cloth and to leave Yale in 1890" and expanded that bare statement for more than a page. His perception of his speaking difficulties seems to have grown during the late 1880s, perhaps along with his taxing studies. A couple of years after he decided to leave, the correctness of his action was confirmed when he overheard two student conference colleagues agree that they could not "understand why Stagg simply can't make a talk." One of the few contemporary judgments about his speaking ability at this time appeared in the admiring *Sporting Times:* "Stagg talked like a slow but sure thinker and in an easy, colloquial manner that won the confidence of his hearers without a doubt."[36]

Stagg had arrived on campus at a propitious time: American religious groups were using new programs and approaches to take aim at the souls and bodies of young people. American distrust of physical amusement, based in Puritanism and other English colonial thought and experience, was dissolving on nineteenth-century college campuses because of the needs of harried administrators and their postadolescent charges. Administrators increasingly welcomed organized sports in order to replace reckless hazing and other undergraduate excesses. Students, in turn, found new meaning and enjoyment in the predominantly student-run athletic associations, and many faculty applauded the helpful degree to which such physical pursuits prepared the young athletes for serious study. Moreover, these developments were undergirded by the general growing belief that physical energy and training constituted an essential feature of manly character.[37]

The missionary impulse, whether applied to religion or sport, has had a significant role in the history of American higher education. The cultural transit of rugby football from England to eastern America in the 1870s was followed by the movement of the new variety westward as intercollegiate football followed the frontier of American academic life. And the cultural transference to the West, and later to the South, was greatly aided when football was linked with evangelical purposes by believer and secularist alike. Graduates of eastern colleges combined their evangelical instincts and vocabulary with their love for football as they journeyed west. One western professor noted in 1895 that at "many western colleges football is comparatively new." He figured, therefore, that it was reasonable to allow men to go from college to college "doing missionary work." Puritan Yale and Presbyterian Princeton led the football missionary effort of the late nineteenth century just as they had led the earlier religious one; Unitarian Harvard lagged, as it had earlier in the century.[38]

Lonny Stagg was a man of strong allegiances and commitment; the loss of one career goal would soon be replaced by another. He had already commenced summer work after his college graduation in 1888 by taking charge of the athletics program at Chautauqua in upstate New

York, where he worked on the staff with William Rainey Harper. In successive summers he served at Dwight L. Moody's student conferences in Massachusetts and Wisconsin, tending to the evangelical young. These self-improvement programs sponsored by American evangelical groups made good use of the decade's best-known college athletic hero as an exemplar of muscular Christianity.

A new opportunity was presented the same year Stagg left divinity school, when the International Young Men's Christian Association Training School was to open in Springfield, Massachusetts. The head of the physical training department was one of the leading spokesmen for evangelical athleticism, Dr. Luther H. Gulick, who lost no time in persuading the Yale all-American to join his student body and staff. The first "class" of four included Stagg and McGill University graduate James Naismith, who invented basketball that winter as a course project. Soon Stagg, along with a suitcase of lantern slides, was on a promotional tour as an instructor for the new school, talking about what he knew best—how to be a Christian athlete. Later, when Stagg went west, the *Chicago Tribune* reported that his "mission is to spread the gospel of football throughout the land, to make the matter so plain that even a child can understand it."[39]

The opportunity at Springfield College proved especially auspicious for the resourceful Yale graduate. Stagg became coach of the new institution's football team, the Christians, and for the next two seasons received widespread recognition as a superb trainer of young men. He also showed the entrepreneurial spirit that was to take him far. He coached his team at the first indoor football game played in America, a midnight contest that was part of an elaborate spectacle at Madison Square Garden. Amos Alonzo Stagg had been well prepared for having breakfast with William Rainey Harper and the most important job interview of his life.[40]

The novels of Horatio Alger were Amos Alonzo Stagg's often-expressed inspiration, and he claimed that "there is something of Alger in my story." He admitted that although he had read little of Alger, he subscribed to "his creed." Stagg thought the Algerian heroes "arrived at their goal by the practice of three virtues—work, courage and honesty." He missed a fourth element—luck—which was perhaps more crucial to the shaky Algerian plot and hero's success than the other three.[41]

Stagg must have believed in salvation by works, which is how he preferred his Alger and his autobiography to read. There was no allowance in Stagg's self-made gospel for some Algerian luck or for Divine Grace. If Divine Grace had been present, Stagg would have been a very different, perhaps more humble and hesitant, man and leader—and his story would be very different and probably not worth the telling. The likelihood that his career at Chicago would provide an instructive universal case study would certainly have been greatly diminished.

The strength and force of Stagg's personality will be demonstrated in the following pages. He had the characteristics of a medieval saint: He was long on focus, short on perspective. And, like the saints, he was not above assuming the martyr's mantle, so much so that he came to identify his own best interests with those of his institution. Stagg's career and contributions demonstrate that he had overcome much with the odds against him (Alger, *The Odds against Him,* 1890). Those searing early experiences had forced him into a siege mentality. It was frequently the five-foot-six-inch Amos Alonzo Stagg facing the world alone (Alger, *Facing the World,* 1893). Therein lay an enormous need and an attendant strength and capacity to move others and to create.

1

The Origins of Intercollegiate Football at the University of Chicago, 1890–94

We will have a college here soon if this keeps up.
—Trustees Secretary Thomas W. Goodspeed
after victory over Michigan, 1893

President Harper and Coach Stagg

President Harper's breakfast of "great importance" had led to Stagg's prayerful acceptance of Harper's handsome offer. But before they could embark on their intercollegiate adventure in physical culture, many a month passed and many a letter was exchanged. A review of the breakfast discussion that morning in New York is necessary to understand these men and their relationship. We have only one record, and it is Stagg's:

> Dr. Harper then unfolded his plans for the University and broached the subject of my heading up the athletic department, first offering me a salary of $1500.00. The whole idea was new to me and I kept still and just thought. Dr Harper did not wait long but said, "I'll offer you $2000.00 and an assistant professorship." Still I kept silent and thought. Decision and action were dominant characteristics in Dr. Harper's make-up and probably thinking that the question of salary, which was furthest from my mind, was causing my hesitation, he enthusiastically burst in with "I'll give you $2500.00 and an associate professorship, which means an appointment for life."[1]

It is a fine story. Unfortunately, there is no record of Harper's sense of the meeting—he was much too busy with his scores of other meetings, but we can form some view of Stagg's veracity based upon subsequent correspondence.

A year after Stagg's master's call to Chicago, the young coach intended to break his commitment to Harper. His 1891 letter to his president was ostensibly candid, but it was also convoluted, coercive, and self-serving. He claimed he was writing to put Harper at ease regarding press dispatches that had reported his consideration or acceptance of posts at Yale or Pennsylvania. Stagg admitted to considering firm offers from both, receiving a committee from Pennsylvania, and at least discussing a position with a Harvard professor. He disingenuously asked Harper's "advice as a good friend to me what I ought to do or what you would do." He then noted that the Harvard and Pennsylvania offers "appealed to me chiefly from the financial side" because he would receive much more than at Chicago. He allowed the Yale proposal had the most appeal, reiterated he was still mindful of his "pledged word to go to Chicago," and catalogued the personal, financial, and physical advantages of the New Haven institution. The last advantage listed was that Yale would give him the "best possible chance for Christian and moral work." Stagg concluded that he felt the "surpassing magnitude" of the Yale position over Harper's Chicago job "in every way."[2]

Then Stagg got down to business: "I must confess also that since the day of my giving you my decision I have had constant reminders in the way of financial offers which have made me feel that I was not doing rightly by myself in agreeing to go to Chicago for so small a salary." He finished his plea by asking Harper, "Does not your unbiased judgment concur with that of all with whom I have spoken that my opportunities are greater and the arrangements more satisfactory at either Yale or the University of Pennsylvania?"

On the day of Stagg's writing, Harper had written to Stagg regarding newspaper reports of Yale's overtures, had nervously likened them to those of The Johns Hopkins University a year previous, and assured him, "We are depending upon you." Stagg had indeed revealed his inconstancy earlier, for newspaper reports indicated that The Johns Hopkins University desired Stagg as physical culture director, and Harper wrote to Stagg "to stand firm for Chicago." In the event, he did stay with Harper, but his variable behavior could not have left Harper thoroughly confident in him. This record of letters, which Harper preserved, should prompt viewing those events or judgments for which there is only Stagg's heavily ghostwritten autobiographical word with some unease, not to say skepticism.[3]

The coach was unsparing of his older colleague. A year later, about four months before the university was to open, Stagg felt Harper was slow with the gymnasium funding so he urged colloquially, "Get a *hustle on* for the gymnasium."[4]

The appointment of Amos Alonzo Stagg as "Associate Professor and Director of the Department of Physical Culture and Athletics" with full tenure was a double precedent in the history of American higher education. It was the first tenured academic appointment of a physical education department head with universitywide responsibilities, and it was the first tenured appointment of a coach of intercollegiate athletic teams. The idea of an intercollegiate "coaching profession" was unknown in 1892, and this innovation began the professionalization of college coaching in America.[5]

The arrangement was remarkable for its time because it reformed the prevailing noxious control of intercollegiate activity by students and alumni and gave stature to the new pedagogy of physical education. President Harper probably vaguely intended the Department of Physical Culture to be a regular academic department, but several structural and cultural factors no doubt mitigated this intention. The department's head, Stagg, was not given the usual "head professor" designation of the other departments, although he was appointed to a fully tenured post. Moreover, a superior faculty body, the Board of Physical Culture and Athletics controlled departmental requirements, course offerings, and finances, and Harper appointed the board. The board also controlled all intercollegiate athletic activities, sometimes meeting in two separately minuted consecutive sessions, one as the Board of Physical Culture, the other as the Board of Athletics. Harper entrusted this new body with large responsibilities, much larger and more complex than the nonathletic president could have realized: Its "business," Harper soon explained, was "to guard with jealous care the purity of college athletics." Finally, many members of the faculty found it difficult to extend full academic patronage to the new discipline, which seemed both too common and too uncommon—it lacked intellectual rigor and academic ancestry. Stagg soon used the intercollegiate activities of his department to gain interest and to disarm the faculty apprehensions regarding the curricular work.[6]

The purpose and place of the Department of Physical Culture and Athletics remained constant during the first decade. The physical education department requirement was the largest of any in the college. Every junior college student (years one and two at the University of Chicago) was required to take three quarters of work each academic year, and every senior college student (those in years three and four) took two quarters of work a year. The regular courses met four and one-half hours a week, and the activities were planned to correlate with each student's needs as determined by physical examinations. The Women's Department of Physical Culture was a subdepartment under Stagg's department. It was led by Gertrude Dudley, who also served as a women's residence hall head.[7]

Stagg concentrated where his personal satisfaction and the public interest lay. As a result, as early as 1901 Harper grew uneasy over Stagg's reported exclusive concern with intercollegiate athletics to the detriment of the physical culture work. The president reported that "it is maintained that the whole attention of the administration" was given to intercollegiate athletics "and is thus given to very few students. The average student has nothing which interests him or really benefits him."[8] Stagg's intense devotion to his intercollegiate enterprise allowed of no appropriate response, and Harper did not pursue the matter; in fact, no response was demanded for about two decades, at which point inattention had produced disaster and the required program was scrapped. Women's physical culture work also suffered from Harper's and Stagg's other interests, and until the 1915 opening of Ida Noyes Hall, women had inferior athletic facilities.[9]

No other department in the new university received as much newspaper comment as Stagg's department. After all, Stagg brought his national reputation to Chicago, a city none too sure of itself when it came to comparisons with eastern cities and their institutions. Hence, journalists perceived the significance of Harper's recruitment of Stagg more readily than they did the president's wooing and winning men and women prominent in academic pursuits. Stagg and the intercollegiate athletic apparatus at the new institution also represented the area that most Chicagoans could readily understand and appreciate as readers and spectators. Football was an excellent vehicle, reasoned the nonelitist salesmen Harper and Stagg, with which to promote the university and symbolize American values.

William Rainey Harper, the "P.T. Barnum of education" whose University of Chicago was "The Greatest Show on Earth," in Professor J. Laurence Laughlin's prickly phrase, realized that the opportunities for popular promotion were great in athletics. Although one journal quoted him as being a "strong believer in the physical culture theory" of required work, most of his attention was given to intercollegiate sport. Harper, the "born propagandist," early dreamed of athletic success— he simply believed that a great school demanded great teams. "The University of Chicago believes in football," he stated. "We shall encourage it here."[10]

Harper's strong views had been a "very pleasant surprise" to Stagg during a talk the men had before the university opened. Stagg wrote that "in answer to my question what his attitude would be towards intercollegiate athletics," Harper answered, "I am most heartily in favor of them. I want you to develop teams which we can send around the country and knock out all the colleges. We will give them a palace car and a vacation too." Stagg's response: "These words have made me very happy, for it means such a vast deal more pleasure to me."[11]

One of Harper's strongest assertions regarding the place of football at the university was provided at a convocation in 1894. No doubt prompted by the nationwide criticism of the sport that season, he addressed the arguments that opposed football on the likelihood of injury and death: "We may grant that limbs are broken and lives lost; but we must remember that there is no form of life's activity which is not attended with risk." He concluded:

> If the world can afford to sacrifice the lives of men for commercial gain, it can much more easily afford to make similar sacrifices upon the altar of vigorous and unsullied manhood. The question of a life or of a score of lives is nothing compared with that of moral purity, human self-restraint, in the interests of which, among college men, outdoor athletics contribute more than all other agencies combined. . . . The University has encouraged athletic sports; it will continue to encourage them. We believe that this is an important part of college and University life.[12]

Harper thus joined Stagg publicly as evangelist of the gridiron gospel, and the president's speech was applauded vigorously. Later, in one of his fullest statements of the 1890s, Harper declared, "The athletic work of the students is a vital part of the student life. Under the proper restrictions it is a real and essential part of college education." Then he set stringent standards for the conduct of student athletics, including the students' personal and academic behavior.[13] My narrative will demonstrate the degree to which Harper's university followed his rigorous prescription.

Stagg's own playing experience, his coaching at Springfield and Chautauqua, and his missionary interests led by 1891 to his threefold rationale for his intended place in intercollegiate athletics. He admitted that he was "very, very fond" of outdoor intercollegiate activity, that he felt it could "create a strong college spirit," and that it was "a fine chance to do Christian work." The young coach-evangelist added to the last-named point that the boys on the sports teams "are sure to have the most influence" on campus: "Win the athletes of any college for Christ, and you will have the strongest working element attainable in college life."[14]

At the same time, Stagg followed dominant American values. First, he did not like to play unless there was a very good chance of winning. He reasoned, "If Chicago University places a team in the field *it must be a winning team* or one which will bring honor to the University. . . . I don't propose to encourage any team from the University contesting with Ann Arbor, Northwestern or any other rival without its having been well trained," he added. "We shall live in quiet until such time as we can make a *good* showing if I have my say about it." Second, Stagg emphasized the aspect of athletics that could be used for personal and university promotion, namely intercollegiate competition. He planned to "develop players for the team" from the curricular work in physical education and thus gain "many skillful players who otherwise would never appear."[15]

Stagg began his duties by claiming in a newspaper interview that his work represented an important educational innovation in "going a step farther . . . than any other institution ever has done," by prescribing "compulsory gymnastic work." The goal was that "all the students in the university" should have "a certain amount of physical exercise every day." It was symptomatic, however, of the relationship of the new institution's educational goals to the larger society's interests that the portion of the article that announced the physical training requirement was buried well down in a column headlined "STAGG ON ATHLETICS . . . No Hired Athletes." The main body of the piece discussed the amateur code in college athletics. Stagg promised, "We will not hire men to come to the university because they are athletes nor will we pay their expenses there because they are athletes," and concluded by charging that "some of the eastern universities" had hired athletes "for years."[16]

Associate Professor Stagg served as a kind of coach-chaplain to the undergraduates at Chicago. Stagg, as muscular Christian, combined the muscular and the moral, embodying the American intercollegiate football coach's preemption of the role of the nineteenth-century campus cleric. A clever student named Madeleine Wallin noted the similarity of the two functions when she observed Stagg leading catechistic football cheers on Saturday and then, early on Sunday morning, "Behold Mr. Stagg, in a black coat and irreproachable tie, leading the first student prayer-meeting, and starting the gospel songs with the same spirit that had sent off the college yells the day before—for Mr. Stagg does what has been irreverently called the 'heavy pious,' combining athletics and religion in a masterly manner, with success in each."[17]

The relatively young all-American contrasted rather sharply in the students' eyes with his older, distinguished faculty colleagues. Marion Talbot, an early dean of women, records that the "prestige of Mr. Stagg in some respects surpassed that of any other member of the Faculty.

Certainly more eyes were turned upon him as he walked through Cobb Hall." Demia Butler, a student from Indianapolis, noted in her diary the attractiveness of Stagg's reputation and personality, recording somewhat dreamily his appearance at her residence hall, his singing of "some ridiculous college songs," and his comic instinct. She reckoned meeting him "a treat," for he was "so full of fun; and still we know him to be so earnest." Shortly, Coach Stagg returned to the women's residence to lecture on football, and the women felt that they "were prepared to enjoy it with greater zest than ever." Elizabeth Wallace, then a graduate student, remembered, "We ached with eagerness to cheer the newborn team to victory" after his appearance. After Stagg's debut in the women's residence hall, Wallace, who would have a long career as a professor, observed, "He became a popular figure, at whose arresting, swarthy appearance many a young undergraduate heart beat quicker."[18]

Stagg, as the most eligible bachelor on campus, soon attended the women's residence Halloween party and was a featured performer again. The coach's eligibility was ended by Stella Robertson from upstate New York. Harper and senior faculty looked with unease at the open campus courtship of the thirty-one-year-old Stagg and the teenaged Robertson, "the youngest freshman woman on the campus." In a later uncharacteristic revelation, Stagg wrote his fiancée of the anguish he had experienced over the criticism of Harper and others, the lack of respect he felt from the academics, and of his desire to go away and study medicine. The strong and resilient Stella rallied him, and the couple persevered. They were wed in 1894 and had a storybook marriage of more than six decades, three children (of whom the two sons followed their father into coaching), and increasing career and financial security. Stella even proved an invaluable coaching assistant and from the 1890s was probably the first woman regularly in the press box at sporting events in America as she charted plays.[19]

The football program started auspiciously on the university's opening day—October 1, 1892. The *Chicago Tribune* reported that three hundred students met at the request of Stagg "to select a 'varsity yell.'" More than fifty yells were submitted, each "yelled with a tremendous shout." The newspaper printed the five finalists' yells and reported that the meeting adjourned to cheers for the enthusiastic Stagg. The report concluded that he had "certainly captured the hearts of the students already." Madeleine Wallin, who was present at the yell meeting, recorded that Stagg appeared in football pants and sweater, "looking decidedly tough." She thought his presence infused a "splendid energy" into "his chorus of boys" and that the experience of mutual exhortation gave her a "feeling of greater personal pride and possession in the university than any thing else can do."[20]

The public showed lively interest in the yell competition. A Loop attorney and university trustee, Eli Felsenthal, wrote Stagg to suggest that as the "University has adopted yellow as its color" why not use "Yell-ow! Yell-ow! Chicago!" which would be "very appropriate and original." The most popular yell, the one that used the "Chica- , Chica- , Chica*go!*" cadence and became synonymous with the football team, was claimed by Stagg as his own. No doubt generations of Chicago Maroon athletes have been thankful that the school color was changed to maroon in 1894, for, as Stagg commented, "The yellow ran, soiled easily and had a regrettable symbolism, which our opponents might not be above commenting upon."[21]

The First Season, 1892: Stagg as Player-Coach

Stagg had to institute a program at the youngest university in the land, where ignorance of football was vast and the challenge for the coach almost overwhelming. The first team started practice late because of the university's new quarter system. Stagg found only "about a dozen" willing, mostly inexperienced boys when he started practice in October of 1892 at a midwestern pasture-cum-city park. The twelve candidates were the total available; no more than six were at most practices. The student editor of the *University of Chicago Weekly* asserted that support of the team was a matter of loyalty to the university, and for those "physically able" that meant trying to make the team. There is a Horatio Alger flavor to the editor's plea: "If you show ability and good training, your prospects of rising will be good. . . . Watch the game, be enthusiastic, post yourself on the rules, do as you are told, and under the coaching of the mighty Stagg we will soon see the vast amount of raw material now on hand, transformed into an eleven that can play football, and that with the best."[22]

"I am taxed to my utmost limit in arousing enthusiasm in football," complained Stagg, noting the heavy classroom commitments of his players, whom he termed "eager students." He soon decreased the length of the practice period to encourage more students to participate on the team, and victories over local high schools were followed by the first game with Northwestern University. Stagg felt it imperative that he play to steady the young team during their games: "I had to do one-half the playing. Our boys are so very green." Conditions were described in an early Chicago song: "Then Stagg was catcher, pitcher, coach, shortstop, and halfback, too; For in those days of 'Auld lang syne,' our good athletes were few."[23]

The season wore on, with many games arranged within mere days of the playing date. The Chicago newspapers greeted each appearance of the team with acclamation. The first game, a tie with Northwestern, was hailed by the *Chicago Times* as a debut in which Stagg's team "covered itself with glory." Another paper described Chicago's defeat by Northwestern in their second game: "Stagg is the Anson of football, as his remarkably strong team . . . would indicate." Still another thought Chicago's tie with Lake Forest demonstrated play "of the phenomenal kind."[24]

The outlines and inherent values of Chicago football became evident even during the makeshift first season when Stagg took his team to play the University of Michigan at Toledo, Ohio. Chicago was defeated decisively, but the idea of journeying to play football at a site some distance from either campus was historically significant, even if not unique to football's national story (Yale, Harvard, and Princeton had moved their Thanksgiving games to where the money was as early as the 1880s). The trip gave Stagg an opportunity to play the best football team in the West; for Harper it was an opportunity to advertise the university in northern Ohio. Only two questions were considered before the trip: Would Stagg's team play adequately enough not to tarnish the new institution's assumed academic reputation, and would the game cover its own expenses?[25]

One of the earliest difficulties that the team encountered was the lack of a home football ground. This required the rental of a field for home games away from the campus, which decreased both student attendance and interest. Newspaper boosters suggested that there was "a superb chance for some millionaire Chicagoan to show his progressive spirit by donating a field."[26] The university community discussed the possibility of providing the Department of Physical Culture and Athletics suitable indoor and outdoor instructional areas during the winter of 1892–93. The secretary of the board of trustees, Thomas Goodspeed, addressed the prospects for an indoor gymnasium: "We do not intend . . . to make any attempt to build a gymnasium until we have the money to put up one that will be a credit to the institution and superior to those owned by any other colleges in the country."[27] The inquiry soon moved away from physical training for all students toward a field for intercollegiate athletes.

The provision of facilities for football fans was highly attractive to Harper and Stagg because additional football sales would enable the financially harried president to cover the costs of the other, less marketable, intercollegiate sports. Marshall Field, the Chicago merchant, responded to a request from Harper and granted the use of some property contiguous to the university on the north. Under the headline

"Stagg Chasing the Mighty Dollar," the *Chicago Times* told of his attempt to raise $1,500. Another headline claimed "Athletics Are Booming," as trustees, faculty, and students subscribed impressively and student labor prepared the ground for use. The field was pronounced in "good condition" early in October 1893, and termed, inevitably, "Marshall Field . . . in honor of the generous donor."[28]

This university effort of money and muscle was like a religious enterprise. As "chaplain" to an increasingly secular collegiate community, Coach Stagg led the community to higher levels of commitment. And as he promoted a collective experience at the university, intercollegiate football was also becoming the proof of campus loyalty and the measure of men at Chicago. Laurence R. Veysey, in discussing "sources of cohesion" in the new American university, noted, "The laboratory, the football stadium, and the dignified presidential suite each claimed a certain legitimacy as the center of activities."[29] This book will trace the strand of the football stadium as the center of activities, but with some attention to the other two strands as all three competed for the attention of student, professor, alumnus, and citizen.

The Second Season, 1893: Instant Tradition

One preview of the 1893 season's prospects was optimistic, asserting that in two years "Stagg claims that he will have as good a football team as there is in the country." Stagg played more sparingly in 1893, a decision based upon the availability of better players and criticism of his participation from other universities. He found a capable replacement for himself at quarterback in Joseph A. Raycroft, a member of the physical culture department, but when Raycroft was injured Stagg immediately put himself in the line-up as quarterback against Purdue and in the final game with Notre Dame. Participation by the Chicago coaches, although not unheard of, was not a noteworthy step toward honorable intercollegiate football.[30]

Several factors promoted the growth of football interest during the second season: the physical culture requirement helped acquaint undergraduates and the faculty with the unfamiliar game; Chicago faculty and students found it easier to commit themselves to a winning 1893 football team than to the losing team of 1892; and the initiation of the big game on Thanksgiving with Michigan drew many in the civic community.[31]

Campus support was reported to have grown in numbers and understanding, and five hundred spectators watched Chicago defeat Michigan at the new ground early in the season. A student reporter characterized the game as "brain against brawn . . . skill, science and steadiness against force, brute-strength and unsteadiness" and left no doubt in his readers' minds which set of attributes represented each of the universities. The writer was enthusiastic about the Chicago crowd's dedication and reported a remark of Secretary Goodspeed's to President Harper after the game: "We will have a college here soon if this keeps up." Harper agreed. "Truly, it was wonderful," the student editors of the popular *University of Chicago Weekly* rhapsodized and judged that the victory provided Chicago "what we most need—a reputation." The *Weekly*'s argument reiterated the familiar, "The best colleges are, as a rule, the leaders in athletic games." The equation would become a maxim of American collegiate culture even if not original; a Queen's College student expressed an early Oxonian attitude around 1600 when he judged "the excellency of his colledge" by a "match at football."[32]

The seductive mystique of American football, a mixture of boosterism and idealism, can be seen in the editorials and articles of the *Weekly*. Football was described and justified as a pastime with valuable athletic and social uses for the university. Football was "the one distinctly college game, into which professionalism can never enter," which "should be upheld by the outside public as well as by the college man." And the fortunate Chicago public was offered the "sympathetic fellow feeling" that accompanies football enthusiasm.[33]

The big game came to Chicago in 1893. The idea was not unique; eastern schools had played such contests for some years. The Harvard-Yale and Yale-Princeton matches had become especially important athletic and social affairs in the East during the 1880s and early 1890s. These contests were big games for many college-oriented Americans of the middle and upper classes but did not excite wide interest among the larger public.[34]

Chicago society and alumni of many colleges responded appreciatively to the announcement of the Chicago-Michigan Thanksgiving game. Newspapers argued that the city needed a football tradition "reaching the importance in the West of the Yale-Harvard or Yale-Princeton games in the East." Instant tradition was the rule; the game was to be only "the first of the Thanksgiving Day intercollegiate matches which will be played every year." Special excursion trains were formed at Ann Arbor for Michigan's followers to accompany their team to Chicago. The *Chicago Interocean* anticipated that the Michigan supporters, seated across the field from the Chicago partisans, would make the day like "the most attractive and exhilarating incidents of the great games in the East, where college yells and songs stir the hearts of the most distinguished persons among the spectators." For the first time in the university's short history Chicago experienced football's capacity to dominate attention: "For the last week nothing but football has been discussed at the University on the South Side."[35]

The final important element in this athletic show was provided by President Harper, who "sent out invitations to many prominent people in Chicago," and "a fashionable company" was expected. Harper used the first big game to involve the Chicago social and financial community with the fortunes of the university, and his personal invitations were well received—a special area was filled with these guests' impressive tallyhos and carriages, from which they watched the game and each other. The score (28-10, Michigan) was not the most important feature, some of the three thousand spectators must have decided, for gimcrackery promotion was aplenty: "Both sides had mascots in the shape of huge strutting turkey gobblers, the one adorned in old gold and the other a symphony in yellow and blue. These majestic birds, secure from the common fate of their kind, celebrated the occasion by gobbles almost as loud and effective as the yells of the rival universities."[36]

Stagg was still working out the form of football at Chicago in late 1893 when he arranged two indoor matches against Northwestern and Notre Dame during December and January. The concept was new to the West, but Stagg, who had helped inaugurate indoor football in America at Madison Square Garden in 1891, forged ahead. American footballers had initially sought to follow the autumn-through-spring British football schedule, but the severity of the North American climate shortened the period; Chicago's indoor matches were no doubt an attempt to prolong the season and the revenues. The games were played at nearby Tattersall's arena on a playing field affording a scant sixty-five by thirty yards. The Northwestern game ended ignobly, with the players picking up glass fragments after a Northwestern player punted into an electric lamp. The Notre Dame game, however, played on New Year's Day, was especially helpful to the athletic enterprise, and "a boom in athletics in the middle of the winter" was reported at the university.[37]

The Third Season, 1894: Nineteen Games and a West Coast Trip on New Year's

A profile of the Chicago team of 1894 indicates they were a mixture of age, size, and dedication to the sport. Coach Stagg felt the number of likely undergraduate players was small compared with other universities and that this put him at a severe disadvantage. The average age of the fifteen "regulars" was twenty-three. The oldest player, a

German immigrant, was thirty; the youngest player, Clarence Hersch-berger, eighteen, was to become Chicago's first all-American. The Maroons were a small team, even by the standards of their day; the men averaged 161 pounds, and only one was six feet tall or over, eight of the team being under five feet nine inches. A reporter described the young men who represented the university in 1894: "They are a mod-est, gentlemanly party of young men. . . . They are exceedingly abste-mious, indulging in neither the flowing bowl nor the fragrant weed and retiring to their virtuous couches at the seasonable hour of 11 o'clock. There are four divinity graduates in the party, which may have an influence on their high moral standards."[38]

The Chicago football eleven was becoming a saleable item for the local newspapers, and 1894 was the year the publishers began to stake their claim. Several papers featured a flurry of charges and denials regarding "signal-stealing" following the Purdue game, which Chica-go lost. The newspapers eagerly promoted the tempest and demonstrat-ed little concern for the possibility of ruptured relations between the two schools, and Chicago-Purdue relations ceased for four years. Chi-cago newspapers were beginning to exact just such a price in return for their partisan cooperation in university and team publicity.[39]

The second big game on Thanksgiving Day against Michigan was a larger production than the first one and featured a campuswide fund-raising campaign to build a grandstand. Students and faculty had raised $1,200, and many also contributed labor. The two-thousand-seat struc-ture was completed just two days before the game and made possible the record attendance. Harper and Stagg employed a charity-benefit organization for the game, which the *Chicago Tribune* noted by listing the "patronesses" of the event. The newspapers competed in naming worthies who attended. Under the headline "Chicago's Four Hundred in Attendance," the *Chicago Interocean* reported: "Society and learning joined in the general enthusiasm of the collegians. The grandstand was packed to its last foot of standing room by professors and writers, merchant princes, and professional men. . . . The crowd was largely made up of college men and ex-college men and their friends."[40] There followed a listing of ninety-two men in attendance (including the young Chicago city attorney, Clarence Darrow); all twenty-four patron-esses; and the thirty-six members, guests, and equipages of the two leading fraternities.

The foundations were now virtually laid at Chicago for a successful intercollegiate football enterprise. Major innovations included the el-evation of physical culture to a place of curricular acceptance, a puta-tive faculty intercollegiate supervisory body separate from student and alumni control, and a founding membership in the Intercollegiate Conference of Faculty Representatives (the first intercollegiate athletic conference under ostensible faculty supervision). If these methods of control appeared solid and impressive, in reality the values and judgments of trustees and administrators, influenced by the entertainment marketplace and by the demands of alumni and other interest groups, prevailed.[41] And in the actual event—the games and the cheering—what had been launched and accomplished on the prairie was derivative. It had already been done back east. In 1894, however, Associate Professor Stagg and President Harper trumped their old eastern colleagues: They invented the football bowl concept.

The most significant occurrence of the 1894 season was the 6,200-mile tour the Maroon players made to the Pacific Coast in December and January. The trip served as a multifaceted model for American intercollegiate football. The distance and duration, the season of the year, the number of games played, and the attendant publicity all demonstrated the enormous possibilities of the intercollegiate game.

The imaginative Stagg worked up the tour. His preparation of the West Coast trip proceeded with no questions raised about the propriety of a college football team making a transcontinental journey to play a game. Stagg's rationale was simple: After noting the tempting larger crowds and dearer tickets on the Coast, he concluded, "And we could use the advertising." He later remembered that "President Harper was entirely agreeable" to the journey, "as he was toward anything legitimate that put the university's name in print, but he left it to me to find the money." The student editor who saw the team as a "traveling advertising organization of the University" had the clearest vision.[42]

The negotiating officials of the West Coast teams, including Walter Camp, Stagg's old Yale mentor who coached Stanford University in 1892 and 1894, and Herbert Hoover, treasurer of the Stanford Athletic Association, were interested in nothing save that the games "would be a great success financially." The twenty-four telegrams between Stagg and the officials gave no intimation of any purpose other than the financial, and only one telegram mentioned the important matter of player eligibility requirements.[43] Arrangements for transporting and feeding the team were completed in a flurry of uncertainty. The team's itinerary was much discussed. Perhaps Butte, Portland, Denver, and Galveston would be visited; perhaps Chicago would make a southern swing on their return journey to include New Orleans. The probable list of games included two with Stanford, one with the University of California at Berkeley, one with the Reliance Athletic Club of San Francisco, one with the Los Angeles YMCA team, and one with the University of Texas at Austin on the homeward leg. One of the few things made clear was that Stella Stagg was to accompany the team on a kind of delayed wedding trip.[44]

A kindly "spinster" volunteered the use of her private rail car, and Stagg accepted the offer without examining the coach. The newspapers vied with each other in their zealous descriptions of the car and its journey, also without investigation. The *Chicago Times* described the interior of the "white coach," the sleeping berth arrangements, the number and placement of the luggage, and gave the names of the chef and the porter. The *Chicago Record* rhapsodized of the "elegantly equipped car" that was "fitted up especially for the convenience of the class of people who are to be occupants."[45]

Coach Stagg and his team saw the carriage for the first time at their departure, and he remembered that the Chicago press must have been afflicted with a merciful myopia: "The car looked as though Sherman has just marched through it. It was a show car, a condemned Pullman that has been sold down the river in its old age. . . . The wheels were flat, the paint scabrous, the body humped at one spot and sagged at another." The journey began. Stagg recalled: "In the middle of the night, at the top of the Rockies, I woke to hear that the car was afire. The coal stove at the forward end, becoming red hot, had ignited the woodwork. . . . While the train toiled upgrade, we fought the fire with axes and water and beat it after a blistering fight." The wooden coach was quietly left at Sacramento, to be picked up on the homeward journey. The difficulties were not reported in the press, and upon arrival in San Francisco the players dutifully described the trip as "a picnic."[46]

The first Stanford game, the most important of the series, was played on Christmas Day. The San Francisco-area football followers were greatly interested in the game, and the Maroons were well received. Chicago defeated Stanford easily, 24-4. One San Francisco paper described the game in a fashion overwritten even for a sports report. The University of Chicago eleven became the "Windy City aggregation of pigskin propellers" who fairly "swooped down upon the . . . gridiron." Again, they were "Dr. Harper's football fiends" who represented "the so-called 'egotistical metropolis,' located on the balmy shore of Lake Michigan."[47]

An incident in the game indicated the rawness of intercollegiate football in 1894. The referee had ruled in the first half that a Chicago play at the goal line was not a touchdown. As the players filed off the field at half-time, the Chicago quarterback charged the official with being "a cheesy sort of a referee," whereupon the referee punched the "offending Chicago jaw." The scuffle was reported somewhat differently by other papers; several versions had the Chicagoan punch the official. When the referee refused to return for more of the same treatment, another official was obtained, and Chicago won handily. The hostile Chicago quarterback was Frank Hering, who later helped devise Mothers Day.[48]

The Chicago-Stanford athletic show moved to Los Angeles in order to draw more money than had the two teams met again in the San Francisco area. And there in southern California the modern bowl concept was born: The teams from the two young universities met at the turn of the year far from either campus and for no discernible educational purpose, but with clear financial and public relations objectives. Chicago lost the game and recessed to the San Francisco area to absorb another defeat from the semiprofessional Reliance Athletic Club, the Pacific Coast champions. The newspapers of the two cities appeared to be describing different Chicago-Reliance games. The San Francisco press saw it as one of the finest exhibitions of football ever played on the West Coast; conversely, Chicago was beaten by the "roughest and most brutal play ever seen" and "the Californians resorted to hoodlum tactics to win," according to the Chicago writers.[49]

The weary team stopped in Salt Lake City on the return home to play the local YMCA team for more gate receipts and to relieve Stagg's concern over trip finances. The game was well attended, played in "snow and slush," and won by Chicago 52-0. The railroad coach misfortunes that plagued the team on the journey to the Coast did not desert them on the return home, and repairs to a "flattened wheel" stopped them in Laramie, Wyoming. There they enjoyed a seven-course meal that their chef prepared from western provisions. The menu included "California Salmon" and "Wyoming Jack Rabbit à la Macedone," the essence of which is evident on Stella Stagg's carefully preserved stained tablecoth from the train.[50]

The journey concluded as it began—with no justification other than the challenge of a 6,200-mile tour and its renown. The dimensions of the accomplishment grew steadily, and the Chicago-Stanford game came to be widely and incorrectly recorded as the "first inter-sectional football contest," despite the prior claims of the Harvard-McGill and Michigan-Harvard, Michigan-Yale, and Michigan-Princeton games of the 1870s. The four games of the western tour ensured that the football season lasted from September to January and totaled twenty-two games, according to the yearbook *Cap and Gown, 1895*. This may be a record season total of games played in intercollegiate history, but no complaints seem to have been made on the campus. Official University of Chicago publications mirrored the proud competitiveness of the young university in recording that its team had completed "the longest football tour on record. It was the first time that a football team had crossed the Rocky Mountains." This concern for primacy and quantity was, in turn, a faithful mirror of the larger American culture, especially on the moving frontier. Within seven months the universities of Minnesota, Wisconsin, and Michigan were rumored to be planning to go either east or west or in both directions to play football.[51]

But the significance of the Chicago Pacific coastal tour goes beyond the Midwest. Gilded Age college athletics had been taking place substantially within traditional university groupings—the goals, scale, and personnel engaged in football were local or regional. At the same time, the pervasive "mentality" of those leading and shaping intercollegiate football proceeded from national cultural trends and methods. Chicago's extravagant trip heralded the faint beginnings of a national commercial enterprise characterized by inter-regional play and parity.[52]

Stagg had written to Walter Camp twice in 1894 regarding the value of intercollegiate football at Chicago. He wrote in response to Camp, who was assembling testimonials for football, which he published in 1894 as refutation of some attacks on the game. "Football has done a great deal toward arousing college spirit where little or none existed," Stagg stated, "so we feel it has been of special value in our university life. In fact our athletics have done more to create a college spirit than all the rest of the student organizations."[53] Few observers in the traditionless university would have disagreed. Football helped to meet such scathing comments as those from the president of Knox College, who noted the rawness of the new enterprise: "There are no traditions. The place seems to have no more character than a new school house."[54]

The wooden grandstand that rose in 1894 by campus subscription and partially by student labor was proof of the uses of football to promote a sense of community. The extra seating for the general public, in turn, demonstrated the Midway community's wish to serve and be served by the larger Chicago community. Further, the impulse to commercialize this gentlemanly leisure-time activity came as naturally to this American university as Harper's professorial raiding had followed John D. Rockefeller's commitment to the efficiency and profit of the monopoly. The Chicago intercollegiate football program was established within the institution's first three years as an amalgam of earlier eastern American models and with considerable promise of new approaches to lodging the game within a major modern research university.

2

The Rise of the Spectator, the Coach, and the Player, 1895–1905

Rockefeller gifts were celebrated like football victories, and football victories like the Second Coming.
  —Milton Mayer

Our profession is one of the noblest and perhaps the most far reaching in building up the manhood of our country.
  —Amos Alonzo Stagg

I have no more fun in practice games. It isn't amusement or recreation any more. It is nothing less than hard work.
  —Chicago player, 1897

Harper's university fostered the growth of football so successfully at the turn of the century that Chicago gained the leadership of western intercollegiate football and won the national championship in 1905. Maroon football had two extraordinary assets. First, located in the largest city of the Midwest (and by 1900 the nation's second most populous), the university could count on many players and spectators. And those spectators ensured the end of the players' innocence, the cessation of play as an end in itself, and the beginning of play as an instrument of larger economic and cultural values. Second, Amos Alonzo Stagg was the perfect athletic entrepreneur to complement William Rainey Harper's academic entrepreneurial movements.[1]

The Rise of the Spectator

The most significant development during the period was the rise of the spectator—the widespread acceptance and use of the Chicago football enterprise by the students, faculty, and alumni of the university community and by the larger civic community. The use and enjoyment of football by American "witnesses," not participants, for whatever civic, social, economic, or vicarious cultural reasons were barely remarked upon, even though they constituted an enormous change from the British educational model. After all, Chicago did not invent these practices; rather, it had eagerly transferred eastern collegiate forms and folkways to the Midway in as intact a fashion as possible. In the event, the university became very successful in selling its athletic product and even at applying monopolistic principles as a kind of "athletic Darwinism." Although some academics grew chary of the strong community interest and nascent control by 1900, most judged that the activity was useful to the university's larger mission.[2]

Certainly President Harper was keenly aware of the relationship between philanthropy and football victory. He dramatically appeared in the Maroons' dressing room at halftime of the 1895 Wisconsin game, with his players down 0 to 12. He challenged the players: "Boys, Mr. Rockefeller has just announced a gift of $3 million to the University. . . . he believes the University is to be great. The way you played in the first half leads me to wonder whether we really have the spirit of greatness and ambition. I wish you would make up your minds to win this game and show that we do have it." Chicago won 22-12.[3]

The period is replete with a kind of yellow sports journalism. Frank Luther Mott notes that "emphasis on sports was characteristic of the yellow press," and that editors "developed for that department a slangy and facetious style." William Randolph Hearst developed sports journalism when he challenged Joseph Pulitzer for New York circulation leadership in 1895. American intercollegiate sports coverage evolved into a permanent feature on the "sporting page" after the turn of the century, displacing the earlier method of including collegiate activity within the social elite's leisure news. The "windy city" newspapers maintained their civic booster reputation with unsupportable claims for Stagg's teams. The journalists themselves were a prime market for the game, even as they became the chief salesmen; they soon believed and printed virtually everything that Stagg told them.[4]

Boosterism came full circle in 1902 when the first "Gridiron Fest" was sponsored by the Chicago Press Club. Coaches, athletic managers, football officials, and players joined the propagandists in the formal unification of the press and the new intercollegiate football industry. The banquet was termed "an entire success" from the "social point of view" by the *Chicago Daily News*, which interpreted the event as changing the "atmosphere entirely between the men actively engaged in football, the greatest of all college sports, and those who have this same game to report for the mass of enthusiasts."[5]

The university's strategy in taking the game to the Chicago civic community was divulged by Horace Butterworth, manager of Maroon athletics, when he discussed schedule-making and the market. He reasoned that early season victories promoted attendance and enthusiasm for the later contests, an approach that accounts for the scheduling from 1896 to 1905 of teams that managed only twenty-seven points in thirty-six early season games while Chicago scored 1,116 points. Butterworth described the Chicago marketplace as possessing two elements— the "society element" and the public. Athletic Director Stagg added a third constituency, "the college people" (he estimated fifty thousand), by which he meant citizens who had attended other institutions and whose loyalty might be partially transferred to the Chicago Maroons. All of these groups, including the press and the noncollege "subway-alumni," were addressed carefully as markets.[6]

The city of Chicago was a limited football marketplace in the early 1890s because few Chicagoans knew the game either as players or spectators. Public interest in football picked up when the sport was introduced into the secondary schools during the 1890s, but the greatest single influence on public perception was the football enterprise that Harper and Stagg marketed. Between 1896 and 1905 almost 90 percent of all Chicago games were played at home, and persistent publicity argued that the honor of the collegiate and civic community was at stake on the Maroon gridiron.

Chicago students readily accepted the idea that the team was "theirs" and that the games provided valid institutional comparisons. The autumn placement of the sport was especially advantageous. Games became a weekly meeting place for the new and old members of the university and promoted a community reconfiguration each autumn. The campus suffered and rejoiced communally over the team's performances: "Rockefeller gifts were celebrated like football victories, and football victories like the Second Coming."[7]

Student support for the Maroons was formally expressed by carefully composed and rehearsed songs and cheers. The prime example, a song entitled "John D. Rockefeller" (sung to "Daisy"), was both audacious and defensive regarding Rockefeller's relationship with the university. The first stanza is brassy.

> There is a Varsity out in the West
> Chicago, Chicago.
> Founded by capital, backed by the best

Go it Chica-a-go.
Headed by wisdom that knows no bo
She's making a wonderful show
And others are longing to share the lot
Of Chica-go-Chi-ca-go-go.

The second verse is defensive regarding the school's ori

They say that he made it by forming a trust
Chica-go, Chica-go,
That may be true but its use is most just
Of this man we are all proud
Be it high or low
For to him we owe our all
At Chica-go, Chica-go-go.

The panegyrical chorus sublimates any unease that might remain.

John D. Rockefeller
A wonderful man is he,
Gives all his spare change
To the U. of C.
He keeps the ball a-rolling
In our great varsity
He pays Dr. Harper
To help us grow sharper
To the glory of U. of C.

An additional stanza was added within a short time and reiterated the chauvinism of the first.

We advise you, kind friends, keep an eye on this place,
It has entered the race and it will set the pace,
Go it, Chicago!
The recourse is long, the world it includes,
And all who would start at the blow,
Must train here with us for many a year,
At Chicago! Chicago-go![8]

These positive and defensive words were no doubt prompted by the widespread image of the new institution as flying the "Standard Oil Colors" and of the team termed the "Rockefellerites."[9]

Rockefeller was also honored with a short yell used during the 1890s:

Who's the feller
Who's the feller
Zip-boom-bah

Rock-e-feller
He's the feller
Rah! Rah! Rah![10]

John J. MacAloon has used the modern Olympic Games to discuss Emile Durkheim's proposition that modern secular societies require secular rituals that provide them meaning and solidarity. The football festival of the campus weekend developed by college communities, with its attendant rituals and abnormal behavior, also meets Durkheim's prescription. Certainly the outlines of Chicago student behavior toward the team were clear and fixed by 1905. Pregame rallies, school songs, football banquets and receptions, celebratory bonfires and parades—all the spectatorial accoutrements to the Chicago football industry—were begun, developed, and refined during the period to such a degree that they changed little over the next decades.

Careful rituals were developed for pregame mass meetings by 1903. The meeting for that year's Michigan game became the prototype; it was planned by six committees, held in Mandel Hall, led by a prototypical cheermaster, Arthur E. Bestor (later to become one of America's leading cultural historians and critics), and followed a special four-page program of the nineteen separate steps of the evening's observance. The meeting began with step one, "The Procession," of fifteen campus organizations whose three hundred members all sat on the stage and concluded with "a series of fights between the freshmen and sophomores," which would have been the twentieth step had it been placed in the program. The alumni met earlier in the evening at a nostalgic dinner that was to become a staple for returning team members and their supporters. The mass meeting was described as the "biggest and most enthusiastic in the history of the University of Chicago," a claim that would be repeated with uniform monotony in future football seasons.[11]

The women of the university took the lead in producing cheers. Dean Marion Talbot, "in behalf of the girls," announced a prize contest for the "best gridiron lyric." As "chairman of the committee on musical cheer," Talbot expected that the assembled students would practice new compositions weekly to improve team support on Saturdays. The committee was none too sure of the quality of the entries. A scale of prizes was set up for the "best composition": $10 if the composition was "satisfactory" and only $5 if "it is satisfactory or not." The women were working out their peculiar role as major athletic advocates on the American campus. Only two years before, the psychologist G. Stanley Hall had dared provide the pioneer analysis of football and female supporters: "Glory, which is the reward of victory and makes the brave deserve the fair, is . . . never so great as when it is the result of conflict; and while the human female does not as in the case of many animal species look on complacently and reward the victor with her favor, military prowess has a strange fascination for the weaker sex, perhaps ultimately and biologically because it demonstrates the power to protect and defend. Power . . . has played a great role in sexual attraction."[12]

Women were shut out of what was becoming one of the surest means to social acceptance on the American campus—intercollegiate athletic participation. The role of women in intercollegiate football and the larger society was graphically evident in 1902 as female students helped lead a rally for the beaten Chicago team in 1902 after the second consecutive loss to Fielding Yost's dominant Michigan squad. The university community met "to show their appreciation for the great fight put up." Over the caption "Coed Rouses Spirit of Defeated Maroons" the *Tribune* ran a photo of Agnes Wayman encircled with posies. Many students and faculty spoke of the discouraged team's courage and pluck, but it remained for Agnes Wayman to strike the right note of comfort and encouragement. She said, "The harder the defeat, the more tender ought to be the treatment the team received at the hands of the university students." She retailed the "faith the coeds had in the team" and concluded with the prediction of great success and joy for the Maroons. Then the *Chicago Chronicle* expressed surprise that "even the coeds had something to say."[13]

The football team's relations with the faculty and alumni also became more regular and formalized during the period. Faculty leaders made frequent appearances at football mass meetings, and some could be counted upon for stirring rhetoric. The 1902 meeting after the Michigan defeat was also noteworthy for faculty response: "Almost every department furnished a representative" to aid the team in assuaging their despair, and none was more convincing than the sociologist Albion Small. The professor mused that everybody connected with the team's valiant effort should be praised, "from substitute to Captain Sheldon and from highest soprano to cheer leader. Rubber, scrubber and cook deserve it, too." Small concluded that "football has got to be played with a combination of brain and muscle" and left no doubt with his audience in which element he felt Chicago superior to her opponents. Law Dean Joseph H. Beale, recently arrived from Harvard, offered "a stirring speech" at the same meeting, and Philip S. Allen, the initiator and managing editor of *Modern Philology,* neatly encapsulated the university's twofold purpose to the delight of his listeners. The two purposes, according to the former Maroon star, were "to spread the light of knowledge over the western world and to 'lick' Michigan."[14]

University Registrar and Secretary of the Board of Trustees Thomas Goodspeed, called "Chicago's oldest rooter," keynoted the largest mass meeting of the 1903 season with rampant enthusiasm and analogy. Michigan could be beaten, he insisted, if Chicago would fight with "the same spirit that animated the old Norse sea kings." Dean George E. Vincent addressed the same audience alliteratively as "heroes, heroines, and heelers."[15]

Both President Harper and Dean Vincent hosted celebratory dinners and receptions. For some years Harper held a postseason dinner for the football team at which the captain for the next season was elected; in 1903 he added a midseason "Victory dinner" at Hutchinson Commons and five hundred male students attended. That same year Vincent's annual Thanksgiving Eve reception for the team members had evolved into a rather formal event by invitation only. The invitations, sent sparingly to the university community and "friends," allowed the recipient "to meet the University of Chicago football team" from 7 to 10 on the eve of the battle. The occasion had the unmistakable air of using the team as a corporate asset.[16]

Professors who showed anything less than wide-eyed, uncritical enthusiasm for the Maroons courted swift unpopularity. The day after an 1896 victory over Michigan, a crowd of two hundred students roamed the halls, cheering and interrupting lectures. Only once did they meet a professorial check, and that by geologist Rollin D. Salisbury, who "shoved the offenders out the door." The students chanted derisively in response, "What's the matter with Salisbury? He's all-right! Nit!" President Harper emerged from his office and ended the confrontation by enthusiastically contributing $10 to start a fireworks fund for the evening rally.[17]

A more serious campus upheaval resulted from a Thanksgiving victory over Brown University in 1899. A number of the faculty, including the political economist J. Laurence Laughlin, required their classes to meet the next day, despite the custom of granting the students a holiday after a Thanksgiving win. Several hundred students spilled into Cobb Hall, where most of the classes were meeting, and shouted for the offending lecturers to dismiss their students. The reserved, anti-imperialist Laughlin's classroom became the focus of this demand, and the man described by a colleague as "the essence and flower of good form" came to the classroom door. "'Mr. Laughlin, give us a speech. Expansion. Expansion.' chorused the students." A shoving match resulted, followed by the use of the professor's fists and a chair he lifted to defend his classroom. These methods having failed, Laughlin demanded the names of the offenders, who boldly handed over their identity cards and continued chanting. President Harper arrived at a poky run, spoke persuasively to the leaders, and the crowd began to drift from the building, accompanied by Laughlin's mutterings of "rowdyism" and "ungentlemanly exhibitions." Most of the campus appeared willing to accept Secretary Goodspeed's judgment that the episode was "simply an outbreak of natural boyish enthusiasm."[18]

The development of consistent support by alumni occurred later than the development of student and faculty support and was contemporaneous with the support of the larger civic community. Chicago was in a unique position during the 1890s; although it opened and functioned as a fully staffed university with a comparatively large student body, it took about a decade of graduations to produce a sufficiently large and interested group of supportive alumni. By the 1902 season 1,866 degrees (70 percent of which were undergraduate) had been awarded. There was also a sizable number of students who had attended the institution during the first decade without taking a degree. The Chicago alumni were joined around 1900 by other universities' alumni to provide enthusiastic backing for Stagg's teams and a collateral desire to demand victory regardless of means.[19]

During the first decade, alumni interest in the athletic fortunes of university teams was informal, and little organization beyond the seating of alumni in the Chicago section of the stands was accomplished. The local alumni club, the largest and most active chapter, planned a dinner in honor of the football team as early as 1899. Soon after, a more formal dinner before the Thanksgiving game became a regular feature. The first successful concerted effort by the alumni to influence athletic policy occurred at that annual dinner in 1902, where some critical remarks were directed to Stagg's alleged ineptitude at recruiting top high school athletes. This alumni influence, combined with the increasing sense of team ownership felt by the civic and journalistic communities, was so strong that Stagg and his staff were stirred to more active recruiting and periodic reports to the alumni. In return, the alumni–civic coalition provided long-running protection for his winning program and rendered Coach Stagg a campus untouchable. Harper and Stagg were more than willing to go along with the demands for victory, even when the result was the bending and warping of the original stated values of their intercollegiate athletic program.[20]

The selling of the Maroon football team went well at Harper's university. The rise of the spectator on the Midway and in the city was so marked that the Maroons did not leave Chicago once for their twelve matches in 1902. They began with two games in September, wedged six contests into October, and finished with four in November. From 1903 through 1905 Stagg scheduled twenty-eight games in Chicago, five away. Football revenue had so outgrown football expenses that the surplus was devoted to maintaining the other activities in the Department of Physical Culture and Athletics. Increasingly, the dependence on football was becoming a major argument for maintaining the large commercial football enterprise at Chicago and elsewhere.[21]

The Rise of the Coach

Amos Alonzo Stagg rose to a position of considerable power in Harper's university. The growing influence of a coach at such a university is perhaps initially difficult to fathom, considering that in 1892 Stagg was an untried administrator and shaky academic surrounded by eminent administrators and scholars. Stagg's rise was due to his special relationship to Harper, his dominant personality, the precedentless department that he headed, the innovative "profession" of coaching of which he was a pioneer, and the enlargement of his national reputation based upon his unparalleled entrepreneurial and football genius.

President Harper and Coach Stagg grew increasingly close and mutually dependent. It was an good marriage because they knew what to expect from each other, and both endeavored not to let the other down. Harper was constantly vigilant about the best way to present the Maroon football show to the paying customers. In 1897, he suggested to Stagg the addition of "a bulletin board" (scoreboard) on the field so that "all can see and understand" the progress of the game and then wondered, "Should there not be a band at the Michigan game Thanksgiving day?" The next day he wrote to Stagg again, this time to ask, "If you could get the team together at any time secretly, without its being public, I should like to make a little talk to them. . . . It must of course be absolutely quiet." He also requested Stagg's presence at the morning Thanksgiving service—"and have all the boys with you." Stagg almost always carried out his president's requests promptly and diligently.[22]

The relationship also had its trials. Harper showed unhappiness over his coach's management in 1895 when a university summer baseball team (one of Stagg's delights was to play in these more informal games), comprised partially of nonuniversity students, played teams the president deemed inappropriate: "We have had a series of games with negroes etc. which has brought disgrace upon us." Stagg seems to have sorted out the baseball issue by the summer of 1896, although many questions are left unanswered. Few African Americans played for him, but few were enrolled at Chicago. Perhaps the most celebrated was Henry Dismond, one of Stagg's sprinters who held a world record.[23]

The Harper-Stagg colleagueship was severely strained at times because the coach was frequently at the heart of a campus imbroglio and often the focus of antagonism. People sometimes viewed his insistence upon what he considered points of "principle" as overly forceful or even tactless behavior. Stagg was a man of imperious character, and he saw issues more simply than his faculty colleagues; he committed himself completely to a position, sometimes squelching those who were less committed or sure of a solution. His sense of personal and departmental prerogative grew with his enhanced reputation, and he became more bold when he dealt with his superiors and increasingly sensitive to what he considered any infringement of his preserve. A number of times his resistance to any interference with the affairs of the athletic department came to the fore, and on occasion his letters reveal a regrettable brashness. For example, Stagg wrote an assertive letter to President Harper in 1896 regarding what he considered the impertinence of University Comptroller Henry Rust in requesting justification for some of Stagg's expenditures: "I understand that I am not to be hampered in any way in my work through this arrangement of finances; that Major Rust is not to request *reasons why* this or that expenditure; that I am not compelled to *explain* to him for what ever purpose certain money is to be used . . . and am not to be called to account by *him* for the same."[24] Harper backed Stagg, and it was not until many years later when the University Council and board of trustees investigated Stagg's special autonomy that his department was brought into line with others.

Another episode occurred when the university's extension department sought the use of the gymnasium bleachers for an outdoor event. Stagg's chief assistant had granted the request, and plans went forward for the occasion; Stagg then denounced the agreement and stipulated a rental fee for the stands. Harper gingerly wrote to his coach that perhaps Stagg was "a little rigid with the University in this matter," confessed that he did "not see why one department should rent timber from the other," and suggested they discuss the issue "as a matter of principle." Stagg's reply was a marvel of technicality, obfuscation, and patent self-denial. He found an analogy in the nonlending of "house furniture" of the university; he admitted "to a degree" the worth of the promise made to the other department but did not feel "absolutely committed"; and he pictured the extension department as disingenuously attempting to "get around" the issue of damage by paying the rental fee he demanded.[25]

Stagg's relationship to the governing Board of Physical Culture and

Athletics evolved during the period. Early on, the coach took care and time to establish his dominance. For example, during Stagg's 1895 summer vacation his assistant Horace Butterworth kept him informed of the board's doings. He reported a good deal of dissatisfaction over Stagg's management among such prominent members as Assyriologist Robert Harper (President Harper's brother) and divinity professor Shailer Mathews. Butterworth described them as "men anxious to make a display of authority," noted that an important meeting of the board was imminent, and predicted that they would "try to take management of affairs out of your hands" and then "crow over it." Butterworth's report stirred Stagg, who began a heated, handwritten letter to President Harper with, "I hope that you will see to it that the Board does not act upon important matters of policy in my absence." He continued, "Frankly, I do not consider some members of the Board capable of wise action, and I don't care to have the work of the Physical Culture Dept. made more burdensome." Stagg finished his argument by referring to the control of policy as "my particular charge . . . for which I have thought and labored and prayed a great deal." Harper acquiesced, and Stagg acquired a virtually impregnable position as a result of this and other test cases.[26]

Stagg's impatience with those who might challenge his point of view was not confined to his relations with university officials. His dealings with the representatives of other universities led to complaints that he had behaved imperiously toward them. The Intercollegiate Conference of Faculty Representatives, the Midwest's pioneer athletic governance organization, had been formed in 1895–96 and provided the context for such protests. President C. K. Adams of the University of Wisconsin leveled extensive charges against Stagg in 1898 to the effect that Stagg's duplicity had ruined athletic relations between Wisconsin and Chicago. A year later Adams wrote a longhand "Personal and Private" plea to President Harper regarding the "assumption of superiority" he felt Stagg had demonstrated toward him, University of Illinois President Andrew S. Draper, and Michigan Professor Albert H. Pattengill at a conference meeting. That Chicago alone was represented by an instructor in athletics rather than Harper or one of the traditional academics at Chicago was an issue that would receive airing and resolution within a decade.[27]

Coach Stagg's successful athletic career and his early physical education training at Springfield had prepared him to serve as the pioneer of a new profession, the college coach. In this development, he was in advance of the gentlemen-scholars who became the businessmen-superintendents of America's public schools in their new profession. The same societal forces behind the "cult of efficiency" that was to convert the schoolmasters into superintendents was a part of the culture that produced the nation's football coaches. Their vulnerability to "the great strength of the business community and the business philosophy in an age of efficiency" was considerable, and these influences molded their work. Few were allowed to remain simply as coach-educators. The professionalization of the college coach is illustrated by Stagg's career. He moved from the player-coach of the first generation of coaches (from around the 1880s through 1900) into the "scientific" coach-manager (from around 1900 through 1920) and the celebrity-entre-preneur-coach (the 1920s) stages of successive generations. Many other coaches followed his model at each generation. Football coaches, for example, assumed control over all other intercollegiate activities as "athletic directors" because of football's dominant economic position on campuses about twenty to thirty years after Stagg had assumed the title. Stagg even led the chosen few toward the final coaching stage— the celebrity-entrepreneurs of twentieth-century American universities. These powerful coaches often occupied a cultural and financial niche well above their college president or state governor and at this stage of development Knute Rockne took the leadership from the aging Stagg. Stagg and his fellow first- and second-generation coaches, especially in the old, elite Anglophile eastern universities, would seem tailor-made to fit T. J. Jackson Lear's description of antimodernism. The coaches were antimodernist, and they claimed to capture "real life" for sixty minutes on the gridiron much as Lears's "pre-modern craftsman, soldier" and "saint" did in their endeavors.[28]

By 1905, Athletic Director Stagg was the best known figure in intercollegiate athletics west of the Appalachians, and Walter Camp had already named him the "dean" of western football. The fame he had gained as a Yale undergraduate was not of a transient nature because he made new conquests of the popular fancy throughout his career as coach and athletic director.[29]

Stagg was lauded by a leading Chicago newspaper, the *Chronicle,* in 1902 as "better known than anyone connected with the University of Chicago, Dr. W. R. Harper and John D. Rockefeller alone excepted." The panegyric continued, "Stagg is hardly ever out of the public eye" and concluded that he was "the genius of the university advertising department." The public enjoyed reading about the spartan Maroon coach. In one earlier case, a journalist described how Stagg coached from the sidelines while holding plump Alonzo Junior in his arms. When needed, he hastily handed the baby to his all-American Clarence Herschberger and "plunged into the line-up." The enthusiastic observer concluded that the "grave coach, carrying the youngster in his arms and initiating the green ones into the mysteries of football is a sight not soon to be forgotten." A mystique surrounded his activities on the gridiron and extended well beyond its perimeter, where Stagg's abstemious behavior was appreciated. It is probable that he personified, for many Americans, a purer, less materialistic, Christian America that had been lost.[30]

Stagg's preeminence lay in the acquaintances and contacts he maintained in the East, as well in his position as a leading coach and athletic director. His coauthorship of the first avowedly "scientific" football book, *A Scientific and Practical Treatise on American Football for Schools and Colleges,* in 1893 had also brought him considerable attention. He knew most of the eastern athletic authorities, and the East continued its hegemony of the West in athletics during the early years of the century. In 1904, Stagg became the first noneastern representative on the Football Rules Committee, which legislated the rules of the sport for the entire nation. The Intercollegiate Conference had elected Stagg as representative in the hope that his prestige and friendship with the six-member Rules Committee might induce his inclusion. Walter Camp soon wrote the Rules Committee's acceptance of the familiar Stagg.[31]

University of Chicago football teams became nationally known because of their precedent-setting inter-regional trips and games. Stagg's 1894 West Coast marathon was followed four years later by a significant eastern foray. The 1898 game with Pennsylvania at Philadelphia's venerable Franklin Field was not only an important Chicago institutional milestone, but also the match "that put western football on the map." Penn was considered the best team in the country that year based on a twenty-four-game winning streak and the presence of three all-Americans. Chicago, featuring the play of back Clarence Herschberger, led at the half and surprised Penn with a new style of play that featured deception and quickness (despite Penn's victory). Walter Camp wrote, "Stagg brought out of the West a decidedly advanced style of play," and the veteran observer Caspar Whitney ranked Chicago equal to the best of the East that year. At the end of the season, Herschberger became the first noneastern player (i.e., the first not educated at Harvard, Yale, Princeton, Pennsylvania, or Cornell) selected by Walter Camp for his all-American team. Chicago football teams met eastern opponents seven times in the four seasons from 1898 to 1901 and served as the first western host of an eastern team. Local journalists expected only path-breaking material from Stagg: In 1904 the Maroons' match with the University of Texas was hailed incorrectly as the first football game between teams of the Southwest and the North.[32]

Perhaps an instinct for profits as well as desire for renown accounted for the fact that Stagg's football teams consistently played more difficult schedules than those of their opponents. Well-known, successful opponents ensured greater revenues, and Chicago regularly played
two or three times the number of major opponents as the other conference members. For example, Chicago's 1904 schedule included sev-
en major university teams out of eleven opponents; Michigan played
two major opponents in nine games, Wisconsin two of seven, Illinois
four of ten, and Minnesota two of ten.[33]

The fact that Stagg's demands were granted regularly despite his
occasional rudeness to superiors and peers indicates the esteem in
which he was held. The 1903 construction of state-of-the-art Bartlett
Gymnasium, with its medieval lines and stained glass, was due to the
coach's dogged insistence on the best from Harper. When a well-known
sports authority accused Stagg in 1903 of using players who were not
amateurs, the charge brought a swift defense from one of the university's most renowned professors. Albion Small angrily termed Stagg's
detractor "a cad sport lacking in manhood" in a speech before five
hundred at President Harper's 1903 football dinner. As Small warmed
to his subject, he stated, "I want to tell you that in this cad sport's whole
body there is not as much of the making of a man as Stagg leaves on
his shaving paper each morning." Small's remarks demonstrate the
depth of Stagg's support among Harper's administrators and some faculty. Stagg took deep pride in his position as football coach: "Our profession is one of the noblest and perhaps the most far reaching in building up the manhood of our country."[34]

The Rise of the Player

The most concise statement of the change in the place of football in
the lives of players at Harper's university came from a Maroon veteran in 1897: "I have no more fun in practice games. It isn't amusement
or recreation any more. It is nothing less than hard work." This development no doubt relieved many American minds; set against their
distrust of organized sport, any physical training that could be seen as
work (or later, as war) was welcome. Hence, the status of players
changed, as well as those of spectators and coaches, and the period from
1895 to 1905 saw student-players become player-students. By 1905
football was viewed as the most jealous mistress of college sports; a
Harper's Weekly commentator compared football with the older sports
baseball and rowing and then concluded, "In those sports high excellence is not incompatible with a residue of strength applicable to oth-

er pursuits. Current first-class football seems to take, while it lasts, everything a lad has in him. The game is his work. His recreation he finds in the hospital."[35]

The role of the football player was becoming an identifiable one; it can be described as the twofold development of the player as a "campus commodity" and as a "campus physical elite." The attitude of the young student-player who complained of the businesslike manner with which he was expected to approach the sport of football in 1897 became an anachronism by 1905, for by then players were required to continue football training year-round.[36]

The basis for Stagg's new cult of player efficiency can be seen in his explanation of the award of the coveted C monograms to Chicago athletes—the Order of the C was "the first athletic-letter club ever formed," he wrote. Stagg controlled the awards, which were based upon "merit, amount of work done, and usefulness to the team and the university." The form letter of notification of membership in the Order of the C was built upon the concept of "athletic service to the university." Hence, "usefulness" and "athletic service" spelled out the rationale for the rise of the player as a campus commodity.[37]

Just as the city of Chicago afforded the university the preeminent football marketplace of the West from 1895 to 1905, an excellent supply of college-level players was also available locally. Chicago was in the median enrollment position among Intercollegiate Conference schools, and after 1902 Stagg had excellent players for years. For example, the Maroons of 1896 averaged 173 pounds; those of the 1905 aggregation, 186 pounds; and the size and quality of the players increased almost yearly. The player commodities were supplied by the high schools and by the Chicago Football League, which sponsored a "prairie" (sandlot) game for youths. Both of these agencies, especially the former, grew rapidly from 1895 to 1905 and were similar to the sources the eastern colleges used.[38]

The Recruitment of the Campus Commodities

Stagg and Harper developed a number of recruiting methods that enabled them to improve the quality of Chicago's football teams markedly. Shortly after the turn of the century they sought to create a special relationship with interscholastic players and officials. Harper himself presented an ingenious plan (no doubt produced by Stagg) to the Board of Physical Culture and Athletics addressed to the "reorganization of the Physical Culture work." The seven resolutions were passed in May 1902 in a form both dignified and vague enough to pass faculty review; their effect was the widespread recruitment of schoolboy athletes. Six of the seven resolutions served as Stagg's manifesto to recruit in a more open manner, and they formed an outline of his future recruitment activities.[39]

Harper proposed using the nine previously "affiliated" university prep schools in Illinois and Indiana as places of future employment for Maroon athletes and as athletic "feeder" schools. Another recommendation cleared the way for using the public schools in much the same way. Recommendation number five was the most cryptic and significant of the seven: "That a system be devised for obtaining information in regard to athletics in secondary schools." The text would appear to provide for a kind of data-gathering regarding secondary school athletic programs. In truth, this recommendation led to a comprehensive card file on high school athletes to whom recruitment letters were sent and followed up. Dr. Joseph Raycroft, a member of the board, provided the rationale for the resolution: "The university, to protect itself, must engage actively in a canvass for new students. Others did it, and we must do it, too."[40]

Finally, the sixth recommendation passed in May 1902 legitimated an event that Stagg had already planned and scheduled. The vague proposal was "that interscholastic meets be held of the Academies and high schools in relationship to the University." Within eight days the "First Annual Interscholastic Track Meet" was history, and about two hundred athletes from forty schools—youngsters who had won state meets in Illinois, Michigan, Wisconsin, and Iowa—competed at Marshall Field. Stagg's varsity track team was put on display for the schoolboys as the Maroons engaged the University of California on the same field. The visiting "young prospectives" were housed in university fraternity houses and entertained in "great style" by the athletic management and by enthusiastic student groups.[41]

The coaching staff's decision to engage in a recruitment drive and capture beefy, speedy campus commodities constituted a change from their public position on the matter. Stagg had often railed against "scouting" by other universities and their alumni; in 1900 he argued that recruiting was contrary to the "spirit of amateurism." Two unsuccessful football campaigns later, Stagg and the board "discovered that something had to be done if Chicago expected to compete with other western universities." He and Raycroft admitted that their "conversion" came chiefly at the hands of Chicago graduates, who challenged them publicly at the 1901 alumni football dinner to initiate thorough recruiting. An older Stagg was to assert that the alumni of the American universities were "the most active agents in developing athletic immorality," even though he had assiduously courted just such a development.[42]

The Chicago coaches, the football captain, and interested faculty members met periodically to assess their recruitment progress. They reviewed past communication with the prospects, charted new letter contacts, and prepared for the fall season. The prospects for the 1902 season had been poor, but the number of football aspirants grew from thirty to nearly sixty by early October. The recruitment success of 1902 was enlarged in 1903 with the prophetic "Maroons Sound Doom of Yost's Great Eleven" due to the snaring of "one of the greatest collections of giants ever collected in the West." Earlier in the spring, "unusual activity" by "several old alumni" was credited, along with the track meet, for the "very fertile" athletic prospects of the freshmen of 1903.[43] Chicago newspapers greeted each Midway acquisition as a civic resource and with bold headlines: "Stagg Gets Sprinter," "Hogenson Captured for the Maroon Team," "Stagg Secures Good Guard," "Stagg Gains Another Star Prep Athlete," and "Stagg Secures Star."[44]

President Harper worked with the coaching staff to initiate the recruiting system. He led the formal organization of the university alumni early in 1904, when he addressed them along with C monogram-winners, faculty, and the team at his annual football dinner in the Reynolds Club on campus. "Bring in freshmen athletes" was the motto Harper "unreservedly adopted" in his speech. "We have 6000 alumni in and about Chicago," he challenged the one hundred alumni guests. "Why do not these alumni see that the university gets its fair share of the athletic material?" Harper then urged that a committee be appointed to organize the alumni into "a recruiting organization." The alumni complied within days.[45]

The interscholastic track meet grew rapidly in its importance for the Chicago football enterprise. In its second year Stagg's meet more than doubled in size, and representatives from Indiana, Ohio, Missouri, and Minnesota joined the states that had previously sent athletes. "Stagg's Interscholastic" was the premier meet in the West by 1905, as Nebraska and Kentucky joined the throng; seventy-five schools were represented.[46]

A battle between Chicago and Michigan erupted in 1903 over recruiting prominent Chicago high school players. It was difficult to make a head count, for some of Stagg's new wards had not completed high school, and it was not always easy to pry them into the university. Coach Fielding Yost of Michigan also recruited his share of Chicago public high school juniors in 1903. Yost had early demonstrated the value of proselyting player talent for his teams—he had managed to shanghai some of his West Coast stars (including the legendary Willie Heston from a neighboring California college) when he made the change from Stanford University to a new academic home at Michigan. President David Starr Jordan of Stanford addressed the North Central Association of Colleges and Secondary Schools in 1903 and recalled Yost as a practitioner of the "kind of corruption" in intercollegiate athletics that colleges should eschew.[47]

This undignified recruiting scramble by two major universities drew some criticism, but not from the eminent academics within those institutions. The criticism came from the public press and from high school administrators and officials. One respected columnist, Henry M. Bates, had described late in 1902 the "new and dangerous development . . . of semi-official recruiting bureaus" as a part of the University of Chicago. Bates argued that even if such recruitment were confined to the supposed "legitimate methods," the activity was "most unworthy of the dignity and purposes of a great institution of learning." Another critic perhaps captured the proper spirit when he suggested that the school boys "should . . . be numbered and driven into an inclosed field," after which the coaches of the Intercollegiate Conference would have a drawing for the lot.[48]

The most telling indictment of the player recruitment chaos came from Chicago Superintendent of Schools Edwin G. Cooley. Cooley was an alumnus of the university (Ph.B., 1896) and an acquaintance of President Harper. The superintendent described the Chicago-Michigan approaches to Chicago school boys in 1903 as "practically stealing boys out of high school for athletic purposes before their high-school courses are completed." Cooley claimed, "There are in the University of Chicago three pupils who are on the team who did not complete their high-school course. At the University of Michigan there are two, while the other universities are also bad offenders."[49]

Cooley and a committee of secondary school teachers and principals drew up a set of resolutions that were presented to the Intercollegiate Conference for approval. The resolutions consisted of three rather general statements regarding "a higher standard of morality in athletics" and two specific ones that required a change in university behavior toward high school athletics and athletes. The Intercollegiate Conference responded by noting that the high school officials should address the individual universities, because the conference had no jurisdiction over admissions policies.[50]

Cooley's committee next addressed the universities individually. At least two of the conference schools indicated a desire to cooperate, but the response from Chicago was ambiguous. President Harper did not acknowledge receipt of the committee's January letter until April; he admitted that he had not even presented it to the Board of Physical Culture and Athletics, and yet his conclusion seemed promising: "the conditions which now hold in interscholastic and intercollegiate athletics are so bad that they need the earnest co-operation of all forces—secondary and collegiate—to keep them within proper bounds. You can always count on the University of Chicago joining forces with other faculties and institutions in any effort to better athletic conditions."[51] Events were to prove, however, that such assurances represented the diplomatic duplicity of the athletic entrepreneur rather than the considered judgment of a leader of a major university. There is no record that Harper presented the Cooley Committee's communication to any Chicago faculty group.

President Charles R. Van Hise of the University of Wisconsin presented a plan similar to the Cooley Committee's to Harper, and the response was again disappointing. Van Hise wrote twice before the Chicago leader answered his proposal that all athletes should spend a year in residence before competing in intercollegiate athletics. Harper dismissed the proposal with "one serious objection": "The inevitable result will be to send all men who are interested in athletics to eastern colleges. The eastern institutions are now vying with each other to secure material from the west. This will be playing into their hands. If we could have the east join with us in this rule, this difficulty would be avoided, but there is little hope that they will do this, and if they do not it is practically an abandonment of the athletic field."[52] The Board of Physical Culture and Athletics, in a rare display of difference with Harper, discussed the Harper-Van Hise correspondence at their next meeting and voted to support Van Hise's reform idea.[53]

Vagabond players peddled their football abilities to the highest-bidding school at the turn of the century, and in the absence of standardized eligibility regulations, the bidders were many. For example, two candidates for the 1902 Chicago team practiced one week, disappeared, and emerged at the Michigan practice field. One of the tourists returned to Chicago's team, followed by the other; Wisconsin was then rumored to have captured their fancy. Finally, one went to Ann Arbor to play, and the other remained at Chicago.[54]

The most difficult recruitment for Chicago's football enterprise occurred in 1905 with the acquisition of Walter Steffen, future all-American, from a Chicago high school. His attendance at the Midway did not end the battle for his services, however, for if the universities of the Midwest attempted to lure young athletes before high school graduation, they did not scruple to recruit athletes enrolled at another institution. According to his father, Steffen had "matriculated, paid his tuition, bought his books and attended classes for a week" at Chicago when he left for Madison, Wisconsin. He was accompanied by Wisconsin coach Philip King and the Wisconsin captain, who had journeyed to Chicago ostensibly to see a Chicago game with Iowa. Steffen's announced reason for the visit was an earlier promise made on one of his two previous trips "to see what they had." To that end, he attended football practice to ascertain the football future that Wisconsin, and perhaps he, could expect. Steffen returned to Chicago after a three-day absence. He claimed that the journey was made "entirely against my will" and that he "was ashamed to make the trip and hoped to get up there and get back before any one would know about it." Captain Vanderboom of Wisconsin retorted that the Madison sojourn "was done on Mr. Steffen's own initiative." When the valuable young man returned to the Maroon practice field, President Harper quietly forgot his threats to require an explanation for Steffen's absence from President Van Hise of Wisconsin; Coach Stagg stated that the athletic department would take "no official notice" of Steffen's confused behavior.[55]

The Retention of the Campus Physical Elite

Retaining players proved as difficult as recruiting them, and the elevation of players to a special status in order to retain their services produced a physical elite on the Midway. The new athletic meritocracy within American higher education should not be viewed as a sole aberration against the backdrop of a pure academic meritocracy. Indeed, that academic meritocracy was itself instituted during the late nineteenth century within the social meritocracy (based upon one's birth, piety, and behavior) of the earlier American college.[56]

In 1896 Thomas W. Goodspeed encapsulated the attitudes that led to the rise of football players at Chicago as physical elite: "What we like about our team is that they are men. They are clean upright men and we are not ashamed of them in the classroom, in the parlor, among men or upon the gridiron." He proclaimed them "heroes, every one of them" and promised that "anything the university had they could have." Goodspeed's promise proved remarkably prescient.[57]

The specter of ineligibility was constant for the Chicago players. At least five of the best players on the 1900 team were found academically deficient in July. One leading player was frustrated enough to charge that "he was flunked by a professor who is opposed to athletics." The charge would be difficult to prove because the Chicago faculty generally showed a benign interest in the football team. Indeed, the player who complained was given a special makeup examination by history professor O. J. Thatcher, who was in constant attendance at team practices. The errant player was soon back on the field.[58]

Special examinations administered by a football enthusiast were only part of the indication of faculty kindness. Another valuable player for Chicago journeyed with the team to West Point, New York, for the 1903 Army game although when he departed he was ineligible. The player's eligibility was reinstated by telegram to Stagg from Dean George Vincent after the team's arrival in New York: "Parry reports satisfactory eligible to play best wishes to team."[59]

The departure of an ineligible player with the team may appear questionable, but the ruling was no more precipitate than those made the morning of a game. Eleventh-hour eligibility decisions were usually made by a small subcommittee of the Board of Physical Culture and Athletics. The composition of the committee during one particularly busy period consisted of three physical culture department members (Stagg, Raycroft, and Butterworth) with the ubiquitous Professor Thatcher as chair. The *Chicago Interocean* surveyed the arrangements at the Midway and concluded, "It seems safe to say that no really valuable man will be lost to the team on account of any little educational deficiency." Another newspaper noted wryly later that season that none of the players was ineligible for the Thanksgiving game with Yost's Michigan team.[60]

The regular academic program consisted of three majors of course work each quarter for undergraduates. Chicago undergraduates could take a baccalaureate degree upon completion of four academic years only if nine quarter majors were earned each year. The academic records of the 1903 football team during the fall quarter show that only three of twenty-three members were registered for the normal three majors of work, and only two of the three members received credit for their majors (the third was in a law program that extended into the next quarter). The athletic and academic authorities exercised "careful supervision" over the athletes to limit their course work to two majors. Eighty-three final grades were given the twenty-three members (most were given separate final grades for "class work" and for examinations). The team maintained a 2.01 grade point average (on a four-point grade scale) as a group, or a C average for the quarter if all final grades are weighted equally. There were few A grades (three, two by one team member, F. G. Burrows, a substitute lineman) and few failing grades (i.e., four no-credit grades, two by Walter Eckersall).[61]

That the players were indeed carefully supervised can be seen also in the memoirs of a young history instructor. When Elizabeth Wallace offered her initial course in Latin American history she found, "Most of my students were athletes." Because Spanish was not a prerequisite, and all relevant readings were in Spanish, she recalled, "It was logically concluded by the keen undergraduate mind that the course would be a lecture course and therefore what was known as a snap. It was."[62]

Coach Stagg himself kept a watch on his players and was not above using an informal conversation with an instructor as an appeal for a player's eligibility. When his captain flunked a course after the instructor had told him, he claimed, that the player would pass, Stagg wrote a protest to Harper. The coach stated he thought the case justified his breaking "a rule of my own not to intercede in behalf of any delinquent athlete." He questioned whether the player's failure after his coach had been told the man would pass was "according to rule and whether it is fair treatment." Because there is a paucity of explanatory materials on the many delinquent players it is unclear how often Stagg felt it necessary to abridge his rule "not to intercede."[63]

The physical elite were given other special considerations as well. Early in the century a set of chimes was installed in newly constructed Mitchell Tower, and Stagg had the idea of a special playing of the carillon for the Maroon athletes, especially for those who tended to miss curfew, and gave a sizable gift toward that end. His gift was to provide "a nightly curfew to the men in training." As he explained, "The thought came to me and filled me with the deepest satisfaction, 'Why not have a good-night chime for our own athletes—to let its sweet cadence have a last word with them before they fall asleep, to speak to them of love and loyalty and sacrafice for their University and of hope and inspiration and endeavor for the morrow.'"[64]

The special nightly ringing of the carillon for the benefit of the athletes was consistent with the new elitist status of the group. The concern for the football players' welfare led to a special diet for them at a "training table." The original training plan was to ask all football candidates to live on or near the campus to enable them to eat together. The concept was extended to their living quarters in 1896, when two flats of a private apartment house were engaged as a training center where the "candidates, coaches, and trainers" would "spend all of their time when not in the recitation-room or on the athletic field." That hope vanished by 1897, when local landlords claimed that the footballers had "played such havoc" that they would not be accepted as tenants again. The university countered this refusal by putting a portion of Snell Hall at the disposal of Stagg's men, and by 1902 the newest and most luxurious residence hall was reserved for the intercollegiate athletic teams. Hitchcock Hall, termed the "millionaires' den," became the site for the training table and quarters for about thirty players. Every resident athlete had to sign a "Training Quarters Agreement," which incorporated the spirit of Stagg and the peculiar calling of the young Maroon athletes. Each athlete pledged "not to bring in nor use" alcohol or tobacco and not to gamble; the "good name of the athletic men of the University" was to be preserved in order to make Hitchcock "a clean, sweet and beautiful athletic home."[65]

The separation of the football team from the rest of the student body was accomplished with no discussion of its effect upon student life and values. The idea of separate and unequal training facilities for the players was viewed simply as an efficient use of the physical elite. But students petitioned the faculty overseers of the Men's Commons to move the athletes and their training table to the midst of the commons so that mutual-acquaintance and "school spirit" could develop properly. Their argument asked for the return to a time when student-athletes were not restricted as to the sphere of their activities and when student spectators were acquainted with the players for whom they cheered. The plea was to no avail.[66]

If the physical man was furnished at the training table and at the training quarters, the mental and emotional man was also served. Academic advice came from the faculty members most interested in the success of the team and from Coach Stagg, who watched his men's study habits carefully. President Harper inaugurated a special tutorial program for football players by requesting instructors to coach them in troublesome areas. The emotional balance of the football team was sometimes strained during the season as the pressures for winning mounted. When the Maroons suffered "Nervous Fits" in 1905, Stagg suspended practice sessions and took the team for a carriage ride through Jackson Park. Later in the season when "lack of sleep and general nervousness" bothered the team before an important contest they were whisked to exclusive Onwentsia Golf Club in Lake Forest for a weekend of relaxation at university expense.[67]

The administration and many faculty members were lavish in their praise of the function the new physical elite performed on campus. The football captain was elected at President Harper's annual dinner and became the most revered undergraduate figure. Maroon captains were usually rewarded with the position of convocation student marshall as "an evidence of the esteem" in which they were held by their university, according to President Harper.[68]

Many members of the university community caught the openhanded spirit promised by Secretary Goodspeed; the *Chicago Tribune* observed after one season that the "gridiron warriors have not yet descended to the level of ordinary students," for they still had "distinctions shown them to which the common 'grinder' cannot lay claim." The players were given postgame theater parties, dinners, and trips to other campuses to view football games, accompanied by proud professors and paid for by the game receipts. Such use of game revenues had clear, if casual, precedent. Philip S. Allen, a language instructor and former captain, recounted the immediate use of gate receipts in 1895 to feed the team at a French restaurant on Clark Street after every game. The Thanksgiving dinner after the traditional Michigan game had an important place on the players' calendar, especially when select female students were included as guests of the young gladiators and themselves became an auxiliary elite.[69]

President Harper and many others on the Midway viewed the players as having greater responsibilities to the institution and the other students because of their position as campus elite. Harper scolded academically conditioned and flunking athletes as lacking in "genuine college spirit" at his football banquet in 1903; he charged that such students did not have "the interest of the university at heart." And athletes were held to a higher standard of behavior, much as the nineteenth-century class deacons at Yale. When ice cream was stolen from a class reception and carried to Hitchcock Hall, three athletes who did not participate in the theft but who helped eat the ice cream were immediately suspended as examples to the student body.[70]

Player Profile: Walter Eckersall

The rise of intercollegiate football players as campus commodities and a campus physical elite can be illustrated in the career of Walter Eckersall, the most acclaimed intercollegiate athlete in University of Chicago history and a consensus all-time all-American quarterback.[71]

The future star was born and grew up in the Woodlawn area of Chicago, adjacent to the university. "We little fellows couldn't buy footballs," Eckersall later recalled, "but we caught the spirit of the game from watching Stagg's players racing around in practice and in real games. We had bully times those days. I guess we all dreamed of being football heroes."[72] The youngster's rare physical gifts became apparent at Hyde Park High School. Eckersall set a ten-second-flat Illinois hundred-yard dash record in 1903 that stood until the future Olympian Ralph Metcalfe broke it in 1928. The football teams on which he played there were nationally ranked and contributed many noteworthy players to American collegiate football. One year Hyde Park played Brooklyn Tech, the best eastern school team, for the "high school national championship" and won 105-0 (fifteen-year-old Knute Rockne sneaked into the ball park to see his boyhood idol Eckersall play that day). Eckersall was the quarterback and leader of those teams and already a favorite with intercollegiate coaches when he was midway through his secondary school work.[73]

Coach Stagg precipitately announced in the autumn of 1902 that he had secured "Eckersall's promise to enter the Midway school" the following year. That claim upon Eckersall was recalled in June of 1903, when it was reported that "Michigan has had secret embassies calling on Eckersall" and that "rare inducements have been offered." An outraged member of Chicago's athletic management was quoted as charging that the "Wolverines have violated every ethic of intercollegiate sport" and have "been stooping to the lowest practices to steal Eckersall from us."

Stagg was probably the strongest inducement for Eckersall to remain in Chicago for his intercollegiate career. An important, if not crucial, factor in Eckersall's decision was Stagg's defense of the young player's "amateur" status during the summer of 1903, when the Amateur Athletic Union suspended Eckersall for playing on a professional baseball team. Stagg was the chief public defender (Yost of Michigan also joined the defense) of Eckersall's amateur status, and he was later reinstated. In the event, the uncertain young man did not make his college decision until just before the opening of the two universities in 1903, and he was aided mightily by Stagg, who later admitted grabbing Eckersall off the platform before he could entrain to Ann Arbor.[74]

Eckersall was the best-known athlete to leave a Chicago high school up to 1903; his athletic records and the AAU contretemps had brought him more notoriety before he had played a game for Chicago than most collegiate performers ever gain. The slight, quiet boy seemed to be made in the hero's mold on and off the gridiron. He even saved the life of a yachtsman in the summer of 1904 after the sailor's boat capsized in Lake Michigan.[75]

Young Eckersall served well as player commodity. He was a selfless performer, marked by complete dedication to the purpose of the American intercollegiate game—victory. Well, almost always. Once he decided to refuse. In a play to be used when the Maroons were within five yards of the goal line, the linemen were to hurl the 136-pound Eckersall goalward through the air. On the first practice attempt, he landed a scant three yards away on his back. The winded and bruised quarterback commented, "The Old Man has gotten up this fine play, but I will be damned if I am ever going to call it." Eckersall's commitment to victory was never more noticeable than in the 1904 game with Michigan, when he fainted of exhaustion in the carriage returning home. His academic dean George E. Vincent said in a speech to students and faculty, "I have noticed that he has always shown extraordinary indifference to the grandstand, and a splendid loyalty to his team." The Eckersall dedication to the game infused his teammates magnificently, according to Stagg: "In his playing, Eckie was very intense and hard working, and he had no patience with a loafer. On the field, and running the team, he was a dominant personality and carried the team along with him. He snapped out his signals quickly and incisively with the command of a general, and did not stand for any dilatory tactics on the part of any of the players."[76]

Walter Eckersall brought more publicity to the University of Chicago than any other student in the institution's history, with the possible exception of the kidnap-murderers Nathan Leopold and Richard Loeb. From his freshman year, when a disappointed Wisconsin newspaper headlined a Chicago victory with "Eckersall, 15; Wisconsin, 6," the young man had a heavy burden of fame to carry.[77]

Intercollegiate football provided the authentic folk hero for the university which it had lacked. The students had gamely tried to make the cadaverous Rockefeller a hero with their songs and praise, but the attempts were characterized by a defensiveness and unease hardly appropriate to a hero's status. Eckersall was a figure who could not be gainsaid, even by the enemy. Michigan composed an Eckersall chant that was wishfully fatal but implicitly laudatory:

> Eckersall, Eckersall!
> running with the ball,
> You will get an awful fall,
> Eckersall, Eckersall!
> Eckie, Eckie, break your neckie,
> Eckersall![78]

Unfortunately, Walter Eckersall was living on borrowed time; he compiled an atrocious academic record but was permitted to pursue that path until his football eligibility ended. In 1905 *Collier's* termed him as "simply an 'athletic ward'" of the university, whose qualifications were well short of the "most poorly prepared freshman." From his first quarter at Chicago as a subfreshman (he had not completed college preparatory work), Eckersall led his teammates off—as well as on—the field in failing grades and total absences from classroom work. He registered for courses with the same instructors the next quarter (winter 1904), but his political science instructor, Charles Merriam, reported that "he never appeared in class" during the quarter. His work in English showed a C average, although he again led the class in absences. Eckersall continued to participate in athletics after his disastrous first quarter at the university. In fact, he and six other first-year students who were flunking participated in intercollegiate track meets for freshmen. Their participation and the press coverage prompted an embarrassed University Council to reconsider the basis of eligibility for freshmen, but the inquiry petered out when Harper assumed responsibility with Stagg for the involvement of the errant students.[79]

The reconstruction of Eckersall's eligibility began during the spring quarter of 1904 to ensure his football play that autumn. He was enrolled in two history courses for Senior College (upper-division) students. His enrollment in "The Renaissance Age" would appear peculiar because the course was described as appropriate for those wishing to do graduate work in history, and such students were advised to take the course in their third year at Chicago. Eckersall's registration would appear peculiar, that is, if the teacher were other than the Chicago athlete's friend, Oliver J. Thatcher. Eckersall was given a C for his work by Thatcher, who did not flunk a single student in the class of sixty-seven, which included a good number of athletes, some of whom had previously experienced academic difficulty. The other course Eckersall enrolled in was "History of the United States: The Later Constitutional Period," taught by Francis Shepardson, a future member of the Board of Physical Culture and Athletics and secretary to President Harper. Work in the course was acceptable for graduate credit, and the largest division of students represented were in the Senior College. Eckersall received a C for his work in the course, which enrolled sixty-six and flunked but one.[80]

Although quarterback Eckersall's football career continued along extraterrestrial lines during the remainder of his four seasons at Chicago, the hapless young man fell to earth and further behind his classmates in his academic career. He maintained his eligibility in intercollegiate athletics but found that after three and two-thirds years of higher education he was still classified in the Junior Colleges (lower division). His lack of the full secondary school preparation for his college work was partly responsible; at least eight of his courses were applied toward making up his admissions deficiencies. At the end of the autumn quarter of 1906, the all-American had earned only fourteen course majors of credit toward the thirty-six required for graduation. He no doubt viewed his academic future with considerable anxiety; the completion of his degree program would have required many years of further study even though his program, the Ph.B. in the College of Commerce, was the least taxing field of study.[81]

By 1905 Eckersall had captured the complete fancy of football officials, sportswriters, and the public. His appearance in the lobby of the Chicago hotel where the Intercollegiate Conference was meeting reportedly provoked a spontaneous ovation. Sportswriters honored him with paeans for special games or performances. Most of the efforts were forgettable sports page doggerel, but one was more revealing than intended. "The Man with the Toe," written before the 1905 game with the Michigan Wolverines, was prefaced with an apology to Edwin Markham and began:

> Bowed by responsibility he's poised
> Upon his toe and gazes at the ball,
> Resolution stamped upon his face,
> And on his back the burden of maroon.
> Who made him dead to censure or applause,
> A man who grieves not and who always hopes,
> Clever and cool, a brother to the fox?
> Who loosened him among the wolverines?
> Whose was the mind that taught him how to kick?
> Whose word that coached his docile brain?[82]

Eckersall was consistently portrayed as the Chicago team leader and star player: "Everything revolved around the skilled kicker," asserted the *Chicago Journal*. The *St. Louis Post-Dispatch* headlined an article regarding Eckersall, "Chicago Sets More Store by Eckersall's Toe Than Rockefeller's Money." The article claimed that "greater even than Mr. Rockefeller's tainted tin about Chicago University is the terrible toe of Walter Eckersall." *Collier's Weekly* thought Eckersall's play was "without a flaw" and that "as captain of a team and field general he has no equal." The *New York Globe* wrote of Eckersall's place in intercollegiate football at the close of his career: "The passing of Eckersall is not only a loss to western football but the eclipse of the brightest star in the football firmament. When it comes to handling the palm to any one player for individual brilliancy Eckersall has no rivals, according to critics of all sections of this country."[83]

The student body gathered in a giant rally to demonstrate their affection and appreciation for Captain Eckersall the day before his last game in 1906. The *Daily Maroon* reported that at the "most enthusiastic mass meeting that has been held this year the cheers for the little captain lasted at times for minutes." The report continued:

Actual tears stood in Eckie's eyes as he told how much gratitude he owed to Coach Stagg, as he praised the team, as he thanked the student body for its loyal support of him and as he expressed his wish for Chicago's success in the future. He had planned to say more, but his emotion made him leave the platform abruptly. He said in speaking of Director Stagg: "It is a privilege to be on such a team as Chicago has. I cannot tell you how great a privilege it has been to spend four years under Coach Stagg. I owe what success I have had to him. He not only trains his men in athletics but he trains their character."

An accompanying *Maroon* editorial spoke of Eckersall's football playing abilities and asserted that "his loyalty, his modesty, his qualities of
leadership . . . have endeared him to his friends." Students at the university were encouraged to "pay tribute" to their hero "by purchasing
the beautiful six-color, 25 × 29, autographic poster of Eckersall." The
buyer was instructed to "hang it up in your room, and always have a
material remembrance of him."[84]

Dean Vincent praised the strength of Eckersall's character in a speech
to that student rally, and the university faculty reinforced his assess-
ment at the player's last game. The faculty presented Captain Eckersall a "time-piece" as a "token of appreciation" of his "services in the
University." Thomas Goodspeed presented him with a gold watch in
front of the grandstand during half-time of the Nebraska game. The
moment was frozen by a photograph: Eckersall, sheathed in a Maroon
blanket, accepts with becoming modesty as he shakes the hand of Secretary Goodspeed, whose round face frames eyes crinkled with pleasure; one prepubescent boy lays his hand gently upon the laces of
Eckersall's football shoe as if to imbibe the wondrous powers within,
and another boy gingerly begins his grope for a share in the anoint-
ment. Eckersall expressed his formal thanks to Acting President Harry
Pratt Judson (Harper died early in 1906). "It is a gift," he wrote, "I shall
cherish as long as I live, not alone for its value as a gift, but also for
the memories it carries with it." The admiration that prompted the gift,
and the gratitude the young man felt toward the donors, were to evap-
orate within two months.[85]

The last term in which Walter Herbert Eckersall was enrolled was
the 1906 autumn quarter, during which he completed his football eligibility. He did not register for the 1907 winter quarter and never again
resumed his studies at the university.[86] Eckersall faded rapidly from the
pages of the newspapers that he had dominated such a short time before. The last athletic exploit recorded of Eckersall on the Midway was
as spectacular as his earlier ones. Bowling in the interfraternity tournament, he broke the university record handily as he rolled a 245 game
score. Within days his difficulty was hinted, but not explained, when
the *Maroon* announced that his bowling scores for his fraternity, Al-
pha Delta Phi, had been abrogated due to his being ruled ineligible
because of his "non-residence."[87]

The demise of Walter Eckersall at the University of Chicago was
superficially sudden, but the crisis was seemingly long in the making.
The troubles he experienced must have gone beyond the academic for
some time, but the extant records are spare and coded. We do know
that a bitter rupture between Eckersall and university officials occurred;

a notation dated January 25, 1907, on his official transcript reads, *"Mr. Eckersall is not to be permitted to register in the Univ. again—for cause.* By Order of Acting President Judson."[88]

The fullest explanation available of this whole affair is contained in a four-page letter written to President Judson on March 14, 1907, by an older friend of Eckersall, George Buckley. Buckley wrote as a representative of some Chicago alumni, who had heard that Judson was "contemplating drastic action" to demonstrate his "disapproval of the many deplorable and unfortunate actions of Mr. Eckersall." Buckley explained that Eckersall had informed the alumni group of a letter he had written to the president. Eckersall, Buckley reminded Judson, had "the object of removing himself from your jurisdiction as well as to call your attention to the fact that the University, through its officers, has been derelict in its duty. Derelict in so far as their having knowledge of his loose morals, and yet willing to use him for advertising purposes until he had completed his college career."[89]

Buckley did not continue this theme of thinly veiled attack on Judson's university. Instead, he admitted the truth of the grave charges against his friend Eckersall, which included bad debts, traitorous personal friendships, and the athlete's letter, which Buckley termed "a nasty thing," to Judson. Buckley undertook to guarantee the reformation of the football star with the help of the other interested alumni and a legal undertaking by Eckersall "assigning every cent of his salary and income for one year to a person who will see to it that all debts contracted by Eckersall in the past will be paid." The goal was that Eckersall execute a "right about face" and "clean house morally."[90]

Buckley alluded no farther to the circumstances under which Eckersall was recruited by the university community and encouraged to put the life of the body before the life of the mind; Judson, after all, had been a major official in the university when Eckersall was at the institution. Instead, Buckley kept his purpose firmly in mind and eased the tone of his letter considerably from his opening; Eckersall became at once victim and victimizer: "He is not altogether to blame; he has never had the right way pointed out to him until the University took action. He had come to regard his friends and admirers merely as persons from whom something was to be had for nothing. In other words, he has been a grafter as well as a monumental liar." Buckley concluded with a plea that no public expulsion or similar action take place until the group of alumni and friends of Eckersall had an opportunity "to make Eckersall a man." There is a bitter irony here, for both Stagg and Eckersall had claimed for four years that such manufacture occurred daily at the football field. Buckley's plea is strong, touching, and patronizingly hypocritical, with, "We believe you do not want to do anything which would in any way handicap this boy in the years to come." Buckley's plea for mercy brought a swift response from Judson—by return mail he asked Buckley to come in for a conference. President Judson subsequently made no public statement regarding Eckersall, and there is no further official university record of their most famous student-athlete.

Walter Eckersall soon became a successful football correspondent for the *Chicago Tribune,* a task in which he could still trade upon his athletic career. He also became a widely employed football game official, frequently of the same game he was covering for the *Tribune* (and earning considerably more at the game as an official than as a writer). He was one of many sportswriters who practiced this conflict of interest, but he seems to have been particularly popular in the role, especially with Knute Rockne, who often successfully managed the selection of officials for his own games and even paid sportswriters as publicists for the games they were assigned by their newspapers. In *Shake Down the Thunder: The Creation of Notre Dame Football,* Murray Sperber notes that Eckersall even practiced "triple-dipping" (as paid game publicist, game official, and game reporter) for Rockne, and that coaches gave many writers (including Eckersall) free tickets, which they resold for a handsome profit.[91]

Although Dean Vincent warned Stagg off further relations with the disgraced Eckersall in 1908 ("It would seem unfortunate to have any association with him or recognition of him by the University"), the coach found it difficult advice to follow. He subsequently took Eckersall with him to help former Maroon halfback and teammate Hugo Bezdek install the forward pass at the University of Arkansas. However, the relationship must have cooled subsequently, because in 1924 Stagg asserted that the sportswriter "has given me the go bye for years." And a long-due loan for $20 and Eckersall's national promotion of cigarette smoking did not help the relationship during the 1920s. There is no record of Stagg's response to the tobacco campaign, but other coaches were outraged: Coach Bill Roper of Princeton attacked what he termed this "exploitation of football for commercial purposes," and Knute Rockne, offered $2,000 for the same advertising campaign, refused: "This attempt . . . to build up increased business at the expense of the youth of the land cannot be condemned sufficiently." The ghost of Eckersall's past as the prototypical player commodity and gridiron hero seems to have pursued him, however, according to an undated memorandum dictated by his old coach Stagg:

In _____, I visited "Wallie" Eckersall at the St. Luke's Hospital, where he was in very great danger of dying as the result of a very severe case of heart dilation brought on as a result of dissipation. I said to him, "Eckie, you are going to turn over a new leaf now, aren't you?" and he said "Yes, Mr. Stagg, I am." It is several years now since this incident occurred, and Eckie has been true to his word. He hasn't touched liquor since his hospital experience and he has become a dependable and good citizen.[92]

Somehow the need for a proper ending to the Eckersall story took precedence over the truth of his obloquy on the Midway. In 1921, a scant fifteen years later, George Matthew Adams, a leading writer of twentieth-century success manuals and a nationally syndicated columnist, confidently wrote: "Many years ago, when Eckersall, the brilliant quarterback for the University of Chicago, finished his college course, he paid this tribute to Mr. Stagg: 'Stagg teaches character, as well as football.'"[93] The apocrypha was enough to warrant that a Walter Eckersall Memorial Stadium be built by the city of Chicago in 1947.

Walter Eckersall received his apotheosis soon after his early death in 1930. It was fitting, perhaps, that this poetic remembrance of him be written in the turgid style of the sports page:

THE QUARTERBACK

It's a long way back o'er the beaten track,
To the football of yesteryear,
Over hill and dale winds the long, long trail
That's misty at times, and drear,
There are lots and lots too, of gladsome spots
Though the gladness just now is stayed
When we think of the cheers not unmixed with tears
When young Walt Eckersall played.
Not the bulky type but your heart would gripe.
When he flashed through a broken field,
And he knew the trick of a placed drop-kick
When a score was a drop-kick's yield.
Reckoned near and far as the quarterback star
O'er the Styx he's gone unafraid,
And the old time grads will say they were lads,
When young Eckersall played.
But he's old Walt now and that battered brow
Is stilled 'neath its laurel and bay.
What can be that roar from the nearing shore?
Why it's men not the Milky Way.
Friends are in the crowd, "God they're crying' out loud?"
They await him, bedecked, arrayed?

> Be sure they recall in Valhalla's hall
> When young Walt Eckersall played.[94]

The patronage of President William Rainey Harper, the spectator and player supply that the city of Chicago offered, and the single-minded "saintly" coach had combined to ensure that the University of Chicago football enterprise was hugely successful by 1905. President Harper had adopted university founder John D. Rockefeller's Darwinian modus operandi closely enough to recruit professors and players alike and to use them successfully in promoting the new academic creation. It was, moreover, Harper's and Stagg's keen sense of the basics of the institution and their artful collaboration in the athletics of Darwinism that promoted football within and without the university. The institution and the sport were now synonymous, stable, and famous. And the fixity of the football undertaking was soon demonstrated, for Stagg and Chicago football were tested severely in 1905–6, along with the national game.[95]

The rise of the spectator, coach, and player over the generation ending in 1905 demonstrates that the order of primacy in American football had been reversed—the student-player lost control of his surpassingly enjoyable pastime—the adults snatched the joy from him, and his campus enjoyment became his campus employment. The voracious appetite of the consumption economy began to take over adolescent sport—the man/child had begun to lose the natural joy of sport to the yawning maw of the acquisitive society.

3

Football's Year of Trial and Triumph, 1905–6

Football today is a social obsession—a boy-killing, education-prostituting, gladiatorial sport.

    —Divinity Professor Shailer Mathews

Success to Camp, Deland, Stagg, and all the kings and leagues of football the country over, that their craft may snatch the noble game from threatened disrepute, keeping it from generation to generation the natural training school of the American boy invincible.

    —*Chicago Interocean*, December 3, 1905

American universities had in effect asked a question of themselves similar to that of William Graham Sumner's *What Social Classes Owe to Each Other*.[1] If Sumner finally answered, "Nothing," the leading football powers answered similarly regarding interuniversity relations, and their attempts to emerge as the fittest were unsparing of each other. The sport by 1905 was characterized by rapid expansion, exploitive use of student and spectator, and a rather smug assurance that this was all a part of inevitable "progress." Administrators and coaches shared the laissez-faire view that the game's development would be best left alone without group sovereignty and interference.

Intercollegiate football at Chicago was, from its origins, an athletic model of the survival of the fittest. Football was superbly fitted for the job: It grew out of a congeries of disorderly campus activities such as hazing; it was intrinsically engrossing as a physically taxing and precarious exercise; its blending of rugged individualism with the need for a militaristic, unified, efficient effort assured it met the need for liberty, purpose, and order in American life; it served as a basis for simple comparisons of complex and diverse academic institutions; and its highly competitive, meritocratic, Darwinian nature reassured those who insisted the American collegiate sporting scene should be freed from the class-ridden, inequitable British models. And, just as with other American institutions founded upon Darwinian principles, intercollegiate football overreached itself through its intrinsic violence and its tendency to be a jealous and greedy companion. In 1905, football joined the economic trusts and political monopolies as objects of unprecedented public scrutiny and criticism. Then American society had to determine the appropriate place of football in university culture.

An American Game, 1905

The 1905 Michigan at Chicago Thanksgiving game provided a vivid demonstration of the development of American intercollegiate football—the strengths and weaknesses of the game were on display that gray, cold November day. The violence on the field and the attendant academic difficulties off the field were representative of the factors that provoked a widespread challenge to the sport; the resulting American reforms can be termed the "athletics of consensus."

The game was significant for football followers, for it "decided" something deemed crucial—the championship of the West. Three decades later, football writers would determine that the game had identified the mythical "national champion" that year. More important, the two well-trained teams, coached by men whose university compensation surpassed almost everyone on their respective campuses, were harbingers of the twentieth-century rise of intercollegiate players and coaches, which would prove of enormous significance for American higher education.[2]

The game featured the legendary Michigan team of Fielding Yost, which had not been defeated for more than four seasons, against an undefeated Chicago team led by all-American quarterback Walter Eckersall. The University of Michigan had been the pioneer of football outside the Atlantic Seaboard and New England. Michigan organized a football association in 1873 and played the first intercollegiate contest in the Midwest when they met Racine College of Wisconsin at the Chicago White Stockings baseball field in 1879. Lacking competition in their area, they journeyed east in 1881 and played Harvard, Yale, and Princeton within six days in the nation's first inter-regional matches. Yost had been unbeaten at Michigan ever since he arrived in 1901, and the last Michigan defeat had been to Chicago in 1900. Yost's teams, from 1901 to the last game of 1905, won 56 games and scored 2,821 points to 40 for their opponents, or an average of more than 50 points per game to .7 points for opponents (only five teams scored against Michigan, and Chicago had scored twelve of the opposition points). Michigan played an impressive inter-regional schedule, including Stanford, Nebraska, Carlisle, and Vanderbilt, and the Wolverines were named retrospective national champion for 1901 and 1902. Chicago had been disappointed for four years in its late-season clashes with its chief rival, and Maroon supporters judged a football season successful only if Michigan were beaten.[3]

The meeting of the two teams elicited the greatest volume of interest in a single game west of Philadelphia to that time, and Walter Camp noted in *Harper's Weekly* that Chicago was "bending every energy toward at last stopping Michigan's conquering ways." One estimate was that only 20 percent who wanted tickets could obtain them, even though Chicago had enlarged the stands. Requests for fifty thousand seats reached the Midway ten days before the contest, and orders continued to flood the athletic offices. Michigan ran short of tickets, for three thousand of their followers were to entrain from Ann Arbor and join another three thousand Chicago residents in the west stand reserved entirely for Michigan backers.[4]

Chicago fans, some two thousand of whom were fresh from a football journey to Madison to see the Maroons defeat Wisconsin, clamored for the Marshall Field tickets. The rapidity of the ticket sales was phenomenal. Chicagoans bought their seats at the rate of one every two and one-half seconds at one source, and Ann Arbor fans bought tickets almost as rapidly. Widespread scalping resulted as the shortage of tickets became acute. "The ticket scalping industry on the Michigan-Chicago game is a record-breaker for a sporting event in Chicago," one newspaper asserted. Even the elevator boys in the Marquette Building were said to be peddling the precious tickets at inflated prices, but the chief culprits were university students who had been allowed special consideration—prime location and early purchase. A Chicago alderman angrily introduced a resolution against scalping, and the mayor, dramatically addressing himself to public safety, ordered police to arrest all scalpers, including students. The Palmer House ticket agent was arrested and made an example—his defense was that he bought them from needy students. John McCutcheon, the *Chicago Tribune*'s popular cartoonist, showed speculators literally putting the gun to hopeful spectators over ticket prices, with "student grafters" serving as suppliers.[5]

President William Rainey Harper knew how to use such a widely heralded event. It was a time to sow the seeds of interest among wealthy Loop businessmen, and it was a time for those who had invested in the school to reap the rewards of a choice spectator position. Some, such as a flush clothier, demanded the best and showed impatience when the best was not delivered. "Mr Henry C. Lytton, my father, having donated quite liberally to the University, feels rather keenly the fact that he is not entitled to any consideration, all of which is due to the management of this sale of seats for the games," wrote George Lytton. Superb tickets from Harper's office were in the return mail. Football was the chief event that caused such spectatorial concern; people would hardly manifest such waspishness over a public lecture by a faculty luminary. Anita McCormick Blaine, a well-known Chicago patroness, wrote after the game to thank Harper and said, "We considered ourselves your guests."[6]

President Harper was ill with cancer, but his condition did not dampen his enthusiasm. Although he was in bed and would be dead within two months, he made plans to view the game from his son Paul's room in the north facade of Hitchcock Hall, across 57th Street from Marshall Field. Harper also quite remarkably managed to give orders in great detail regarding arrangements for ticket-selling, building and grounds guards, seating conditions, and ushering.[7]

Coach Stagg prepared his team inside a specially constructed "stockade" some twelve feet in height, where he conducted secret nocturnal practices by electric lights. The one building that afforded a view into this field was patrolled by a corps of watchmen.[8]

Thanksgiving Day 1905 was cold (about ten degrees above zero), and a light snow fell intermittently throughout the game. Michigan was favored two to one over Chicago, and it was estimated that $50,000 had been wagered. Speculators received $20 a ticket by game time, and a university student was arrested for trying to peddle his tickets at the inflated price. The stands were sprinkled with partisans two hours before the kickoff, and the cheering sections of the two schools broke out new taunts and songs for the occasion. The maize and blue stands of Michigan yelled a prediction that "there'll be a hot time in Ann Arbor tonight," and the Chicago section answered across the frozen field, "Maroon, Maroon, Maroon . . . show the Michiganders how Chicago goes."[9]

The contest was viewed by twenty-seven thousand people, including Walter Camp, creator of the all-American player idea. Interlopers viewed the game from the windows of the Home for Incurables across 56th Street and from the temporary stands on the roofs of the houses across Ellis Avenue, for which privilege some had paid handsomely. The largest gathering of students without tickets was gaping from the student rooms of Hitchcock Hall. Women were allowed into the men's rooms for the occasion, and "jolly" room parties proceeded during the game. President Harper was too ill to get up to his son's Hitchcock room, and language professor Elizabeth Wallace, who took turns with Mrs. Harper sitting with the president during the game, wrote that telephone lines came from the field, where a "press agent" reported the action to the ear piece on Harper's pillow. She continued:

> Finally the stentorian voice of the press agent said in metallic measure. . . . "Michigan team comes on the field . . . Chicago team comes on field . . . Chicago wins the toss . . . chooses north goal, wind in back . . . teams line up in center of field. . . ." When we reached this point I noticed that Dr. Harper was trembling with excitement and his hands were cold; so I gently but firmly took the telephone away, and said that I would listen and report, as that would lessen the strain by at least one remove. He meekly acquiesced. Once in a while when we made an unusual gain, we had to give a little cheer all by ourselves, and once Dr. Harper tried to hum, "There'll be a hot time."[10]

The event offered two important developments that represented a kind of democratizing of the game: Chicago newspapers described it primarily as an athletic and not a social event, and women attended in large numbers and showed their enthusiasm in much the same manner as their male escorts. Chicago society was again out in force, but they had to be content with regular grandstand seats because the elitist front boxes of previous years had given way to the more democratic and profitable tiered seating. Women "fought for tickets and points of advantage around the field" as they emulated the male spectators, and the newspapers made heavy photographic use of their presence. One writer described a Michigan student as "a demure young woman" with "progressive ideas." Her "escort was the proprietor of a silver flask. The woman carried it in her muff. Every little while, feeling chilly, she would touch her muff lightly to her lips. Then with ingenuousness written all over her pretty face, she would hand the muff to her escort. He, too, would apply it to his countenance."[11]

The game was superlatively played. Both teams were trained and coached to a fine precision, and it soon became apparent they were nearly equal that afternoon. These well-meshed groups of young men were symbolic of the demise of free-ranging individuality and creativity on the gridiron. Teams as successful as these were due to the subjugation of such expression to the group purpose. One football expert described the Michigan team as a wondrous "machine," and Yost also referred to it as, "my . . . beautiful machine." The nature of this leisure activity changed mightily when aggregations of student-athletes became "machines" of athlete-students. The demise of the swift-dealing individualists and the rise of the machine in the American intercollegiate football garden was sealed with the *Chicago Tribune*'s announcement after the game that Stagg had "out-machined" Yost's eleven. The match was so closely played by the two machines that only a human error of judgment could afford a break in the impasse.[12]

The "nonmachined" element was provided by Michigan halfback Dennison Clark as he attempted one flash of rugged individualism that afternoon. Catching an Eckersall punt at his own goal line, he pluckily tried to advance with it and was carried back into his own end zone by the tackles of two Chicago men. The resultant safety yielded two points to Chicago and was the only score of the day.[13]

The safety did not occur until late in the game, and at halftime both coaches endeavored to talk their teams into victory. Stagg's effort was especially impressive, he remembered, because the bedridden Harper sent the team a message that they "must win this game." He had become so agitated by the scoreless game at halftime that he dispatched Professor Wallace to the locker room to deliver the message to Stagg, who recalled giving the message to the men and "pleading with them to win for the dying president's sake." It is an all-American story; unfortunately, the most reliable eyewitness, Professor Wallace, recorded her disappointment at finding an empty locker room.[14]

The 2-0 victory over the Fielding Yost Michigan dynasty in 1905 was the opening of two decades of Chicago leadership of the Midwest and the university's being a significant factor on the national scene. The victory brought about the highest level ever of campus and public enthusiasm over football at the university. An impromptu parade of 2,500 Chicago students and alumni led by the university band formed immediately after the game. They marched to President Harper's house and sang the "Alma Mater" followed by nine "rahs" for him and cries for a speech. Harper was too ill to make an appearance, but his eldest son, Samuel, read a statement of thanks from his father. Bonfires flickered against the grey gothic of the campus in the early sunset. The celebrations were extemporaneous, fragmented, and continuous the first night. During the next day, students scurried about the campus and Hyde Park, searching for firewood. By late afternoon a woodpile "as large as a house" stood north of Ryerson Hall, awaiting its torching. Class attendance was limited to the "grinds" as students continued to celebrate and fete the victorious warriors in their midst. That night, the woodpile, containing representative bits of many Hyde Park garden fences and out-houses, glorified the Chicago football players. The bonfire was accompanied by "a nightshirt parade and war dance."[15]

The official celebration of the football victory was held on the Monday night following the game. Virtually every part of the university was represented in the planning, the program, and the audience at the "Monster Football Mass Meeting" in Mandel Hall. The alumni club of the city of Chicago asked members to gather fifteen minutes early in their alumni room, Hutchinson Tower, to ensure that they made a unified, dramatic appearance. Not inappropriately, all alumni were instructed, "Bring Your Rattle!" Amid the many and diverse speakers was a steady parade of graduates who had played football in the "olden days"—some ten years previously.[16]

This binge at the Midway was an important corporate activity. The university had been established after the abolition of compulsory chapel in most American academic communities and at the time the elective system was gaining wide acceptance. The secularization of the campuses combined with the new elective systems left many institutions without a means of corporate focus and cohesion. Intercollegiate athletics, especially football, helped the schools to reclaim their constituencies.[17]

The victory over Michigan increased the university's sense of community, and that community gave testimony to its common faith at the game's end, when fans sang a Doxology written by a Chicago halfback. The song announced a Chicago gridiron paradise and was sung to a tune of Baptist utopia, "Beulah Land!":

> We have reached the day of turkey and wine,
> And we have been winners every time,
> Here stand undimmed one happy day,
> For all our foes have passed away.[18]

The Michigan postscript to the game was provided by the life and death of the young halfback Denny Clark. The blame placed on the unfortunate Clark was widespread and pointed. "It may be said, and said truthfully," one newspaper sermonized, "that Clark of Michigan defeated his own eleven." Other newspapers termed it "the wretched blunder" and a "lapse of brain work"; Walter Camp was quoted as describing the play as a "rank blunder." Clark left the Michigan team quarters after the game and was missing for a time. His despondency was so great that suicide was mentioned as a possibility; Clark was quoted as moaning, "Oh, this is horrible. . . . I shall kill myself because I am in disgrace."[19]

Fielding Yost, in a nationally syndicated article in 1925, remembered the incident and noted that a year previously he had met the middle-aged Clark in Portland, Oregon. Clark recalled his error constantly during their reunion, and Yost tried to set him at ease. Yost concluded that "only Dennis still feels the pain of it." The pain ended for William

Dennison Clark seven years later; he shot himself through the heart. In a suicide note to his wife he reportedly expressed the hope that his "final play" would be of some benefit in atoning for his error at Marshall Field.[20]

There was a paradox in the response of many thoughtful Americans to the game of intercollegiate football in 1905. Anita McCormick Blaine was one such who was present at the epic Michigan-Chicago match. She saw Eckersall fouled after one of his punts and the Michigan offender ordered from the field, and she was no doubt aware of the possible loss of the eye of the Chicago songwriter-halfback. After the game, she wrote her host, President Harper, that the game "certainly should not be played quite as it is," but she hoped the game would be saved by amended rules. Blaine felt the Chicago team demonstrated excellent sportsmanship in their victory—that they battled "so magnificently" and "so valiantly"—and concluded, "It was a great day!" This mixture of abhorrence and attraction to the sport was not unusual in the critical year.[21]

National Reform

Criticism of American football had been building during the season of 1905. The principal elements of the institution of football at the University of Chicago—the intense degree to which students, faculty, and alumni identified with the fortunes of their teams, combined with the resultant academic dysfunction, the physical violence on the field, and the overblown publicity—were all present on that day of Thanksgiving in Chicago and were present on campuses and gridirons across America.

Sir Thomas Elyot's assertion that football offered nothing but "beastly fury and extreme violence" to sixteenth-century England can also be applied to American intercollegiate football up to the reforms of 1906.[22] There were two basic criticisms since the beginnings of intercollegiate football in America: that it was unnecessarily violent, and that it was deleterious in various ways to the student-player and his academic environment. Harvard had temporarily abolished the game in 1885, essentially because of the latter criticism; the argument regarding violence was added during the widespread attacks on the game in the early 1890s. In 1905, most of the criticism by the general public noted the brutality issue, and the academics' criticism was concerned with academic erosion.

Cornell University president and historian Andrew Dickson White earlier had regarded football as a "vestige of barbarity," and one observer termed the 1890s the "barbarian age of the game." Slugging, especially at the line of scrimmage and in the frequent pile-ups, was developed to a fine craft, and many players excelled. Game officials exercised scant control over the players; they sometimes stood toe to toe with offending players, exchanging blows in an attempt to enforce decisions. Wrangling was constant and game stoppages frequent. Unnecessary roughness and brutality were such a part of the game that their absence was usually remarked upon. The "mass momentum" plays (i.e., when the offensive players would mass together and gather momentum to hit the defensive line or kick coverage) were at the heart of the problem.[23]

Hoping to construct a defense to the reformers of the 1890s, Walter Camp created and chaired a committee comprised of Harvard, Yale, and Princeton trustees and alumni and the Reverend Endicott Peabody, Groton School's founder-headmaster. The group surveyed virtually all former players from their three colleges and Pennsylvania and also queried many former schoolboy players. Camp rushed the results into print with his 1894 football apologia *Football Facts and Figures,* but he may have received more than he bargained for in the nearly one thousand survey responses. Although they enthusiastically supported the game, many players and observers (notably the headmasters) hoped that the new mass play that Camp had recently engineered would be replaced by the earlier, more "open" game they preferred. In 1894, Harvard, Yale, Princeton, and Pennsylvania met and agreed to cut violence by outlawing "momentum," but they let the massing of players alone. Predictably, creative coaches such as H. L. Williams of Minnesota, George Woodruff of Pennsylvania, and Stagg developed new formations that were successful but extended the violence. There was continued pressure in the middle- to late-1890s to end all mass plays, but the four leaders were slow to respond because they could not reach unanimity. Stagg pressed his old mentor, Walter Camp, for one set of football rules. Yale and Princeton favored further reform, but Harvard and Pennsylvania, with brilliant new offenses that took advantage of the 1894 rules changes, resisted. This led to the final breakup of the domination of the four universities in the early twentieth century due to their disunity and the new national interest shown in the issue.[24]

The problem was not confined to the universities; it presented larger implications for American views of sport, especially because the colleges had begun to market their activity to a larger public. The public press relished the prospect of a bloodletting and sometimes appeared disappointed when such did not occur. Walter Eckersall later wrote of the 1890s and early 1900s that "even when the rules were strictly observed, there was the roughest kind of play." A member of the eastern rules committee allegedly admitted that "grade crossing slaughter is as nothing to the mass play slaughter," and Knute Rockne remembered the pre-1906 game as a "modified shambles."[25]

It was common for an entire team to attempt to injure the opposing team's star player badly enough that he would have to leave the game. A Princeton quarterback admitted, "We're coached to pick out the most dangerous man on the opposing team and put him out in the first five minutes of play." The degree to which this barbaric code was publicly acceptable can be seen in the complimentary statement regarding Chicago's all-American back Clarence Herschberger. The trainer of the Michigan team said after the 1896 game, "The very first time I went out on the field with a sponge, I told the men that they would have to get rid of him, but they couldn't touch him. . . . He is a wonder and I give him full credit for his good work." Walter Eckersall was always a marked man as well, and it is remarkable that the 136-pounder was never seriously hurt during the many games on which money was wagered that he would be put out.[26]

President Theodore Roosevelt took a leading role in the 1905 American football controversy even before the season began, and a nationwide alarm was raised when a survey of the 1905 season tolled 18 dead and 159 serious injuries. His thoughts and actions were characteristically candid and exaggerated, and they afford the opportunity to view an unusual American mind at work. Roosevelt spoke not only for himself but also gave expression to ideals of others; he was "preacher-at-large to the American people."[27]

The most effective criticism of intercollegiate football in leading Roosevelt to his public position on the sport appeared in *McClure's Magazine* in June and July 1905. Henry Beach Needham approached the intercollegiate sports industry much as Ida Tarbell and Lincoln Steffens were approaching John D. Rockefeller's monopolistic petroleum industry and Boss Cox's lucrative Cincinnati political industry in the same magazine. Needham's first article, "The College Athlete: How Commercialism Is Making Him a Professional, Recruiting and Subsidizing," earned him an invitation to visit the president at the White House in June. Roosevelt appreciated the muckraker, and his silence on the importance of Needham's articles in prompting presidential actions later in June is of a piece with his attitude toward the influence of Tarbell, Steffens, and Upton Sinclair.[28]

Needham's second article, "The College Athlete: His Amateur Code, Its Evasion and Adminstration," extended his attack to the prevalent unnecessary roughness and the evasion of the amateur ideal in the game of football. His essay abounded with names of institutions, players, and dates of transgressions. Needham observed that even those Americans who were asking for rules changes did not desire the revision to produce a "cleaner" game, "but for a more open game—one the spectators can enjoy." He stopped short of extending his critique to the whole of the society that created the sport; his articles did not view the rampant commercialism of the sport as symptomatic of American values.[29]

Shortly after Needham's visit, President Roosevelt used the occasion of a Harvard commencement speech to address the evils of American intercollegiate football. His most scathing denunciation concerned excessive roughness and violence: "Brutality in playing a game should awaken the heartiest and most plainly shown contempt for the player guilty of it." His speech was a statement regarding the proper function of an institution of higher learning in a democracy; the presence of the game on many campuses, Roosevelt argued, was despoiling the purpose of the institutions.[30]

The president led the 1905 attack until he discovered that many academics were taking his criticisms seriously and that abolition of intercollegiate football was being considered and carried out. New York University and Columbia University led the prominent schools that abolished the sport; Stanford and the University of California led those who wished to substitute British rugby for the American game. And when Charles W. Eliot, president of TR's beloved Harvard, moved to abolish the game at Cambridge, Roosevelt ceased his attacks and defended the sport. He wrote harshly of Eliot's intentions: "I think Harvard will be doing the baby act if she takes any such foolish course as President Eliot advises."[31]

Theodore Roosevelt made a last criticism of "brutality and foul play" on November 20, but his statement resembled more an apology for the sport than a call for sweeping reform. He called a member of the University of Pennsylvania's Board of Athletic Control to the White House and used him as a mouthpiece to announce that Roosevelt "emphatically believes in continuing the game." Roosevelt had taken sober note of the rumors regarding abolition of the game at many colleges, and his statement was meant to stay such radical moves. "It would be a real misfortune to lose so manly and vigorous a game as football," he argued, and insisted on "the far greater relative danger of many other sports and pastimes." Roosevelt returned to his square deal: "Brutality and foul play should receive the same summary punishment given to a man who cheats at cards, who strikes a foul blow in boxing."[32]

The politician in the White House emerged as spokesman for one of the two main football reform movements that became delineated by November of 1905. Roosevelt led those who believed in the athletics of consensus—a compromise that would abrogate the most glaring faults of the game but would retain those elements that appealed to the American mind and spirit. The other movement was comprised of those who believed in abolition because there were fundamental faults in football that could not be righted by a revision of the existing rules.

The University of Pennsylvania, after the presidential prompting, circulated a letter to introduce the athletics of consensus to the "heads of all universities, colleges, and schools in the United States which are interested in athletics." The athletics of consensus was frequently accompanied by the proposition that football could be reformed by "giving the public what it wants." This corollary proved especially seductive; most American reformers did not wish to reject a profitable enterprise.[33]

Walter Camp's Football Rules Committee, a self-elected and self-perpetuating "old boys" group (the membership remained exclusively eastern with the exception of Camp disciple Stagg), was meeting regularly by the time of the controversy of 1905. The committee proved to be reactionary with regard to rules revisions, and President Eliot expressed the feelings of many when he told Roosevelt that they needed "to get rid of the existing Committee on Rules." A chief reason for the reactionary attitude of the Rules Committee members was that they served the interests of the student-alumni-controlled athletic associations of the East and were substantially free of faculty or administration control. In 1897, the Intercollegiate Conference had pressed for important changes by appointing its own rules revision group and corresponding with Camp. Camp's committee had three responses: First, Camp disciple Stagg was invited to join the committee; second, most western rules changes were incorporated into the new Camp committee rules; and third, Camp selected his first noneastern all-American, Hershberger of Chicago. Overall, the Rules Committee had the appearance of an eastern trust to many observers, who looked to the president to rid the game of its tentacles.[34]

The reform controversy of the 1890s had produced the Football Rules Committee, and the 1905 controversy produced a rival, more representative rules committee that forced reform upon the older group. Representatives of sixty-two colleges and universities attended a series of meetings emanating from Chancellor H. M. McCracken of New York University's call for a football conference. They organized the Intercollegiate Athletic Association of the United States (later to be known as the National Collegiate Athletic Association) at the end of

December 1905. The association also selected a reform-minded rules committee of its own. Camp's original rules group was forced to meet with the new body when Harvard officials instructed their delegate, William T. Reid, Jr., to withdraw from the older committee and affiliate with the newer, more representative and reform-minded one. The meeting led to a merger, but any change in the control of football proved more apparent than real: Members of the old committee were elected to dominant positions, and an eastern majority prevailed until the late 1920s.[35]

The all-American athletics of consensus were never more apparent than during this entire procedure of broadening the base of the committee and in ensuring rules changes, a development that continued to 1912, when more rules further opening the game were passed: The forward pass was encouraged, the ball streamlined, and touchdowns increased in value. The rules changes agreed upon were the ultimate defense to the football critics because the consensus approach ensured that the new rules met the largest possible area of criticism without lessening the attractiveness of the game. In fact, the most significant changes, those requiring ten instead of five yards for each series of downs and legalizing the forward pass, were destined to prove among the most successful marketing moves in American history. One Chicago review prophetically observed, "The forward pass promises sensational plays." The rules changes, the result of increasing democratization of the gentlemen's leisure activity, stranded the radical advocates of reform by promising more "open play" and hence less violence. The revisions of 1905–6 and the continuing reform to 1912 were so effective that the abolitionists had to return to the fold of American intercollegiate football after unhappy experiments in trying to live without the sport or with substitutes for it.[36]

Regional Reform

The national controversy over intercollegiate football in 1905 also had its regional-level discussions. The most noteworthy developments occurred in the Intercollegiate Conference of Faculty Representatives, of which Chicago was a founding member. The conference had been founded at a meeting of seven midwestern university presidents early in 1895 (an earlier, smaller group had met in 1892), in good part because of the paralysis of the eastern rules group. In organizing the conference, academics had attempted to control an area of institutional life that threatened the maintenance of traditional values. The group drew up twelve resolutions that were so well drafted that they formed the working basis for many years of intercollegiate activity in the Midwest and were used as a model for similar associations elsewhere.[37]

The presidents' conference of 1895 followed two general principles in the drafting of the twelve resolutions: Each university was to place faculty control over its intercollegiate activities and select faculty representation for subsequent conferences, and local institutional autonomy was to be protected by allowing each university to define its degree requirements and other internal mechanics. The faculty members selected as representatives of the seven universities met in 1896 as the official "Intercollegiate Conference of Faculty Representatives." The guarantee of autonomy encouraged quite different concepts of eligibility, and this difficulty was later seemingly met by the creation of the office of conference "arbitrator" and an eligibility committee. When that faltered, the office of "commissioner" was founded, with questionable impact, in the 1920s and 1930s.[38]

Spectator Reform

The rise of the spectator presented the conference schools with complex problems that were difficult to solve. The desire of all the universities to procure the most profitable site for their games was the root of most of the controversies. The prime issue of discontent revolved about the University of Chicago's control of the finest football marketplace—the city of Chicago. Chicago's rivals were all located in much smaller cities, with corresponding game receipts. President Harper and Athletic Director Stagg used these advantages to dictate the division of game revenues and the venue of Chicago's games, thus creating an engrossment of the Chicago market within the conference. Chicago's conference opponents frequently yielded to the demands, sometimes even consenting to pay half of the improvements for Marshall Field in order to increase its seating capacity and their take-home receipts. Hence, Stagg came to control the most lucrative football marketplace west of Philadelphia, and his insistence upon playing at Marshall Field most of the time was grudgingly accepted by the rivals, whose own greed was seldom mitigated by the ideal of providing their campus constituencies with a local game.[39]

Chicago's principal conference opponents, the universities of Michigan, Wisconsin, and Illinois, grew restive by 1899 under Stagg's yoke and pressed for a more equitable arrangement of schedules and revenue-sharing. President Andrew Draper of Illinois, President Charles K. Adams of Wisconsin, and Professor Henry Pattengill of Michigan met Stagg and asked to have equal rights with Chicago in determining game sites and in the division of the football revenues. The meeting went badly, and President Adams then wrote to Harper that the universities were "agreed in thinking that we cannot continue athletic relations with Chicago if the attitude taken by Professor Stagg is insisted upon." Harper and Stagg then seemingly adjusted their position if not attitude; they agreed to divide the Marshall Field game revenues equally and consented to play return games at the opponent's field. Chicago would insist, however, upon being guaranteed—and paid—the difference in receipts for playing in the poorer football market compared to what the Maroons would have earned at home. The predictable rejection of Chicago's hard proposal by the three rivals followed.[40]

Michigan, Wisconsin, and Illinois boycotted Chicago during the season of 1899 in an attempt to bring it to their position. In the event, Chicago did not lose the fight to play where the money was, and Stagg uncovered several allies in the process. The lure of big revenues at Marshall Field ensured that the other conference universities of Minnesota, Purdue, Northwestern, and Iowa played there during the season of boycott. Moreover, Stagg looked for prime eastern opponents, and Cornell University, Oberlin College, the University of Pennsylvania, and Brown University journeyed to the Chicago marketplace to play, ensuring the most profitable season ever.[41]

The victory for Chicago's aggressive policy was evident in its Marshall Field schedule: The Maroons had played an average of one game away for the seasons 1895 to 1898; after the boycott, they played fewer than one game away for the next eight seasons. The coup de grace to the 1899 boycott was applied well after the season seemed completed. Chicago emerged unbeaten from its long (thirteen games) and difficult schedule, and Wisconsin was beaten but once, and that by Yale, 0-6. Pressures mounted in Madison and Chicago to arrange a western championship between the two schools; Chicago was patently willing, and Wisconsin was forced into the match, which broke the boycott. What principles of conference financial equity and faculty control that remained at the kickoff were effectively disposed of in the cold December drizzle; Stagg's team overwhelmed Wisconsin on the Badgers' home field, 17-0.[42]

In 1906, the Intercollegiate Conference met the problems occasioned by the rise of the spectator by attempting to separate the activity from simple financial considerations. Among its reforms, the conference placed a price ceiling on the sale of tickets by any member to its own campus constituency; it ruled that the season must end before Thanksgiving and include no more than five games; and it strongly urged that "receipts and expenses of athletic contests" be reduced. The conference hoped that any "athletic surplus" would "be devoted as far as possible to permanent University improvements" and voted that the financial management of intercollegiate athletics "be entirely under the control of the Faculty" and the financial statement be made public. These resolutions pertaining to the rise of the spectator accounted for seven of the fourteen major reforms that the Intercollegiate Conference of Faculty Representatives passed in 1906.[43]

Coaching Reform

The conference also dealt with the problems occasioned by the heightened importance of coaches. "Coachers," who were paid by the institution or by an athletic association and gave instruction only to intercollegiate athletes and only during the period of intercollegiate competition in a specific sport, were usual in the Midwest by 1900. These men maintained no other contacts with the institution whose athletes they taught. Coaches vied with each other to begin training their teams early, and their use of training quarters and training tables helped professionalize their players as well. Such professional dedication to football victories necessarily led to much misunderstanding among the conference schools. Stagg had pushed Chicago's preliminary practice sessions to September 4 by 1900, and other conference schools retaliated. Michigan sent twelve players to the northern lakes for early training, and other institutions planned August practices. In 1906, the Intercollegiate Conference of Faculty Representatives attacked every one of these areas of overemphasis: training quarters and training tables were abolished, common preseason practice dates were scheduled, and the problem of the seasonal coach was faced by requiring a regular academic appointment and at a moderate salary.[44]

Player Reform

The rise of the player produced the conference's oldest and the most common and complex controversies. Further, because the problems over player eligibility were quite visible, the press often dealt summary sports page justice, which placed the conference schools in an undignified light.[45]

Faculty representatives tried to legislate and control two facets of player behavior: that of the "amateur ideal" and that of proper academic standards. The amateur ideal was widely respected even if it was never sufficiently defined. The 1895 presidents' conference had tried to cover this area by prohibiting "any gift, remuneration, or pay" for "the collegian's services on the college team," and intervening years saw a continual evolution toward a more sophisticated rule. One of the most egregious violations of this prohibition must have occurred when the secretary of the Chicago board of trustees publicly presented a gold watch to Walter Eckersall. The presidents had sought to promote proper academic standards with the requirement that only a "bona fide student doing full work in a regular or special course as defined in the curriculum of his college" was to be permitted intercollegiate competition. The wide variation of the universities' admissions and grading standards made this approach inconsistent, but the principle of institutional autonomy was deemed more important than consistent application.[46]

The faculty representatives responded to the controversies of 1905 with stricter rules on player recruitment and eligibility: Conference coaches were limited in their contacts with prospective players, entering students at conference schools were no longer eligible for intercollegiate play during their first year of academic residence, and under no circumstances could students participate in athletics for more than three years.[47]

Coach Fielding Yost and Michigan constituted the most complicated of all challenges to these reforms. The other universities probably wanted Michigan to follow the new rules and remain in the conference, where their considerable prestige and gate receipts were much appreciated. In the event, the Michigan regents, as representatives of the football-mad citizenry, took charge of athletics; the ostensible point at issue then became proper faculty control, a sacred part of the conference charter. When the problem could not be sorted out, Michigan resigned from the conference in 1908. When it returned in 1917 after unsuccessfully trying to go it alone, its offending 1908 governance apparatus (including Yost) was essentially intact, save for an unusual understanding that gave the faculty veto power over the regents' athletic decisions. The 1906 reforms, skeletal and shaky though they were, indicated that the Intercollegiate Conference of Faculty Representatives had progressed further in its control of football players than any other group in the country.[48]

Reform at Chicago

The manner in which members of the university responded to the challenge of 1905 demonstrates that football had ceased being an experiment at Chicago. The leaders of the football business worked out a local version of the athletics of consensus that fitted football for a continued place in the university's life.

Before 1905, the most extensive opportunity for the academic leadership to consider the place of intercollegiate athletics had been initiated in the University Congregation (the most comprehensive representative body) by a minority faculty group termed the "Harvard gang." Robert Morss Lovett and Carl Buck in 1900 presented briefs supporting the proposition that "the present increasing interest in athletics in the University is undesirable." Their awareness of rampant student interest had been heightened by the campus response to the 1899 championship football team. Lovett's main point was that "far more beneficial than the training of special athletic teams, which was the prevailing method of the present athletic policy, was the general participation of the largest possible number of the students in athletic sports." The discussion by the members of the congregation soon lost sight of Lovett's basic critique of policy, and the intercollegiate athletic apologists succeeded in passing three resolutions, the first of which indicates the tone of the others: "That, on the whole, the Congregation believes that the advantages of college athletics as at present conducted outweigh their disadvantages."[49]

The blunting of the reform impulse manifested at Chicago in 1905–6 must be viewed against the backdrop of the relationship of William Rainey Harper and Amos Alonzo Stagg; their friendship proved a crucial factor in the defense of football. The early acquaintanceship between President Harper and his former divinity student had grown into a friendship of affection and mutual trust. Harper's support of his athletic director remained constant, even when Stagg became embroiled with leading academic lights or when he violated the letter or the spirit of the institution's athletic code.

During the last years of his life, President Harper seemed to increase his dependence upon men such as Stagg with whom he shared a religious faith and pre-Chicago experiences. Stagg's painful sciatica increased the mutuality, and Harper assured his ailing coach during the 1904 season that "we are more devoted to you than ever before. . . . We think more of you than we should of a whole season of victories in football or in anything else." The men exchanged warm letters during the remainder of the 1904–5 academic year, and when Harper underwent surgery for his malignancy, Stagg wrote encouragingly, "We rejoice in your courage and in your brave fight. . . . Our hearts are all with you." And the dying president's need of Stagg was expressed during the 1905 football season: "I should like very much to have you come over some morning and talk with me a little while," implored Harper in October, "I am not able to talk much but I should be exceedingly glad to see you."[50]

The emotional impact of Harper's last months was enormous because so many in the university community had cast their lot on the Midway due to his presence and vision. That they might feel bereft in the extreme is not surprising, but the sense of the forsaken invaded un-expected hearts. Even Robert Herrick, whose disdain for Harper was unfolded in his novel *Chimes,* was affected. Herrick's sketch of the dy-ing president noted that "he seemed another kind of being, with a dignity, a grandeur about him that Clavercin had never suspected all these years."[51]

After the 1905 season and within weeks of Harper's death, an at-tack upon western intercollegiate football appeared in an influential national publication, *Outing Magazine,* and included a disparaging note regarding Stagg's superiors at Chicago. Editor Caspar Whitney charged: "I am convinced that if Stagg was entirely free of any higher up influ-ence there would never be a questionable man on the Chicago team." The article hurt Harper deeply. He was "not conscious of having done anything to interfere with your ideal," he wrote to Stagg. "Will you not write me a letter on this subject to relieve my mind?" he pleaded. Stagg responded that the criticisms could not properly be directed at Harper and assured him of his devotion and gratitude:

> I can speak out of a heart full of gratitude to you, my dear President Harper for the loyal and generous support which you have always shown in the affairs of my department I can assure you Mr. President that I have not one unpleasant memory to look back upon in connection with your relationship to me and my ideals but on the other hand the memories of your many helpful suggestions and your invaluable support and your words of commendation so generously given to me at various times, I shall always treasure as among the sweetest things of my life.[52]

Hence, the special relationship with which President Harper favored Athletic Director Stagg was especially intense during 1905, and as crit-icism of intercollegiate football mounted that year, Harper's friendship and illness provided invaluable protection for Coach Stagg and foot-ball at Chicago.

The most significant local response to the national and regional challenges to football in 1905 was the reappraisal of the sport prompted by the University Senate, the highest legislative academic body on campus. The senate's handling of the problem is revealing of values and power in the institution. Two days after the much-heralded Thanks-giving Day victory over the University of Michigan, amid the general celebrations of the team, William G. Hale, a classicist, moved the fol-lowing in the senate: "In the opinion of the Senate, the game of foot-ball under rules permitting either mass-play or tackling should be abol-ished." The spare minutes reveal little, but the discussion over this approach must have been long and heated. The influential football apologist Albion Small finally got senate approval, and Hale's "consent," to the following alternate resolution: "That in the opinion of this body it will be the duty of the University to refuse to sanction participation by its students in intercollegiate football contests unless changes be made which will eliminate the flagrant moral and physical evils at present connected with the game."[53]

The passage of such a senate resolution after more than a decade of benign neglect, while Harper, Stagg, and Harper's Board of Physical Culture and Athletics (including Small) ran the athletic enterprise, indicates that the senate was quite alarmed over the nature and dimensions of the sport at Chicago and elsewhere, even at a high-water mark of intercollegiate football success at Chicago. We know all too little of the professors' thinking and comments, but if the careful and thoughtful Divinity Dean Shailer Mathews's statement to the *New York Times* earlier is indicative of widespread feeling, intercollegiate football was in mortal peril at Chicago: "Football today is a social obsession—a boy-killing, education-prostituting, gladiatorial sport." The senate promptly voted enabling legislation to the Small compromise, including a request for an investigative football committee pursuant to the approval of President Harper.[54]

Harper disapproved. A special meeting of the senate was held a scant two days later "to consider a communication from the President, in modification of the resolutions upon the football question." The stricken Harper had prepared (surely with the aid of Stagg and members of the athletic board) a seven-point "Preliminary Statement" and two resolutions that he wished substituted for the senate's own statement. Harper's proposal contained the substance of Small's diplomatic compromise and added several strong commendations of Stagg.[55]

The faculty senators operated decisively on the Harper "Preliminary Statement" at their meeting held the day of the official university rally for the Michigan victory. Harper's statement denied that the Chicago "athletic management" or "University authorities" were responsible for the state of affairs; instead, he placed responsibility for the evils of football upon the fans for their "intense popular interest" and upon the faculties because their "vigilance" was lacking. This must have struck the professors as defensive and fatuous. It was the first and only time the university's faculty senate challenged the football program of Harper and Stagg directly, and the senators' message was clear: They excised every commendatory word for Stagg that Harper's document contained.[56]

The senate had spoken clearly on the issue, but Harper's enabling resolutions shifted the action to a committee headed by his appointee and containing two representatives each from the senate, the University Council, and the Board of Physical Culture and Athletics. The death of William Rainey Harper occurred before the formal report was made, but as the Intercollegiate Athletic Conference was to meet soon, the football issue was dealt with in the midst of the mourning period. The first report of the "Joint Committee on the Football Question" was given to the senate at the next meeting. Despite campus circumstances, they rejected it and concluded with a recommendation to the Intercollegiate Conference: "The Senate of the University of Chicago is therefore of the opinion that intercollegiate football, if not all intercollegiate contests, should be discontinued for a term of years."[57]

President James B. Angell of the University of Michigan (James B. was the father of Chicago's Professor James R., who later served as Yale president) called a special meeting of Intercollegiate Conference officials in late January. The Chicago delegate to President Angell's meeting was Acting President Harry Pratt Judson, who was instructed by the senate to recommend that all intercollegiate sports be examined critically and that, at a minimum, football competition should cease for some years.[58]

The Angell conference prepared a group of far-reaching proposals for the individual institutions to address but did not call for the suspension of football. Chicago dealt with the proposals at a combined meeting of all university faculties, which again instructed its delegate, this time Albion Small, to press for the suspension of the game. The Chicago faculties then proceeded, however, to approve most of the Angell conference proposals that looked toward reform, not suspension. It was clearly a time of intense politicking set against the background of mourning the fallen leader, and because the leader had fervently attempted to mitigate criticism of Stagg and Chicago football as one of his last duties, the vigor of the criticism must have been considerably enervated.[59]

During this period, the Chicago Alumni Club (the group Harper founded to recruit players) discussed the Angell conference's recommendations and petitioned the senate toward moderation. The alumni assured the senate that their "policy" would be "at all times to promote amateurism in athletics." This action proved to be an effective pressure for reform rather than suspension.[60]

The University Senate had one more opportunity to change the direction of football at the Midway. The Joint Football Committee made its final report to the senators on the day before the Intercollegiate Conference was to meet and act upon the Angell reform program. And the momentum of the conference proposals was strong enough that the senators responded favorably to them. The issue in the Joint Football Committee report that prompted the most discussion was the problem of paid coaches. The Intercollegiate Conference was to consider the following recommendation the next day: "That no coach be appointed except by University governing bodies on the recommendation of the Faculty or President in the regular way and at a moderate salary." Michigan had curiously already gone on record as opposing recommendation number ten because they believed "that professional coaching of any kind is objectionable"; they hoped "to abolish all paid coaches" (which would have sent Fielding Yost packing and may have been President Angell's true intention). That the Chicago senators were discussing and voting on Stagg's job was clear to all as they tried to find a resolution they could support. Four motions or substitute motions were offered, two of which (by Professor Hale and Professor of Paleontology Samuel Williston) would have resulted in the abolition of Stagg's job. In the end, the senate voted support for the Intercollegiate Conference proposal.[61]

The University Senate's desire to suspend football at Chicago had been blunted by Harper's stout defense, partially beyond the grave, of the local football business. At the same time, newspapers headlined, "Maroon Students to Protest against Football Changes," and much antireform student agitation was reported. The senators' reform enthusiasm was further mitigated by the alumni petition, the long period of intrainstitutional maneuverings, and by the apparent thoroughness of the Intercollegiate Conference reforms. As to intrainstitutional politics, Stagg's top assistant, Dr. Joseph Raycroft, revealed how that group had fought the battle: "The longer we can hold this thing off and prevent it from coming to a definite issue the more chance we have of arriving at a sane conclusion." He claimed to have had just such an influence on professors Albert Michelson and John Coulter at their daily "progressive lunch party at the Quadrangle Club." Moreover, Stagg's assistant admitted to "balling up" procedures to such an extent that the Board of Physical Culture and Athletics could not act at all on a reform measure. His avowed purpose was to gain time and allow faculty disinterest to grow.[62]

The Board of Physical Culture and Athletics met soon after the reform program had been submitted by the Intercollegiate Conference to its members—they approved the reforms and recommended the same action to the University Senate. The campaign of reform launched by Professor Hale's dramatic resolution in December 1905 came to an end on March 17, 1906, when the University Senate briskly minuted: "The action of the Board of Physical Culture was approved by the Senate." The football controversy of 1905 had produced the "rebellious-ness but not rebellion" that Richard Storr described as occurring in the senate over an earlier issue.[63]

The Effects of Reform at Chicago

The effects of the conference reforms that dealt with the rise of the spectator had some initial effect at Chicago, although hardly the last-ing effect intended. The financial arrangements of the athletic enter-prise were already under the control (if remarkably autonomous) of a department of the university; hence, reforms in this area were at least formally met. The price controls on tickets and the fixed number of games affected Maroon revenues immediately, but the next decade proved such reforms transitory. The one lasting change was that which banned Thanksgiving games—Chicago never again played on that day.

The position of the football coach at Chicago during the reform year of 1905–6 was ostensibly above the criticism leveled at the part-time, completely extracurricular, positions that other universities maintained. The Board of Physical Culture and Athletics had adopted just such a smug position in their response to a sweeping University of Illinois indictment of college coaching practices in 1901. Hence, the effects of the conference reforms on coaching were nonexistent at Chicago, al-though the real place of the coach on the Midway deserved such at-tention, as the graphic concerns of the senate had made clear that year.[64]

Coach Stagg had described his position and evaluated his perfor-mance just before the football season of 1905 in a letter to Harper ask-ing for a raise in salary. The letter is recognizably Stagg's: It is a bit heavyhanded with recollection of the greener gridirons he could have trod, it is full of reminders of his self-denial for the university, and it includes a scheme whereby Harper could increase the coach's salary handsomely without touching "regular" university monies. Stagg knew Harper well. Hence, he suggested that part of the requested $6,000 salary "could very properly come from the Athletic Fund," for the "out-look" was that the fund would be "sufficiently prosperous" to provide his increase (football ticket revenues accounted for most of the ath-letic fund). Harper agreed, and the board of trustees accepted his rec-ommendation that Coach Stagg be paid $6,000 a year by paying $3,500 of it from the athletic fund, with only $2,500 "paid by the Universi-ty." This salary placed Stagg among the institution's highest-paid per-sons, just behind some of the founding head professors but well above some notable head professors, for example James R. Angell of the

Department of Psychology ($4,000) and James H. Tufts of the Department of Philosophy ($4,000, one of Tuft's full professors, George Herbert Mead, earned $3,000 two years later).[65]

The comparative state of Stagg's salary can be further seen in a 1907 study by the University Senate and presented to the board of trustees. At Harvard, the maximum salary for a full professor was $5,500, and at Chicago the twenty highest-paid full professors received an average of $5,400. Harvard's first paid head coach, Bill Reid, received $7,000 in 1905 and 1906, although half came from public subscription. Yale's first paid coach was given a $2,500 salary in 1909, and one of Stagg's few coaching peers, Glenn S. "Pop" Warner, was reportedly paid $4,500 ten years later at Pittsburgh. Hence, Chicago had much to reform if it were to bring its position of coach into line with the conference reform, particularly because the university was encouraging a rampant professionalism in its intercollegiate athletics by rewarding its coach in relation to the size of the football revenues, the very connection the reform was supposed to halt.[66]

The consolidation of Amos Alonzo Stagg's power within the university and his prestige in the public mind went well beyond the natural limits of his position. Stagg was the exemplar of amateurism in intercollegiate sport. In the *Chicago Tribune*'s view, "His rugged honesty, his regard for truth, and his simplicity in life and manner have made him beloved of all who have associated with him. . . . one could not fail to notice his home life, for that of no man can be more beautiful." Harper appended his own tribute to the piece and spoke of Stagg's "intense love for pure sport, his incorruptible spirit, his indefatigable effort, his broad minded zeal and his absolute fairness of mind and honesty of heart."[67]

Chicago players were affected by the conference reforms but, as with the coaching reforms, the reality was far from the public image that Harper and Stagg promoted. The conference reform that abolished football matches with all secondary schools was aimed at discouraging early recruitment of the high school team members. The ban of such games would diminish the accessibility of the schoolboys to the depredations of Yost, Stagg, and the other coaches. The conference reforms that limited the participation of a new student to three years and required his academic residence for one year before playing in an intercollegiate activity proved to be wise and precedential.

The effect of the post-1905 season reforms on the issue of eligibility standards at Chicago is difficult to ascertain. It was claimed that the school was limited in its reservoir of player talent because of comparatively higher entrance requirements and eligibility standards than other Intercollegiate Conference colleges. Generally the assertion may have been valid, but the statement should be viewed in the light of the exceptions that were permitted, for example, Stagg reasoned if one prospect could "enter the University of Michigan, he certainly ought to be able to enter the University of Chicago." Harper "instituted an investigation" into the matter and concluded that it would be possible for the young man to meet Chicago's requirements by the next fall if he were watched closely, or in Harper's words to the boy's principal, "Let us keep our hands upon him and see that he is properly prepared to enter here next fall."[68]

Young instructors gave their testimony regarding the athletes before and during the reform period. A Maroon athlete in 1900 had stated his purpose at Chicago was "solely for athletics," according to his French language instructor. The teacher admitted that he had protected another athlete who was doing "unsatisfactory" work because "he had been told that in the case of men in athletics *much leniency was to be shown.*" Another instructor complained to Dean George E. Vincent in the spring of 1906 that Stagg's captains had pressured him to ensure the continued eligibility of failing team members, including Eckersall. Two starring teammates of Eckersall's quit the university after their last football season when the proposed three-years conference rule appeared to halt any more intercollegiate sports participation for them.[69]

One of the reforms had an immediate and direct effect upon player life at Chicago—the separate but unequal training quarters and diet were abolished. Other conference reforms brought about an indirect effect at Chicago—the requirement that each school publicly define that "full work" meant, or appeared to mean, that the lessened course work of the athletes had to cease. The requirement that no student could participate in intercollegiate athletics without "meeting the entrance requirements of the College of Liberal Arts of his institution or its equivalent" would in future aid those, like Eckersall, who never were made to meet such standards and fell hopelessly behind their classmates.[70]

Athletic scholarships were also affected. The death of Harper and the general desire to bring Chicago's athletic industry into line with the spirit of the reform measures combined to stop the practice partially. The university, through the covert partnership of Harper and Stagg, awarded tuition scholarships to athletes for "student service." There were early discussions between Harper and Stagg in the 1890s regarding campus awareness of such arrangements, and they wished to keep secret from faculty and other players the financial help some players were receiving. Stagg wrote to Harper before the academic year began in 1904 regarding financial arrangements for the Department of Physical Culture and Athletics and noted, "Provision should be made so that eighteen new students can work out their tuition free. This is very important." Harper promised by return post, "We will of course do what is necessary to be done."[71]

Collier's magazine had charged in early November 1905 that Chicago was a leader in football corruption and that "over one hundred persons" via "the instrumentality of 'student service'" were receiving remitted tuition. "Student service" was the means by which Chicago students were given general maintenance, housekeeping, and secretarial tasks in return for which they received part or full tuition, and all needful students were theoretically eligible. This and other challenges after the season of 1905 moved the University Council in 1906 to ask Dean Francis W. Shepardson of the Senior College (Harper's former secretary) for an explanation of any such financial aid to athletes. His response revealed that the university had awarded, and continued to award, oxymoronic athletic scholarships: "Mr. Shepardson made a statement to the effect that the University had appropriated twenty-five scholarships to be given to athletes without the requirement of any service . . . and that this matter had been administered by him." He had "arranged" the student service scholarships for Stagg's men, according to Harper's instructions.[72]

Stagg's old friend Dean Vincent wrote to the coach urgently within six months of Harper's death and during the council's investigation. Vincent was not writing "officially," he warned Stagg, "but personally in order that you may be aware in advance that there seems to be a change in the policy" of awarding scholarships; they were now to be given "solely on the basis of scholarship and their need." Vincent thought Stagg should defend his interests and "bring up immediately the question as to whether Athletes are to be given any special consideration." Harry Pratt Judson investigated the use of student service scholarships for athletes, but the results of his inquiry are as elusive as Harper's and Stagg's creation and administration of the program. The faculty were little concerned with intercollegiate athletic issues after the eruption of 1905–6. Perhaps they thought such protestations futile; for whatever reason, they did not continue to force the attention of the administrators in that direction. Hence, the University of Chicago was poised on the threshold of the period when Stagg and football became the measure of the institution for many Americans and for a remarkably large proportion of students, scholars, and administrators within the grey city.[73]

Ironically, the consensus reforms of 1905–12 legitimated the sport's existence and set the stage for its mass market appeal. The reforms led to the unleashing of the spectator, coach, and player—united only in developing the collegiate golden goose of cultural and economic aggrandizement. And this preemption by emerging bureaucratic structures led later to the NCAA's cartelization of American universities as a means of preventing player price competition. After the "reforms" and new-found rationales were set, the race was to the swift and the clever—the democratization, nationalization, and commercialization of football followed and combined to produce the mass entertainment industry of the twentieth-century American university.

4

Stagg's University: Intercollegiate Football as a Way of Life, 1906–24

There is no danger at Chicago of athletics getting out of bounds; that was taken care of at the outset by providing rigid faculty control and direction.

—Amos Alonzo Stagg

President Judson and Coach Stagg

Acting President Harry Pratt Judson (he was made president in 1907) was an original member of Harper's faculty and administration, although he was never one of Harper's best-paid "Head Professors." The relationship of Judson and Stagg in their correspondence from 1892 to 1905 appears to have been one of mutual respect, although the letters deal exclusively with administrative procedures until Harper's illness. Judson was generally careful in the expression of his opinions, and his statements regarding the values of intercollegiate football were much more restrained than those of Harper or Stagg. Judson, who admitted that he was "not an enthusiast in disposition," followed the enthusiast Harper, and the new president was not given to the extravagant public gesture of which Harper was so much the master. If Harper would go to the locker room at halftime to flail the team toward victory, Judson almost never ventured near the squad. A Judson attempt to meet the team after a game met with oblique criticism by the *Chicago Tribune:* "President Judson of the University of Chicago did a rare thing—for him—in extending the hand of congratulation to the Midway players in the gymnasium basement after the clash."[1]

"As dean and President," Richard Storr wrote, "Judson was a skilful and meticulous craftsman, the conservator of an institution." His

approach to intercollegiate athletics at Chicago was cautious and prin-
cipled; his careful tending of the athletic enterprise was similar to his
work with other areas of university life that he found to be in need of
such cultivation. In fact, Judson faced the considerable challenge of
mastering Harper's perennial deficit, which he did, much to the relief
and warm appreciation of the Rockefeller family.[2]

The acting president found that he had to deal with football upon
his accession—he was forced to expel Chicago's out-of-control football celebrity Walter Eckersall within his first few days in office. Judson had been a member of the University Senate and other administrative bodies that had already dealt with the volatile issues raised after
the 1905 season. Characteristically, he had been allied neither with the
attackers nor the defenders of the Chicago football industry. Judson's
specific contributions to these bodies is unknown, but his opinion on
the issue of football reform shows him to have been a moderate practitioner of the athletics of consensus.[3]

President Judson's first quarterly statement to the university community gave more attention to football than to any other topic. "To those
who believe in the value of athletic sports and of intercollegiate contests,
as I do," he declared, "it is of first importance that these shall be carried
on under such conditions that all suspicion of professionalism shall be
eliminated; in short, that amateur sports may be what they purport to
be, the sports of amateurs." Earlier, Judson had written an absent university official that "football reform has gone quite beyond what in my
opinion is desirable" and admitted that he was "more and more afraid"
that "suspension of the game for the present is inevitable."[4]

The relationship of the acting president to Stagg was marked by
uneasiness from the beginning of Judson's tenure. Judson found himself the moderator between the senatorial reformers and the indignant
Stagg and soon began gingerly to review the "special" relationships and
policies that Stagg and his department had enjoyed. The confident
coach responded with assurance by quoting Harperian precedent.

The clearest index to Stagg's power at Judson's accession to the presidency was his direct appeal in 1906 to the trustees over Judson's office when he felt that the senate and other bodies were intent upon
eroding his position. Stagg was incensed that the new president could
not, or would not, offer him the kind of protection he had come to
expect from President Harper. The senate's editing of the resolution that
Harper submitted after the season of 1905 was a clear vote of no-con-
fidence in Stagg and his athletic policies, but Stagg chose to style the
battle as one of principle on his part and one of internecine meanness
on his opponents' part. He counterattacked immediately from his post-

season site in Florida when he received word of the senate action. In his appeal to the trustees, Stagg termed the University Senate's action "manifestly unfair and un-American" for legislating on matters regarding his department in his absence, although he admitted that the senate possessed such legislative powers under university statute.[5]

Judson tried to pacify the absent coach, pointing out that he (Judson) had been "steadily resisting" the football abolitionists and those favoring football suspension on the Midway. He further reported to Stagg that the reformers constituted "an overwhelming majority of our Senate and Faculties," and that "a second line of attack" had been made specifically at Stagg "on the ground that he is a professional coach and nothing else." Stagg continued to press for his departmental prerogatives and the Harperian precedents, and he did not express any gratitude to President Judson for the defense of the department and practices that were being widely attacked.[6]

Coach Stagg reasserted his claim to his university constituency with the appeal to the trustees and the recent past. His most passionate letter to Judson indicates that he was fighting for his career, and he refused to consider the resolutions of the senate as descriptive of any reality:

> I have been greatly hurt by the action of our faculties in taking such extreme attitude in the recent discussions implying to the public by so doing that the University was among the worse offenders athletically. It seems to me that my 13 yrs work at the University should have stood for something especially as Pres. Harper for several years back has taken occasion publicly and privately to commend my department. From the beginning it was a rule that nothing of importance to my department should be brought up and least of all passed upon without his first informing and consulting with me as Director. . . . I have been more hurt than I can express that such vital actions to the department for which I have almost crippled myself can be discussed and passed without my even being asked to venture an opinion. . . . if I felt that this handling of the affairs of my department and this disregard of myself as Director were done intentionally, I would withdraw at once from the University.
> The financial responsibility of the department has been my especial burden.[7]

Judson attempted conciliation by patiently, but firmly, explaining some educational principles at the Midway that should not have escaped Stagg's attention for thirteen years. "It is not simply a matter of department by any means," Judson told Stagg, "the whole subject goes much deeper than that and bears on the subject of the relation of athletics to the university as a whole as an educational question." Judson warned that petty departmental maneuverings were out of place, for the "question has resolved itself simply into this—Shall football be lost altogether, or shall it be saved by making certain definite and rather drastic reforms?" Judson assured Stagg, "Personally I have been in favor of saving it. If you had been here you would have realized that I have been fighting for the game and that I have been fighting for you."[8]

The president noted that the attack on intercollegiate football was initiated by the senate, "not by me," and that "I ought to remind you that the University Senate under the statutes has the right to take up in the first instance any question within the University which it regards as having an educational character." Judson added that he could not interfere with the senate's right in the matter. The president was grieved by Stagg's direct appeal to the trustees and reminded the coach that when his "protest went to the Board of Trustees, it being present-ed to the Board without my knowledge," he asked for—and the board agreed to—a place on the senate for Stagg. Earlier, he had been given a place on the joint university committee chaired by Dean Judson to consider the football question. Judson concluded, "I am sorry that you felt hurt about the way in which the faculty have acted," because the critical action by the faculty "would have been much more drastic if I had not brought a strong influence to bear."[9]

Stagg's counterattack continued after the senate accepted the con-ference reforms. He publicized a plan, which he termed the "Chicago Idea," for improved interinstitutional athletic relations and compiled a list of former Maroon players who held athletic directorships and coaching positions at other schools. The Chicago Idea was based upon an agreement made by Minnesota and Chicago for their 1906 football game and was signed by the presidents and athletic directors of both schools. Stagg's initiative was a masterstroke. It provided an uneasy university community with an acceptable rationale for the sport and encouraged their visions of intercollegiate athletes engaging in ama-teur good faith and fellowship. Judson found this approach commend-able and announced the plan in his first *President's Report*. He expected "large results from it for the bettering of athletic conditions," and the public use he made of the plan demonstrated that he felt Stagg had met the attacks of the football critics.[10]

The Chicago Idea stated as its "end" that intercollegiate games "shall be arranged, prepared for and played in the spirit of fair play which characterizes gentlemen." There was little original or concrete in the plan; there was much that was nostalgic, and the inclusion of a ban-quet given for the visiting team was the sole innovation. Coaches who had played for Chicago were listed in the 1905–6 *President's Report* to demonstrate "the influence" that Stagg's department was "exercising on the gymnastic and athletic interests of other educational institutions." Stagg brought home that influence even more graphically the next year when he reported "there were a number of places at salaries of $1,000" and noted that "most of the men now placed receive more than $1,200." This intrusion of mammon seems not to have bothered President Judson, and he duly published Stagg's financial claims for his disciple-coaches in the next *President's Report*.[11]

The cautious Judson required some years to make the presidential transition to a place of confidence and power when he succeeded the dynamic Harper. At the same time, Amos Alonzo Stagg was strikingly successful in obtaining acceptance of his intercollegiate football enterprise without substantive change in Judson's university within a comparatively short period. Judson's unease over football was effectively relieved by the reforms of 1906 and by Stagg's Chicago Idea.

This record of the relationship of Judson and Stagg may encourage overlooking the extent to which they were both committed to the continued existence of strong intercollegiate football. Harry Pratt Judson's thought and talk on the subject, although clearly not as uncritically enthusiastic as that of Harper or Stagg, were still quite enough to guarantee the activity on campus. Moreover, Judson's careful course in dealing with the enterprise in his early years as president and his promotion of the athletics of consensus ensured that Chicago football was much less susceptible to serious criticism for many years. Football was more firmly established than either Judson or Stagg, in the midst of their tense correspondence, could appreciate.

Intercollegiate football at Chicago was marked only by moderate adjustments from 1906 to 1924; its presence at the Midway was accepted generally as a way of life. The reforms of 1905–6 fulfilled a consensus, as the absence of significant movements of further reform at Chicago demonstrated. After the flurry of reform and abolition activity, the issue rested—the critics became few and quiescent, the champions of football increasingly evident and sure of its value to the university. Moreover, the Chicago experience was but one of countless others in America in which a general acceptance and enthusiasm over the sport displaced the former unease now that the proper progressive consensus reforms had been administered.

Football fatalities at the national service academies in 1909 prompted a brief reform stir, but abolition was seldom mentioned. In fact, the students' *Daily Maroon* was almost alone when it attacked the "win at any cost" spirit of college football and presented the issue as one of retaining the game with its characteristic physical danger or of doing away with it. Most observers in Chicago deferred to national Football Rules Committee member Stagg's promise that the committee would make proper adjustments, and the *Chicago Tribune*'s football expert Walter Eckersall applauded this "wise and conservative" approach. On the national scene, *Collier's Weekly,* a leader of progressive reform, combined its crusade to dump House of Representatives Speaker Joe Cannon with a campaign to retain the game it judged "too valuable" to lose. The weekly also carried a survey of American university presidents, and all but David Starr Jordan of Stanford felt that football was "too valuable" to abolish; Jordan, however, simply wanted others to join Stanford in playing rugby.[12]

President Harry Pratt Judson's attitude toward intercollegiate football seemed representative of the university community in 1909. He thought that the game existed among midwestern schools as "a branch of the recreative life of students," which was "a form of genuine amateur sport." Judson's statement was the lead quotation in the *Collier's Weekly* survey. Earlier, Judson made one of his boldest assertions regarding football (and one very like that of Harper in 1895 regarding injury and death on the gridiron) when he responded to the death of an Army player in the Harvard game of 1909: "The death of the West Point player is unfortunate and will give football a black eye with some persons. It has not changed my attitude. Accidents may occur in any sport, but I think they are less frequent and less dangerous in college football than in any other branch."[13]

The *Daily Maroon* again attempted to reform Chicago football in a 1911 crusade. Attacking overblown student enthusiasms and undue pressures upon the athletes, the editors charged that football dominated "the fundamental purpose of college—which is education." They concluded, "The evils of the system are so inherent that they can be cured only by extirpation of the entire system." Few on campus took note of the *Maroon* position except the coach. Stagg was incensed by what he termed the "absurd editorial," written "as if the Athletic department of the University had gone back to the practices of the Roman Arena and were sacrificing the students of the University for the glory of victory." He was alone among administrators to take public notice of the *Maroon.* Dean Vincent counseled restraint by Stagg, and the paper soon concerned itself with the reform mayoralty campaign of the popular university professor Charles E. Merriam.[14]

The early years of Judson's administration were marked by a careful reexamination of some of the procedures of the Department of Physical Culture and Athletics. Judson moved gingerly here, as with other departments, trying not to give offense. His corrections or rulings regarding Stagg's department were seldom substantive; they were more often procedural. The new leader refused to extend free tuition to university coaches not holding regular appointments; he attempted to bring some of Stagg's departmental physical facilities under the aegis of the superintendent of buildings and grounds; and he questioned Stagg's keeping the team in Minneapolis over Sunday after a Saturday game. A caveat is in order: Intercollegiate football impinged very little upon Judson's time after 1906. There are thirty pieces of extant correspondence between the president and Stagg during the reform year of 1906, but the years from 1907 through 1910 yielded an average of only five pieces regarding football.[15]

The relationship between President Judson and Coach Stagg was characterized by the goodwill, restraint, and patience of the former. Judson continued to pacify his coach as he had during the critical year of 1905–6. For example, when Stagg wrote to protest a change of curricular policy that he had read about in the *Maroon* and would affect his department, Judson answered soothingly, "There has been no change. . . . The Maroon is not an authority on University regulations." Although a relationship such as Stagg enjoyed with Harper was not possible with Judson, the two men did manage to increase the confidences they shared. Judson returned from an eastern trip, carefully noted suggestions on football rules reform made to him by Princeton President Woodrow Wilson, and asked Stagg's response. Another time, Stagg candidly wrote his president that a proposed game with Cornell in 1908 would aid Chicago's "prestige" and check "Michigan's asperations [*sic*]."[16]

President Judson, however, was forced to address another issue—Stagg's serving as Chicago's faculty representative to the Intercollegiate Conference—which, despite the president's diplomatic approach, strained their relations. Judson broached the topic to Stagg after attending a conference meeting at which other members expressed unhappiness because Chicago "alone of the nine was represented in the regular conference by its coach." Judson explained he did not wish to displace Stagg; he wanted to send an additional delegate from outside Stagg's department to meet the criticism. Stagg curtly answered that such representation "should properly be one of my duties. . . . I can perform it better than any other man that I know of in this University" and reminded Judson that Harper had felt the same. Stagg concluded, "I am either worthy or unworthy to represent the University. . . . if the former then I expect to continue to fill the position with the dignity which my title in the University merits." Judson hastily assured Stagg that he would not "press this matter against your judgment."

Amos Alonzo Stagg sitting on the "Yale fence" in his football uniform—about 1889, the year he was selected on the first all-American football team. The Department of Special Collections, the University of Chicago Library

Stagg posing to show his physique, late 1880s, much in the contemporary style used by artists such as Thomas Eakins to study the figure and by physical educators to study musculature and movement. Newspaper publishers may have had other purposes. The Department of Special Collections, the University of Chicago Library

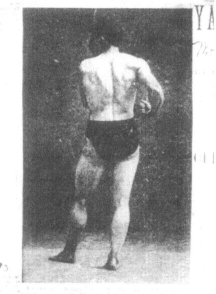

"What Hath Oil Wrought?"—Founder John D. Rockefeller and President William Rainey Harper leading a procession at the decennial celebration of the University of Chicago in 1901. The Department of Special Collections, the University of Chicago Library

1892—The first football team at the University of Chicago. Coach Stagg holds the ball, center. Joseph Raycroft, sitting directly in front of Stagg, soon served as a coaching assistant and later became the Princeton athletic director. The Department of Special Collections, the University of Chicago Library

Captain Stella Robertson Stagg, holding ball, and her basketball teammates, 1897. The Staggs were married in 1894. Stagg Collection, Amos Alonzo Stagg High School, Palos Hills, Illinois

Oct. 29-1899.

A proud papa Stagg with his first-born, six-month-old Amos Alonzo, Jr. The Department of Special Collections, the University of Chicago Library

The Chicago all-American quarterback Walter Eckersall on the practice field, about 1904. He was named to the All-time All-American football team in 1969, college football's centennial year. The background building is the new, state-of-the-art Frank Dickinson Bartlett Gymnasium (1904). Chicago Historical Society.

Marshall Field during a late-fall game, possibly the titanic clash between Michigan and Chicago in 1905. Note the horse-drawn carriage, center foreground, of the type hired by fraternities for the day. The university buildings just across 57th Street are, from left, John J. Mitchell Tower (1901), Charles L. Hutchinson Hall (1901), zoology (1897), Cobb Gate (1900), anatomy (1897), and Charles Hitchcock Hall (1902). The physics building just behind zoology was the work site of America's first Nobelist (1907), Albert A. Michelson. The Department of Special Collections, the University of Chicago Library

Walter Eckersall, bareheaded right center, running loose at Marshall Field about 1905. Note the longitudinal markings which, along with the lasting latitudinal ones, gave the early field the "gridiron" appellation. Mitchell Tower and Hutchinson Hall are in the background. The Department of Special Collections, the University of Chicago Library

Coach Stagg on the sidelines of a 1905 game, with the band just behind. The zoology building can be seen in the background over the east stands. The Department of Special Collections, the University of Chicago Library

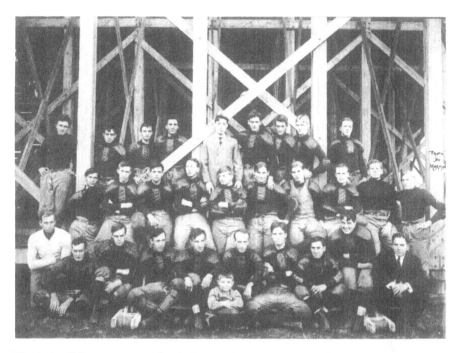

The 1905 Chicago Maroons football team. They were undefeated, untied, and scored 212 points to 5 for the opposition. They won the Intercollegiate Conference title and were named retrospective national champions by the Helms Foundation in the 1930s. Note Amos Alonzo, Jr., with the football in front. Eckersall and Stagg are to the right on the front row. Leo DeTray, who lost the vision of an eye to football that season, is in a suit at the rear. DeTray's left hand is on the shoulder of Hugo Bezdek, future Arkansas and Penn State coach. Second from the left, middle row, is Jesse Harper, backup quarterback to Eckersall and later the most important Notre Dame coach until his former player and assistant, Knute Rockne, succeeded him. The Department of Special Collections, the University of Chicago Library

University Board of Trustees Secretary Thomas W. Goodspeed and Walter Eckersall in front of the stands at halftime of the 1906 Nebraska game—the quarterback's last home game. Goodspeed presented Eckersall a gold watch in appreciation of his football career at the university. Within two months, the three-time all-American was expelled from the university. The Department of Special Collections, the University of Chicago Library

Unsuccessful in convincing Stagg of the need for change, Judson allowed him to be the sole representative. If Judson found the matter impossible, the conference did not: A conference reform in 1912 barred any athletic department member from serving as a representative.[17]

The Spectator and Football as a Way of Life

President Harry Pratt Judson stated a "distinct University policy" in his *President's Report* of 1913–14: "It is not the function of the University to provide at great cost spectacular entertainment for enormous crowds of people." If Judson's policy was distinct, it was ignored in the event. The same *President's Report* noted a newly constructed west stand that seated 13,500 and contributed to the new attendance record for the season of 1913. In fact, a new stadium had been on Judson's and the trustees' shopping list since 1910. And before Judson's statement was published, the championship game of 1913 with Wisconsin had seen the erection of additional bleachers that pushed the capacity to twenty-five thousand. The same game was noteworthy for another index of the importance of the spectators: Chicago players wore jerseys with numerals, probably the first such use in the country. By 1920, the Intercollegiate Conference voted to require them at all conference games.[18]

The growth of spectator facilities at the athletic field was constant, despite Judson's public caution. The capacity was more than thirty-two thousand, and seating encircled the field by the season of 1922. Stagg's rationale for increased seating was simple; he described the "great need which exists for a larger seating capacity to accommodate the friends of the University who wish to attend the football games." The construction of the handsome crenelated west grandstand and wall in 1913 was perhaps more significant than Judson realized. At its completion, the facility was the most significant structure of its kind after Harvard's Soldiers Field Stadium. The inauguration of the Yale Bowl and Princeton's Palmer Stadium the next year ensured that the eastern leaders and Chicago had staked their futures upon the accommodation of spectators and had legitimated the approach for other colleges.[19]

The record of the financing of the grandstand at Chicago reveals the shifting policies and economic difficulties that characterized the relationship of the university and the spectator. Even Stagg remembered "considerable unfavorable comment" by faculty over the expansion, and the physiology faculty across 57th Street coined, "Thousands for de fence but not one cent for test tubes." The trustees paid for the 1913 stand and wall from general university funds; the athletic fund was not touched. The principle was an important one: Increased facilities should be viewed as a part of the university's educational function and should not bear any relation to the game revenues. The impressive principle proved impossible to follow. In 1921 during a period of financial stringency the trustees cast covetous glances at Stagg's independent athletic fund. The fund showed a surplus of about $70,000 that year after paying the way for the entire intercollegiate program and most of the curricular work in physical education. The trustees decided to use retroactively the athletic fund surplus of the 1920s to pay the equivalent of the cost of construction of the grandstand in 1913. The direct relationship between game revenues and spectator accommodation was then formally established, just as those revenues had been linked to Stagg's salary sixteen years before.[20]

Chicago student-spectators became of lesser importance to the football business as facilities were enlarged and game revenues rose. Students had to compete with the general public if they desired single-game tickets. They were offered the quarterly C Book that included admission to various sports and was priced at a level commensurate with the Chicago football marketplace and at the top of the price scale of the Intercollegiate Conference. But Chicago students who possessed the C Book found themselves seated in the end zone in deference to the public seated at the center of the field. The undergraduate council complained formally to the Board of Physical Culture and Athletics in 1920 of not being "treated fairly and squarely as regards the purchase of tickets for games." The board subcommittee report on the student remonstrances rated the importance of the game revenues well before the spectatorial rights of students, a position the board adopted. Further student agitation finally produced an improvement in the placement of student seats eighteen months later. An undergraduate council survey of other colleges documented the degree to which the football enterprise at Chicago had been removed from the control of the students: "No other institution with the exception of Bowdoin has so small a number of seats reserved for students."[21]

Chicago continued to dominate the Intercollegiate Conference financially from 1906 to 1924. Athletic Director Stagg instructed his ticket sales manager in 1913 not to publish the football profits because "our rival institutions have considerable jealousy," and "such a statement of our prosperity would tend to intensify it." Chicago extended its scheduling prerogatives based on gate receipts; the Maroons played ninety-five home games, only twenty-seven away, and most of these arrangements had been legitimated by 1924 with conference rulings. Stagg's team played at home exclusively during two seasons (1906 and 1923) and scheduled the final game of the season at Chicago every year from 1911. The size of the Chicago football marketplace was noted in the Intercollegiate Conference Commissioner's Report of 1922, which said the Princeton game at Stagg Field had prompted ticket applications four times in excess of the field's thirty-two-thousand capacity. Admission prices climbed steadily to the preform 1905 levels and above. A top price of $3 was usual after the Great War, and the average revenue per ticket for major games in 1921 was more than $2. Football profits soared at Chicago from a yearly average around $30,000 in 1915, 1916, and 1917 to $211,796.46 in 1924, and Stagg predicted a profit increase of $100,000 for the 1925 season.[22]

Stagg's university had been the architect of the approach that encouraged stronger universities to prey upon weaker ones by either insisting on all home games or ignoring the institutions and refusing to play them. This policy of "athletic Darwinism" was expressed by the sociologist Albion Small after the University of Iowa athletic control board addressed Chicago's athletic board with a 1917 proposal to handle the problem of equity. The smaller universities found they could not obtain "a satisfactory Conference schedule" with the richer schools. The Iowans wanted to initiate a rotating schedule for all conference schools on a home and home basis. "From the standpoint of fairness," they argued, "there should be absolutely no objection to this schedule." Chicago's board briskly disposed of the Iowa idea by endorsing Chairman Small's statement, which did not mention "fairness." Instead, Small argued that the yearly schedule-making on the open market ensured the survival of attractive games played by the strongest teams. He concluded of the Iowa proposal, "If we wanted to kill the game I can think of no more certain way of doing it." Chicago firmly controlled what had developed into one of the most lucrative football marketplaces in the nation, and Stagg's insistence upon playing at Marshall Field was finally accepted by league rivals who also appreciated a bigger payday.[23]

Stagg's Years of Mastery

Amos Alonzo Stagg proved himself one of the ablest intercollegiate football coaches and certainly the most creative tactician and entrepreneur in the country from 1906 to 1924. He also gained considerable respect as a basketball, baseball, and track coach in his years on the Midway; of those other sports, track was the most noteworthy. Stagg served as a member of the American Olympic Games Committee from 1906 in Athens to 1932 in Los Angeles (he was the coach of the four-hundred- and eight-hundred-meter runners at Paris in 1924). When he came to Chicago, he had brought the new game of basketball, devised by his Springfield College classmate James Naismith. Stagg was the early coach and Chicago was a national center for the sport's development. In 1908, Chicago won the first "national" intercollegiate championship as the midwestern champion when the team beat the western champion, Brigham Young University, and the eastern champion, Pennsylvania.[24]

But Stagg's reputation was built mostly upon football; his teams compiled the best record in the West. Chicago played more Intercollegiate Conference and other major opponents and won more of the games than any other team during the period. During the four-year periods between 1906 and 1909 and 1921 to 1924, the Maroons dominated their opponents. They recorded 90 percent victories in the former period, 84 percent victories in the latter. In only two of the eighteen seasons (1918 must be discounted because the war effort upset normal schedules) did Stagg-coached teams lose more games than they won (1910, 2-5, and 1920, 2-4; major university opponents only).[25]

Stagg received more coverage and adulation in the popular press than any other person at the University of Chicago, and glowing descriptions of his abilities were carried over a wide area. Among the tributes he received from newspapers and magazines after the championship 1913 season were: "The gridiron genius . . . reached the pinnacle of fame and happiness"; "His master mind triumphed"; "It was a great year for the 'old man of the Midway,' who not only achieved success but deserved it"; and "Stagg is the greatest coach the game has ever produced."[26]

Stagg was the paragon of western coaches and destined to become "the most remarkable figure in all the history of American football," according to long-time football journalist Allison Danzig of the *New York Times*. His regional influence rapidly became national because he already had widespread eastern contacts and no one had a more sustained impact upon the game. Stagg was the most prolific creator of game strategies and play tactics during the last decade of the nineteenth century and the first twenty-five years of the twentieth. His multifarious contributions ranged from his earliest remembered innovation (a new tactic added to the old wedge formation at Yale in 1888), through his "ends back" idea in 1890 and 1891 at Springfield and his "tackles back" formation at Chicago in 1894, to his especially fruitful period between 1895 and 1913, when he developed the shift formations and the forward pass. These strategic and tactical breakthroughs were an important part of the widespread influence Amos Alonzo Stagg enjoyed and shared with his university.[27]

Stagg's most significant contributions occurred in two major areas of the development of intercollegiate football: the "open game" and the forward pass. These proved to be lasting features of the twentieth-century game and became irrevocably tied in the American mind with the nature of the sport.[28]

The open game evolved early in the century as the thinking man's counterthrust to the older mass-momentum style of play that was based upon size and strength. The new approach emphasized quickness and cunning—an appropriate combination for college teams that found themselves with more brain than brawn—and this style of football featured the shift formations. A few men began the development, and many copied and perfected the shift into the 1920s. Knute Rockne brilliantly mastered the formation during the 1920s with his "Notre Dame shift." Rockne steadfastly claimed, however, that Stagg was the chief architect of the idea; he credited the Chicagoan for the "revolution in football that gave us the shift," which he termed the "dramatic equalizer between 'big' teams and 'little' teams." In fact, Rockne dominated the 1920s' game until new rules blunted the Notre Dame shift's hegemony, and even then the "Rock" stayed ahead of the others. Rockne provided his most comprehensive statement on the origins of his system to the *New York Telegram* in 1929: "The game which I have taught, with some important changes, was brought to Notre Dame by Jesse Harper, whom I succeeded in 1918. Harper was one of Alonzo Stagg's best quarterbacks at Chicago. Stagg brought his game from Yale. Ergo, just as we all trace back to Adam, so does Notre Dame football go back to Stagg and to Yale."[29]

As to the forward pass, Coach Stagg wrote with remarkable vision in 1906 regarding the possible uses of the newly changed football rules. "I have been doing a good deal of experimenting with the forward pass," he reported, "and I believe it is going to have quite an influence upon the game." He created at least sixty-four forward pass plays for the first season it was legal (1906), and between 1906 and 1909 he developed many of the tactical maneuvers that use the forward pass or its possibility. His team led western football during those years because of his open play and forward passing offense. The significance of the new style of play was gauged accurately by W. E. McCornack of Dartmouth College, who refereed the overwhelming Chicago victory over Illinois in 1906: "Chicago's display at Marshall Field was the most brilliant exhibition I ever saw on a gridiron. . . . This is the style other teams must cultivate or Chicago's system is going to beat them."[30]

Later, when Notre Dame had generally been credited with the introduction of the forward pass, Rockne remembered Stagg's pioneer work and asserted that "Notre Dame received credit as the originator of a style of play that we had simply systematized." Sports writers and sports historians have understandably worked hard to describe Stagg's contributions adequately. The following homely comparison from *Collier's Magazine* in 1930 is representative: "If Walter Camp is the Father of football, Stagg is its Thomas Edison."[31]

Allison Danzig's survey of the origins of the forward pass places Stagg chronologically just after Eddie Cochems of St. Louis University and alongside Glenn "Pop" Warner of the Carlisle Indian School. The issue of which coach's player first used the overhand spiral forward pass is of some moment and is widely disputed, with the strongest evidence naming a St. Louis University player against Kansas on November 3, 1906. Chicago's all-American Eckersall used some of Stagg's sixty-four available forward pass plays on November 17 of the same year in the defeat of Illinois 63-0. And the Maroons used the forward pass to win the Intercollegiate Conference championship in 1907 and 1908. Perhaps Stagg's own measured comment is most helpful: "I have seen statements giving credit to certain people originating the forward pass. The fact is that all coaches were working on it."[32]

Coach Stagg's contributions to game strategy and tactics were widely disseminated through his charges who entered coaching after graduation. The former Maroon players who coached across the country were responsible for much good will toward their old coach at their new institutions, and he reciprocated when he could by including those schools on the Chicago schedule. A prime example of this kind of influence was Stagg's early relationship with Notre Dame when that institution needed friends. The small Catholic school had difficulty scheduling major opponents and was greatly aided when Stagg agreed to meet its team four times during the 1890s. The Notre Dame student editors noted that their players were "grateful to him for his many kindnesses," which included running clinics for them. By 1899 the editors recorded the "old familiar way" of victories by Stagg after four defeats of their team. And his former players and coaching disciples, Frank Hering and Jess Harper, served as Notre Dame's most important coaches before Rockne took over in 1918. Stagg's disciples remained markedly loyal to the master and returned periodically to the Midway for his latest developments; among those training developments were wind sprints, tackling dummies, and the diagnostic uses of the x-ray (operated by Nobelist Albert A. Michelson). During this early period when intercollegiate coaches were still generally traditional liberal arts graduates, Stagg's disciples were as numerous and visible as any other coach's.[33]

A campaign to name the athletic field "Stagg Field" was initiated in 1913 by the *Chicago Tribune* shortly after the newly built stand and wall were formally named "The University of Chicago Athletic Field." President Judson had offered to rename the field after any donor of $100,000 toward the cost of construction. The *Tribune* did not wait for the donor to appear and headlined the rhetorical, "Why Not Call It Stagg Field?" The campaign gathered momentum outside the university and received the backing of the Chicago Alumni Club and old grads like Harold Ickes, who encouraged the *Tribune*, "keep plugging away and you will bring it about." That season's football dinner became an occasion to put successful pressure upon the university administration regarding the naming of the field; Stagg Field thus became the first "memorial" dedicated to a living, working university employee and a strong reminder at the heart of the campus of Coach Stagg's place at Chicago.[34]

Amos Alonzo Stagg remained an imperious entrepreneur during the period in which intercollegiate football was a way of life at Chicago. The years of mastery on the gridiron combined with his years of service at the Midway and his temperament ensured that there would be no diminution of the coach's authority without a memorable battle.

Stagg's conflicts with university administrators were usually based on his long-held presumption of his personal and his department's autonomy. He fought the University Council's special Committee on the Financial Administration of the Division of Athletics in 1908 when they recommended the fiscal procedures of Stagg's department be regularized under the aegis of university officials. The Stagg-dominated Board of Physical Culture and Athletics finally acceded to the council committee, which decreased the degree of independence that Stagg exercised over the financial transactions of his department in order to bring the "Athletic Division financially more into accord with the other financial administrations of the University." There was no suggestion of financial peculation within the department although there was implied criticism by the council committee of many of Stagg's procedures. The athletic fund does not appear in official trustee financial records until July 9, 1918. The reason must have been trustee desire to bring Stagg's baliwick under some semblance of university control based on a tax report they received. Federal authorities had ruled that the income from football ticket sales were "not taxable if proceeds go into University funds."[35]

Other developments regarding game management followed the partial loss of financial control in 1908. Stagg's department had managed the ticket sales and crowd control of all athletic events from the beginning, and his department's increasingly antiquated procedures prompted criticism from the university community and the public. But Stagg took such umbrage to the criticisms that university officials did not insist on change. Finally, after a particularly chaotic Saturday in 1921, President Judson was forced to write to Stagg: "The many infelicities with regard to the conduct of football games of the season has caused much distress on the part of the Trustees, and it was thought best at the meeting yesterday to have the administration of the field put in the hands of the business department." Judson's letter was another diplomatic wonder, and it did the job for a time of soothing the feelings of the combative veteran.[36]

These administrative changes probably alleviated Stagg's work load considerably, but he could not appreciate that improvement. For him, an arrangement that had worked in the 1890s was a procedure that should serve well in the 1920s. In 1922, just as another successful football campaign had closed and Stagg was preparing for his annual Florida stay, he heard that Judson and the trustees were intent upon further streamlining his creaky ticket sales management. Stagg erupted. He protested to Judson and then appealed over him to Harold H. Swift, the board of trustees' head and a long-time football supporter: "I feel very deeply about this matter. . . . It seems kind of tough to have to go away with a sick wife and have this trouble on the eve of my starting. . . . it means a lot to me and I would like to give the remaining years of my life as wholeheartedly to the service of the University as I have in the past." Swift noted in pencil at the bottom of Stagg's plea: "Hold No-Answer." Stagg soon explained his outburst to Swift. He did not want to be subjected to "a penurious attitude which would break up my organization for the sake of a very small saving." He had written as "feelingly" as he did "because of my realization that this was an entering wedge, that the President's plan was the beginning of producing conditions under which I would be unwilling to work."[37]

Stagg's appeal over Judson to a trustee might be considered an extraordinary move had Stagg not done it before and had that trustee had been other than Harold Higgins Swift (1885–1962). Swift, '07, one of the principal heirs of the meatpacking firm, had been the first Chicago alumnus elected to the board. He took his place as a trustee in 1914 and served until his death in 1962, a good deal of that time as the chief executive (the title was alternately president and chairman); he was easily the most influential and powerful trustee from the late 1920s through the mid-1950s. And because of Swift's commitment to football, Stagg always considered him a friend in court. The 1922 ticket sales change did take place, Judson wrote to mollify his coach, and the threat to resign was not carried out.[38]

Athletic Director Stagg claimed these conflicts proceeded from an illicit desire of the other administrators "to get hold of our athletic funds." The burgeoning game receipts from about 1908 to 1924 were indeed a tempting target for trustee and president alike. Oddly, the trustees also led in the quest to improve the hot dogs at Stagg Field. Hot dogs and such are hardly the areas of concern over which trustees might best spend their time; it is probable, however, that Judson and his successor leaned on the trustees, especially Harold Swift, to take some of the pressure off them in their dealings with Stagg. And by 1924 Stagg's authority was little diminished, despite the apparent losses over the sales of tickets and hot dogs. In fact, he used the occasion of the trustee use of gate receipts to pay for the old stadium to press for the construction of a new one. He predicted the athletic fund "could contribute yearly a sum amounting to not less than $200,000 to $300,000" for a new stadium, an argument that was to prove hard to resist.[39]

Stagg's control over student activities of all types was nearly complete. The annual Spring Athletic Festival became a point of contention between him and the student council in 1913. The council, with the encouragement of some of the academic deans, asked to be given control of the student body's annual campus exhibition of classes, dancing, and athletic events. Stagg claimed the student council had "grabbed" the event by taking "the affair out of our hands discourteously" and threatened not to allow the council use of the athletic facilities unless his department continued to receive the financial proceeds. A compromise was soon effected that soothed the coach's feelings. Another area of conflict occurred because of Stagg's assumption that his athletic events should have primacy in campus scheduling. The Board of Student Organizations asked for a more equitable procedure to prevent conflicts from developing between athletic and social or cultural events. Dr. Dudley B. Reed, a tenured member of the physical culture department, thought that some accommodation by the department was possible, but Stagg would not agree: "Mr. Stagg's feeling," Reed explained, was that "the present system of having the other interests avoid athletic dates had been in use for twenty years" and no change was necessary.[40]

Football Coach Stagg represented, and to an impressive degree affected, an important segment of the university community. His constituency was now centered in the alumni, just as in Harper's university his backing had been centered in the president's office itself. President Judson was careful to provide honors and special perquisites to reward his athletic director. When Stagg's salary was increased, as it was three times during the early 1920s, his and Harper's creative linkage of his salary and the football receipts was continued. In addition to Stagg's lengthy winter stays in Florida during the academic year, the trustees granted Judson's request that, because of "continued ill health," the coach be given a leave of absence for the spring and summer quarters of 1913 with pay. Stagg's portrait by Oskar Gross was placed in the Bartlett Gymnasium Trophy Room in 1917, and the same year he was honored as one of sixteen faculty selected to serve on the Twenty-fifth Anniversary Committee appointed by the board of trustees. Stagg's influence with the alumni and his untarnished community image in Chicago meant that his value to the university grew during these years. Harold Swift saw the place of Coach Stagg clearly when he advised, "I believe his feeling disgruntled has a direct influence on very many alumni and believe we are justified to go to rather extreme lengths to avoid hurting his feelings."[41]

Player Recruitment as a Way of Life

The Carnegie Report on *American College Athletics* (1929) stated that their investigation of the evidence provided them at Chicago showed the athletic authorities there had never engaged in active recruitment by correspondence: "As regards the University of Chicago, among hundreds of letters examined, only one, which recommended candidates for rushing by fraternities, remotely suggested recruiting." No time limits on the investigation were noted, but the general tone of the report indicates that records of several decades were examined, and at Chicago, as elsewhere, the Carnegie investigators were dependent upon the access and documents provided by the college officials. A survey of Stagg's correspondence with high school athletes leads to a different conclusion from that of the Carnegie investigators.[42]

Stagg had pursued a cautious course with regard to the recruitment of athletic material until about 1902. He did initiate correspondence with promising athletes, but typically informed them, "We do not give scholarships or tuition for work in athletics." By 1902 he began to accentuate the positive, as he paraded the charms of the University of Chicago, including the "millions of dollars of endowment" that ensured them "greater opportunities for development and for gaining a reputation than you can secure elsewhere."[43]

Coach Stagg recruited zealously by correspondence once he and Harper determined to improve the team early in the century. He even initiated correspondence with athletes already enrolled in college elsewhere; for example, he wrote to James Lightbody, an outstanding athlete but a shaky student (who was deficient in his studies at DePauw University) that "it would be easy" to get him admitted to Chicago.

Stagg did not mention the no assistance for athletes rule when the youth asked to "be fixed up"; instead, he informed the prospect that the university "furnishes opportunities for considerable help to students who need it by what is termed student service" and advised his future Maroon and Olympic star to apply for "a position on the University Choir." In 1903 Stagg addressed Oley Kintz, a college athlete in Des Moines, Iowa, and, after denying any desire to get the young athlete to switch schools, continued, "But should you decide to come here we shall be glad to do everything we can to develop you and enable you to make a reputation for yourself commensurate with your size and ability."[44] By 1907, Stagg openly tried to obtain "scholarships" for his athletes. He made the ultimate argument to a muscular prospect that same year, promising that E. S. Turner would be used "in a combination of plays in which you could make yourself famous," and such "a reputation in athletics would be of pecuniary value to you."[45]

The direct recruitment of players by the misuse of the university's student service program was ostensibly ended by two developments, one at the local level, one at the conference level. After an investigation demanded by the faculty, President Judson ruled in 1908 before the Board of Physical Culture and Athletics that athletic scholarships through student service should cease. But Judson's ruling did not affect the physical culture department's control of many building and grounds jobs for their needy athletes or their athletes' application for regular student service aid.[46]

The Intercollegiate Conference passed a resolution in 1912 that neither directors nor coaches were to "initiate correspondence or interviews" with high school athletes. The rules proved difficult to enforce.[47] At Chicago, Stagg followed an inconsistent approach to the regulation. Usually, he was careful to follow the letter and the spirit of the no-initiation rule, and to the less gifted he declared that nothing could dissuade him from observing conference regulations. But if he genuinely wanted an athlete he managed to communicate that desire to the prospect. For example, Stagg wrote instructions for a prospect named Setzer to a neighboring Chicago alumni family in Washington state:

> Make sure that the boy arrives about a week ahead of time so that we can take him to the Bureau of Self-help and have access to some good jobs before the main body of students arrive. . . . We will see that he is taken in charge and well guided in every way. . . . On account of the Conference rule against athletic coaches initiating correspondence or conversation with prospective athletes, I am writing directly to you rather than to Mr. Setzer. . . . P.S. . . . Have the boy look me up as soon as he arrives.[48]

The athletic enterprise developed two major methods of attracting players to Chicago apart from the promises made by Stagg in his contacts: baseball tours to Japan and continuing interscholastic meets and tournaments. Many of Stagg's footballers also played baseball.

The more unusual of the two recruitment developments was the Asian tour, which had its genesis in 1909 when athletic officials of Waseda University invited the University of Chicago to send a baseball team to Japan during the late summer of 1910. President Judson chaired the meeting of the Board of Physical Culture and Athletics at which Stagg presented the invitation, which the board deemed "inadvisable to accept." The matter was again discussed "informally" at the next meeting of the board and the last of the academic year, "but no action was taken toward a reconsideration of the vote." Within two weeks, a "special meeting" was called (undoubtedly by Stagg) to reconsider the Waseda initiation. This meeting, held while the university was not in session, attracted six members of the seventeen-member board (four of whom were holders of the C) who successively voted to reconsider the invitation and accept it; the approval included a return visit by Waseda to Chicago in 1911. President Judson found that the visits by the Japanese could be made into impressive university publicity, and the first series of visits were followed by tours in 1915–16, 1920–21, and 1925–26.[49]

Stagg used the Pacific trips to lure schoolboy athletes to Chicago. An athletic department publication addressed to high school boys around 1924 described the tours. "A unique distinction, much as our eastern games in football, is the international baseball series . . . a tour of Japan every five years. What an experience for red-blooded young fellows to travel across the Pacific in a jolly group—all expenses paid—and touring the Orient, where games, sightseeing, banquets, and hobnobbing with Nipponese dignitaries are part of the program."[50]

The discussion in the Board of Physical Culture and Athletics to arrange for the series in 1920–21 revealed Chicago attitudes toward the intercollegiate enterprise; in turn, the action of the board demonstrates the power Stagg wielded. The trip was proposed in much the same manner as previously, with an important exception: The tour would be taken during the spring quarter, necessitating the absence of the players from their academic work for the entire quarter and the cancellation of all conference baseball games. Albion Small demurred from approving the plan, noting that although no formal opinion had been given by other Intercollegiate Conference representatives, his "impression was that that body was not in sympathy" with Chicago's baseball barnstorming at the expense of other schools. Dean Henry G. Gale argued that a spring trip would be "inconsistent" because the university had earlier granted "war service credit" to these students; to schedule a baseball journey that would require their further absence from campus would be questionable. Gale added that the proposed cancellation of the Maroon's Intercollegiate Conference schedule for an entire season was "most unfortunate." President Judson, however, backed the trip and spoke obscurely of the "political and military significance of the matter." A committee was appointed to study the proposal and returned a favorable recommendation, with the sole provision that "adequate financial guarantee is to be provided." The journey was approved, undertaken, and still finished with a deficit of more than $6,000. The only other time the Japan tour was questioned was due to the poor quality of the 1924 team, which finished last in the conference. The trip was approved anyway but somehow Stagg delayed until the next year, when the baseball team finished second—and that team also journeyed to Korea after Japan.[51]

The most fruitful method of recruitment continued to be the series of interscholastic meets and tournaments planned and managed by the Department of Physical Culture and Athletics. Stagg spelled out their rationale: "The original motive which led me to start the . . . [meets] was that we might profit athletically." Harold Ickes was one of the early organizers of interscholastic meets for Stagg, and he claimed many of Chicago's "outstanding" athletes had been attracted during their visits. Director Stagg maintained complete lists of all participants, their college preferences, and his record of interviews with each. Like so much else pertaining to athletics at Stagg's university, he made the track meet highly personalized, and it was termed, "Stagg's Interscholastic."[52]

The interscholastic track meet served best as a recruitment approach to top football prospects, and the growth of the meet ensured a continual supply of material for Stagg's teams. The meet grew from the few-score boys who participated in 1902 to more than a thousand participants in 1924. It was staged so that the glories of Stagg's intercollegiate enterprise were constantly before the youngsters. The athletes arrived a day early, were given tours of the city, and attended the interclass dance "at its height," according to the *Daily Maroon*. An impressive banquet in Hutchinson Commons was staged after the track competition the next day. Old "C men" reminisced of past victories, Stagg presented letter sweaters and blankets to the current Maroon heroes, and the schoolboys were awarded their trophies. The entire university community seemed, at times, to be bent upon securing the young athletes. The *Maroon* editors published an "Interscholastic Extra" for the young visitors that was filled with chatty descriptions and pictures of university life and buildings and glowing reports of Stagg and the athletic teams. Stagg appealed to all Chicago alumni to attend the meet. "We have got to make strong impressions on these boys if they turn toward us," he wrote the alumni; he asked them to show their loyalty "to the great effort the university is making to get splendid men and good athletes to accept her beneficent [*sic*] opportunities." Stagg's effort included the following claim to the prospective athletes: "Many an athlete has awakened Sunday morning after the meet to find himself famous throughout the athletic world." One orphan from Oklahoma came, conquered, and was kept at Chicago from June until he was safely enrolled in September.[53]

A basketball interscholastic tournament was added in 1917; it grew rapidly, attracting thirty-two state champions for the playoff by 1925. During the 1920s the University of Chicago promoted interscholastic championships in indoor track, outdoor track, basketball, swimming, wrestling, and tennis. The promotions' early losses were made up by a grateful Stagg from the athletic fund; Chicago's athletic teams reaped large rewards from the flourishing activities that were also financially profitable by the mid-1920s.[54]

Player Retention as a Way of Life

Player eligibility proved the most difficult intercollegiate athletic issue confronting the universities. From the moment the student-player gave way to the player-student, outside interests and values tended to invade the academy forcibly, frequently with noxious results. President George E. Vincent of the University of Minnesota (formerly Dean Vincent of Chicago) described the "extremely bad" eligibility conditions among most universities in 1915; he hoped for "a uniformity of theory and practice" among conference institutions. And Chicago's dean of the faculties, James R. Angell, admitted the situation there was lacking in uniformity: "There was considerable variation in the interpretation of the eligibility rules as administered by the individual deans."[55]

The conference regulation that all colleges publicly define what constituted the "full work" of that school had caused Stagg some anxious moments in 1909. He discovered that the Chicago definition, that is, three major courses per quarter (necessary in order to obtain the baccalaureate degree in four academic years), would render ineligible twenty of his thirty-four probable football candidates if the new rule were applied retroactively. If the rule were so applied, he argued, "It will be almost impossible for the University to have a football team this fall." The rule was not so applied.[56]

Athletic Director Stagg, members of his department, and the team captains tried to ensure that few Maroon athletes were lost because of academic failure after their careful recruitment. Captain H. O. "Pat" Page reported in 1911 on the condition of returning football players who remained in summer school to try to become eligible for the fall quarter. Sometimes young Page found the task formidable, as when Stagg asked him to watch a player "we absolutely cannot get along without." Page found it necessary to live with the errant player in order "to get him straightened out." The arrangement met with less than enthusiastic response from the valuable player, and Page complained, "I can't believe a thing he says, and simply have to watch him all the time. . . . He is certainly one big liar."[57]

The coaches felt that the academic leaders were too inflexible with regard to eligibility problems. There were ways of aiding valuable players to regain eligibility, however, and Pat Page, now an assistant coach, presented his plan in the summer of 1915 for rescuing a young man whom he likened to his earlier "big liar." The unfortunate footballer was not expected to come through his three courses very well, so Page told Stagg that "Lovett [Dean of the Junior Colleges Robert Morss Lovett] has to be hoodwinked into letting him take a little correspondence work during September while still on probation."[58]

The athletic staff was not isolated in their attempts to field a winning team. University Recorder and Examiner Walter A. Payne, who took a warm interest in Stagg and his athletes, arranged a special summer examination by Professor of History Andrew C. McLaughlin for a football player in order to make up a deficiency. When the absent professor had still not received the examination after a month, McLaughlin awarded a B to the halfback, deciding it would be unfair to keep the boy out of football just because the postal service was uncertain, and that anyway, the player "will pass all right."[59]

Two significant cases brought to the Board of Physical Culture and Athletics for judgment in Stagg's university—those of Milton A. Romney and Franklin Gowdy—provide a graphic and unflattering picture of Chicago eligibility procedures during the early 1920s. Both cases concern the traditional paragons of football programs—team captains—and in both cases Stagg conspired to have them drop out of college for a quarter or so in order to prolong their football careers. Romney was the captain-elect for the 1922 football team when the issue of his eligibility arose in early 1922. At the end of his present quarter (winter), he would have earned 34½ majors of the thirty-six majors of credit required for the bachelor's degree. Stagg's plan for the young man was that he would drop out of the university for the 1922 spring and sum-

mer quarters and return for the fall quarter to lead the team and graduate. Dean David Robertson of the College of Arts, Literature, and
Science raised the question before the athletic board and asked for
instruction. He stated that Mr. Stagg had called Robertson's attention
to a resolution passed by the Intercollegiate Conference of Faculty
Representatives in 1920. Stagg claimed the 1920 resolution would allow Romney to proceed as just outlined, for the resolution "repealed"
the following older part of the conference eligibility code that clearly
would have debarred Romney from such a scheme: "No student . . .
shall be considered eligible who prolongs his undergraduate course for
the purpose of extending his period of eligibility."[60]

President Judson immediately declared "that such action would
appear to him to be dictated only by a desire to participate in athletics
and should not approved by the Board." Stagg was undaunted and
"emphasized" that if his interpretation of the conference eligibility code
were followed, "the question of motive is eliminated." Dean Small, as
the university's faculty representative to the Intercollegiate Conference,
"expressed emphatic disapproval of the suggestion" by Stagg, "stating
that he would be greatly embarrassed if required to take that position
at the meeting of Faculty Representatives."[61]

Despite Judson's and Small's arguments, Stagg's motion to declare
Romney eligible was almost passed, five to seven. No roll call was giv-
en for the board's vote, but on the basis of the arguments and interests advanced by the members present over the period of their membership, it is likely that the following four members voted with Stagg:
Professor of Political Economy Harold Glenn Moultin, Professor of
Mathematics Gilbert Ames Bliss, Assistant Professor of New Testament
History Fred Merrifield, and Associate Professor of Physical Culture
Dudley B. Reed. Professors Moulton, Bliss, and Merrifield were all
holders of the C, and Reed worked for Stagg. At the conclusion of the
vote, Judson and Dean Robertson "announced that Mr. Romney would
accordingly be declared ineligible."[62]

But the issue would not down. At subsequent meetings of the board,
Stagg and his supporters raised procedural points surrounding the vote
on Romney. Stagg pressed Trustee Chairman Harold Swift into service
on Romney's behalf; Swift subsequently advised Judson in March that
"the case should be carefully handled." Swift justified his intervention
with a reference to Romney's "standing as a man and his importance
to the team." President Judson seems not to have appreciated this intrusion and assured the chairman of the trustees that the issue would
be fairly handled. A penciled underscoring and question mark applied
to Swift's letter was no doubt made by the harried president. The un-

derscoring occurs at *"and his importance to the team"* and is accompanied by a marginal question mark. The case of Romney's eligibility, which seemingly could not be handled by administrators who felt constrained by the leader of the trustees not to thwart Stagg, was finally presented to the Intercollegiate Conference, where it was handled with dispatch—Romney was unanimously ruled ineligible.[63]

Franklin Gowdy was the captain-elect for the season of 1924. He had been in residence during the 1923 autumn quarter and played football. He planned to be out of residence during the winter quarter of 1924 in order to prolong his degree program into the fall quarter of that year. The board of athletics met early in 1924 to deal with his eligibility for the upcoming season. The same conference eligibility rule applied as in the Romney case that was punted to the conference in 1922. This time, the board handled the issue itself and did not send it on to the conference; they voted that Gowdy would be eligible for the season of 1924.[64]

As it turned out, the decision to render Gowdy eligible was made on the basis of inaccurate or incomplete information. Sometime later, Gowdy's dean, Basil Harvey, claimed the evidence presented regarding Gowdy's curricular program was "a mistake." He explained that Gowdy "could have graduated in June, 1924" had he completed his work with "satisfactory grades" and followed the course sequence drawn up by Harvey. But Gowdy's low grades in two courses and his voluntary absence during the 1924 winter quarter made it possible for him to extend his academic residence and play another season. This new information, contrary to that originally given the board by Stagg, did not change the decision; in fact, there is no further reference to Gowdy's eligibility in the board's minutes. Gowdy led the Maroons to a conference championship in 1924, made the all-American team, and was called "one of the outstanding linemen in the country" by the *Chicago Tribune*'s Walter Eckersall.[65]

Chicago and the Closing of the Football Frontier

The most significant development in American intercollegiate football during the period when football was a way of life at Chicago was the closing of the cultural frontier of the sport and the subsequent cultural ascendancy of the non-East. Chicago led the development of parity but was left behind during the subsequent period of cultural reversal. The frontier was closed during the 1920s when noneastern teams gained parity with the East in game strategies, play tactics, and player techniques and training. In the larger cultural sense, noneastern sources also came to dominate the period. Midwestern, southern, and western state universities and some private universities such as Notre Dame were major forces in the democratization and nationalization of the sport; these both led to intercollegiate football becoming an important factor in the assimilation and upward mobility of America's immigrants, especially those of the New Immigration from the 1890s to 1914.

Chicago made a significant contribution soon after the rules reforms of 1906 when the innovative Stagg used the new open game successfully and demonstrated more graphically than any other coach the path football strategy and tactics would take. As an eastern expert observed in 1906, "Chicago's system means a new era in constructing defense." When Stagg's assistant, Dr. Joseph E. Raycroft, went to Princeton University as athletic director in 1911, his appointment was a precursor of the future cultural reversal. Raycroft soon wrote Stagg his views of eastern football; he described the "conservatism not to say stupidity of the plan of attack" that Yale employed and said that Yale's opponents need not fear the attempt of anything "unconventional." He summarized the place of the new forward pass in eastern offense: "Generally speaking the forward pass is not only not used as a ground gainer—but it does not even threaten sufficiently to keep the defense uneasy and a bit opened up."[66]

The season of 1913 was a harbinger of the closing of the intercollegiate football frontier. Rules changes in 1910 and 1912 had greatly increased the utility of the forward pass, and those western coaches who already used it were delighted. The ball could now be thrown from anywhere behind the line of scrimmage and to a receiver at any distance beyond the line of scrimmage, even into the end zone—all of which had previously been proscribed. Jesse Harper, a Stagg disciple and former Maroon reserve quarterback, provided the most dramatic demonstration of the western use of the forward pass when he took his Notre Dame team east to play the school's first intersectional game. The opponent was Army, which, like Notre Dame, was not a major team (Army's schedule earlier had included up to two major teams, but they had retreated to a schedule of no major opponents by 1913). The game, however, was covered by some eastern sportswriters who were impressed with the passing tactics of Notre Dame in their 35-13 upset victory. The significance of the game as initiating the forward pass has been exaggerated. The game was important primarily in dispelling eastern ignorance of the possibilities of the new rules permitting open play, especially the forward pass. At the same time, Notre Dame quarterback Charley Dorais and his two ends, Knute Rockne and Fred Gushurst, had developed a precision passing game that yielded large gains against a shocked Army team. Other western teams played major eastern teams that year, and young Grantland Rice informed his eastern readers that the overall record strongly favored the West.[67]

Walter Camp, the thirty-year veteran of Ivy League football, wrote for the first time that year of the superb western teams and their dominance of the eastern teams. Chicago was the finest noneastern team in 1913; the Maroons continued to play the most trying schedule in the West and emerged undefeated and untied. Some called them the best team in America, but when Harvard, led by the famous kicker Charles Brickley, emerged from the season undefeated and untied, most observers rated the Crimson at least even with the Maroon. The two teams played a type of football representative of their regions. Harvard employed the traditional mass play tactics and perhaps the last of the great kicking games; Chicago used a more modern game of quickness and attack.[68]

There was great ferment in the West, for despite the keen national interest in comparative regional play, the teams in the Intercollegiate Conference "Western Conference" had been honoring their agreement not to play intersectional games, even with the premier eastern universities. They confined their schedules to conference and regional opponents.[69]

Stagg's university not only flagrantly breached the conference understanding but also provided the most dramatic proof of cultural parity when a home and home series with Princeton University was arranged in 1921 and 1922. Coach Stagg introduced an "informal proposition" from Princeton authorities to the Board of Physical Culture and Athletics in 1920 for a home and home series of four years' duration; it would be the first time a "Big Three" team agreed to a game played in the West. Albion Small and Henry Gale, both of whom had succeeded Stagg as the Chicago faculty representatives to the Intercollegiate Conference, were the only critics of the matches; they worried "as to the probable effect of such action on the Conference." Stagg countered by retailing the "public reports" that other conference schools would like to make a similar schedule. He claimed that the home and home arrangement would meet Chicago's objection to playing Harvard in 1914, that objection being, Stagg said, Harvard's refusal to return the visit. Stagg had not been present at the Board of Physical Culture and Athletics meeting in 1913 which voted not to accept Harvard's invitation, and his argument was fallacious. The reasons for not playing Harvard were clearly stated at that time. The board felt it was not wise "to schedule football games outside the Western Conference" and "especially at so considerable a distance." These objections were still applicable to the proposed Princeton series in 1920, but the board authorized the determined Stagg to plan the games.[70]

Stagg soon completed the arrangements by abruptly dropping traditional conference rival Michigan from the 1921 schedule. He argued that the series would prove "the most important intersectional athletic contests that have ever been held in the country." The *Chicago Tribune* agreed on the importance of the games but noted that other members of the conference were critical of Stagg for dropping Michigan to play Princeton, especially as he "always had advocated sticking to Conference games." It would be hard to prove the *Tribune's* premise regarding Stagg's respect for conference rules; it would not be difficult to argue that Stagg was continuing to set precedents in the application of athletic Darwinism to intercollegiate relationships. The other schools soon rallied; Indiana scheduled Harvard for 1921, and most conference schools began shopping for prestigious eastern matches.[71]

The 1921 Chicago at Princeton game was played early in the season and became the "game of the week" for most journalists. The enthusiastic *Chicago Tribune* admitted that the eastern writers were not as excited about it as the westerners because few easterners accorded Stagg's Maroons any chance of victory. Westerners were not dismayed, however, and a special train carried supporters from Chicago. The state's two U.S. senators were at the stadium, along with President and Mrs. Judson and a throng of thirty thousand. America's finest sportswriters attended and described the game: "Romantically it might be said that the invading eleven came out of the West like Lochinvar, or more realistically that it slaughtered Princeton like a steer," reported Heywood Broun; Damon Runyon wrote that Stagg "unwrapped an outfit that played hoops around Princeton, both on attack and defense." The significance of the game was headlined by the *Boston Globe*, "Western Football's Greatest Triumph"; the *Boston Herald* noted that Chicago was the first western team to defeat one of the Big Three.[72]

The effect of Chicago's 9-0 victory and the subsequent success of the Princeton team against eastern competition was the general recognition that non-eastern football was at least equivalent in quality of play. The New York-based *Outing* canvassed a national sampling of coaches for its annual "Roll of Honor," and the result was a list that was heavily western. This recognition, combined with the notable lack of a single strong Atlantic seaboard eleven in 1921, even intimated that parity might be developing into western hegemony. Enthusiasm for football in the West was unprecedented, and attendance in the Intercollegiate Conference was "uniformly record-breaking."[73]

The impact of the Chicago-Princeton series was increased in 1922, when Princeton defeated Chicago 21-18 at Stagg Field in an extraordinarily close finish. Some sportwriters in their enthusiastic manner termed the match the "greatest game of the century." It was certainly a popular engagement, for Chicago received well over a hundred thousand ticket requests. The incredible Princeton finish, after being battered by the Maroons for three quarters and entering the final period behind 18-7, ensured it wide news coverage. Paradoxically, Chicago won in 1921 using the traditional eastern ground-oriented play, and Princeton won in 1922 by playing the modern western game. Princeton alumni were to remember the outmanned Tiger team of 1922 as their "team of destiny." Chicago alumni consoled themselves in a typical American swirl of game statistics proving clearly that the best team did not win.[74]

The Chicago-Princeton series was a significant stimulus to college football becoming a national game. Chicago's action in breaking the Intercollegiate Conference agreement regarding intersectional games was an important element in the economic and cultural takeoff of football, which paradoxically would leave Chicago far behind over the next fifteen years. Neither President Judson nor President John G. Hibben of Princeton had initially opposed the series. Afterward, Judson wrote that he was "greatly pleased" and Hibben that the "interchange" was "most delightful," but both admitted that the series was unwise and gave the impression of exploiting their football teams. If the presidents of Princeton and Chicago felt that transregional games were deleterious to their educational objectives, they proved to be in the minority and seemingly helpless before the alumni enthusiasms that the games awakened. The Intercollegiate Conference formally decided in 1924 to follow an open policy on intersectional games. For the moment, however, the East wanted Stagg's Maroons, and Chicago led the West in number of games played with the Big Three (six), and with all eastern schools (thirteen), for the period from 1921 to 1932.[75]

The period during which noneastern teams closed the frontier of the intercollegiate football culture and gained cultural parity with the East occurred about 1919–24. There are a number of indices of the parity that the West achieved during the five-year period: (1) *Outing* magazine's postseason "Roll of Honor" of outstanding college players included more noneasterners than easterners by 1919; (2) a higher percentage of noneastern than eastern players were placed on the various all-American teams, including the first Pacific Coast representative and a few from the South; (3) many western teams made eastern tours, sometimes to play several colleges before returning home; (4) Walter Camp judged that the West led in innovative play and that the quality of football was improving nationally; (5) by the mid-1920s a secondary Pacific Coast and southern football frontier joined the primary midwestern frontier, and a tertiary southwestern and Rocky Mountain frontier had been established that was mostly staffed by graduates of the earlier frontier schools; and (6) the Football Writers Association in 1969 selected a list of "All-Time All Americans" to mark intercollegiate football's centennial. The writers picked a pre-1919 team and a post-1919 team in order to make a neat fifty-year period for the "old" and "modern" eras. The 1869–1919 team consisted of seven easterners and four non-East members (Eckersall of Chicago was listed at quarterback). The 1919–1969 team, however, consisted of eleven non-East players (Berwanger of Chicago was placed in the backfield).[76]

Nationalization and Democratization of American Football and Western Hegemony

Western confidence was built as the result of the growing number of intersectional battles. Western teams soon dominated American football to such a degree that the cultural parity changed to cultural reversal. This new assurance was pungently expressed in a *Chicago Tribune* editorial, "Where Does Yale Get It?" It chided Yale snobbishness in scheduling and scored Old Eli for its effete football. The clumsy editorial title was explained, "Where does Yale get the idea that it can meet superior western teams only on its own grounds . . . at its own pleasure?" The *Tribune* declared western teams should play eastern teams of "class" and refuse to play Yale, "which anyone could lick." The editorial concluded by hoping that Yale "learns the modesty which is the best dress of mediocrity."[77]

The University of Chicago led the closing of the football frontier, but Chicago would not prove to be the long-term leader, and it would soon fade from its role as pioneer in the cultural hegemony of the noneast during the 1920s and 1930s. The scale of the football enterprise on the Midway remained more like that of the elite eastern schools; Chicago and those eastern teams found themselves far behind after the nationalization and democratization of football in America had its effect by the late 1920s.

Some private universities, for example, the University of Southern California and the University of Notre Dame, were among the nonelite leaders, although large state universities furnished most of the thrust toward democratization. These public institutions had their beginnings in the promise of serving all the people, and football became the most effective means of communicating with state universities' constituencies. At the same time, many private Roman Catholic schools found the formula useful in their service among Irish Catholics and the New Immigrants who looked to those colleges for cultural symbolism and upward mobility. For such institutions a restricted admissions policy in academic or social terms was untenable and unpolitic. This ensured that their student bodies would be more a part of the mainstream of American life than those of the eastern elite colleges. The *Chicago Tribune* explained the reason for the eastern decline: "Athletic supremacy" would reside in "the state universities of the midwest," for those institutions "have the wealth of a sturdy population behind them." Interest in football "was more widespread among all classes than ever before." A Norwegian Lutheran immigrant from Chicago, Knute Rockne of Notre Dame, expressed a widely held view when he declared, "Western supremacy in football is a triumph of the middle class over the rich." Rockne (who as a twenty-two-year-old postal worker and high school dropout went to the only college that would accept him) and his Notre Dame became the most potent symbol of the upward striving of millions of Americans, the "Curbstone Alumni" whose families had been in America less than three generations. And at a time when there were few national Catholic heroes save for the brief heyday and defeat of New York's Al Smith, Notre Dame and Rockne filled the bill. More than thirty years before a Catholic could have a real chance at capturing the presidency, Knute Rockne dominated the 1920s, a football dominance that was the most complete and lasting of any coach or institution before or since.[78]

Rampant commercialization accompanied the democratization of football. The collegiate leisure activity played best by the student-athletes of eastern elite schools became a campus business done best by many nonelite universities from coast to coast, whose athlete-students came from and then played before, and for, the masses. The football season of 1924 demonstrates the maturation of these developments and the beginnings of overwhelming western cultural ascendancy. Cultural parity was recognized belatedly because of an eastern orientation of the press, but the recognition of western superiority was hastened with the heavy intersectional schedules. The reasons for the importance of the season of 1924 are various and include:

1. A western team, Notre Dame, became the first clear national champion because it defeated opponents from the major regions of football importance.[79]
2. Western intercollegiate football heroes—Harold "Red" Grange, the "Four Horsemen," and Knute Rockne—became national heroes on a par with the professionals Babe Ruth and Jack Dempsey.[80]
3. Walter Camp failed to select any representative of the Big Three on his all-America team for the first time (the effort was his last—

he died within three months).[81]

4. The leading season attendance figures moved west in 1924. Only three of the top nine universities in attendance were from the East; five (Michigan, Notre Dame, Ohio State, Chicago, and Illinois) were from the Midwest; and a new national single-game attendance record, ninety thousand, was set on the Pacific Coast.[82]

5. The dominant and most successful playing systems employed in 1924 were almost exclusively noneastern, and the trend would continue.[83]

6. Both the members of the all-American teams and the teams selected as "consensus" national champions, from 1924 on, demonstrate the change.[84]

Chicago's Last Hurrah

In 1924, all of Stagg's years of mastery and all of the years of building the Chicago football tradition came together at Stagg Field on a cold, blustery November day. Stagg's task was to stop halfback Harold "Red" Grange, then in his second season of gridiron immortality at Illinois. Grantland Rice described his extraordinary athleticism: "Grange runs . . . with almost no effort, as a shadow flits and drifts and darts. There is no gathering of muscle for an extra lunge. There is only the ghostlike weave and glide upon effortless legs with a body that can detach itself from the hips—with a change of pace that can come to a dead stop and pick up instant speed, so perfect is the co-ordination of brain and sinew." Generally called the finest runner in intercollegiate football history, Grange, the "Galloping Ghost," had been spectacular that year leading up to the Intercollegiate Conference putative title game with Chicago. A bare three weeks before, Grange had scored four touchdowns on runs of ninety-five, seventy-five, sixty, and forty-five yards against Michigan within the first twelve minutes. That performance, the most remarkable in football history and at Michigan's expense, was enough to bring Fielding Yost out of his short retirement—and it did.[85]

Illinois coach Robert Zuppke, the "Dutch Master," had built his team around his junior runner by 1924 and used what he called the "Grange Formation." His line was comparatively light—Chicago outweighed them fifteen pounds a person—and swift, so they could lead Grange's sweeps around end or block downfield on his reception of swing passes and spring him for his long gallops. No other coach had managed to solve the Grange problem or even come close to a solution.[86]

Illinois was heavily favored over Chicago, but Stagg was quoted as asking, "Did you ever see Grange score without the ball?" Hence, Stagg's tactics were built on the premise that Chicago should hold the ball as long and as successfully as possible in order to deny Grange the opportunity to handle it. The plan worked to perfection in the first quarter, as Chicago dominated the game with the repeated hammering by fullback Austin McCarty of the lighter interior Illinois line. McCarty's remarkable succession of five-yard thrusts that day earned him the nickname "Five-yard" McCarty. More important, Grange did not touch the football during that quarter, which was marked by long Maroon marches (one ended with a fumble at the Illinois five), one touchdown, and the ball in front of the Illinois goal line at quarter's end, just six inches from another Chicago score.[87]

The first play of the second quarter produced a touchdown for the Maroons and a Chicago lead of 14-0, but as Stagg remembered, "Up to now Illinois had not carried the ball once. Where is Grange? Here he is and there he goes! On successive plays the galloping ghost ran the ball down the field on forward passes for Illinois' first touchdown." Chicago recommenced the attack on the Illinois line, interrupted only by a surprise twenty-eight-yard pass, and pushed the score to 21-7. Three runs by Grange put the ball on the Chicago seventeen. Then Grange made a nifty lateral to his fullback Britton, and Britton passed to the right end, who, in turn, passed to the sprinting Grange (Zuppke was renowned for his multipass innovations), who was stopped at the four-yard line. On the next play, Grange out-raced everyone around end for the score—Chicago 21, Illinois 14 at the half.[88]

Coach Zuppke challenged his team at halftime by charging that their rugged fullback, Earl Britton, had been playing the Maroons "like a piano—with his fingertips." That talk and the installation of a new backfield box defense (which had previously worked well for Ohio State against Chicago) blunted Chicago's attack in the second half, and they did not score again. After both teams were stymied several times by solid defenses in the middle of the field, Chicago cleverly quick-kicked over defensive safety Grange's head and pinned Illinois at their own twenty. But that position merely meant that Grange had more field in which to dash through the Maroons, which he did, in a beautiful zig-zag run marked by the speedy Illinois linemen blocking cleanly downfield for the eighty-yard touchdown—Chicago 21, Illinois 21.[89]

After Grange's touchdown, Zuppke's inspired pianist Britton kicked the ball off by clearing the Chicago goal posts. Both teams gained yards in the middle of the field but had to be content with only two scoring threats and failed field-goal efforts the rest of the way (Chicago tried one from the twenty-seven, and one of Illinois' two was a sixty-fiveyarder by Britton that was on-line but short). Grange's game-breaking fifty-yard run was called back by a holding penalty on a substitute lineman, and the game ended 21-21. Three eyewitnesses, Grange, Stagg, and Walter Camp, later assessed the game:

> The Illinois-Chicago classic of 1924 was the toughest football game I ever played in college. Every time I was tackled I was hit hard by two or three men. At one point in the game I was so exhausted I fell flat on my face as the Maroons were running off a play. I was no exception, for the entire Illinois team took a terrific beating. I don't believe the Illini in my day had ever been in such a ferocious football game. (Grange)

> Taken all in all—the expected one-sided victory, the over-shadowing reputation of Grange, the irresistible sweep of Chicago from the kick-off, the tremendous upset in the first quarter, the seesaw in the second quarter, Grange's magnificent response in which he brought the Illinois score from 0 to 21 virtually single-handed, the breathless dead-lock in the final quarter, with both teams narrowly denied the winning touchdown, made it one of the greatest football dramas ever played on any field. (Stagg)

> Harold Grange is the marvel of this year's (1924) [all-American] backfield. His work in the Michigan game was a revelation, but his performance in the Chicago game went even further when by his play—running and forward passing—he accounted for some 450 yards of territory. He is elusive, has a baffling change of pace, a good straight arm and finally seems in some way to get a map of the field at starting and then threads his way through his opponents. (Camp)[90]

The Illinois postscript was allegedly provided by the Dutch Master, who had hitherto recruited only his favored small, quick linemen. Zuppke told his freshman coach and recruiter Milt Olander to "voik on the beeg boys. The little ones are no good."[91]

After the Illinois tie, Stagg's team had to wait for several more games played by both teams to be awarded the undisputed conference championship. When Chicago finally won the Intercollegiate Conference title in 1924 they set a new conference and institutional attendance and revenue record, netting more than $200,000 on a gross of about $236,000, and were seemingly kings of the gridiron hill.

5

The Decline, 1925–38

Maroon supporters do not come to the Midway for entertainment. They come out of a grim sense of duty, as if they had the
obligation of sitting up at an old friend's wake.
    —*Chicago Herald-Examiner*

After the 1924 Intercollegiate Conference championship season, a confident Stagg predicted an even more impressive football and financial
future. He had already promised the trustees that the athletic fund
"could contribute yearly a sum amounting to not less than $200,000
to $300,000" over expenses to the university, and now he expected
even more. He immediately scheduled the best teams in the East, Pennsylvania and Dartmouth, for the 1925 season in order to make good
his promise. Although the future of football on the Midway looked
secure, Chicago had been a leader in creating attitudes and forces in
American intercollegiate athletics that would erode the university's
position swiftly. The team of 1924 was the last championship one at
Chicago, and that season was also the last in which the vaunted Maroons won more games than they lost.[1]

During the mid-1920s, professors, administrators, and trustees found
themselves trying to deal wisely and rationally with an academic excrescence that had been cofounded by their founder, was still led by a
founding coconspirator, and that now, alarmingly, defined the university for millions. And cofounder Stagg constituted a phenomenon that
had never been checked by the usual methods of the academy because
he was an original whose own external constituency—and its control
of scarce resources—had grown more rapidly than the university itself. Many Chicago academics would no doubt have taken a stand if
the phenomenon's enterprise were failing, but most found it more
expedient to wait for the decline, even for the fall from grace so dra-

matic that sensitive souls averted their eyes and attention. In time, many remained in place for the kill, albeit in the absence of the Old Man. But surely many, if not most, would have preferred that the football of the early part of the century just take leave of the Midway by the 1930s, after the radio network announcers, the film-makers, the promoters, and the press lords had moved in for the golden profits of the 1920s. Intercollegiate football, however, was much too fond of Harper's and Stagg's university, and the university, in turn, of the seductive battle, for any such simple solution to have taken place. So the game remained on the Midway through the period in which the new consumer culture displaced the earlier production economy and the gridiron work and entertainment ethic was established from sea to shining sea.

There was one quite lone Chicago administrator who wanted to broach the issue of substantive football reform in the mid-1920s. Dean of the Colleges Ernest H. Wilkins asked the big questions of football at the wrong time—few Americans ask them in a time of prosperity—and he investigated football at Stagg's Chicago while the team was winning championships. After his investigation, he wrote to his president in November 1925: "Many phases of the football problem have become so acute here . . . that we can no longer rightly defer a frank and courageous study of the problem." But there were many at Chicago, as Wilkins's embarrassing memorandum was passed from president to trustees and back again, who were not ready to study football. Wilkins's plan to lead the faculty in a discussion of the issue was blunted and postponed by his president and by trustee leader Harold Swift until Wilkins's move to the Oberlin College presidency effectively brought an end to his sticky initiative. Dean Wilkins's words, however, deserve resurrection; his memorandum was a careful fifty-seven-point, eighteen-page indictment of football as conducted at Chicago. It was written mostly from the perspective of what was best for student-players. For example, Wilkins's survey of the 1923 and 1924 players' grades led him to charge in his memorandum, "This exceedingly discreditable record indicates either that the football men are mentally of low grade, or that the conditions under which they live during the football quarter are such as to prevent them from doing their work properly." He concluded, "I may add that in my own opinion the situation calls for drastic and extensive reform, but not for the abolition of football." Wilkins also warned presciently that his reform measures were "the only possible means of saving intercollegiate football from the abolition which it will certainly incur if allowed to continue in its present course." Instead, a long, difficult fifteen-year estrangement of academy and football commenced after the Intercollegiate Conference title in 1924. Perhaps no one was either blameworthy or innocent during those years because larger game and more lucrative issues were abroad and available for spectator, coach, and player—and who would presume to change the human condition?[2]

Wilkins's abortive reform occurred just as football was formalized and made permanent as American education's own mass entertainment industry by an almost universal stadium building boom in the 1920s. When this was topped off with the spread of radio and newsreels, the resulting market take-off ensured industrial-strength football virtually everywhere.

Early in the 1920s, Presidents James R. Angell of Yale (the former Chicago psychology professor and dean), John G. Hibben of Princeton, and A. Lawrence Lowell of Harvard corresponded with President Judson to express grave reservations about intercollegiate football. Angell was representative when he admitted that "a source of appreciable anxiety to me is the existence of our great Bowl here, holding nearly 80,000 people, which, with the great momentary interest of the public in football, brings it to pass that once a week we stage a great public entertainment during the autumn." Although Yale and Stanford had the largest ratios of stadium seats to student matriculation, most of the stadium building took place on public university campuses, where leaders had discovered the most successful, if precarious, way in which to communicate with citizen tax-payers and legislators alike. The stadium building boom across the country provided the most graphic evidence of the enlargement of place that American football enjoyed during the early 1920s. The mammoth brick and concrete-grey structures blended into the ersatz gothic or federal of the universities and dominated the horizons of the campuses as completely as the medieval cathedrals had their world. Carillon towers were sometimes added on the campuses to complete the cathedral-like illusion. And the expensive construction and stadium maintenance, in turn, ensured that the institutions would attempt to increase America's commitment to the game.[3]

Intercollegiate football declined in position and influence at the University of Chicago from about 1925 as measured by spectator attendance, the quality of players, and the place of the coach in the university. By the time President Judson retired in 1923, the issue of a new stadium had been pressed by Stagg and Chicago's football apologists of every occupation and stripe for well over a decade. Judson, no doubt emboldened by his recent eastern presidential correspondence and by his imminent departure, finally declared to the board of trustees that year, "The construction of a great stadium would be an emphatic notice" that "educational ideas . . . are of secondary importance." The subsequent arguments and methods of the persons who led the planning of new spectator facilities on the Midway revealed much regarding the future of football at Chicago.[4]

Ernest DeWitt Burton was the last University of Chicago president to have been present at the creation of the institution. He was one of President Harper's most elusive professorial candidates in 1891–92 and proved a canny, successful negotiator. President Burton has been described as the founder of the more dominant of two branches of biblical scholarship at the early university, and he had a significant impact on American New Testament criticism. His administration was short (1923–25), but the number of projects studied and commenced made his tenure an impressive one. A childhood friend remembered that, for Burton, baseball "had no attractions" because of "the vigorous physical efforts required by the game," but his views on intercollegiate athletics were unknown when he acceded. One old C man and alumnus, A. R. E. Wyant, was chary of Burton and wrote the new leader that some alumni were concerned about his "attitude toward athletics." Burton replied that he would not take any "rash or extreme positions" in that regard. Ignorant of athletics though he was at his accession, Burton expressed a desire to learn, and he attended football games to that end. Within two years of his appointment, he was "persuaded that there is a legitimate place for athletics, and even for spectacular games as a part of a programme of college education."[5]

No Giant Stadium

The effects of the growth of spectator interest surfaced at the University of Chicago at the conclusion of the successful season of 1924 and became an important part of the university's first formal development campaign. The university, after taking the lead in 1913 with an expanded Stagg Field, was one of the last Intercollegiate Conference institutions to announce plans for increased spectator capacity in the 1920s; as early as 1922, eight of the ten schools were planning or completing stadiums. Chicago's plan for enlarging the existing facilities at Stagg Field rather than building a new facility was announced in a handsome eight-page booklet sent to the alumni late in the football season of 1924. "The Program for Athletic Development at the University of Chicago" opened with a reproduction of a handwritten letter from Stagg "To the Alumni." Stagg informed the alumni that the "announcement marks the realization of our hopes for the development of athletic facilities at the University." He assured them that "in my opinion it is an adequate and satisfactory solution of our difficulties and I commend it to you all." The trustees had committed the university to a "two-fold plan" that included the erection of a new field house and then the construction of increased seating at Stagg Field, roughly to double the present capacity of thirty-two thousand.[6]

The scheme was made public just before the climactic 1924 game with Illinois and was a special feature of the annual alumni football dinner. President Burton regretted his inability to attend the dinner but wrote the diners of his "great satisfaction" over the trustees' action, which, he noted carefully, "has Mr. Stagg's hearty approval." When Chicago tied Illinois that Saturday en route to the championship, Burton wrote Stagg of his "great satisfaction" with the team and judged their showing "at this particular point in the University's history . . . is of great significance and value to us."[7]

Alumni supporters assumed that the stadium enlargement meant that the Chicago administration was dedicated to a heightened scale of football activity, but the truth lay elsewhere. In a letter to his friend and former colleague George E. Vincent, President Burton asserted the new plan was "far from" a victory for the stadium advocates because "it involves the abandonment of the proposals made by those who favored a stadium." The new stadium supporters, with Stagg's backing, had pressed for a stadium south of the Midway costing $3 million, which would have "a prominent place" in the development campaign. Burton explained that a trustees committee had drawn up a plan that called for an expansion of existing facilities, every step being financed by athletic receipts; "no money" was to be raised for the athletic work during the campaign. Stagg had been forced to set priorities between a field house (the newest form of athletic conspicuous consumption led by Michigan's structure) and the stadium and to grant his acceptance of the projects being paid from his well-guarded athletic fund. Burton argued that under these conditions the scheme was "not athletically top-heavy," for "to have persuaded the strenuous advocates of a $3 million stadium plan to accept this modest programme was really a great victory." Vincent, now the president of the Rockefeller Foundation, wrote his agreement. He thought that "staving off" the new stadium idea and "securing support of the alumni for a purely educational program" was unique in American higher education. The Chicago trustees had indexed the new construction with the economic progress of the football business at the Midway, which provided, in the event, an effective brake on expensive new construction without alienating Chicago spectators. Most significantly, the divorce of the intercollegiate football industry from any education rationale was both contrary to Harperian precedent and left the activity without justification if the athletic revenues became insufficient to support it.[8]

The separation of the development campaign from the expansion of the stadium proved a difficult distinction to make with football-hungry donors. When a rich Chicago merchant sent a $500 check to Stagg for the stadium in order to "express better than words the admiration" the man had for the coach, Burton was faced with the difficulty of following the stated policy that the stadium would be financed entirely with athletic receipts. The president wrote to Swift, asking, "Can we skilfully turn this money into some other direction?" Swift's reply was a balance of diplomacy and opportunism: Burton should take the opportunity to request a talk with the donor about the "interesting problems in connection with our athletic and educational development" and still leave the way clear for a larger sum (up to $25,000).[9]

The heady years of financial success due to the winning Chicago teams of the early 1920s formed the backdrop to the decision to enlarge the football seating facilities. Stagg had urged the construction for more than a decade; "Personally, I am a strong believer," he stated in 1923 to the trustees, "in the building of a stadium," and he predicted that a new facility would ensure continued prosperity. He repeated his pleas until the trustees partially accepted them in their plan of 1924. The new north stand was to be augmented with collapsible bleachers on the south and east to bring Stagg Field's capacity to about sixty thousand. The north stand was to be strongly constructed to allow a second deck to be added when the sixty thousand seats were no longer adequate, as Stagg confidently predicted.[10]

Burton and Swift were no doubt wise to fend off Stagg and the $3 million stadium advocates in favor of the lessened expenditures. Of course, here Chicago was getting caught in the same bind that other universities experienced: When the physical plant and athletic program are indexed to game revenues, the pressure for spectator-pleasing winning seasons becomes the priority. When the profits for the 1924 season proved to be on track, if at the lowest end of his prediction, Stagg was pressed to provide more turnstile-bursting matches.

The trustees' plan for the twofold development of the athletic facilities began in 1925 with the ground-breaking for the new field house, and that was as far as the construction got. The ground-breaking had been scheduled before they had financed the building. The order of the trustees' scheme was then reversed, and the enlargement of Stagg Field went ahead. Harold Swift explained later that the purpose in changing the priorities "was so that we could the more quickly have money to build the field house. We were up to capacity and expected to make the bigger stands pay us well." Chicago's trustees shared the financial optimism of the period; even so, they built later and more cautiously than other university boards. Finally, the lack of a winning football team ensured that the Stagg Field enlargement signified the end of a glorious era, not the beginning of another.[11]

The Decline of the Spectator at Chicago

American intercollegiate football experienced its greatest growth period in history during the 1920s. Between 1921 and 1930, the activity enjoyed a doubling of attendance and a trebling of total gate receipts, and the Intercollegiate Conference ("Big Ten") may have "experienced the most significant growth over this period" among all groups. But after some healthy growth midway in the decade, Chicago began to move in the other direction—the Stagg Field enlargement saw a portentous development within two seasons—the conference teams that Chicago played in 1927 drew fewer spectators than in 1926. By 1930, a projection of $225,000 in receipts for eight games proved to be nearly $70,000 too high. The swift drop was due to the team's poor performance and accelerated by the depression; the total 1926 football receipts of almost $400,000 dropped to $157,000 in 1930. The decline had begun, ironically, just as the new facility was readied to handle increased crowds. During the 1930 season, Vice-president Frederic Woodward observed, receipts were "barely sufficient to pay the current expenses and there is no immediate prospect of a change in this regard."[12]

The rapid plunge in Chicago's football fortunes was comparative and absolute. The victory-hungry fans of the marketplace deserted the Maroons after the team suffered two seasons of mediocrity after the 1924 championship. In 1925, Chicago led the Intercollegiate Conference with net receipts of $248,867.13, and the new facility enabled it to lead again in 1926. Three seasons later, however, it ranked eighth, and as conference football receipts more than doubled from 1923 to 1929, those at Chicago dropped more than 50 percent from 1926 to 1929. Student season ticket sales were increasing at most conference schools, but they decreased on the Midway. The proportion of the student body who held them became the lowest in the conference.[13]

Although Chicago remained one of the finest American cities in which to sell a football team, an important factor in the university's rapid loss of the marketplace lay in the number of alternative games offered in the metropolitan area. Some natural law of gridiron supply and demand seemed to be operating. If the University of Chicago could not supply an attractive football product, others would. The Chicago Bears professional football club steadily increased their following (especially due to their signing of Red Grange in 1925), Northwestern University and the University of Notre Dame experienced an unparalleled period of football success during the late twenties, and even interscholastic games outdrew the Maroons. The municipality of Chicago built one of the largest stadiums in the world during the building boom—Soldier Field in 1925—and the apprehension Midway officials felt over its construction was not misplaced. The new field, located on the lake front about four miles away, furnished direct competition to Stagg Field and offered games that attracted the largest crowds in American football history. Chicago's football market can be appreciated by noting that in 1937 120,000 fans attended the annual championship battle between the public and Catholic high schools, constituting "the largest crowd for a team sports event in American history," according to the historian Steven A. Riess.[14]

Stagg's often-beaten Maroons were hardly a fit competitor for the nationally prominent teams that played at Soldier Field. The 1928 Iowa game at Stagg Field, for example, competed with the Navy–Notre Dame contest at the municipal stadium and a Northwestern match in Evanston. The Notre Dame game drew about 120,000 spectators, Northwestern had 50,000, and only 30,000 attended at the Midway. And the problem intensified. By 1933, Northwestern played two of its "home" games at Soldier Field; in response, Chicago looked seriously, but in vain, at scheduling their 1933 Michigan game there.[15]

The institution that took the market position in Chicago previously held by the Maroons was Notre Dame. The two schools had little in common despite Stagg's early relationship, and the Roman Catholic college was located in South Bend, Indiana, about ninety miles from Chicago. Notre Dame authorities saw the uses of intercollegiate football early in the 1920s, and they determined to make the neighboring metropolis a second home town. At the time Maroon fortunes were rapidly diminishing, Notre Dame usually played its home games in Chicago. It was a natural alliance, for many citizens of Chicago were Roman Catholic, and many were New Immigrants; they responded enthusiastically to the Fighting Irish. By 1929, the president of the Chicago Association of Commerce wrote to tell Coach Knute Rockne that he regarded Notre Dame as a "Chicago institution."[16]

The degree to which the University of Chicago team had lost the affections of spectators could be seen during the season of 1931. Virtually the only point of interest that writers could find on the football field that year was Stagg's fortieth year of coaching. The headline, "Maroons Are Willing, But Team's Weak," was indicative of the lack of promise. Early in the 1931 season, the Maroons met Michigan at Ann Arbor and set an attendance record—the game was viewed by the fewest spectators in the stadium's history. The team's Stagg Field appearances followed the same pattern. The 1931 loss to Indiana "was transacted in remarkable privacy for a game involving two members of the Western Conference," said the *Chicago Tribune,* beneath the headline, "Private Battle." The Purdue loss proved to be another private contest; one writer described it as the most sparsely attended game on the Midway since the 1890s. The next week's engagement with the University of Arkansas broke the week-old record. More than fifty thousand Stagg Field seats were empty, and fewer than two thousand spectators paid to see the match. The University of Illinois lowered the price of their tickets for the Chicago game to $1, but only twelve thousand sat in the sixty-five-thousand-seat Illinois stadium. And Chicago's traditional homecoming game drew only twenty-two thousand dispirited followers. "Maroon supporters do not come to the Midway for entertainment. They come out of a grim sense of duty, as if they had the obligation of sitting up at an old friend's wake," observed the *Chicago Herald-Examiner.*[17] The decline of spectators was a symptom, not a cause. Attendance dropped, in Stagg's words, because of a "series of bad years." That record was the result of many factors, the most important being the quality of the players.[18]

The Decline of the Player

A period of study and change had begun when President Burton obtained trustee acceptance for his commission to study the undergraduate work of the university in 1923. The graduate divisions still held rank among the nation's finest, but Burton had grown concerned with the place of the college at Chicago. The two men who led in the development of the studies were Ernest H. Wilkins and Chauncey Boucher, successively deans of the Colleges of Arts, Literature, and Science from 1923 to 1931 (Boucher assumed a new title and duties of dean of the college in 1931). An organization and curriculum were devised that emphasized the importance of good teaching and voluntary learning; year-long courses were instituted that did not require attendance and were completed by sitting comprehensive examinations at the end of the spring quarter. President Robert Maynard Hutchins, who inherited the "New Plan" in 1929, saw the university's ruling bodies finally accept it in 1931. Ironically, Hutchins has generally been given credit for the scheme that took eight years to develop, almost all before his arrival.[19]

Coach Stagg encapsulated the effects of the educational changes on his work by telling an athletic prospect that it was "hard to get into and hard to stay in" the college. He also spoke of the drastic "decline in material in 1926 largely due to the raising of entrance scholarship at the University." Such pessimism replaced Stagg's earlier enthusiastic assurances to athletes. This gloom was justified, for studies at Stanford, Columbia, and the University of Minnesota in the late 1920s indicated that football players performed comparatively poorly in their academic work. The raising of entrance and academic standards at Chicago during the 1920s and a new generation of Chicago administrators determined to interpret the rules strictly occurred at the same time the Intercollegiate Conference created an office of commissioner to oversee a move toward controlled recruitment. In fact, this proved a futile attempt at rules enforcement, and the commissioner reported, "We are not making very rapid progress in discouraging illegitimate recruiting." Hence, Chicago began to restrict recruitment during the period that the practice became more widespread elsewhere.[20]

Chicago's tuition rate also discouraged young athletes, a problem that did not rest only with the need for more skilled players on the athletic teams. Associate Dean of the Faculties David H. Stevens admitted in 1929 that there was difficulty in carrying out the new admissions and scholarship policies because the number of applicants for admission had decreased sharply.[21]

Player Recruitment

The athletic management at Chicago had developed some recruitment methods that they enlarged and retained tenaciously in the face of growing criticism. The primary means after the mid-1920s were the intersectional games, the Japanese baseball trip, and the interscholastic basketball and track meetings. The intersectional games increased in number, and Stagg wrote prospects that he "hoped" they would be on his team when Yale and Princeton were met in the coming seasons. Exchange visits to Waseda University by the baseball team were continued through the mid-1930s and continued to be used as a carnival-like attraction for the Chicago athletic business.[22]

The interscholastic meets were the chief means of attracting athletes to Chicago. As the Maroons faded as a threat in conference athletic races, Stagg's publicity for the meets became more brassy, or "terribly sophomoric" in Vice-president Woodward's phrase. The official program pushed the claims of Maroon uniqueness to absurdity: "How

Chicago met Princeton in the East and turned her back 9-0 will never be forgotten, and how she met Princeton at Chicago and lost . . . is equal glory that will never pass." It declared Chicago was supreme in the West "even though the War left Chicago crippled for four years," and the Stagg authorship was apparent. The information booklets regarding the tournaments carried the Maroon *C* on the cover and the modest appraisal, "The World's Greatest Basketball Interscholastic." The track meet was still billed as "Stagg's Interscholastic."[23]

By 1927, high school authorities were publicly expressing dissatisfaction with the Chicago basketball tournament. As state and national secondary school federations grew in size and unity, all college-sponsored recruitment events appeared to be anachronistic or hurtful to the health and autonomy of interscholastic programs. The campaign waged by school officials to stop the events and the position of Stagg on the matter constitute one of the most dreary affairs in the history of Chicago athletics.

The National Federation of State High School Athletic Associations asked Chicago to abandon the basketball tournament a number of times between 1928 and 1930. The University of Iowa, Washington University in St. Louis, and other universities had discontinued their events for schoolboy athletes in response to a similar request. A boycott of the Chicago meet grew during the two years, and by the spring of 1930 only six "state champions" were included in the thirty-six-team field, a dramatic decrease from the thirty-two state leaders of former years. The remainder of the field were private schools and public schools who did not accept the eligibility standards of the state associations and were "not members of their state athletic associations and in no sense 'represented' their states." Hence, the university found itself, under Stagg's approach, encouraging a lack of cohesion and eligibility requirements among American high schools.[24]

Vice-president Woodward addressed Stagg in February of 1930, noting the resolutions of the National Federation that criticized interstate basketball. Woodward wrote that President Hutchins and he felt "we ought not to continue to hold the national interscholastic basketball after this year." Stagg responded with renewed public attacks on the National Federation and explained the motives of his opponents: "It's just plain jealousy, the national federation wants to run my tournaments and I won't allow it." Soon the North Central Association of Colleges and Secondary Schools joined the National Federation in opposing such tournaments, a position that most of the faculty representatives of the Intercollegiate Conference supported. Sportswriters described the actions of the education associations in much the same manner as Stagg, although one ingenuously admitted not having heard of the North Central Association until the controversy. James Weber Linn, a Chicago English professor who was noted for his support of intercollegiate athletics, claimed the development of opposition to the tournaments was a "racketeering attack" on Stagg and constituted "a kick in the pit of the stomach from a fellow educator." No other members of the faculty expressed themselves so elegantly in the press.[25]

The entrance of the powerful North Central accrediting agency into the controversy finally forced action upon the hesitant Midway administration. The Board of Physical Culture and Athletics discussed a letter from the accrediting group condemning the interscholastics and decided to survey the 269 schools that had entered the basketball contest during the period it had a "national character." Only 25 percent of the school principals supported the "continuation of the tournament." This compelled the committee to its finding that "the only possible recommendation . . . is to discontinue the tournament." The principals also expressed unhappiness with Stagg's interscholastic track meet, and the committee also advised the discontinuance of that event. It was left for Woodward to write gingerly to the aging Stagg that as there was "a strong current of adverse opinion among the high school principals," it would be "unwise for us to insist upon the continuation of these tournaments." Stagg finally accepted the cessation of the national meets but insisted upon continuing his basketball tournament as a Chicago-area series.[26]

Amos Alonzo Stagg's actions should be set in their context—he was struggling to maintain his successful football enterprise under difficult conditions. The university still wished him to wage the good warfare, but he was limited by a diminishing arsenal. Policy and procedural decisions regarding the college had demolished Stagg's recruitment opportunities and apparatus during the late 1920s and early 1930s until the interscholastic events were about the last effective method of recruitment. He held stubbornly to his meets until he and the university were the objects of professional scorn.

It was widely recognized that recruitment of quality football players was the most important factor in building a successful intercollegiate program. And many were the colleges and conferences across the country who made their peace with methods that would not have been countenanced earlier. Perhaps the ethos of college football was best captured in 1930 by a *Literary Digest* article, "What Football Players Are Earning This Fall."[27]

Chicago steadily lost ground in the competition for players. Northwestern was the only other private institution in the Intercollegiate

Conference, and its football fortunes were on the rise. Northwestern developed a unique approach; almost fifty "alumni counselors" were appointed to scout for students. Opponents claimed that the system, combined with "loans" to freshmen to cover tuition, was responsible for the advance of the Wildcats' gridiron prospects. The method proved difficult to control, as a number of cautionary letters from President Walter Dill Scott to his enterprising athletic director, Kenneth "Tug" Wilson, demonstrate. Some of the football captains had difficulties graduating (including their greatest star, Ernest "Pug" Rentner), and some Northwestern alumni got the impression that the athletic officials "go out and get them regardless of their scholastic ability." And, of course, the other Chicago competitor, Notre Dame, was in a unique position. The symbolism of Rockne's school continued to ensure national interest in the success of his program. The mystique of the Lutheran coach (who converted to Catholicism) and his institution's service to the Roman Catholic church provided an informal national scouting network. This network combined with relatively low admissions requirements and financial help to ensure a continual and impressive supply of players. For example, a Pole in San Francisco wrote Rockne an "annual letter" regarding players; a seminarian in Rome wrote news of a prospect from Boston; and the father of a player from California requested a special tutor (whom he got) for his son. Even when Rockne exhausted the number of "student jobs" for his athletes, the influx continued. The network of priests and laity barraged Rockne with nearly two hundred scouting reports during the spring and summer of 1929, and the system continued into the 1930s even without him.[28]

Player Retention

The curriculum and eligibility standards at Chicago were as important as the admissions policy in determining the number and quality of football players on the Midway. The period of decline threw the deficiencies of the Department of Physical Culture and Athletics into sharp focus, and its importance was diminished absolutely and comparatively.

By the mid-1930s, most American universities had developed a physical education major in response to required physical education in most school systems in America. The required physical education program was accomplished by educators who managed finally to place the sound body alongside the sound mind as goals for American schools. Coaches soon worked out programs that attracted a steady supply of muscular prospects who majored in physical education and returned to the schools as physical education instructors and coaches;

these coaches, in turn, sent promising players to their alma maters. The arrangement constituted a new supply aspect of the football business, which grew apace among the other Intercollegiate Conference institutions. The inauguration of the physical education major began at Wisconsin in 1910, and by 1929 Purdue was the ninth school to begin a baccalaureate program in the field. The possibilities of the circular commerce were endless, and conference schools attracted and lodged large reservoirs of physical talent in their courses. There were almost four hundred male undergraduates majoring in Athletic Coaching and Physical Education at the University of Illinois in 1930–31; Purdue, Wisconsin, and Indiana enrolled 108, 109, and 90 males, respectively, as physical education majors in 1935. Indeed, the use of the physical education major (or other majors, such as business administration in the 1950s, communications in the 1970s, and sports management in the 1980s) in such a way meant that even comparatively rigorous institutions could file their athlete-students in a safe and nonthreatening place.[29]

Chicago did not meet the competition. Stagg came to the physical education major idea late, and his department only then prepared proposals. The nearest the proposals came to reality was in 1923, when President Burton "evinced interest" in the program, according to Stagg. Although Charles H. Judd, a Chicago professor of education, was a leader in the national movement toward accreditation of these programs, his university did not follow. In fact, physical education of any sort did not expand in the Chicago curriculum; it decreased. Physical culture at Chicago had been precedential in 1892, but Stagg's subsequent emphasis on intercollegiate athletics proved to be at the cost of sound curricular development. The lack of interest shown by the students in their required work was a matter of concern, and even Judd suggested the lowering of physical culture requirements as early as 1912.[30]

The deliberations regarding all Chicago undergraduate work initiated by President Burton and concluded by President Hutchins proved to be devastating to the independence and importance of the Department of Physical Culture and Athletics. The record of the Board of Physical Culture and Athletics during this period is of a body divided: Stagg's disciples (declining in number and affiliation every year) tried to salvage some compulsory work in physical education as others, led by Dean Boucher, tried to bring the physical culture work into line with the voluntaristic philosophy of the New Plan. In 1932, the University Senate eliminated compulsory physical education, prompting a decrease in the size of Stagg's faculty, a number of whom were primarily coaches and not committed physical educators. Hutchins's administrative reorganization plan placed the department under the control of the dean of students (a new office) and the Board of the Coordination of Student Interests. The senate attempted to deal positively with the physical health and enjoyment of the undergraduates when it abolished the compulsory work by planning an emphasis on student medical examinations and an enlargement of intramural activities; both areas had been poorly developed by Stagg's department.[31]

A pointed 1914 query from Divinity Dean Shailer Mathews, "What is being done to bring the general student body into athletics?" had brought Stagg's disappointing answer that contained nothing new and nothing whatever of an intramural nature. The effects of the slow development of intramurals were not clearly seen at Chicago, but most schools recognized the relation between a strong intramural program and the discovery of athletic talent on campus.[32] Princeton and Amherst students led the first formal organization of intramural competition in 1909; in 1913–14, Michigan and Ohio State organized programs under their intercollegiate athletic departments. Football was a favorite intramural sport; leading universities provided complete uniforms for upwards of five hundred men (Michigan equipped more than a thousand) and boasted 80 percent intramural participation among their male student bodies. Chicago was not only behind the large public universities, but also in arrears of the private universities of its class; Harvard and Pennsylvania had large programs.[33] Albon Holden, former Chicago student and editor of the *Big Ten Weekly,* informed a concerned Harold Swift of the paucity of intramural development at the Midway. Holden declared that Chicago was "ten years behind" the other schools; he termed the phrase with which Chicago described its intramurals, "athletics for all," (borrowed from Michigan) a "travesty." Chicago's intramural expenses during the autumn quarter of 1930, for example, were less than the cost of seasonal intercollegiate game officials or for painting the bleachers at Stagg Field.[34]

Intramurals were formally recognized on the Midway in 1924; Dr. Charles Molander, an athletic department physician and former Maroon basketball captain, was put in charge. Molander was largely unsuccessful with his frequent pleas for adequate funding because all requests went first to Stagg, who showed little interest and sometimes hostility, and then to the Board of Physical Culture and Athletics. Intercollegiate athletics consumed more than 90 percent of the board's time; neither intramurals nor physical education was mentioned or alluded to at many meetings. The first sustained attempt by the board to increase the scope and value of the program did not occur until 1927; it remained for the senate's action to ensure significant progress.[35]

Walter Camp had noted in 1923 "a great increase in the number of special players—that is, the tendency to inject into the game a player for some particular specialty" and "an additional increase in the number of men playing in any one game through the continual injection of fresh players for tired ones." But at Chicago the development was reversed: the result of raising the academic quality of the undergraduate student body was a decline in the football player reservoir just as the game required more specialization and a larger player pool.[36]

Michigan's Fielding H. Yost, who had watched and played a generation of Chicago teams, asserted that the comparatively large university enrollment at Chicago (still number one in the conference as late as 1924) was a misleading index of player numbers because neither transfer students in their first year nor graduate students were eligible.[37] Knute Rockne thought that Stagg accomplished an outstanding coaching job in 1929, despite the fact that he had "practically no prospects" and "no material of experience." And the peripatetic Glenn S. "Pop" Warner, whose coaching career spanned about as many years and victories as Stagg's, stated in 1932 that Stagg no longer had "a sporting chance to win many of his games because of lack of materials." Many others agreed with these judgments and cited such factors as the low average age of Chicago players (nineteen in 1933) or the inability of the university to attract as many football players from the Chicago area as Illinois, Notre Dame, or Northwestern. Most authorities agreed that Chicago's player problems were "hereditary" not "environmental," and one wag suggested, after an allusion to the poor eyesight of the Maroons in 1935, that the entire Chicago team be equipped with "shatter-proof smoked goggles—and possibly rear-vision mirrors" to remedy nature.[38]

Chicago had the smallest pool of players in the conference according to approximate enrollment figures of eligible students from the late 1920s. The reservoir was about one-sixth that of Michigan; one-fifth that of Illinois, Minnesota, Wisconsin, and Ohio State; and one-third that of Iowa, Purdue, and Northwestern. Michigan boasted hundreds of football candidates, and Northwestern had awakened from its athletic somnolence by 1931 with more than 120 candidates for their freshman team and seventy for the varsity. The largest number of Chicago men to report for varsity football practice in 1932 was thirty-four, and by 1937 there were only a handful of good Maroon players, according to one football writer. Finally, enrollment figures showed that only a few of the promising lower-classmen athletes survived to play as seniors at Chicago.[39]

The Decline of the Coach

Coach Amos Alonzo Stagg, who had been respectfully termed the "Old Man" before his fortieth birthday, enjoyed continued popular adulation during the period of the decline of his football enterprise. At the same time, however, members of the university community were showing more critical interest in the material used for the construction of the Stagg living monument. Although Stagg was not given to educational theory, his assertion in 1908 that the purpose of the university was "to teach truth and educate manly men" had seemed to suffice for thirty highly successful years. Now, it must have seemed to him, upstarts were substantially changing the rules by which he had played the game. Increasing numbers of administrators and faculty who had not been present at the creation of the institution were more likely to challenge some of the traditional perquisites Stagg, and no doubt other veterans, enjoyed. An example of the new administrators was Dean David Robertson, formerly secretary to President Judson, who was certainly aware of the difficulties that Stagg's behavior had meant for Judson. For their part, Stagg and the physical culture department viewed Robertson as distinctly unfriendly to the athletic enterprise.[40]

Stagg had become a invaluable symbol of the institution; one index of his magic name was its use six times over in the official university song book. He was the only person who served as the sole subject for a song during the period ("John D. Rockefeller" was dropped after 1920):

"Grand Old Stagg"
(to George M. Cohan's "Grand Old Flag")

He's a grand old Stagg tho we don't like to brag
And his worth we will prove to you soon
He's the idol of the team we love
That fights for the dear old Maroon (rah, rah, rah)
We will stick for him
Tho we lose or we win
And our faith in him can't lag
Tho other coaches be forgot
Take your hat off to grand old Stagg.[41]

Stagg's public role in the university's $17 million development campaign of 1924–25 went very well. He spoke widely on behalf of the campaign, and Burton received much correspondence indicating his popularity. After his championship season of 1924, the vigorous, white-haired coach was easily the most publicized university speaker available for alumni and general groups, and he was given special responsibility for the C men. Examples of distinguished C men who maintained contacts with Stagg and the university were Harold Ickes, Donald Richberg, and Hugo Friend. Stagg continued to keep in touch with the men who had played for him; as a result, they probably felt more a continuing relationship with the university than any other alumni group. This was an important factor in an institution comprised of a graduate and professional student majority who seldom thought of Chicago as deserving of their first loyalty.[42]

The world of Amos Alonzo Stagg changed more rapidly within a decade than would have been thought possible in 1924. The decline in the place of the football coach at Chicago was more real than apparent due to Stagg's unique place and reputation. It was not until another man took his position in 1933 that the reality surfaced, but there were a number of indicators of unease and stress during this period of decline.

The Department of Physical Culture and Athletics had always been highly personalized around Stagg, without clear delineation of the responsibilities of his inferiors beyond their subservience to the Old Man. One of the most sensitive areas for apportioning responsibility was the health of student athletes. Player health had been an issue for some years due to the confidential reiteration of charges by Harold Swift, beginning in 1915, that Stagg sometimes used unfit football players in games. Upon Swift's complaint, Judson inquired of Stagg whether "we are so eager to win games that we have permitted students to play who ought not to have played." Stagg's response to Judson, along with that of his medical assistant Dudley Reed, indicated the lack of proper procedure. Stagg admitted the possibility of a mistake in the handling of one athlete and excused himself as having been "so crippled" he could not keep close watch. And Reed's reply to Judson was hardly calculated to put his or Swift's fears to rest; Reed declared that "usually" Stagg was "quite loath to use an injured man." Upon Swift's urging, Judson requested the establishment of clear lines of responsibility and procedure in this critical area.[43]

That a trustee would involve himself in such a matter might be thought unusual, once again, if the trustee were other than Harold Swift. The thirty-year-old Swift no doubt was in a position to know about player health in 1915; he was an extraordinary trustee in his active care and feeding of members of the football team, and he occasionally attended practice. For example, he ordered his executive officer at Swift and Company in St. Paul, Minnesota, to provide for the comfort of Stagg and the team when they played at Minnesota later in the 1915 season, including good beef, and he often invited members of the team to his nearby home for dinner. Swift never married, and he spent much time with the activities of his fraternity, which had a good share of athletes as members.[44]

The lack of proper care for player health appeared at its most unfortunate during the period of the decline of football. The lines of controversy over the matter were drawn in 1929, perhaps because Dr. Reed was no longer under Stagg's direction; he was now director of the health service and professor of hygiene and bacteriology. Vice-president Woodward annually wrote to Dr. Reed to remind him of his responsibility for player health. Woodward noted one year that due to the large "hopes" for the season, "there may be more than the usual temptation to use men who are not in good condition." Reed's reply to Woodward in 1929 must have detailed past incidents in which the medical advice had not been followed, for Stagg was angered by it. Stagg's letter to his former department member is defensive regarding circumstances that Reed divulged to Woodward. Stagg stated that Reed's letter assumed "that it is our practice to override orders of the Medical Department," and he coolly corrected Reed, "That is not true." Then Stagg discussed two incidents in a convoluted fashion. He admitted asking one of the injured boys whether "he thought he could return to the game and suggesting that he do so," and he admitted "going contrary" to Reed's advice in the second case. The exchange seemed not to have solved the problem, and Reed wrote Stagg again in 1932 "to make it clear" that an injured player should not play for four weeks. Reed reported that the boy was put in a "difficult place" when "the surgeons tell him he ought not play" and "the coaches give him the impression that he would play if he had the real stuff in him." In both cases, Stagg's disappointing replies to Reed were full of prideful self-justification—the lifelong habit had become intensified with adulation and age.[45]

The decline of intercollegiate football at Chicago was accompanied by the late rise of intramurals, and the conjunction of the two areas produced conflict in Stagg's department. Intramural Director Molander proved to be a constant irritant to Stagg; he promoted student participation and interest in intramurals with a constitution partially drawn up and carried out by them. Stagg had never liked the idea of student involvement in such matters, and he styled the plan a surrender of "the authority" to the students. When the demise of compulsory physical education seemed imminent, he carried out a plan to protect his varsity coaches (who had previously enjoyed sinecures as physical education instructors) by reorganizing the department. His coaches would take over the intramural work, even though they had evinced little interest in that activity in the past. The student leaders of the intramural program were opposed to this action, and one wrote to Stagg that he had never appreciated his policy toward intramurals as subordinate to intercollegiate athletics. "Coaches with the intercollegiate viewpoint are simply not interested," the student argued, "the only interest" a varsity coach could have in intramurals "is that of securing recruits for his varsity squad." The changes in the college could hardly have spoken more clearly to Stagg, and he did not like what he heard. He attempted to silence the student critics, whom he termed "very odd and mulish," by reminding one of the young men, "you are putting your view . . . up against the point of view of the Director of the Department who has been working for the Department forty years and who has spent his life in sacrificial building up of the Department."[46]

Chicago students began to criticize Stagg in an unprecedented fashion. In an "Open Letter to the Old Man" during the 1931 football season the *Daily Maroon* pleaded with Stagg to depart before he was asked to do so and claimed that the plea represented a good amount of campus opinion. The letter, signed "Undergraduate," touched off a minor controversy. James Weber Linn called for the *Maroon* editor's resignation for "conduct unbecoming a gentleman" and forgot to discuss the merits of the case. Team captain Sam Horwitz did discuss the merits of the case in a letter to the editor and used the occasion for a derisive attack on the "attitude of that great student body of ours." Horwitz indulged in the cant that sometimes passes for moral wisdom in American athletics: Would Stagg "turn over the reins when the going is the toughest?" asked the captain. "No," Horwitz answered himself, for Stagg was not a "quitter." The *Phoenix,* an irreverent student publication, addressed the issue of the aging coach in a thinly veiled satire that referred to Horwitz as the "Defender of the Faith." The piece noted the decline of football and laid it at Stagg's feet: "Now in his advancing years Sir Elkk grew feeble, and the company of champions commenced to disband. No longer did the straightest backed and longest limbed youths come to his banner, but instead sought out the banners of his foes. But still, because of the fame that had been his, and the honor due his greying beard, he held much kudos, and was revered as a sage and a builder of men."[47]

The position of football coaches in America had undergone a thorough professionalization by the early 1930s. One of the most lucrative methods by which they capitalized on their fame was the publication of football articles, usually ghostwritten. Stagg had asserted many times that college coaches should not use their fame to obtain additional income, and he publicly refused to write for newspapers during the 1920s. His own weekly Hearst column, however, appeared nationally in 1931; he wrote the syndicated Saturday piece (with the same agent) that Knute Rockne had written before his death. Stagg's point of view could have done little for morale when Maroons read his column the morning of a game. He frequently chose the opponent of the day to defeat his own team: "The fast-scoring machine of the Boilermakers is certain to be too much for the comparatively weak Chicago team," and "Wisconsin outclasses Chicago and can safely be relied upon to win the game at Stagg Field."[48]

Coach Stagg enjoyed a number of helpful relationships with university officials during this period. None was as trustful as the one he had enjoyed with President William Rainey Harper, but they served the Old Man and his department well. Harold Swift continued as counselor and friend, although he tried to take care that his relationship with Stagg did not undermine larger university interests. The two exchanged confidential letters regarding the university, as when Swift wrote chatty notes of the appointments of Presidents Burton and Mason, and when Stagg wrote pleas to Swift if he felt personal or departmental preserves were invaded. Swift usually allowed himself to be used as a sounding board by Stagg only to help the administrators disarm the volatile coach.[49]

When the biblical scholar Ernest DeWitt Burton became president of the university he had less knowledge of intercollegiate athletics than had his predecessors. Burton's tenure is not well known, but it was marked by unusual vitality and importance. A well-tailored, gentle professor with dancing, humorous eyes, Burton initially had some difficulties making sense of the place of Stagg and his football players in the larger university purpose. When Stagg wrote Burton, on summer holiday, of an administrative slight and protested, "I feel humiliated by this action and the sweetness has been taken out of my work," the quiet scholar caught on fast. He was also carefully instructed by Thomas Goodspeed and Harold Swift on the importance of Stagg. "Mr. Swift feels that a thoroughly cordial understanding with Mr. Stagg is indispensable to alumni cooperation," wrote Secretary Goodspeed for Swift, who regarded such "cultivation" as "of the greatest moment, hardly second to any of the great duties that are so pressing you." Such cultivation could prove taxing. When Stagg appointed his eldest son, Amos Alonzo, Jr., to the coaching staff in 1923, the Trustee Committee on Expenditures "were indisposed to approve it," according to

Burton. The result was "considerable emotional disturbance," Burton remembered, because the elder Stagg "took serious offence at a suggestion of doubt on their part." The appointment was approved reluctantly, "Even though on general principles it is precisely the thing that ought not to be done," wrote Burton. Then Burton permitted himself a characteristic tongue-in-cheek remark to trustee Scott Bond: "The Father and Son Movement is a good one, but not applicable to University appointments."[50]

Burton was careful to advise Stagg and be advised by him upon matters that had any bearing on physical culture. The scholar assured his correspondents and the coach's friends of his high regard for Stagg's contributions, attention that paid handsomely and led to the Old Man's ready acceptance of being designated a featured speaker for the development campaign.[51]

President Max Mason, recruited from the University of Wisconsin, where he had been a star athlete and influential professor, had such an uneventful and short tenure (1925–28) that Stagg had relatively few dealings with him. Mason's most significant step was probably the appointment of history professor Chauncey Boucher as dean of the college, a position in which Boucher took up Burton's quest for a revitalized undergraduate institution and carried it successfully into the 1930s. Stagg seemed to find nothing in their brief relationship to change his early judgment of Mason as "a corking fine new president" whom he remembered as an athlete.[52]

Mason seldom challenged Stagg and at times was almost submissive in his approach. When Stagg decided that Northwestern athletes were not "clean" enough to play his team, it was President Walter Dill Scott of the Evanston college who informed Mason. Mason then engineered an awkward accommodation not only ensuring continued athletic relations but also obliquely supporting Stagg, who had shot from the hip at Northwestern. Mason's action was more reminiscent of the uncritical way in which Harper backed Stagg than the more careful approaches by Judson and Burton. But one peculiar story (related in 1938 in the student magazine *Pulse*) indicated a more activist President Mason, who allegedly asked Stagg to open the campus tennis courts for student play on Sunday. Stagg, whose own sabbatarian beliefs had always controlled the courts, refused and threatened to resign over the matter. Mason countered somewhat oddly, if not precariously, with the threat of *his* resignation if Stagg did not act. A compromise resulted in which the courts were opened to the students, but not during the hours of Sunday worship.[53]

President Mason persisted with Burton's fund-raising initiative, and an extensive opinion survey was completed in 1928. The surveys, undertaken among alumni and the college-educated middle-class, addressed general university matters and also moved into the area many respondents knew most about—intercollegiate athletics. There was considerable opinion that the University of Chicago was an excellent graduate academic institution, but, suggesting a consistent future criticism, that the college was overly academic at the expense of the social side. Opinion regarding athletics followed closely upon that track and suggested that the current intercollegiate situation, particularly football, was "deplorable." A good number of the athletic critics felt that Stagg and other coaches should be replaced. The most unexpected response came from Pat Page, Stagg's former stalwart captain and coach, now football coach at Indiana University. Page, whom Stagg would soon bring back as an assistant, regarded Stagg as well past his best but also noted that a number of his leading Indiana players from Chicago-area high schools had initially tried to enroll at the University of Chicago and couldn't meet the admissions standards. It was a plaint that would be repeated frequently throughout the next decade. As to Stagg's presence, Mason honored Burton's early commitment that the Old Man would not be forced to retire at age sixty-five; this meant that the dreaded duty of forcing Stagg's retirement was left to Mason's successor. Mason resigned in 1928 to join the Rockefeller Foundation, where he later became the president.[54]

Mason's successor was Robert Maynard Hutchins, of whom many apocryphal and true stories would be told regarding his aversion to physical activity and athletics, even if he would also be remembered as a competitive tennis player. Hutchins discovered early in his administration that Coach Stagg was an important man on campus, and the new president soon approved a Yale football game at Chicago in 1931 to celebrate Stagg's fortieth anniversary of coaching. The Yale University Alumni Association of Chicago staged a mammoth testimonial dinner for the Old Man on that occasion, and Hutchins, in his dual capacity as Yale alumnus and Chicago president, spoke at the event. He praised Stagg as "the greatest coach in the country" and noted the important place which Stagg had filled at the university. Hutchins was hardly ignorant of the uses of football to maintain the interest of alumni; as secretary of Yale University he was involved in this area and frequently attended the Yale games.[55]

By the time Hutchins arrived at Chicago, however, institutional and personal forces were already in place that would seem to leave little room for either Stagg or the new president to alter the course of athletic history there. Hutchins was elected in 1929, the same year that the Carnegie Foundation published the most comprehensive study ever completed of intercollegiate athletics. After definitively demonstrating the impossibility of control, the report "illogically called for college presidents and faculties to lead a crusade for institutional self-restraint." In fact, that final plea to those presidents who themselves had led the rush to intercollegiate gold and institutional celebrity over the past decade had all the wisdom and odds for success of the Children's Crusade.[56]

Stagg's extension of service from the university trustees at age sixty-five meant that he and his admirers lobbied for another extension at seventy. When the extension was not granted in 1933 there was the predictable response from alumni, sportswriters, and the public. C man Walter Steffen claimed there was "much adverse criticism" of the university downtown; one sportswriter termed the offer of a university development job to the aging Stagg "Chicago's ruthless relegation of an honored employee to a desk job." Actually, something quite different occurred.[57]

Coach Stagg wrote President Hutchins more than three years before his seventieth birthday (as he had written Burton well in advance of his sixty-fifth birthday) in order to ensure his future at Chicago. It is an unusual letter, or would be had Amos Alonzo Stagg not written it: "I may be frank in saying," he said, "that I have often felt that, in fairness to myself, I should resign from the University and take a position where I would have a favorable chance to recoup the loss in prestige which I have suffered as a football coach." The two began discussions in early 1932 regarding the coach's relation to the university. Stagg submitted an extremely audacious plan in which he would "retire" from the faculty but be given the new position of "Director or Chairman of Intercollegiate Athletics." He would be responsible only to the president of the university, have no relation to regular faculty overseership, and be separated from the Department of Physical Education. He pressed for control of "athletic budget," "schedules," "increased control of financial part of athletics," "appointment and control of coaches," and for himself, "coach football for five years at least—1936 [sic]." The reorganization would save his job and enlarge his power over a newly autonomous intercollegiate enterprise. However, the scheme would also have constituted the most flagrant admission in America of the ultimate professionalization of the football coach. Hutchins then diplomatically suggested instead two public relations positions for his coach; one, working with high schools and alumni; the other, as university representative to intercollegiate athletic meetings.[58]

Stagg did not respond to the presidential offer for eight months. When he was prompted to do so by Hutchins for the second time, he wrote his refusal to accept either of the jobs in a cool one-sentence letter. The Old Man retold his dealings with Hutchins to his old Springfield College classmate James Naismith: "I turned down President Hutchins' offers because one of them was not in my line and the other was not any kind of a job." Stagg continued, "I know he could have arranged" for more coaching years "if he had wanted to." The coach concluded, "Then, I asked [T. Nelson] Metcalf [the newly appointed athletic director] to appoint me for one year but I think the President butted in there and he did not do it. My reason for wanting to coach was to regain some of the prestige I had lost."[59]

If Hutchins's public position and comments were respectful and circumspect, it is probable his private feelings about Stagg and his demands were otherwise. Earlier, when Stagg lost a letter for two months from Yale University regarding the 1931 game, Hutchins wrote his Yale friends an apology: "I am sorry you have been inconvenienced by the eccentricities of the University of Chicago." His old Yale classmate and lifetime friend, playwright Thornton Wilder, who served as campus confidante, recalled years later the circumstances of Stagg's departure, "Do you remember when you broke Alonzo Stagg's heart? We thought we'd never survive the humiliation. Just pine away." Another confidante and a memoirist of the Hutchins years has asserted that "The Old Man was sacred" and that he "was untouchable—and so, therefore, was football" when Hutchins arrived. Hutchins no doubt felt that football would be considerably less untouchable with Stagg out of the picture.[60]

Officially, the decision not to retain Stagg as football coach came from Stagg's successor as athletic director, T. Nelson Metcalf. Hutchins punted when he instructed Metcalf, "This is a matter for you to decide." Metcalf admitted that the "easiest and pleasantest way out" of the situation would be to recommend Stagg's reappointment, but he bravely told Stagg, "With a new coach of football I shall feel much freer than I otherwise would to make certain changes in the departmental organization, teaching assignments and program." Metcalf referred to Stagg's plan to retain his coaching duties: "To consider coaching as a 'special duty' not falling under the university's retirement ruling is to my mind a backward step to which I do not care to be a party." The diplomatic difficulties associated with the Old Man's leaving led to Hutchins taking the low road. He explained Stagg's retirement by noting that the distinguished theologian Shailer Mathews was also "retired automatically" in 1933—in fact, the board minutes show Mathews was offered the choice of continuation.[61]

The aging and confident coach wrote of his feelings to his newspaper column agent, "I have no idea where I shall locate. . . . confidentially I would eat my shirt if I could not coach better than nine-tenths of the big leaguers. . . . If somebody was smart enough, they would grab the opportunity to get me."[62] If the Old Man could not coach at Chicago, he would go elsewhere, and his subsequent coaching career at California's College of the Pacific promoted that small, unknown institution to undreamt athletic heights. Pacific adjusted quickly under Stagg to the realities of the competition for players. The local Pacific Alumni Club developed the Pacific Athletic Revolving Loan Fund, which was "to assist deserving athletes." Within six years, Stagg had lodged enough fine players at Pacific to schedule universities such as the University of Southern California and Notre Dame; within ten years, he was elected coach of the year when his team, now augmented by military trainees, became nationally ranked. He was forcibly retired from Pacific when he was eighty-four but continued to coach into his nineties. Reporters flocked to his door at every birthday to record his austere prescriptions for a long, rewarding life. Popular admiration and respect changed into a kind of awe when the nonagenarian Stagg was reported mowing his lawn or refusing, once again, to allow his life to be made into a lucrative movie. He died in 1965, full of years and honors and bereft from the recent death of his beloved assistant coach, Stella.[63]

The World of Robert Maynard Hutchins and T. Nelson Metcalf

President Hutchins, like the first Chicago president, came of age in a Protestant family that lived in Ohio, albeit one several sociocultural and denominational rungs above Harper's more rustic home. His father Will Hutchins studied at Oberlin College and Yale, where he attended William Rainey Harper's popular biblical literature classes; after a Brooklyn pastorate, he returned to Oberlin as professor of homiletics, where he burnished his superb reputation as speaker and man. He was a naturally impressive gentleman whose later "stewardship" (as he would have termed it) of the Berea College presidency (1920–39) was noteworthy for his courageous stand against Kentucky's Jim Crow legislation and his simultaneous embrace of Appalachian whites.[64]

The Hutchins family tradition of intellectual and social rigor flowed in all three sons who grew up in the Oberlin College community after their early experience as preacher's kids in Brooklyn. Robert Hutchins's elder brother Will left his advertising career after attending Oberlin and Yale in order to teach. He had some difficulty making peace with the compromises necessary in teaching the children of affluence, but finally settled in at Asheville School in North Carolina. His younger brother Francis became a teacher-missionary in China for many years and succeeded his father as Berea College president in 1939. And Robert's mother, Anna Murch Hutchins, supplied her own special leavening of wit, which appealed especially to one of Hutchins's earliest Oberlin College friends, Thornton Wilder.[65]

The result of all these enlightened evangelical influences was a young Robert Maynard who would always find the world more complicated and ambiguous than he would have wished and who would forever judge his own contributions wanting in his efforts to bring order to the messy twentieth-century world he helped lead. If Cecil Spring Rice's Teddy Roosevelt was the perpetual boy, the improbably handsome Robert Hutchins was the perpetual adolescent. He was unfailingly idealistic, with an inimitable swagger, yet he was basically conservative and had a penchant for authoritarianism. Hutchins and his utopian college vision rejected truth and beauty as organic and evolutionary, and when the Chicago faculty did not catch on, the young president grew tired of his duties of casting pearls before swine and raising money from the philistines in the Loop (or, as his father sympathized, "the lifting of funds from the pockets of the impious is a sorrowful task"). Despite his general setbacks at Chicago, Hutchins was predestined to discover that intercollegiate football was one area over which he could wield an old-fashioned Scottish Presbyterian "root and branch" solution.[66]

Robert Hutchins of the Yale Law School, which he led as the youngest dean in the land, appeared as a late dark horse candidate on the list of University of Chicago presidential hopefuls in 1929. Then, perhaps illustrative of his own later modest appraisal that it was only "through an inexplicable concatenation of accidents" that he was elected, he provided the trustees a stunning interview. Up to his appearance, the trustees and the Faculty Advisory Committee had been apprehensive over the presidential candidates available. The interview earned him a 7 A.M. telephone call from Harold Swift on a whim to check Hutchins's claim to early office arrival. When the law dean answered on the first ring, Swift had a new university leader, even if it would take some effort to convince his colleagues of the opportunity to take a risk on youth but dare to be great. The last time the university had taken such a risk was at its creation, and the precocious Harper had proved both a 5 A.M. scholar and a nighthawk.[67]

If Hutchins is to be believed on the subject of the state of his mind at his inauguration in 1929—and this man was such a charming smart-aleck, frequently using self-deprecating humor to illustrate his ideas and to keep away from entangling personal alliances, that he is probably having us on—his own education still needed some attending to by such as Mortimer Adler and the "great books" to which Adler introduced him. Reminiscent of President Harper, he probably did not have a firm philosophical model in his mind of the university he wished to create when he arrived. Certainly no one on the search committee expected Hutchins to try and change the mission of the university, but then they never do. It is likely that his views on the relation of intercollegiate athletics to the university evolved considerably during his first five years or so as he sought fervently for an educational faith he could preach as "once for all delivered unto the saints."[68]

The world of the new athletic director Thomas Nelson Metcalf was very different from the world of Stagg. The Metcalf clan, like the Hutchins, was large and impressive; many Metcalfs, male and female, had for generations pursued careers in education and social service after graduation from Oberlin College. The Metcalfs had welcomed Will Hutchins's family to Oberlin early in the century, and the families were well acquainted. Metcalf's experience in intercollegiate athletics was much less high powered and flamboyant than was Stagg's, but he was a consummate educator. Metcalf enjoyed a fine personal and athletic reputation as a student at Oberlin College, and he had also completed graduate work at Columbia University. He returned to Oberlin, where he coached and taught physical education. Although he had not been a part of a highly commercialized football program before he came to Chicago, his underpowered Oberlin football team had upset mighty Rose Bowl–bound Ohio State in 1921.[69]

Metcalf's Chicago was a place of little glamour and of much improvement toward the physical education ideal, and the quiet educator was comparatively dull and lifeless after the volatile Stagg; one campus publication said he was soon called "pinch penny." He was cautious, and his mind did not race to self-serving conclusions. His statement on physical education, which he gave his new constituency upon arrival on the campus in 1933, was typically forthright and unelaborate: "The chief responsibility of the physical educator at the college level should be to develop game skills, play interests and habits of regular exercise which will protect the health and add to the enjoyment of life both in college and later."[70]

Metcalf's views regarding the intercollegiate program indicate that Hutchins had selected carefully: "There is no necessity for athletics to be over-emphasized to the extent of interference with academic work. I believe in light schedules, playing natural rivals only, with a minimum of absence from classes and with short practice periods."[71] These views, combined with his pointing to recruiting and subsidizing players as the "greatest evil" in college athletics, indicated the direction in which the Chicago football program would go. There were some inconsistencies under Metcalf; for example, nonconference games were played with Missouri, Nebraska, Vanderbilt, Butler, Harvard, the College of the Pacific, Virginia, and Oberlin, none of which could be termed a "natural rival." On the whole, however, his 1933 statement formed the framework of Chicago sports. Hutchins's reorganization of the entire university had already affected the physical education department by placing it under student services simply as the "Office of Physical Education." Metcalf's arrival also heralded a kind of athletic declaration of financial independence: Acting perhaps on principle and certainly upon the dire financial record of the recent past, his athletic department was now to operate independently of the influence of gate receipts or, as he explained later, it was "able to prevent commercial interests influencing athletic policy."[72]

The 1930s at Chicago were a time of financial stringency, and the new athletic director no doubt felt the pinch more dramatically than others. In fact, the losing football team's greatly diminished revenues cost the university dearly, and at least one student recalled the paltry expenditures available for golf, a varsity sport. Metcalf, in his single position of director, was not a lobbyist of intercollegiate athletics as was Stagg, who had emphasized his own varsity coaching interests and duties. Rather, Metcalf viewed himself and his department more critically, and Hutchins would not have to worry about his new director bombarding him with new ideas and creative initiatives regarding intercollegiate athletics. If Hutchins was not challenged by his new athletic director and his new coach as his predecessors had been by Stagg, he would also, unlike Harper, Judson, and Burton, be able to say little about athletic triumphs when he gave speeches. Metcalf was very much Hutchins's man, and in the transition the university lost much of the spirit and verve that had characterized Stagg's administration. As a result, Metcalf was largely unknown to the undergraduates and alumni as he faithfully tended his underfunded preserve.[73]

Athletic Director Metcalf hired University of Minnesota graduate and football star Clark Shaughnessy to replace Coach Stagg. Shaughnessy had coached successfully at Loyola and Tulane universities in New Orleans, but those successes hardly prepared him for the challenge on the Midway. The Maroon football operation that Clark Shaughnessy inherited in 1933 was in dire straits: It had no dependable supply of quality raw material; its product was barely competitive; it had a decreasing share of the market; and the executives of its parent company were less sure of the value of football than any of the previous administrators had been. The importance and power of the coach at Chicago plummeted after Stagg left, and the realities of the football decline were clearly seen. For the first time in university history, the office of football coach was being viewed on its own merits, without the surpassing reputation of Stagg. If Robert E. Sherwood's Franklin Delano Roosevelt had "a good act to follow" in Herbert Hoover in 1933, Clark Shaughnessy had an extremely difficult one.[74]

Accelerated Decline at Hutchins's Chicago

The story of intercollegiate football at the University of Chicago from 1933 to 1939 is a continuation and, finally, an acceleration of the decline that marked Stagg's last eight years there. It is a tale of annual hope, ill fortune, and despair. A simple but graphic narrative of those years can be reconstructed from the writing and memories of some of the players, their fellow students, their professors, and from the pages of university publications, which were widely read during the period by members, friends, and alumni of the university.

It was predicted in the summer of 1933 that the New Plan of undergraduate education would bring "a restoration of football," and the impressive freshmen players were termed "Swift's premium Hams" because of Harold Swift's activity in recruiting young men from California as well as locally. The presence of the new coach also prompted hope for the coming season; it was thought the change to a younger man would surely improve the dreary record of the past eight years. The season was completed without victory against the five Intercollegiate Conference opponents.[75]

There was "much jubilation" over the prospects for the 1934 season. Shaughnessy's players were termed "greatly improved," and the coach admitted that he had a promising group. The team began the season by routing Michigan (27-0) and Indiana (21-0), and Chicago hopes soared along with the reputation of triple-threat back Jay Berwanger. Attendance climbed to its highest level in years but averaged only about fifteen thousand at home (up from eleven thousand in 1933); that meant that thirty-five thousand Stagg Field seats went unsold. The final four conference games were lost.[76]

The 1935 team was said to possess "more promise than the run of Chicago squads for the last decade," and Harold Swift had done his best to ensure a good harvest of first-year players. But Maroon followers had to be content with all-American Berwanger's Knute Rockne Memorial Trophy, the inaugural Heisman Trophy (as emblematic of the finest college player in America), and with the team's promise—the team beat only two of its six major opponents. After his last game, Berwanger took a different route from the Granges before him and the multitudes of athlete-students who were to follow; he graduated with his class, refused to play professional football even though George Halas drafted him for the Bears and urged him to sign, and he pursued a stable and profitable business career. Berwanger's accomplishments with a losing squad were so extraordinary that in 1969, to mark the centennial celebration of intercollegiate football, he was placed with Walter Eckersall in the backfield on the All-Time All-American team. Eckersall was selected for the first fifty-year team, and Berwanger for the modern squad, giving Chicago the distinction of being the only university with two backfield men on the all-time team.[77]

There were some "anticipatory whoops" over the prospects for the 1936 season, the "First Year after Berwanger." There were more candidates for the team than usual, with a superb complement of sophomore backs, including Lew Hamity and Saul Sherman, both of whom later played for the Chicago Bears. The team won one game (Lawrence College), lost five, and tied one.[78]

More prospects were out for practice in 1937 than for many years. Freshman Coach Nels Norgren, who had played and worked under Stagg, claimed he had "the best material in five years." The newly enrolled players were called the "Harold Swift Boys" and constituted the last group openly recruited by the trustee president and his friends. The Michigan game provided a demonstration of the comparative lack of depth of the Chicago team; the Maroons withered after leading by two touchdowns with four minutes to play. One critic noted that the small band of quality players had to bear the entire brunt of the difficult seven-game schedule. The team lost all six of its major games and later in the academic year lost a large proportion of the Harold Swift Boys because of grade deficiencies.[79]

The team of 1938 showed the "promise of being the best of the past several years," according to Assistant Coach Jay Berwanger. The fifty boys out for practice were the largest number since 1931, but most were so inexperienced that Shaughnessy had to use six or seven first-year men on his first eleven. That year Coach Shaughnessy introduced his own modern T formation to the Maroons, having already done so as a consulting coach with the Chicago Bears. But even one of the most important innovations in football history could not make a difference with the willing but wanting student-athletes. No conference or major teams were defeated, and the team barely managed a tie with Bradley Polytechnic Institute. And yet prospects were good for 1939, some

Maroon supporters claimed, for the conference schedule was to be limited to three games.[80]

One game during the 1938 campaign epitomized the season and much of what was symbolic for the future of football at Chicago. The visit of Amos Alonzo Stagg's College of the Pacific team to play Clark Shaughnessy's Maroons at Stagg Field was arranged upon the initiative of the western college as a tribute to Stagg's fiftieth year of coaching college football. The college in Stockton, California, had been greatly helped financially by the publicity and recruiting program that Stagg brought with him. Stagg's Pacific teams were soon to defeat some of the largest schools in the West, and in the phrase beloved of sportswriters, he was putting the academically undistinguished college "on the map." Although not a regional or natural rivalry, the game at Stagg Field generated a great deal of interest among sportswriters and old graduates who had been paying scant attention to the often-defeated Chicago team. The *Chicago Daily News* ran a series of biographical "Intimate Stories" of Stagg, and other newspapers also repeated much of the Stagg legend already publicly available.[81]

One sportswriter admitted that the game itself was insignificant, especially in view of Chicago's winless record with major opponents and Pacific's schedule of mostly minor opponents. The material the sportswriters churned out does, however, indicate the state of football on the Midway. One writer, verging on hysteria, predicted that the "Old Man will live in all his memories next Saturday," and that "it won't be a football story. It'll be an epic." Another noted the "jubilating" over the university's "homecoming for its Grand Old Man"; the writer hoped the electric car with steering tiller that Stagg had used around campus could be resurrected for the occasion. The writer, erroneously reporting that Stella Stagg would make the trip with her husband, correctly termed their relationship, "without a doubt, the grandest and sweetest football romance of all time."[82]

Local football enthusiasts and the western visitors were engulfed by a heady round of entertainment from the moment "the incredible Stagg's train arrived." The campus tried to respond appropriately to the superlatives and breathlessness of alumni and writers. The night before the game a homecoming rally was followed by a dinner in honor of Stagg. A bonfire, torchlight procession, and the inauguration of the "Stagg Shag," a dance created for the occasion ("Shag" was Shaughnessy's sports page nickname), completed the evening. Ticket prices were raised to the highest level of the season for an expected crowd of twenty thousand. Director Metcalf said Chicago had not been noticed by national newspapers for years, and the volume of reporters was the largest since the last time Stagg was honored at Stagg Field in 1931.[83]

The reality of that Saturday in 1938 was something less than the sportswriters had promised: fewer than six thousand tickets were sold, and about 85 percent of the seats were empty. Otherwise, the day belonged to Stagg and the past in every way. He was presented with a cowhide scroll from the Order of the C proclaiming him the "All-Time, All-American Coach"; he heard "Big Bertha," Chicago's large bass drum, often proclaimed the "world's largest," boom forty-one times in honor of his years at Chicago; he saw the prime Maroon football relic, his old electric car, wheeled around the stadium; and his team overwhelmed Chicago 32-0. Lewis Hamity, the captain of the 1938 team, remembered Shaughnessy as particularly despondent after this loss to Stagg, especially because the coach had pioneered his sophisticated T formation system for that season. The celebration, led by a thousand old C men, partook only of the past; nostalgia was substituted for substance. The *Daily Maroon* captured the essence and dimension of the pseudo-event with a tiny-type headline surrounded by much white space and black border: "Shucks Fellas!"[84]

If the students could deal with the College of the Pacific disaster with a caustic headline, many alumni could not. Much unhappiness, not to say outrage, over the result was reported from old graduates and C men, especially as the game festivities had stirred them to recapture the glory days of Stagg. And John W. Chapman, president of the local alumni club, announced an ambitious program to do just that. He claimed the club would organize all alumni as recruiters, perhaps lessen the level of competition until their recruiting took effect, and also ensure larger interest and attendance at future games. The *Chicago Daily Times,* which carried Chapman's scheme, was not convinced and concluded in a manner more akin to the *Maroon:* "In short, nothing will be done about anything pertaining to the game."[85]

The New, or Chicago, Plan, which many football followers at Chicago had welcomed as the sport's salvation in 1933, proved to be a disappointment. Among other problems, the New Plan substituted yearly comprehensive examinations during the spring quarter for the traditional end-of-term course examinations, and this conflicted with spring football practice. Spring practice became shorter each year until it was abolished; only eight of the thirty-nine players reported for spring practice in 1937. The spring preparation was especially important so the players could learn Shaughnessy's complex offensive system; hence, much autumn practice time had to be devoted to introducing what should have been mastered in the spring. The year-long courses and comprehensive examinations also made it impossible to shepherd academically marginal players through easier term courses in the autumn. The athletes could no longer anticipate two or three easy off-season terms in which to regain their eligibility. And yet, many student-athletes of the 1930s did make good use of the comprehensive examination system; they remembered it as allowing them virtually to ignore their studies during the taxing gridiron season. At the same time, the Chicago Plan encouraged younger, brighter entrants into the college. The team of 1936 had three eighteen-year-old sophomores in the starting lineup, whereas a typical opponent, Butler University, had no starting player under twenty. And the trend toward younger undergraduates was formalized and accelerated in 1937 when Hutchins enlarged the definition of the four college years to include high school juniors and seniors who entered after their second or third year in secondary school. Of course, Stagg had done something similar when he welcomed husky talent before they had graduated high school in the early 1900s, but Hutchins thought his approach original. One student leader from the 1930s remembered the "early entrants" on campus as hardly participating in the usual extracurricular social and athletic activities at all. These innovations proved a long-term failure; although some impressive sixteen-year-olds were attracted, most parents and college advisers were unimpressed. The college size shrank alarmingly and graduation rates continued low until the early 1950s, when the policy was strongly deemphasized and recruiting efforts were once again concentrated on high school seniors.[86]

The college in the 1930s was "a wonderful place to be young," according to many graduates; it enrolled an increasingly clever and middle-class student body, and one that was comparatively free of enrollment bias. Yet from virtually its inauguration in 1931 the New Plan suffered from a poor reception among the larger public. One newspaper columnist responded to Harold Swift's query about that perception: "The average impression seems to be that the school is a place where some new-fangled sort of stunt is being tried out with no very certain results and that about all a boy going there can look forward to is a year of 'bookworming' after which he will be flunked out." In sum, the kind of athlete-students required for the football fortunes to be resurrected were simply not attracted to the college of the University of Chicago during the 1930s and were even less likely to be attracted during the 1940s.[87]

The New Plan did see an increase in the number of transfer students, but conference rules disallowed their participation for one year. The rule had been initiated to discourage the "tramp athlete" from enrolling at

Big Ten schools; it hardly was meant to apply to the students who transferred in great numbers to Chicago. For example, for the year of 1935–36 about 65 percent of all the baccalaureate degrees were awarded to students who had attended another college before matriculating at Chicago, and it is hardly likely that any of them had changed colleges to play football for Shaughnessy. Chicago's enrollment of eligible athletes fell hopelessly behind those of other universities in the conference, and Chicago continued to demand arguably the highest level of academic performance of the athletes to remain eligible. After six years of the Chicago Plan, the majority of the transfer students gave the new plan of study as their reason for entering, although some who had entered as freshman claimed they were but little aware of the New Plan.[88]

There was unanimity among the press and the public that Chicago practiced "less" proselyting and subsidizing of athlete-students during the 1930s than the other schools, at least in part because Chicago alumni had divided loyalties (most had been either graduate or transfer students on the Midway), although one writer thought Chicago alumni probably had "more mature" interests. Director Metcalf, with considerable diplomacy and unintended humor, stated, "Others do legitimate recruiting, which we do not." Chicago certainly had far more students on athletic scholarships than other conference schools did, but they must have been selected on an entirely different basis or those who selected them were guilty of unimaginable incompetence.[89]

President Hutchins and Dean of Students George A. Works carefully watched the activities of university groups and individuals that had the look of recruitment, especially the C Club. Their vigilance was successful, because most of the players of the 1930s learned of Chicago from rather natural means and not through unnatural acts of the coaching staff. None could remember personally or through rumor that Clark Shaughnessy had recruited a single player. The future all-American Jay Berwanger chose Chicago because of the strong recommendation of alumnus Ira Davenport, a Dubuque, Iowa, neighbor. And this after Northwestern's all-time great "Pug" Rentner and others had journeyed to Dubuque and inquired of the young track star's college plans. Another player, captain and honors student Lewis Hamity, who had been an all-Chicago high school star, was "recruited" by an older friend and teammate who preceded him from Hyde Park High School to Chicago. The recruitment, however, was oblique in the extreme; two players recalled how impressed they, as middle-schoolers, had been years before with Kyle Anderson, a mid-1920s Maroon player with whom they became acquainted through an after-school recreation program and who served as an assistant football coach in the 1930s.[90]

Once these football prospects found their own way to the Midway, their view of themselves was expressed by Jay Berwanger: "We weren't special; we were just students." And yet football players who needed tutoring were provided it; one former player felt "there was no way anybody could help us stay in college, given the system, besides tutoring us." Moreover, Coach Shaughnessy depended upon his captains to ensure that the players met their academic responsibilities. And the football players' lives were certainly different from their nonplaying classmates. Several players recalled that they attended as few as one class session in the fall because the New Plan required only the comprehensive examination at the end of the spring quarter. This was just as well, because the team leaders remembered working almost daily on plays with Coach Shaughnessy in his blackboard-lined apartment through the lunch hour and seldom attending afternoon classes. They also reported little study before practice (which lasted from mid-afternoon to 5 or 6) and less study after the exhausting session. Weekends could not be used to catch up because virtually the entire weekend (and sometimes Friday for away games) was scheduled with game preparation, the game, and the inevitable recuperation on Sunday. Players remembered fondly the severe Dutch-uncle talks they received from young professors when attendance or attitude seemed wanting; the same professors sometimes stopped by practice on their way home. Halfback Berwanger remembered that young Humanities I instructors Norman Maclean and James Cate insisted upon meeting with him at Christmas break, "where they gave me what for for not coming to the Humanities I discussion sections." When they tried to demonstrate his ignorance of the course by asking, "Who was Thucydides?" he disappointed them by giving an acceptable answer he recalled from his unusual ancient history course in high school.[91]

Former Maroon players of the 1930s could not recall any "gut courses" or "jock professors" who gave easy grades to athletes; in fact, the required comprehensive courses with no attendance requirement and common year-end examinations graded anonymously made such approaches impossible. Lewis Hamity remembered being told to be careful with the freshman English course because it was an important building block in his four-year program, but that was surely unexceptional advice. Professors of the time described an identical world to that remembered by the student-athletes. The only occurrence of "special treatment" that the players, students, and professors interviewed could remember besides the plentiful tutoring had nothing to do with student-athletes' playing football for Chicago; it was a case of an impecunious star player having his required first-year texts provided anonymously by a classmate's parents after they heard of his plight.[92]

The craggily handsome Clark Shaughnessy, whose previous success-es had hardly prepared him for the insuperable difficulties at Chicago and the unceasing seasonal sanguinity and disappointment, remained markedly loyal to his Maroons. He resolutely refused coaching offers elsewhere and discouraged talk of his leaving. He admitted that his players were not the most talented, but typically observed, "I have never known a squad that had a finer spirit and attitude." Shaughnessy was remembered by his players as a man of remarkable football intel-ligence, "a great theorist," a "genius of offensive football," who sur-rounded himself with "high-grade fellows" as assistant coaches. They also remembered that he was not a gifted motivator and that his at-tempts at locker-room oratory were stale. Perhaps the job of flailing this thinking football team's emotions to a fever pitch was impossible; at least one player remembered the respected coach's attempts as "if not laughable, at least snickering material." Still, they especially appre-ciated his "skull sessions," when he would think aloud at the black-board as he outlined tactics, and his relationships with the players were lasting and full of mutual respect. Jay Berwanger recalled the day Coach Shaughnessy turned to the beloved team physician and story-teller, Dr. Pat Shannon, when the coach had done his best to talk the team into top performance and felt they needed some levity to take the edge off their nerves before the kickoff. "Tell the boys a story," he asked the doctor. The doctor complied and the story fell flat. "Now, tell 'em a good one—come on!" Shaughnessy pleaded. Dr. Shannon did—a risqué story that embarrassed the strait-laced Shaughnessy so mark-edly the players howled with laughter and Berwanger went out and received the kick-off through tear-filled eyes.[93]

If Clark Shaughnessy's world on the Midway was different from that of Amos Alonzo Stagg, his record on the football field was not appre-ciably different. Stagg's winning percentage for his last eight years (those after 1924) of Intercollegiate Conference games was 21 percent; Shaughnessy's percentage for his seven seasons was 17 percent.

Hutchins's Chicago would not consider the one alternative that might have enabled Shaughnessy to produce stronger teams despite all these liabilities—there would be no physical education major. This aging possibility had been broached again, if in an unseemly and an-gular manner, by one of the downtown alumni sideline superinten-dents of the football program at the annual meeting in 1937. John Schomer, a C Club member and well-known Big Ten game official, pleaded for a return to the glory and methods of the Stagg years. In a transcribed report that was sent to Harold Swift, Schommer "favored giving the athlete all possible aid with his studies, such as tutoring, taking over exams whatever number of times it took to pass them, etc.

He said other universities had Ag Schools and Physical Education Schools which any moron could muddle through (meaning athletes) and, in addition, received the benefit of the doubt in grading, so he didn't see why the University could not be a little more helpful where athlete's grades are concerned [sic]."[94]

The *Chicago Tribune* weighed in with an editorial soon after the depressing loss to the College of the Pacific and summarized the lessons of the 1938 season under the title "Football as Higher Education." "The University of Chicago is offering one of the most brilliant spectacles of adjusting football to the intellectual requirements of the university. In a proper system of rating the Maroons would be easily the country's number one team. The season was not what the players would regard as a success but the university continues undisturbed and unblemished."[95] The *Tribune*'s message had to have been an enormous encouragement to all on the Midway who supported Hutchins's policy.

Hutchins's utopian university professed an essentially intellectual nature, unaffected by the needs and taste of the public. And while much about the university hardly matched Hutchins's blueprint, John Dewey characterized the Hutchins approach as "the greatest possible aloofness of higher learning from contemporary social life." The university's principles under Harper included athletic success, those of Hutchins's university did not. If the price paid for athleticism was steep in Harper's university, it was even more dear in the 1930s, and it was far more than Hutchins wanted to pay.[96]

The Future of Football at Hutchins's Chicago

President Hutchins was forced to discuss the future of football on the Midway during a public meeting with anxious alumni in 1936. He assured his questioners that the university would remain consistent in its approach to the activity. "The future of intercollegiate athletics at Chicago depends partly on what the University does and partly on what other institutions do. . . . It will not depart from its principles to gain athletic success. . . . it will not subsidize athletes; it will not discriminate against them."[97] In fact, Hutchins was enunciating a policy that had only evolved into the university's approach to football over the past few years. Hutchins's assertion that Chicago would never "depart from its principles" was many leagues from Harper's assurance to Stagg over the use of student work aid to subsidize athletes—"We will of course do what is necessary to be done"—except that Harper's principles started with the goal of "athletic success," and his and Stagg's practices followed rather logically. It is also apparent, if only through heavy

historical lenses, that Judson, Burton, and Mason and their administrators had nudged the institution in the direction of Hutchins's final
stated policy in 1936.[98]

Hutchins publicly expressed his views on higher education through
lectures, books, and articles, and his concept of the place of football in
college life had evolved by 1936 into the declaration he made to the
Chicago alumni. That policy, Hutchins might have argued, and the
consistency with which it was followed, combined with the disastrous
athletic and financial state of Chicago football, ensured that Chicago
would have to consider the continued existence of the game by 1939.
It is probable, however, that Hutchins had determined to abolish football at least as early as 1936 and was awaiting events to force others
to join him in that conclusion. The master rhetorician seldom asked a
question without having an answer well in hand; in October 1936 he
asked an 1899 graduate and former Maroon stalwart the rhetorical,
"What would you think of our withdrawing from the Big Ten or from
intercollegiate football altogether?"[99]

The first formal presentation by an administrator to a university
body regarding the enormous problems connected with the future of
football was made by Director Metcalf in 1937 at the Board on Coordination of Student Interests. Prompted by Hutchins, Metcalf discussed
the alternatives open to Chicago and noted that Hutchins favored "immediate withdrawal" from the conference. The board's chair, Dean of
Students George A. Works, appointed a Special Athletic Committee,
chaired by Metcalf, to investigate further and report. In early 1937 the
committee recommended continuing Chicago's membership in the
Intercollegiate Conference, a reduction of the number of "big" football
games, and a commitment to "adult recreations" for more students.[100]

Hutchins drew the lines of conflict over football at Chicago after the
1938 season. It was widely suspected that he and his administration
were opposed to intercollegiate football; accordingly, he received many
letters that blamed him for the team's sorry record. Then his crystal-
line article, "Gate Receipts and Glory," appeared early in December in
the *Saturday Evening Post,* a favorite vehicle of the outspoken president.
He argued that money was the root of the evils of intercollegiate football in America. He admitted that physical education might have a
proper place in higher learning, but he attacked what he termed the
"myths of Athleticism" that were a part of intercollegiate athletics; one
he named and excoriated was that football provided a unique experience for its collegiate adherents. For all who wanted Chicago to regain
its football leadership, the article was proof that Hutchins was as "radical" on the football issue as they had feared.[101]

The Fall, 1939

Football has the same relation to physical culture that bull fighting has to agriculture.
—Thorstein Veblen, ca. 1900

Football has the same relation to education that bull fighting has to agriculture.
—Robert Hutchins, ca. 1939

Intercollegiate football at the University of Chicago fell in 1939 because of the convergence of four factors: (1) Stagg's mythic purity as a university legacy against which to measure the present; (2) a university leadership willing to abolish the game; (3) the ultimate disastrous season; and (4) university constituencies willing to consider and accept the abolition of football. In September 1939, only the first two of the four factors were in place.

Stagg's Mythic Legacy

The place of Amos Alonzo Stagg in American athletic lore was fixed by the time of his departure from Chicago in 1933. Stagg was no doubt deeply pleased that there was a distinct Horatio Algerian flavor to the many uses writers and coaches made of his legendary life. The stories grew more apocryphal, from the story of Harper's hiring of the financially innocent Stagg to the tales of inevitable character-building through football. Businessmen testified that they "determined always to play square" after an encounter on the playing field with the Old Man. The panegyric done by the *New York Times* writer Allison Danzig upon the occasion of Stagg's one hundredth birthday in 1962 is representative: "But it is not because of his prowess as an athlete that

Alonzo Stagg is being feted this week as has been no other American in sports. . . . It is for his unparalleled service in teaching the young to shoot square for seventy years; the spartan ruggedness and simplicity of his life in devotion to an ideal, and the granite-like integrity that never compromised for victory and set new standards of sportsmanship in college athletics."[1]

It was this Stagg legacy that formed the ever-present backdrop against which football at Chicago would be judged during the late 1930s. A number of the Maroons of the 1930s had grown up "with Stagg's songs and legend." For example, the Chicago quarterback in 1938 remembered Stagg was "venerated, to a mythical degree." And a student editor wrote before the College of the Pacific game that year, "To a good 95% of the student body Amos Alonzo Stagg is little more than a myth." The myth became reality on that Saturday in 1938, and a student reporter captured the scene: "Amos Alonzo Stagg, the Grand Old Man, was back. With him he brought a flock of memories, a strong suggestion of past glory, and, most important, a small, fast, well-coached football team." A long-time campus observer, Nels Fuqua, wrote a thoughtful essay at the same time that managed to record and try to explain the Stagg myth, but which in turn became the myth's victim. "Our alumni have been treating themselves to an orgy of sentimentality about Stagg," Fuqua began. He noted many of these orgiasts had ten years earlier been "the most articulate hunters" of Stagg's "scalp":

> It was they who yowled loudest about the endless string of Moral Victories which always left the Maroons on the short end of the scoring stick; it was they who christened the "Grand Old Man" the "Old Old Man."
>
> But the years intervening have been kind to Stagg's reputation; he is now seen only through the enchanted haze of affectionate recollection. Strange he should be so canonized since his viewpoint is about as contemporary as antimacassars, daguerrotypes and the Family Bible on the table in your great-aunt Julia's front parlor. This viewpoint is woven from a warp of Puritanism and a woof of sentiment. . . .
>
> Why is it that the Grand Old Man still holds such a grip on the affections of alumni? Is it not, perhaps, because he is a symbol of our forgotten ideals, of our lost innocence?[2]

The Stagg myth of a pure football utopia overwhelmed the campus in 1938, and perhaps the greatest victims of that myth on the weekend he brought his California contingent to Chicago were the Midway team. They and Coach Shaughnessy attended the pregame dinner that honored Stagg; they and their coach sat silently while old grads and Stagg spoke at length. Some of the speakers "grew so extravagent and long-winded in their glorification of 'the old days' and 'the old fighting spirit,'" according to one sports editor, "they depressed the Midway team, sitting there and listening, and sent them away most dismal." A leading player responded to the oratory: "I thought they were OUR alumni and would want us to beat Pacific, but I guess they were just 'Stagg Alumni.'" The sports editor concluded that the old grads "see everything through a mist of sentimental nostalgia for the only thing they got out of college, football" and hoped the undergraduates could keep in perspective "the melodramatic and sophomoric antics of the football idolators of a generation ago." The sports editor need not have worried about the perspective of student editor Edward W. Rosenheim, a fraternity and literary leader who edited *Pulse* ("Official student magazine of the University of Chicago"). He honed in on the issue of the weekend binge when he asked, "Why was it ever scheduled?" and offered his evaluation:

> If it was arranged to build up Stagg's ego and to gratify the sentimentality of a few wistful old grads it was a pronounced success. If it was designed to add to the morale of the team, to increase the enthusiasm of the student body, to pep up the coaches, or to add, in any way, to the prestige of the University, it was a failure—and a stinking failure. . . .
> . . . Meanwhile the student body knows that the days of Chicago football glory are dead and gone.[3]

The national press had made much use of the underdog Pacific victory over the "Monsters of the Midway" as a dramatic demonstration of the Stagg legacy. One regional paper, the *Pasadena Star News*, managed to muddle the facts—"Stagg's team beat Chicago, a school 30 times its size," and Stagg's great days at Chicago were interrupted only when "a young man, who had been shipped out from Harvard," forcibly retired the saintly Stagg—and to draw its inescapable moral regarding Stagg's triumphant return to the proud Midway with a victory that "caps the glorious career of Amos Alonzo Stagg, now in his 49th year of coaching. It tells deeper the story of what spirit and courage and a clean heart can do."[4]

And if President Hutchins chose not to make heavy use of the myth in the 1940s, his two successors used the Stagg past upon occasion to buttress their present purposes. President Lawrence Kimpton wrapped himself in the Stagg mantle almost before Hutchins had departed. He stated categorically to the Order of the C dinner in June of 1951: "I'd like more athletics on this campus, but in a manner that would meet the approval of the great old man, Alonzo Stagg." Midway through Kimpton's presidency, he continued to judge athletics present against his version of athletics past: "The presence of the 'Old Man' on our campus this evening is filled for us with sentiment and meaning. It reminds us of a day when 'On Chicago' meant something, and meant something that no sane person can laugh off. But it reminds us also of a time when football was played by students who were amateurs and played for the love of the game. This was what the 'Old Man' stood for, and if he were forty-five instead of ninety, football would still mean this for us and for the Middle West."[5] Kimpton's successor, the Nobelist George Wells Beadle, also found uses for the university's athletic legend: "In 1892 William Rainey Harper said, 'Sports will be conducted for the students, not for the spectacular entertainment of enormous crowds of people.' Ever since, participation sports have been firmly entrenched in the University's program."[6]

But the mythic innocence of that institutional past served first as the backdrop to events in 1939; that invented past provided the perfect foil against which the messy present of Maroon football in 1939 could be compared and found grievously wanting.[7]

University Leadership

President Hutchins did not have to persuade the administration and faculty that football must go. Hutchins had his own team of administrators by 1937. He also had a propaganda machine of impressive proportions with the addition that year of millionaire advertising executive and Muzak promoter William B. Benton as a university vice president and a direct pipeline to former Yale classmate Henry Luce of *Time-Life*. Moreover, Hutchins inherited the work of men who had already begun to ask difficult questions of the football business in the train of president Burton's large institutional questions of purpose and curriculum, and these men, Deans Wilkins and Boucher, had consistently reduced the influence of Stagg's department in the 1920s. Hutchins's own appointments, for example, Athletic Director Metcalf, Dean of Students Works, and Dean A. J. Brumbaugh, helped to erode further the place of intercollegiate athletics at the university.[8]

The university trustees constituted both leadership and a constituency to be persuaded. The trustees had the power to abolish football as interpreted by Presidents Hutchins and Swift. Theoretically, the faculty and administration should have been able to make a decision regarding this aspect of their educational program because intercollegiate football had been founded as a part of the academic department of Physical Culture and Athletics and then reestablished as a student program under the dean of students in Hutchins's university. Hence, it ostensibly remained under faculty and administrative control. But this American academic invention had assumed such extraordinary dimensions in the larger society that Hutchins found it wise to share the responsibility with the trustees.

Harold Swift described his board as the "top business men of Chicago" in 1939. Swift noted that thirteen were graduates of Chicago and that many of the nineteen others had been educated at the "cream of the eastern colleges." Two important trustees, Paul S. Russell, a former Walter Camp all-American quarterback and captain of one of Stagg's Maroon squads, and Vice-president William Scott Bond had already gone on record that they did not "feel, as many do" that "a winning football team is a matter of grave importance." The trustees proceeded on the football issue as they did in most other areas: they left the educational policymaking to the university administration and to the small group among themselves who had assumed leadership by philanthropy and dedication to the institution. Chairman Swift had been the major influence in bringing the thirty-year-old Hutchins to Chicago and proudly backed his educational initiatives and innovations.[9]

Trustee Profile: Harold Swift

Harold Higgins Swift, in fact, was a big man on campus for a longer time than anyone else in university history, with the exception of Amos Alonzo Stagg. From the trustees' proper spheres of institutional policy, finances, and fund-raising, Swift at times moved over the line into the faculty and administration operations area. We have witnessed his intervention on the issue of player health in 1915 and the university archives provide many examples of Swift's extraordinary inquiries and action into many facets of the university's operations. When Swift became trustee leader in 1922 he was invested with considerable prestige and even more authority for following his predilections.

President Swift taught Presidents Judson, Burton, and Mason much regarding the proper handling of Coach Stagg over the years, but as early as 1927 he drafted a list to "consider things that should be changed when Stagg retires and try to have them all put in shipshape at same time." Swift's list included taking away all ticket sales from Stagg's department (basketball and other events remained there after the earlier tortuous removal of the football sales), purchasing supplies through the regular university purchasing office (Stagg continued to insist upon his own departmental purchasing), and "adopting definite method of awarding C's" (Stagg controlled the letter awards as a one-man monopoly, based in part on his perception of the men's character). When Stagg's retirement was imminent, Swift pressed Hutchins to make the administrative changes "overnight,—at the close of the Stagg regime and before the Metcalf regime."[10]

Swift instructed Acting President Frederic C. Woodward in 1928 to provide more postseason rewards for the players, noting such activities were "none too good for them" and concluding, "Am of the opinion we err on the side of conservatism in trying to give our football men a good time." After the Metcalf regime was instituted, Swift continued to involve himself in the operations of the athletic department, especially the football program, to a degree that could hardly be considered wise or expedient. At times, for example, he gave approval to the schedule, ticket prices, and the handling of the press; he took the lead in arranging a series of games with Dartmouth College in 1937; he suggested the possible hiring of some of the recently dismissed Michigan coaching staff in 1937; and he was even involved in the choice of radio broadcasters for the games in 1938. At the same time, Swift was a loyal follower of the Maroon, and he saw clearly the philanthropic uses the game provided. He took pains to host his friends and those who might become friends of the university at home and away games, even to the point of overseeing the seating arrangements of spectators at Stagg Field in order to facilitate his social and financial ends. He relished rail trips to away games. On one occasion, he hosted upward of fifty guests in two private rail cars to an Illinois game in Urbana, providing luncheon and dinner en route. All in all, it was no surprise when the Swift family head asserted that Harold's full-time job was not at Swift and Company—it was at the University of Chicago.[11]

But the story of Harold Swift and football revolved most remarkably around his attempts to produce winning teams at Chicago. The board president was the chief of the most sustained and energetic player recruiting effort during the late 1920s and the 1930s, of which he was "deeply proud." Many of the players, students, and professors of the time remembered Swift as an active recruiter, especially in California, but the written outlines emerge only sketchily. Swift introduced his system to Metcalf soon after his arrival. An important part of the effort was Swift's old friend from the college, Norman Barker '08, who, as a high school track coach in Long Beach, California, had "sent" many football players to Chicago. Swift offered Metcalf excerpts from a recent Barker letter that complained that Stagg and his coaches had lost players to ineligibility because they did not have a close relation to them. Both Barker and Swift hoped that Metcalf would ensure better attention to this business. Swift's California pipeline was likely responsible for seven players in 1933, which was more than the five from other states outside Illinois combined, and constituted almost 25 per-

cent of the thirty-member team that year and about 50 percent of the
starting eleven. Swift also recruited locally, as when he provided tickets to a Chicago all-star secondary school game so that a Chicago delegation, including three varsity players "who will be helping . . . in
contacting high school students" could represent the university. The
leader of the recruiting delegation was Keith I. Parsons, who assured
Swift that he could meet "at least a half dozen of the boys who played"
in the all-star game at the annual alumni dinner. Parsons, a former
varsity football and basketball player who won six letters and held a
Phi Beta Kappa key, was the "Assistant to the Secretary of the University" from 1934 to 1937. In that capacity he arranged admission, scholarships, and on-campus jobs for athletes, although most of his work
was with regular prospective students. Parsons was perhaps symbolic
of the Hutchins College; the man in charge of what recruitment of
athletes took place was a Phi Bete graduate to whom Hutchins never
mentioned football when interviewing him for the position.[12]

If Swift actively sought out promising football players, there is little
conspicuous record of anyone else joining his effort, and the record of
the team indicated that even his efforts were futile. In fact, the scholastic mortality rate of scholarship-holding football players was quite
high; the outstanding group corraled in 1935 proved not up to the
academic level required and well over half flunked out and played (and
presumably studied) elsewhere. Swift was engaged in a task that was
inevitably set against the backdrop of a rapidly evolving American
college with distinctly un-American characteristics. In addition, the
Hutchins administration was increasingly known for its insistence on
the primacy of the mind, and Hutchins's often-quoted remark, that he
rested whenever the urge for physical exercise overtook him, was taken
as the gospel of the new order. But Swift, for whom football was an
important element in university and fraternity life, was convinced that
the Hutchins administration was handling the athletic program "inef-
ficiently." This inefficiency might be calculated, Swift intimated, to
make the sport an easy target for criticism. The issue rankled Swift, but
he refused to write his opinions on the matter to the administration
so as not to get himself "stirred up" or "to say things which might cause
resentment."[13]

At least one other man on the Midway campus was as frustrated by
the football picture, present and future, as was Swift. Clark Shaughnessy wrote to Swift confidentially and cautiously in January 1938 to
request "a chat with you—unofficial—about our football situation." The
coach first assured the president that "personally" he had no complaints: "I appreciate sincerely the dignity and security of my position

at the University of Chicago." His problem, Shaughnessy explained rather fuzzily, was that he was "puzzled by a seeming difference in— shall we say—hopes—for football, that exists in the various groups of the university."[14]

Swift answered Coach Shaughnessy somewhat cryptically, "I don't see any reason why we shouldn't talk over the matter mentioned in your note of Monday." The meeting took place and led to Shaughnessy's bare statement of "Difficulties," which Swift filed with their exchange of notes. The litany of problems Shaughnessy offered is powerful, if casual and chatty, and even though the list is notably silent about the "seeming difference in . . . hopes" that their meeting was meant to address. The coach stated ten difficulties that Chicago faced in mounting a "successful," that is, winning, program. The picture is a gloomy one indeed. His "Lack of Material" included inferior numbers, age and maturity, experience, and native ability, which left little save mental processes in which his players were adequate. He noted the poor practice facilities and lack of time for off-season work. He listed inadequate coaching, by which he meant that "too many" of his assistants were part-time and had other, primary interests, and yet he was chary of making changes that would run afoul of "certain personalities and their friends." He noted "lack of interest on the part of the student body and the faculty," which merited an extended discussion. Shaughnessy thought the lack of backing for football was deleterious because the game throve on emotion, of which he found comparatively little on the Midway. One unusual complication was that, for the players, there was the sirens' song of a "multiplicity of interests, attractions and temptations, due largely to our location in a great city." He also explained the "financial difficulties of those boys most inclined to play football. . . . It is *IMPOSSIBLE* generally speaking for an average student to earn his way through the University of Chicago *AND* take part in athletics." Shaughnessy's final major difficulty was the lack of the three course majors in the Chicago curriculum most attractive to football players nationwide: agriculture, physical education, and engineering (surely a distant third), which, he averred, were crucial to a successful football program.[15]

The most telling result of the Swift-Shaughnessy conference was the confidential letter the coach wrote to his board president later in 1938 as he prepared his team for the football season. "I thot [*sic*] perhaps you would be interested in a report, covering the football situation since our 'conference.'" He announced he had "lost" four players, possibly five (all rated in his top fifteen), until at least mid-October due to academic ineligibility. Shaughnessy continued:

I was greatly surprised because I saw _____ frequently and he always told me he was getting along fine—and besides I personally—gave him money to employ all the tutors he could possibly use. We saved all the promising freshmen—by *helping* them get tutors—I guess this would be against the principle of the rules—but it was an emergency—I am going without Christmas money this year to make up for this splurge—but they are good boys in every way and I felt that I wanted to encourage them *practically*—they had enough advisers. _____ and _____—are at present ineligible but will most likely be alright by practice time. I have had to adopt _____—to make my efforts to keep him going legal. He has absolutely NO backing or help from his home at all. . . .

I suppose—my personal efforts—to help our boys stay in school and stay eligible would be criticized in some quarters—and thus probably should not be known at large. My reason for mentioning it is that I wanted you to know that I am doing everything within my power to keep football alive at the university. . . .

Kindest regards,

Clark Shaughnessy

One can be pardoned for wishing fervently that Swift had written a letter to Shaughnessy detailing all *he* had done toward the same end.[16] Perhaps most important, Harold Swift had identified himself so thoroughly with the football and fraternity interests on campus for nearly four decades that he provided the perfect trustee leader to investigate the issue and, if Hutchins could manage it, to find intercollegiate football wanting. And if Swift would not aid Hutchins's campaign against football, he nonetheless chose not to obstruct the project. By mid-December of 1939 his official neutrality was changing to a wary agreement to deal with the issue at the next trustee meeting. On the whole, the trustees were not part of the antifootball leadership; rather, they were the most important constituency to be persuaded.[17]

University Crisis: The Season of 1939

The inevitable early-season predictions of a "come-back" for Midway football fortunes ceased when Chicago lost their first game to Beloit College, 0-6. The major opponents on the 1939 schedule were Harvard, Michigan, Virginia, Ohio State, and Illinois. The Maroons did not score against any of them, and their opponents averaged sixty points each game, despite their using reserves. It was a season of "moral victories" for Chicago. The moral victories were not enough, even with columnist Heywood Broun's assurance that because a winning football team was a priori evidence of stupidity, the 1939 Chicago team had to be comprised of incomparable scholars. The performance of the team went beyond the comic of previous seasons to become tragic in the eyes of Maroon supporters and now assumed the proportions of a crisis that demanded solution.[18]

University Constituencies

As we have seen, the New Plan, adopted in 1931, resulted in a brighter, more critical undergraduate student body and one much less likely to have participated in athletics at secondary school or on the Midway. Football and fraternities were closely intertwined, and the combination accounted for much campus social life; at the same time, many students were more politically active and some never attended a game. The college was clearly changing, and the community, to a degree, behaved in a manner not generally seen elsewhere until the 1960s: sorority and fraternity rushing declined; some classes decided not to organize due to lack of interest or candidates for office; a debate over the purposes of education, starring Mortimer Adler and scientist Anton Carlson (attendance was no doubt encouraged by the perception that the young Adler was Hutchins's champion, challenging a reactionary viewpoint held by an older generation), drew more students than a varsity basketball game; and the *Maroon* campaigned for the abolition of traditional letter grades.[19]

The *University of Chicago Magazine* in 1938 carried a statement by a member of the first New Plan graduating class in 1935 that indicated the change in the college. The recent graduate addressed the chief objection of many older graduates to the college—the poor football team. He suggested a possible corrective: "Fifty thousand dollars will buy an All-American team. . . . It would be the easiest and surest business venture in the world. The alumni would be happy, the University would make money." The young graduate concluded with some assertions regarding higher education that may never have been heard before by those who graduated when football was a way of life: "But the University has curiously felt that it is not in the business of promoting professional athletic contests. And as a matter of business ethics, it wouldn't be fair to compete with the Chicago Bears. . . . The simple and obvious fact is, of course, that, at a University, athletics should be subordinate to the main purpose of education. At Chicago this happily is the case."[20]

The changes wrought in the student body by the New Plan and Hutchins's experiments, however, can easily be overestimated, as student response to *Daily Maroon* editor William H. McNeill's eloquent antifootball campaign in 1937 demonstrates. "It is a depraved system," he announced, "which has to depend on the prestige of eleven men to attract students to the university or to uphold the university's name." But only 6.8 percent of McNeill's fellow students supported his *Maroon* platform for the "abolition of intercollegiate athletics" when they were surveyed. The heavy majority (64 percent) preferred the status quo of intercollegiate competition; however, the seasons of 1937, 1938, and 1939 probably pressed this majority to a more decisive position. Significantly, more than twice as many students in 1937 wanted the university to subsidize athletes (24 percent) than wanted to abolish intercollegiate athletics or to withdraw from the Big Ten (12 percent). Crusading editor McNeill confidently interpreted the poll: "First, that there is more intense 'college spirit' here than one would guess from performances at pep sessions and football games. Second, that college students, like the rest of mankind, put their reason to one side when traditional attitudes are called into question." McNeill's abolition plea inspired little save a brief boycott of his paper; he playfully insisted upon having the last word on the matter that year at the annual football banquet, where his speech was entitled "The Moral Obligations of the Necessity of Getting Circulation." He admitted that his campaign to abolish football had met at least temporary defeat; the six hundred football enthusiasts present responded with "deafening applause." He concluded by suggesting an alternative to football that would guarantee excellent income and no eligibility problems at Chicago—horse racing. The applause was not deafening.[21]

Perhaps the most remarkable football statement from a student came in 1939 from Editor Rosenheim of *Pulse*. Rosenheim observed that Hutchins had informed the students they were at Chicago "to receive an academic education" and that football and extracurriculars were secondary. Still, the editorial deplored the university's lack of a better reputation with "the public" and observed that "throughout the country we are classed either as 'Reds' or as insufferable highbrows. . . . To be respected the University must conform to the popular values as completely as possible, so long as such conformance does not sacrifice our educational ideals. The chances are that Mr. Hutchins' excellent pronouncements on football or anything else would be given greater weight and attention if the Maroons were a winning football team. We do not say that such a condition is right; we feel that it is necessary. We feel, equally strongly, that it can be attained without sacrificing our educational ideals."[22] Rosenheim's position would seem to have been shared by the clear majority of those students who responded earlier to the *Maroon*'s opinion survey.

Chicago back John Thomas testing the Princeton 1922 "Team of Destiny" line. The game at Stagg Field marked the first time one of the Harvard-Yale-Princeton triumvirate journeyed west to play football. Seeley G. Mudd Manuscript Library, Department of Rare Books and Special Collections, Box 14—1920s, Princeton University Libraries

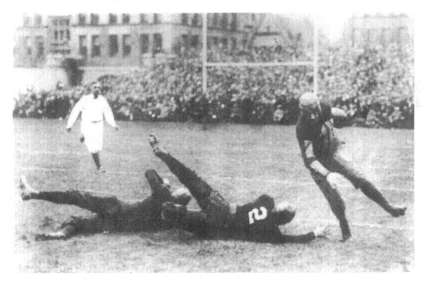

Harold "Red" Grange leaving fallen Maroons in his wake, Illinois at Chicago, 1924. Cobb Gate is behind the goal posts. The Department of Special Collections, the University of Chicago Library

Walter Camp congratulates his former player Stagg after the 1924 Illinois game. Camp and Stagg were the two most significant figures of the first and second generation of American football.

The nearly seventy-year-old Stagg demonstrating blocking fundamentals during a 1931 football practice. Chicago Historical Society.

This Jay Berwanger photograph probably served as the model for the Heisman trophy. The Maroon halfback won the inaugural award in 1935, which was shortly after named for John Heisman. Berwanger was named to the 1969 centennial All-time All-American team along with Eckersall, thus making Chicago the only university with two all-time backfield members. The Department of Special Collections, the University of Chicago Library

1939: Michigan slaughters the Maroons 85-0 in the Stagg Field gloaming of Chicago football. The background crenelated tower is part of the west stands. The Department of Special Collections, the University of Chicago Library

Ten years after the abolishment of football, President Robert Maynard Hutchins suited up in a Maroon football uniform for the first, and last, time. The occasion was the Quadrangle (faculty) Club Revels of 1949. The Department of Special Collections, the University of Chicago Library

Amos Alonzo and Stella Stagg at their golden wedding anniversary, September 10, 1944. The Department of Special Collections, the University of Chicago Library

The long-neglected west stands after World War II. The squash courts beneath the stands were fitted up as laboratories by Enrico Fermi and the Manhattan Project during the war. A plaque later noted that on December 2, 1942, they "achieved the first self-sustaining chain reaction and thereby initiated the controlled release of nuclear energy." Note the ventilation exhausts that had served Fermi's laboratories. The Department of Special Collections, the University of Chicago Library

Demolition of Stagg Field. The Department of Special Collections, the University of Chicago Library

Joseph Regenstein Library (1967) with Bartlett Gym at left background and Hitchcock Hall in right background. This photo was taken from the same building as the 1905 photograph of Marshall Field. The Stagg Papers in the Special Collections wing of Regenstein Library are stored below what was the football field. Author's photo, 1994

"Nuclear Energy" by Henry Moore (1967). The sculpture is on the site of the atomic reaction under the west stands. Hitchcock Hall is in the background. Author's photo, 1994

Faculty opinion was less evident than student opinion; after the death of the popular James Weber Linn in 1938, there was no acknowledged faculty football cheerleader. Some professors, such as James L. Cate and Norman Maclean, were still avid followers of the Maroon, still others enjoyed criticizing the winless Coach Shaughnessy; most, however, appeared not to consider football of great moment at their university.[23]

The alumni were a disparate constituency that ranged from baccalaureates in commerce to those who had obtained the Ph.D. Football was frequently a significant part of their memories. For example, an alumna listed her turn-of-the-century recollections in 1939, and football games and players were especially vivid as she recalled the latter being blessed by a top-hatted President Harper after a Mandel Hall Sunday service. The alumni were one of the least malleable of the constituencies, and many old graduates used the memories of Harper and Stagg to legitimate the activity on campus in the 1930s.[24]

An indeterminate number of alumni had been unhappy and vociferous about the changes taking place on the Midway during the 1930s. A 1909 graduate may have explained the feelings of many Republican alumni in 1938: "They have passed the stage of disapproval and are beginning to feel resentment at this New Deal on the Midway." One alumnus complained, "The spirit and the advertising are all directed towards the children with thick lenses and an inferiority complex." And another charged, "Regardless of its protests to the contrary, the University is becoming a school for intellectual geniuses and bookworms only." An older graduate wrote that he did not approve of present athletic policies, that his "greatest regret" was he was "not a member of the Order of the 'C'," and he thanked the editor of the *University of Chicago Magazine* for providing "an outlet for a great deal of suppression which has been going on in my mind for many months." Harold Swift noted in 1937 that his alumni conversations and correspondence indicated why they were critical of the Hutchins's college: "Many alumni . . . criticize us for being too highbrow and not being interested in the fine type of 'red-blooded American,' who, parenthetically, may be a little dumb."[25] The decline of football served as an especially painful symbol for these alumni, and they were provoked to new heights by President Hutchins's *Saturday Evening Post* "Gate Receipts and Glory" article on the evils of the game. Twenty-seven alumni "read it and raged" enough to dash off letters to the *University of Chicago Magazine*. About 40 percent of Chicago graduates, however, were involved in the educational profession; they were much less vociferous over football and can properly be termed the "silent alumni."[26]

The informal divisions of opinion among the graduates were more formally expressed in 1939 by the membership of the four leading alumni organizations: the Alumni Council, the Alumni Foundation, the Chicago Alumni Club, and the Order of the C. The council and the foundation were encouraged and officially recognized by the university; they represented all alumni, and their leadership was selected from the most distinguished graduates. The Chicago Alumni Club was an unofficial university organization comprised of males who had attended the university and who resided in the Chicago area. This was the club founded by President Harper to help produce winning teams, and it had remained steadfast to that singular purpose. The smallest, most exclusive and cohesive alumni organization was Stagg's original Order of the C, which pledged "enduring support of her athletic honor and tradition." Predictably, many in the latter two groups were loud and persistent critics of the athletic policies and personnel on the Midway during the football decline.[27]

The University of Chicago had a particular need to be aware of public opinion toward any decision regarding intercollegiate football. The institution was about to launch the largest fund-raising campaign it had ever organized, and most of the money would have to be obtained from persons who had no prior educational relationship with the school. By 1939, the American public was well prepared for the dramatic move by Hutchins and the board of trustees in abolishing football. Hutchins was an effective popularizer of educational issues, and many Americans knew him because of his contributions to the *Saturday Evening Post.* During 1937 and 1938 he had criticized and caricatured American higher education in a rambling series for *Post* readers, using his unique style of education evangelism. For instance, he attacked with characteristic alliteration, "football, fraternities, and fun."[28]

There was considerable support among American newspapers for the Hutchins-Metcalf approach to football. The editors of the *Cleveland Plain-Dealer* applauded the "unique distinction" of the university's athletic policies in 1937; they commented that "to one great American university athletic reform and sound physical education are something more than a name." Other editorials also acclaimed the Chicago experiment, and the lopsided scores in 1939 were cited as proof that Chicago was alone in trying to maintain amateur sport.[29]

Football reform attempts by educators and social critics were frequent during the 1930s. Readers of popular magazines were provided an ample diet of articles regarding the heavily recruited and rewarded college teams. A number of institutions abolished the game, and the public was no doubt aware of the better-known ones, such as Antioch, Reed, Emory, and DePaul and Loyola of Chicago, although none of America's major universities had taken that course.[30]

Conversion Period

The elements necessary for the abolition of intercollegiate football at the University of Chicago were in place by the end of the disastrous season of 1939: Stagg's mythic legacy, a committed university administration and faculty, and unusually literate and understanding constituencies. The ball was now clearly in President Hutchins's office.

Robert Maynard Hutchins was an educational evangelist who sought the conversion of others to his vision of what higher learning in America should be. He had called for "an evangelistic movement" in 1936; its object was "the conversion of individuals . . . to a true conception of general education." The influence of his father, as preacher and professor of homiletics, can be seen in the young president's homiletical speaking and writing methods. Hutchins, addicted to alliterative triads, usually sought to demonstrate a grievous need, provide an answer to the need, and conclude with a challenge for conversion (a classic example of this is Billy Graham's sermon, "Made, Marred, and Mended"). The generalist seemed to be working, albeit he denied it, for an artistic (rhetorical) end, not an intellectual one; he sought an emotional rearrangement, not a restructuring of the mind. In the case of football, the method was apt. "I despair of converting our graduates and trustees," Hutchins wrote midway through the autumn 1939 conversion period of his congregation, from believing "the excellence of a university is determined by its football scores." But he vowed, in the manner of St. Paul, to keep the faith and continue the good fight.[31]

The change of the trustees' attitudes in 1939 toward football at Chicago was due to the dogged efforts of President Hutchins and Trustee John Nuveen, Jr. In Nuveen, Hutchins found an excellent and perceptive aide for his campaign. Nuveen was an alumnus of the university, a highly successful stock broker, and Chicago's youngest regular trustee, being only a few years older than Hutchins. He was the chair of the alumni council and one of the most important leaders of the newly formed alumni foundation. The *Denver Post* commented after one of his appearances, "As Nuveen talks, one might think he is a member of the faculty of the university."[32]

Nuveen followed Maroon football avidly, and he had to be convinced both of the necessity to review the situation and of the wisdom of ending the game. Hutchins began to make headway with Nuveen about the middle of November; the trustee wrote the president that he had just reread "Gate Receipts and Glory" and admitted that the article contained "a lot more significance for me now than when I first read it." He then presented his president with a draft of a possible statement by the board of trustees for "our temporary withdrawal from Big Ten competition." He was moving toward Hutchins's position, and his conversion to the view that the abrogation of football was the logical end to the disastrous season occurred soon after. The president's campaign with the trustees went swiftly once Nuveen was converted.[33]

Hutchins and Nuveen showered the other members of the board with memoranda and antifootball literature; they included articles and editorials from the nation's press that indicated a recognition, sometimes grudging, of the point the winless and distinctly amateur Maroons were making. Nuveen's favorite article appeared in the *American Mercury* that fall. The author, John Tunis, was a friend of Vice-president Benton and others in the university's public relations office; with their help, he had previously done a piece extolling Chicago's educational innovations. Now, Tunis's muckraking approach to college football made the Maroons' abysmal record something to boast about.[34]

The alumni were of primary concern for Hutchins and Nuveen because the trustees were worried over the possibility of financial reprisals by graduates if football were abolished. Nuveen, as an alumni leader, was crucial in convincing the trustees that the graduates could be handled if the trustees took the step Hutchins pressed upon them; to that end, he spent two months that autumn interviewing alumni. One graduate, an academic dean in a southern college and a former Maroon track captain, wrote Hutchins that "it hurts the Alumni to see Chicago beaten by such decisive scores." He noted that it was "impossible to keep an amateur standing and have a winning team" and asked, "Would it not be a fine thing for Chicago to be one of the first great institutions to abolish this sport?" The alumnus concluded by predicting an enhanced national reputation if the university made such a decision. Hutchins thought the letter, one of the few from the silent alumni, the most impressive he had received; he distributed copies to all members of the board and mused, "It will have some effect."[35]

The leadership of the alumni council and the new alumni foundation engaged in frequent and prolonged discussions of the football situation during the season of 1939. The coming fiftieth anniversary celebrations had the effect of encouraging them to consider long-range consequences, and the discussions were mature and impressive. John Nuveen, fulfilling important roles in both groups, carefully recorded the points of argument and agreement. The alumni council's governing board demonstrated an almost unanimous agreement on two points: (1) the university should be scrupulously honest in intercollegiate football; and (2) the university should have a successful team, if possible. These were hardly helpful as alternatives, for the existing policy meant to follow the two points. Aside from these points, the twenty-five council leaders were uncertain about concrete alternatives; they agreed only on the need for "action" regarding football.[36]

The smaller executive committee of the alumni foundation contained some of the most successful and influential graduates of the university. They proved to be as uncertain as the council. The executive committee unanimously agreed that they did not wish to "continue as at present," but they voted down all five alternatives presented in a November questionnaire. They would not take the easy route of playing musical chairs with the coaching staff. They agreed that the lack of players was the "principal cause" of the problem but refused to countenance recruitment and subsidization of players. They preferred not to "lighten the schedule," because they felt there was a "danger" that Chicago would be "associated with the smaller schools in scholarship and educational rank." The two most extreme alternatives—withdraw from the Intercollegiate Conference in football or abolish intercollegiate football—were rejected unanimously (9-0). Hence, the foundation and the council wished "action," but they refused to accept any of the alternatives.[37]

Most of the officers of the Chicago Alumni Club and the members of the Order of the C had regarded Hutchins's article, "Gate Receipts and Glory," as an outrage and a call to action. They determined to recruit promising schoolboy athletes despite official university disapproval. These alumni did not act covertly; they raised money openly to aid athletes at Chicago, always asserting that all players subsidized would have to meet the usual entrance standards. In turn, the rationale and boldness with which the victory-hungry graduates operated displeased other alumni. One described those who would pay the players as motivated "primarily for the satisfaction to their personal vanity, which a good football team gives them."[38]

William V. Morgenstern, an alumnus who had termed the football-conscious downtown businessmen the "LaSalle Street Coaching Staff" when he worked as a writer for the *Chicago Herald-Examiner,* later claimed they were not representative of Chicago alumni. Rather, Morgenstern stated, they were "fringe sects whom no one took seriously." Another observer described them as slow-witted and sophomoric. The veteran English professor Edward W. Rosenheim, the student editor in the late 1930s, remembered years later that the LaSalle Street Coaching Staff tried to stir student leaders up over the football issue to no avail; even then, Rosenheim noted, it was obvious to the students that the LaSalle Street crew were "not the University's finest, most successful alumni."[39]

The most important leader of the alumni attempt to lure schoolboys to the Midway was Alumni Club officer John William Chapman, class of 1915. Chapman, who had not received a C in any sport, had asked boldly and unexpectedly to meet with the trustees in 1937 to tell them of "my plans, hopes and expectations for the 1938 football banquet." Swift, who, of course, had been doing his best for the team, lateraled to William Benton after writing to Chapman that his appearance before the trustees for football "would not be wise, and it might not even be fruitful, to try to stir up their particular interest in our athletics." Chapman was not easily put off, and in his preparation for the 1938 banquet, he told one reporter that at the 1937 occasion, attended by a hundred high school prospects, President Hutchins "was practically discouraging to their desire to enter Chicago [sic]." Some of the sporting press delighted in the prospect of a Maroon bloodletting and encouraged the LaSalle Street coaches: "One wonders just how long the alumni, if it has any power or anything at all to say about it, is going to stand idly by and see a great institution continue to be the laughing stock of college football."[40] The indefatigible Chapman bent to the task and warned his 1938 banquet committee that he had been "informed by a member of the University staff" that "there may be no football team at the University next year" and hoped their efforts might recapture "the athletic glory" of "days gone by." Chapman's timing proved perfect, as it followed the College of the Pacific debacle by a month. The 1938 banquet, with Hutchins and Swift noticeably absent, was attended by 450 persons (of whom 144 were specially invited high school football players) and concluded with film of Walter Eckersall in action. When the results were in, it was clear that Chapman had engineered, in Trustee Paul Russell's wry telegraphic words to Swift, the "BEST FOOTBALL DINNER IN ALL HISTORY." Hutchins admitted later, "I am scared to death of the LaSalle Coaching Staff."[41]

Chapman wrote to John Nuveen to reiterate his plea for the restoration of quality football and his hope that the trustees would cooperate with his alumni group in providing it. He appealed to the Stagg legacy and proudly revealed that the reason he attended Chicago was "almost entirely due to the fact that Mr. Stagg was coaching football" there. The recruitment of athletes, Chapman patiently continued, could be accomplished with the aid of the trustees. First, there should be a return to the "old fraternity system." Second, Chapman suggested that "some interested alumnus who knows something about the football records of high school boys" should sit on the scholarship committee that rewarded "leadership potential." He might have had himself in mind for the position because he boasted he had been "interesting [*sic*] good high school students who were proficient in playing football" to enter the university and claimed to possess a list of 111 such boys. Nuveen, who managed to suffer fools more gladly than Hutchins, wrote a diplomatic reply that included a valiant attempt to instruct Chapman on "the real purpose for which our universities were founded."[42]

While the small group of willful men made plans for the restoration of Maroon gridiron glory and their place in it, President Hutchins watched and waited as the disastrous season made its own converts. The effect of the team's humiliations in 1939 was that many faculty and alumni came to feel that abolition was the only sensible solution. Professors became deeply concerned when their students, including one so "badly battered," Edward Shils remembered, as if he "had been in a concrete mixer," appeared in class on Mondays. Typical complaints came from an alumna who was moved to protest for the first time; she pleaded with Hutchins after the Michigan defeat of 85-0, "Such a farce of a football game . . . should be *forever* stopped." After two opponents had scored 146 points to nil for Chicago, an alumnus wrote his concern to Hutchins of the effect on the players—the experience was "too great a heartache for any group of football men to have to suffer." Another graduate ceased attending games that season because he feared the Maroons might be injured severely or fatally. And dispassionate football journalists had come to much the same conclusion: "The material at Chicago is simply not up to Big Ten standards, and the boys shouldn't be asked to break their hearts against Grade A competition," wrote the *Saturday Evening Post*'s Francis Wallace early in the season.[43]

University leaders felt the pressures from the public to yield to the requirements of victory, although they tried to keep the matter in perspective. Trustee Paul S. Russell advised, "The public who still reads the sports page" was not "of sufficient importance to make us change any of our policies." One belligerent fan wrote Hutchins that his old college "won at *least* every other game, & still our scolastic standard was as high as Chgo [*sic*]." The disturbed fan challenged the president, "As the leader of the U. of C. what is your answer?" Hutchins's penciled marginal response: "My answer is nuts."[44]

The American public was kept remarkably well-informed of the university's football policy even if the message was sometimes delivered in the most unorthodox fashion. The most dramatic use of the

Maroons' sorry record was *Look* magazine's selection of the entire Chicago eleven as its all-American team for 1939. The sports editor explained:

> Working on the naive assumption that college football is an amateur sport, this writer has chosen an amateur All-America team. . . . I name the University of Chicago varsity eleven. This team is unique in that it is composed of students who look upon football as recreation. . . . There isn't a single hired hand on this eleven. From end to end, from quarterback to fullback, the players are unsalaried and unsullied. Not one of them has an athletic scholarship. None is majoring in poultry husbandry, appreciation of music, butter and egg judging, blacksmithing or tire vulcanizing.[45]

Hutchins could not have overwritten it better himself.

The Alternatives

The alternatives to the state of football at the university that were available and discussed by the constituencies were: (1) a new coach, (2) new players, (3) new opposition, (4) a new scale of participation, and (5) abrogation of the sport. And alternatives three or five were the only possible ones at Chicago in 1939.

Alternatives one and two addressed internal university values and procedures. The university could not dismiss the tenured Clark Shaughnessy as coach because the institution had claimed publicly that coaches at Chicago did not have to win, and there was expert opinion that he was an excellent coach. Moreover, founding President Harper had somehow created the model for what became the Frankenstein creature of the modern American campus: the football coach-athletic director who answers to nothing save football success as measured by victories and who is paid on a scale unrelated to any other position on the campus (including the president) or to any other public position in the state (including the governor). Of course, if Harper's original idea of placing the coach of the most important intercollegiate sport under academic tenure was meant both to encourage and to control that person and football, his later pragmatic model of tying Stagg's salary to the football revenues led directly to the modern mischief.[46]

The enrollment of better football players, alternative two, was not a possibility for the university unless it dealt in the methods and employed the standards of competing schools. This Hutchins refused to do. The disastrous season of 1939 had merely proved anew what seasoned football observers had been saying for years: "There have rare-ly been, in recent years, more than two or three Maroon regulars who could make the second or third teams at other Big Ten schools." Chicago authorities had tried another approach in the spring of 1939 when Dean of Students Works and Athletic Director Metcalf submitted a proposal to the Intercollegiate Conference to ask permission for Chicago to use graduate and transfer students in order to enlarge its player reservoir. The representatives refused the request, probably because of the impossible precedent that would be set and because it was remembered that Chicago had been unsparing in its relations with the other members of the conference while it was in the dominant athletic and commercial position. Then, too, Hutchins's notoriety, partially based upon his barbed criticism of the modern occupationally oriented university, which all eight of the public universities in the conference represented, would hardly have predisposed them to be helpful to Chicago's football woes.[47]

Chicago could initiate the third alternative by withdrawing from the Intercollegiate Conference and playing schools with nonprofessional football programs. *Daily Maroon* editor Deadmon had put this course forward in 1938 as one of the alternatives; Coach Shaughnessy and Dean Works were reported to be in agreement, and Director Metcalf also chose a lessened schedule as the solution in 1938. But this alternative was rejected by Hutchins because he was concerned that playing small schools would diminish Chicago's status as a premier university, or, as he admitted, it was "worse to be beaten by Beloit and Oberlin." This was an odd and inconsistent point coming from Robert Maynard Hutchins, who had frequently declared, "The football situation has nothing to do with the academic reputation of the University." The fourth alternative was hatched by inexperienced alumni who suggested that Chicago should commence the season with intramural football, to be followed by an "all-star" intramural team that would play the traditional intercollegiate games later in the season. It was rejected as unworkable, but the scheme did betray the enormous ignorance and naivete prevalent among some of the alumni football followers who seemingly wished to combine democratic player selection with a major schedule.[48]

The final alternative remained. The chronology of events in the fall of 1939 swept toward the meeting of the board of trustees on the twenty-first of December. Early in November, Hutchins had written a sketchy outline, "Notes on Football." It was the beginning of the argument he presented to Trustee Laird Bell's Committee on Instruction and Research later in the month. The president outlined the problems and alternatives, and probably for the first time Hutchins formally told a group of trustees that there were "dangers" in continuing intercollegiate football "on any basis." No minuted record of their response is available, but it was favorable and he was encouraged to take his argument further.[49]

The Decision

Two factors appeared in early December to force an immediate decision by the board of trustees: flamboyant player recruitment and imminent alumni fund-raising. A perceptive sportswriter noticed that "various Maroon alumni have been busy getting high school athletes to come to the Midway, and have been offering to find them jobs, etc., etc., all probably within the letter of the law against 'professionalism,' but certainly an embarrassing move to the University administration." The most embarrassing occurrence for the Hutchins administration was once again the annual football banquet sponsored in 1939 by the Alumni Club of Chicago and the 55th Street Business Men's Association. What had been launched in 1902 by Harper and Stagg came home with a vengeance as the special guests, 125 high school seniors, arrived in late afternoon on the Midway for a tour of fraternities and the university. The fraternities provided entertainment at the dinner, and coaches, former star players, and alumni salesmen once again spoke of past Maroon glories and their dedication to the future of Chicago football. It was left to an overheated alumnus to cap the evening's oratory with a declaration of which the university administration and trustees had to take notice. John William Chapman's pronouncements as an officer and past president of the Alumni Club had a kind of official standing to the uninitiated that night, especially to the schoolboys he addressed. "A real spirit exists at Chicago to get a winning football team," Chapman thundered as he promised the Midway moon to the youngsters. The folly of such histrionics was graphically demonstrated by President Hutchins and the trustees within the month.[50]

The football banquet gave final public warning to the university administration and the trustees that some alumni were going to recruit and subsidize football players regardless of official university policy and method. Hutchins's benign indifference would no longer suffice; a decision was necessary before Chapman and his allies gathered in a new crop of expectant athletes. A promising young journalist, Irv Kupcinet, later reported that the 1939 recruiting proved highly successful; the city's top schoolboy player was to enroll, and the 55th Street Business Men's Association had guaranteed good jobs for all the recruits.[51]

The second factor forcing Hutchins's hand was that John Nuveen and the other leaders of the alumni foundation's drive planned to begin the most intensive stage of their canvass in January. Nuveen urged Swift that it was of the "greatest importance" that a decision on football be made before the invitations to the capital campaign kickoff dinner in January were mailed.[52]

On December 20, President Hutchins appeared before the faculty board on student affairs and requested approval of a proposal to the trustees that intercollegiate football be abolished. Predictably, that board approved. Hutchins met the next day with the trustees and submitted his argument for the cessation of football. His formal eight-page memorandum devoted seven pages to the problem and alternatives facing them. Hutchins added little to the arguments he had already advanced in November before Bell's trustee committee. He disposed of the most attractive alternative, that of playing small college competition, but explicitly admitted the relationship between academic reputation and football that he denied publicly: "Our scholastic reputation and our geographical position make it hard for us to play small-time football. We do not like to be classed with Monmouth and Illinois Wesleyan. We are too far away from the New England colleges to make them the backbone of our schedule."[53]

Hutchins concluded his argument by setting the alternative of abolition against an alternative the trustees had already rejected: "Since we cannot hope to win against our present competition and since we cannot profitably change our competition, only two courses are open to us: to subsidize players or to discontinue intercollegiate football. We cannot subsidize players or encourage our alumni to do so without departing from our principles and losing our self-respect. We must therefore discontinue the game."[54] Hutchins then stated the positive benefits of abolition: "We shall get rid of an important handicap to education. It is hard for an educational institution to live in a satisfactory way with football, win or lose." The Chicago Alumni Club's football zealots supplied the ammunition for another positive benefit, which Hutchins foresaw: "We shall avoid the danger, now close at hand, of uncontrollable subsidization by our graduates." Hutchins described the constituencies that he thought abolition would favorably impress: "We shall secure the support of many alumni and lose interest of fewer than we think; we shall arouse the enthusiasm of that large and growing section of the public which is disillusioned about intercollegiate football." The president declared that this large section of the American public included the "major donors to the University." Finally, the decision would "confirm the pioneering reputation of the University and at one stroke do more to make clear what a university is than we could do in any other way."[55]

Robert Hutchins closed his memorandum with the request that the trustees authorize him "to discontinue intercollegiate football." Swift, who voted against the resolution, remembered the discussion of the Hutchins proposal was "prolonged" and that the opinions expressed by the group followed no age, occupational, or educational lines. The deliberations became "so predominantly one way as to suggest and secure unanimous action on a second vote." The deed was done. Football was abolished at Chicago.[56]

Epilogue: After the Fall

The press release that announced the trustees' action began, "The University of Chicago has decided to withdraw from intercollegiate football," and continued, "this action was taken by unanimous vote at a meeting of the University's Board of Trustees." The release vaguely noted that the university "believes in athletics," but that "its particular interests and conditions are such that its students now derive no special benefit from intercollegiate football." The statement said that more students were participating in intramural sports on the Midway than ever before; that Chicago had been the only Big Ten university participating in all thirteen intercollegiate sports scheduled by the conference; and that "the University trusts that its withdrawal from intercollegiate football will not require termination of its long and satisfactory relationship with the other members of the Intercollegiate Conference."[1]

The immediate response to the action of the board of trustees was both favorable to a degree that they did not foresee and favorable to a degree they did foresee, and no doubt planned carefully. The unforeseen favorable response came from the public and most elements of the university constituencies, which, with predictable exceptions, either supported enthusiastically or respected grudgingly an American university that moved decisively in this difficult area. The foreseen and planned response came with the dramatic announcements of a spate of gifts to the university during the last ten days of December. These amounted to about $8 million and included the large estate of Albert Lasker, the American advertising pioneer and a university trustee. The well-timed gifts silenced criticism of the effect that football abolition might have on fund-raising and provided an excellent basis for the public launching of the ambitious development campaign in the new year.[2]

The Response of the Public

The reaction of the public is difficult to determine precisely, but there is much evidence that the "educated" public respected the university for its action. President J. William Fulbright of the University of Arkansas extended to President Hutchins "sincere congratulations on your courageous defense of the university and its true function." The future governor and Senate leader felt that such courage in attacking one of the "worst excrescences of our educational system" entitled Chicago to "the place of honor and leadership in our profession." Others wrote their support, including a superintendent of an Ohio high school at which Intercollegiate Conference schools aggressively recruited athletes, and the former chair of the conference alumni committee that had unsuccessfully tried to end illegal recruiting in the Big Ten. Further, the Chicago Bears' later appropriation of the Maroons' *C* emblem as well as the "Monsters of the Midway" description must have denoted a kind of respect for the university's football tradition.[3]

The portions of the public critical of the trustees' action were not as well prepared to discuss educational policy as those supporting the trustees. One local critic wrote to the *Chicago Daily News* to justify football, "What I mean to say is to be really educated a person ought to absorb an occasional kick in the pants along with his Plato and Shakespeare." The correspondent capped his argument with unconscious humor: "Football comes closer, perhaps, than any other element of college life to providing the missing link in most college educations."[4]

The newspapers of America found the issue of football at Chicago compelling—so compelling that a surprising number wrote editorials about the matter, and, according to John Nuveen, about 98 percent of the editorial comment applauded the action. There was unanimity through the several score editorials regarding the hypocrisy of intercollegiate football, the uniqueness of the Chicago amateur experiment and final decision, the courage of the Chicago trustees and President Hutchins, and a concern that the university not be penalized unduly for moving decisively.[5] The *Milwaukee Journal* was an exemplar of these views. "The Man Who Abolished Football" was the title of a lengthy *Journal* editorial on January 15. The paper admitted that it did not agree with all of President Hutchins's educational views but noted that he was "fighting a pretty hard battle these days" that the paper wanted to join. The reason he was attacked, the paper thought, was that he had "educational ideas and he put them into practice." The *Journal* argued that his "real work" in making a university primarily a place of learning was ignored, and the attack on the football decision was led by sportswriters who were angered by his interference with their sport. The newspaper's strongest criticism was reserved for the response of the other Big Ten presidents, who had not discussed the educational issues, preferring to give defensive statements to the press indicating the purity of their own athletic businesses.[6]

The shadow of Amos Alonzo Stagg over the decision to abolish football at Chicago was still considerable, even if his quoted response to the effect that intercollegiate football still contributed much to young men and ensured alumni interest was uncommonly measured. Grantland Rice, America's most famous sportswriter, quoted and then marked the Old Man's statement with, "Lonnie Stagg still thinks that football at Chicago could have been saved," but, Rice concluded, "I don't believe so." The *Philadelphia Inquirer* addressed the Stagg legacy: "It may be hard for alumni, still mindful of the glories of the Stagg era, to contemplate it but withdrawal of Chicago from the Big Ten, under present policies, is unquestionably for the best." Harold Swift met the Stagg response directly when he wrote a critical correspondent who had quoted Stagg as "one of our great men of Chicago." Swift said, "I, too, like Stagg's statement which you quoted. I have to say, however, that I think he hasn't told the whole story, and that intercollegiate football as practiced in some of the Big Ten institutions has done much to undermine character and learning, which in my judgement it is the university's responsibility to foster."[7]

The Response of the Sports Industry

Most of America's athletic industry responded predictably. Some sportswriters demonstrated the ignorance of higher education and the academic insensitivity that was so much a part of intercollegiate football. The *Chicago Tribune*'s sportswriters began a campaign against the Chicago trustees and president immediately after the decision was announced that was quite at variance with the *Tribune*'s editorial commendation in 1938. Wilfrid Smith wrote of student, faculty, and alumni opinion "in Chicago and out of the metropolitan territory" in sweeping generalizations. That opinion "was almost unanimously opposed to the action," he claimed, and then he offered two student comments in support of his declaration. Smith included a statement from a Winnetka graduate of 1912 as proof of his thesis: "If it is a fact that undergraduate men of the U. of C. desire and have repeatedly voted to play football, then the sophomoric decision of the board of trustees in abolishing football ignores the bill of rights and sincerely flatters both Stalin and Hitler."[8]

The *Chicago Tribune*'s premier sportswriter and athletic entrepreneur, Arch Ward, announced the university's abolishment of intercollegiate football in the sports page style that passes for argument: "Shades of Walter Eckersall, Wally Steffen . . . ! The school where they achieved gridiron immortality has abandoned their sport. . . . Can you imagine those men quitting when things were breaking badly? . . . They belonged to an era when men were men and the University of Chicago wasn't afraid of competition [*sic*]." The *Tribune* sometimes combined its sportswriters and comics on the same pages; Ward's column was accompanied by a cartoon of a stretcher-borne battered body—"Chicago Football"—being carried off Stagg Field by a chesty, pompadoured boy needlessly labeled "Hutchins" and a tearful "Alma Mater." The *Tribune* sports staff's campaign to make the Midway safe for football was later terminated when Colonel Robert McCormick, the newspaper's publisher, found the aid of Robert Hutchins invaluable in his isolationist crusade to keep America First.[9]

The response of some members of the Intercollegiate Conference was, as the *Milwaukee Journal* asserted, disappointing. The conference commissioner, John Griffith, attempted to penalize Chicago for its decision, which he interpreted, no doubt correctly, as an implied criticism of the purity of conference athletics. He and the conference athletic directors were infuriated by a widely reported assertion from an "anonymous" Chicago official (soon identified as Hutchins) that "you can't play Big Ten football without being crooked." They postponed the scheduling of Chicago's conference basketball games for the next season as a form of sanction.[10]

Another point of contention for the athletic directors was a Nuveen alumni brochure that included reprints of magazine articles critical of some Big Ten practices—hence, the directors sought in some manner to punish Chicago for publicizing public documents. Commissioner Griffith attempted to obfuscate some of the issues surrounding the exit of Chicago. He released conference figures regarding the number of varsity athletes at each school receiving scholarships. Chicago had the largest number; hence, the implication of Griffith's statistics, quickly seen and used by the city's sportswriters, was that this proved the university also "paid" its athletes. The figures were correct allowed Nuveen in a letter to his sympathetic friend Joseph Raycroft of Princeton, but the "insinuations are absolutely incorrect." The crucial factor, Nuveen noted, was not the amount of scholarship aid but the basis of the awards and the standards of eligibility applied to the athletes. Although Commissioner Griffith continued his public outbursts against President Hutchins, a clear majority of the men who controlled the conference, the faculty representatives, felt that the continued inclusion of Chicago in all sports but football was acceptable and that the conference could well use the prestige of a major private research university.[11]

The Response of the University Constituencies

The response of the university constituencies can be divided into two chronological periods. The records of university officials to January 15, 1940, indicate that correspondents were about evenly divided over the football solution. Those who felt the trustees' action was in error tended to be emotional because an aspect of the campus life that they valued highly was being removed from their university. One angry C man and graduate announced to Hutchins from Philadelphia: "I will not send my son to the University of Chicago!" He felt that the New College was "over stressing" the "academic life on the campus," for "red blooded young men and women demand a well balanced environment." Perhaps the most candid and perceptive plea to the trustees to change their decision was from a Colorado sheep rancher and alumnus who reminded Swift that he had waited on Swift's fraternity table when they were in the university. The handwritten letter continued:

> So the other day, when you threw in the towel and quit the Big Ten, that sort of made us groggy.
>
> I had counted a lot on my boys going to Chicago U. We rubes need more than hours in Harper [Library] and classrooms. Football doesn't hurt us. . . .
>
> I do wish you Trustees would reverse yourselves and continue to play Big Ten football.[12]

A former Chicago professor wrote just as feelingly in support of the decision: "I hope yet to see the day when the grey prison walls of Stagg Field will be laid low, the abominable bleachers dismantled, 56th Street given back its sunshine and the former quiet, the memory of those maddening football mobs forgotten and forgiven."[13]

The second wave of response to the decision of the trustees heavily favored the solution. A University of Missouri faculty member assured Hutchins that his experience as a faculty member of a state university had instructed him that many administrators have to accept the football situation "as an evil to be endured for the sake of a rather vaguely-defined greater good." A former student congratulated Nuveen on the "courageous step taken by the University" and was proud the college was "maintaining its integrity." A female graduate wrote Nuveen warmly of her respect for the decision: "It is highly gratifying to discover that those are not idle words in the Alma Mater—that the University really 'could not love her sons so well / Loved she not truth and honor more.'"[14]

The most important factor prompting the widespread support of the silent alumni after the first of the year was the arresting twelve-page brochure, "Concerning Football," that John Nuveen as chair of the alumni council sent to all Chicago alumni. The brochure included photostatic reproductions of articles attacking intercollegiate football and of editorials backing Chicago's unique approach. By the first of February, Nuveen estimated that "eighty percent of the 47,000 alumni are outspokenly in favor of the break."[15]

Harold Swift may have had misgivings at the time of the decision, but he backed the action with his considerable prestige among the alumni. He was agitated by some graduates' charges that he and the other alumni trustees were "railroaded" by Hutchins and the nonalumni trustees into the fatal solution. Swift addressed the complainants in language that showed his ire: "I say you were never more wrong in your life," he told one, and added, "your statement is foolish." The board chair typically used four to five pages to answer the critics, and he usually informed them that the trustees "are independent thinkers, and they have guts!" He admitted that they came to their decision with trepidation, but "the protests have not been as numerous as I, at least, expected, and there has been a wave of commendation which I didn't at all anticipate."[16]

John Nuveen joined Swift in dealing with the critical alumni. He demonstrated repeatedly that his combination of patience and argument were invaluable factors in the move for abolishment and the alumni acceptance of it. A critic wrote Nuveen that the trustees' decision was wrong because it violated the writer's "Freudian opinion" that humans need and demand competitive sports. Nuveen disclaimed any workable knowledge of Freud but stated, "Even though human interest in competitive sports may have not been diminished since 1400 B.C., there is no logical association between that interest and the work of our universities." He argued that if the institutions would cease mounting sporting spectacles they would

> remove one of the greatest obstacles of understanding on the part of students, Alumni, and the American Public as to what the true function of the University is. It is very apparent that a large part of the Alumni still do not know why they went to college, and successive generations of high school students are being handled in a way to keep this knowledge from them also.

It is, perhaps, not going to be easy to attract them to a real institution of learning instead of a Country Club, but it is a worthy ideal.[17]

Six months after the abrogation, Nuveen handled the complaint of
John William Chapman that Chicago was becoming too intellectual:
"Whenever I can be convinced that the University is on the way to
becoming a haven solely for grinds and bookworms and that recruiting a couple of dozen pro football players for the rest of the students
to watch will reverse that trend, then I will get in a pitch for that. As
long as there is evidence of increased participation in all athletic sports,
any trend in the direction which you fear seems to be amply refuted
for the present."[18]

The end of the financial drive by the alumni foundation in September 1941 showed that Chicago alumni had given more than the goals
set by Nuveen and other leaders; however, the general Fiftieth Anniversary Campaign was completed about $3 million shy of the $12
million goal. Robert Hutchins pronounced the final judgment to another university president contemplating the abolition of football: "We
have had no disturbances about football here since it was abolished.
Alumni support in our Fiftieth Anniversary Campaign exceeded our
expectations." Of course, development goals are set to be surpassed,
and if not surpassed are reset to be surpassed, and we shall never know
the true impact of the abrogation of football on the fund-raising effort.
Whatever the reasons, the University of Chicago during the twenty-
one-year Hutchins administration lost its place as an endowment leader
in American higher education, and for most of that period the institution experienced significant financial problems.[19]

The responses of the faculty and students to the abolition were less
dramatic and intense than those of the alumni. Newspaper reporters
seeking pungent quotations moved over the campus like an invading
army after the decision was announced. There was unanimity, except
for the *Chicago Tribune,* that the decision met with remarkably little
opposition on the Midway. Most faculty would not talk to the reporters, but there was widespread, if wary, support for the abolishment.
Some of the students were happy to talk to the journalists. Football
and fraternities had become inextricably linked at Chicago. A majority of men who were not in fraternities seemed to approve the action,
although many seemed otherwise occupied, some with political action.
Fraternity members were uniformly displeased; most felt the decision
lessened their social schedules and the opportunities for alumni to
return and "feel old sentiments return," including the urge to contribute and keep the houses solvent. Some members of the varsity foot-

ball team termed the decision "a dirty trick" and "pretty awful," but Director Metcalf interviewed most of the football players when they returned from Christmas vacation, and all planned to stay on the Midway despite the absence of their sport. In the event, forty-eight of the fifty-eight 1939 freshman team members returned to college in September 1940. One freshman player wrote Hutchins after the decision, "Many of the players felt a distinct personal loss, but we agree with you that the first purpose of an educational institution is to educate, with football of secondary importance. We, the players, are proud of you and of the University of Chicago." The sports editor of the *Chicago Daily News* described student reaction: "Many talks with Midway students and with men who know the students have convinced me that the majority of the undergraduates do not care a whoop about football. A very strong minority, perhaps a majority, actually look down on the game as something that has been puffed up all out of importance in relation to a college education."[20]

The issue of student opinion may have been academic from the beginning; that constituency was the least important to Hutchins. After the act of abolishment, which occurred when the student body was on Christmas vacation, the issue seemed closed. There were some petitions and other unease in evidence when the students returned, but Hutchins made a particularly impressive speech to them in January, which prompted the withering away of criticism. If intercollegiate football was an important cultural symbol for most American universities, the undergraduates at Chicago soon made its absence a significant symbol. Within twenty-five years, the use of this symbolism had become so important that one student discussed the rumored restoration of football in 1963: "Until this year, the absence of intercollegiate football was an important symbol of . . . [our] unique character and spirit. With destruction of the symbol may come the destruction of that which it symbolized."[21] The point had been made before, if less narcissistically, by those members of the university's constituencies who argued for the retention of the activity and its symbolism in 1939.

In fact, a new campus myth, that of Hutchins's college, may well have displaced the Stagg myth by the 1960s, and a new generation of post-Hutchins administrators labored to correct it. Dean of the College Alan Simpson responded none too diplomatically to the student concerns with, "The issue of football" is "being blown up by students who feel that the absence of the game on this campus is a unique and precious thing. This is a ludicrous viewpoint." When the football "class" began to schedule "laboratories" that took place at Stagg Field during the fall of 1963, some students took note and action. At the fourth and last of the scheduled matches with outside competition, and no doubt provoked by the presence of CBS-TV national coverage of "the return of football to the U of C" arranged by administrators, two hundred students, some bearing placards announcing "HUTCHINS IS OUR LEADER," sat down on the fifty-yard line. Many refused to move, even after a rather civil discussion of the rights of (Maroon) man led by the dean of students, a philosopher. Chicago police were asked to cart off those who remained, but no one was arrested and the protesters' point had been driven home: The absence of football was sacred on the Midway, and its open return as a NCAA Division III activity would have to await another decade and a different climate.[22]

Dean of Students Warner A. Wick later addressed the students on issues he deemed basic to the football imbroglio. He included a history of the Hutchins college, noting the demise of the early entrants in the early 1950s and the baccalaureate degree then offered—"not recognized by any graduate school"—and concluding that, by the end of the Hutchins era, "we were in terrible trouble." Dean Simpson, with an almost Hutchinsesque ability for the memorable phrase, had already described undergraduates of the early 1950s and their leftovers as "prigs, eunuchs, and maggoty-minded monks."[23]

The Response of Other Universities

The University of Chicago's discontinuance of football did not prompt any other major universities to emulation. The abolishment was a luxury that few American institutions of higher learning could afford by 1939. The *Topeka State Journal* explained this clearly in an editorial entitled "Not Rich Enough to Be Honest." The newspaper noted a Chicago trustee's statement that the school was fortunate "in that it had no debt for stadiums and gymnasiums and other buildings" and described other schools' financial predicaments and their need for the football marketplace.[24]

An Overview

The story of football at Chicago demonstrates the tension in American higher education between egalitarian and elitist viewpoints, which, in turn, but mirrors one of the most significant tensions of the modern democratic state. The early university of Dewey, Veblen, Michelson, and Mead was marked by intellectual quality and ferment; it is striking, however, how easily some of America's seminal minds accommodated themselves to, or ignored, the difficulties football occasioned.

Harper's university decided that the principle of "becoming all things to all men" was more important than academic elitism and consistency, and Stagg's university demonstrated that principle's application most efficiently and seductively. But Hutchins's university decided, aberrantly among the major universities, to rid itself of the most popular manifestation of the earlier principle. Harper's forcible ideal of football as "the altar of vigorous and unsullied manhood" in 1894 became a tarnished, even tawdry, Hutchins image by 1939—and even *Look* magazine's "unsullied" Chicago all-American team of 1939, despite its rhetorical uses, seemed terribly out of date.

Despite the quality of the arguments and personnel surrounding the football problem on the Midway, the Chicago academic community had discussed the root and branch abolition of the sport after their championship seasons only once, and that but briefly in the face of Harper's rebuff. Indeed, it took a series of dreadful seasons and a mythical view of Chicago's past to carry a sufficient number of university constituencies along with the decision. Most institutions seemed to dwell in a different world from Chicago's; the president of Notre Dame admitted publicly that he had advised Hutchins that if Chicago could rid itself of the sport, it should do so. That president and most other American university leaders would never seem to have the opportunity.[25]

But a large question about the nature of the American university remained. Even if every Midway constituency, all the other universities, and the entirety of print and electronic media in the land had agreed that Chicago had done something unexpected but noble in its abrogation of an embarrassing sports business, a future problem remained: Because the demise of football at Chicago effectively left the university without the most popular means that most American universities (of all regions and academic levels) use to communicate and keep in touch with American society, what would or could Chicago develop to fill the place of football in its history? Perhaps the erosion of both the institution's endowment and academic ranking during the course of the Hutchins administration provides at least part of the answer.[26]

One of the few Chicago intellectuals to address this issue has been William H. McNeill, the crusading antifootball editor of the *Maroon* during the 1930s. After teaching and researching at Chicago for more than forty years, McNeill, as a distinguished professor emeritus, published "a memoir" in 1991 that aimed "to set forth the convergence of institutional and sociological circumstances with intellectual and personal aspirations that made the University of Chicago such a special place in the 1930s and 1940s." His *Hutchins' University* is an informative, affectionate, elegant, and, upon occasion, eccentric tribute. Perhaps his most unusual judgment is directed to his old bugaboo, football:

> Of all the actions Robert Maynard Hutchins took in his twenty years as president of the University of Chicago, the abolition of intercollegiate football, announced in December 1939, provoked the loudest reaction, both among alumni and across the country. . . . Football overshadowed everything else, and the university's popular reputation as a place where radical intellect had snuffed out red-blooded, all-American games became an unhappy, half-underground counterpoint to [William] Benton's celebration of the university's cultural and public roles.
>
> In retrospect, it is clear that withdrawal from big-time football involved significant loss for the university. . . . The loss for the university was and remains real.[27]

McNeill's final comments are challenging and remind us that the University of Chicago continues as a place of enormous diversity of opinion: "Hutchins muffed a chance to continue Harper's tradition of pioneering in sports and cashing in on the public attention football commanded; and the student body lost the chance of supplementing their superior intellectual prowess with a more visceral but very valuable sort of collective identity, based on association with famous athletes and cheering them on—thus associating themselves and the whole university with another, quite genuine kind of excellence."[28]

The rise, decline, and fall of big-time football at the University of Chicago demonstrates the arresting nature of the game for the American mind, the vulnerability of American universities to the extracurricular activity, and the fragility of the values of American higher education after the activity had become lodged on campus. Football produced a subculture in American higher education that proved capable of creating and altering academic standards and values, indeed, of defining higher education for many Americans. The American community impinged on the American university and college more graphically at the football stadium than in any other sector. And, in turn, football proved one of the most signal marks on American society provided by the American university.

Appendix 1:
University of Chicago Football
Schedule and Scores, 1892-1939

Season	University of Chicago vs.	Scores
1892		
Oct. 22	Northwestern University	0-0
Nov. 2	Northwestern University at Evanston	4-6
Nov. 5	Lake Forest University	18-18
Nov. 12	University of Michigan at Toledo	10-18
Nov. 16	University of Illinois	10-4
Nov. 19	Purdue University at Lafayette	0-38
Nov. 24	University of Illinois at Champaign	12-28
1893		
Oct. 14	Lake Forest University	0-10
Oct. 18	Northwestern University	12-6
Oct. 21	University of Michigan	10-6
Oct. 25	Purdue University at Lafayette	10-20
Oct. 28	University of Cincinnati	26-0
Nov. 4	Oberlin College	12-33
Nov. 8	Northwestern University at Evanston	6-6
Nov. 11	Armour Institute	18-6
Nov. 18	Lake Forest University	14-14
Nov. 30	University of Michigan	10-14
Dec. 16	Northwestern University at Tattersalls	22-14
Jan. 1, 1894	University of Notre Dame at Tattersalls	8-0
1894 (three preseason games with Chicago high schools)		
Sept. 12	Chicago Athletic Association	4-12
Oct. 6	Northwestern University	46-0
Oct. 11	Rush Medical College	14-6

Season	University of Chicago vs.	Scores
Oct. 13	Beloit College	16-0
Oct. 17	Chicago Athletic Association (2d team)	20-0
Oct. 20	University of Wisconsin	0-30
Oct. 24	Chicago Athletic Association	0-30
Oct. 27	University of Iowa	18-18
Oct. 31	Prairie Athletic Club	26-0
Nov. 3	Purdue University	6-10
Nov. 6	Englewood Y.M.C.A.	4-0
Nov. 10	Lake Forest University	28-0
Nov. 21	University of Illinois	10-6
Nov. 24	Northwestern University at Evanston	36-0
Nov. 29	University of Michigan	4-6
Dec. 25	Leland Stanford Junior University at San Francisco	24-4
Dec. 29	Leland Stanford Junior University at Los Angeles	0-12
Jan. 1, 1895	Reliance Athletic Club	0-6
Jan. 4	Salt Lake Y.M.C.A.	52-0
1895		
Sept. 21	Eureka College	28-0
Sept. 28	Chicago Athletic Association	8-0
Oct. 5	Lake Forest University	52-0
Oct. 19	Northwestern University	6-22
Oct. 23	Armour Institute	24-4
Oct. 26	University of Minnesota	6-10
Nov. 2	University of Wisconsin	22-12
Nov. 9	Western Reserve University at Cleveland	14-0
Nov. 16	Northwestern University at Evanston	6-0
Nov. 28	University of Michigan	0-12
1896		
Sept. 19	Wheaton College	47-0
Sept. 26	Eureka College	46-0
Oct. 3	Monmouth College	43-0
Oct. 7	Hahnemann Medical College	34-0
Oct. 10	University of Iowa	6-0
Oct. 14	University of Notre Dame	18-0
Oct. 17	Oberlin College	30-0
Oct. 21	Armour Institute	36-0
Oct. 24	Northwestern University	6-46
Oct. 31	University of Illinois	12-0
Nov. 7	University of Wisconsin at Madison	0-24
Nov. 10	Lake Forest University	0-0
Nov. 14	Northwestern University at Evanston	18-6

Nov. 26	University of Michigan at Coliseum	7-6

1897

Oct. 2	Monmouth College	41-4
Oct. 9	Lake Forest University	71-0
Oct. 13	Armour Institute	24-0
Oct. 16	Beloit College	39-6
Oct. 23	Northwestern University	21-6
Oct. 30	University of Illinois at Champaign	18-12
Nov. 6	University of Notre Dame	34-5
Nov. 13	University of Wisconsin	8-23
Nov. 25	University of Michigan at Coliseum	21-12

1898

Sept. 24	Knox College	22-0
Sept. 28	Rush Medical College	8-0
Oct. 1	Monmouth College	24-0
Oct. 5	Physicians and Surgeons College	22-0
Oct. 8	University of Iowa	38-0
Oct. 15	Beloit College	21-0
Oct. 22	Northwestern University	34-5
Oct. 29	University of Pennsylvania at Philadelphia	11-23
Nov. 5	Purdue University	17-0
Nov. 12	University of Wisconsin	6-0
Nov. 24	University of Michigan	11-12

1899

Sept. 23	Knox College	40-0
Sept. 30	Physicians and Surgeons College	12-0
Oct. 4	University of Notre Dame	23-6
Oct. 7	University of Iowa	5-5
Oct. 11	Dixon College	29-0
Oct. 14	Cornell University	17-6
Oct. 21	Oberlin College	58-0
Oct. 28	University of Pennsylvania	5-5
Nov. 4	Purdue University	44-0
Nov. 11	Northwestern University	76-0
Nov. 18	Beloit College	35-0
Nov. 25	University of Minnesota	29-0
Nov. 30	Brown University	17-6
Dec. 9	University of Wisconsin at Madison	17-0

1900

Sept. 22	Lombard College	24-0
Sept. 26	Monmouth College	29-0
Sept. 29	Knox College	16-0
Oct. 3	Dixon College	23-5
Oct. 6	Purdue University	17-5

Season	University of Chicago vs.	Scores
Oct. 9	Rush Medical College	40-0
Oct. 13	University of Minnesota at Minneapolis	6-6
Oct. 20	Brown University	6-11
Oct. 27	University of Pennsylvania at Philadelphia	0-41
Nov. 3	University of Iowa	0-17
Nov. 10	Northwestern University	0-5
Nov. 17	University of Wisconsin	5-39
Nov. 29	University of Michigan	15-6
1901		
Sept. 21	Lombard College	38-0
Sept. 28	Monmouth College	23-0
Oct. 2	Milwaukee Medical College	12-0
Oct. 5	Knox College	6-0
Oct. 9	Illinois Wesleyan College	22-0
Oct. 12	Purdue University	5-5
Oct. 19	University of Illinois	0-24
Oct. 26	University of Pennsylvania	0-11
Nov. 2	Beloit College	17-17
Nov. 9	Northwestern University	5-6
Nov. 16	University of Michigan at Ann Arbor	0-22
Nov. 28	University of Wisconsin	0-35
1902		
Sept. 20	Lombard College	27-6
Sept. 27	Monmouth College	24-0
Oct. 1	Soldiers at Fort Sheridan	53-0
Oct. 4	Knox College	5-0
Oct. 8	Cornell College	21-0
Oct. 11	Purdue University	33-0
Oct. 18	Northwestern University	12-0
Oct. 25	University of Illinois	6-0
Nov. 1	Beloit College	18-0
Nov. 8	Indiana University	39-0
Nov. 15	University of Michigan	0-21
Nov. 27	University of Wisconsin	11-0
1903		
Sept. 19	Lombard College	34-0
Sept. 26	Lawrence University	23-0
Sept. 30	Monmouth College	108-0
Oct. 3	Indiana University	34-0
Oct. 7	Cornell College	23-0
Oct. 10	Purdue University	22-0
Oct. 14	Rush Medical College	40-0

Oct. 17	Northwestern University	0-0
Oct. 24	University of Illinois	18-6
Oct. 31	University of Wisconsin at Madison	15-6
Nov. 7	Haskell Indians	17-11
Nov. 14	Army at West Point	6-10
Nov. 26	University of Michigan	0-28

1904

Sept. 17	Lombard College	40-5
Sept. 24	Lawrence University	29-0
Oct. 1	Indiana University	56-0
Oct. 8	Purdue University	20-0
Oct. 15	University of Iowa	39-0
Oct. 22	Northwestern University	32-0
Oct. 29	University of Illinois	6-6
Nov. 5	University of Texas	68-0
Nov. 12	University of Michigan at Ann Arbor	12-22
Nov. 24	University of Wisconsin	18-11

1905

Sept. 23	Lawrence University	33-0
Sept. 30	Wabash College	15-0
Oct. 4	Beloit College	38-0
Oct. 7	University of Iowa	42-0
Oct. 14	Indiana University	16-5
Oct. 21	University of Wisconsin at Madison	4-0
Oct. 28	Northwestern University at Evanston	32-0
Nov. 11	Purdue University	19-0
Nov. 18	University of Illinois	44-0
Nov. 30	University of Michigan	2-0

1906

Oct. 20	Purdue University	39-0
Oct. 27	Indiana University	33-8
Nov. 10	University of Minnesota	2-4
Nov. 17	University of Illinois	63-0
Nov. 24	University of Nebraska	38-5

1907

Oct. 12	Indiana University	27-6
Oct. 19	University of Illinois at Champaign	42-6
Nov. 2	University of Minnesota at Minneapolis	18-12
Nov. 9	Purdue University	56-0
Nov. 23	Carlisle Indians	4-18

1908

Oct. 3	Purdue University	39-0
Oct. 10	Indiana University	29-6
Oct. 17	University of Illinois	11-6

Season	University of Chicago vs.	Scores
Oct. 31	University of Minnesota	29-0
Nov. 14	Cornell University	6-6
Nov. 21	University of Wisconsin at Madison	18-12
1909		
Oct. 2	Purdue University	40-0
Oct. 9	Indiana University	21-0
Oct. 16	University of Illinois	14-8
Oct. 30	University of Minnesota at Minneapolis	6-20
Nov. 6	Northwestern University	34-0
Nov. 13	Cornell University at Ithaca	6-6
Nov. 20	University of Wisconsin	6-6
1910		
Oct. 8	Indiana University	0-6
Oct. 15	University of Illinois at Champaign	0-3
Oct. 22	Northwestern University	10-0
Oct. 29	University of Minnesota	0-24
Nov. 5	Purdue University	14-5
Nov. 12	Cornell University at Ithaca	0-18
Nov. 19	University of Wisconsin at Madison	0-10
1911		
Oct. 7	Indiana University	23-6
Oct. 14	Purdue University	11-3
Oct. 21	University of Illinois	24-0
Nov. 4	University of Minnesota at Minneapolis	0-30
Nov. 11	Northwestern University at Evanston	9-3
Nov. 18	Cornell University	6-0
Nov. 25	University of Wisconsin	5-0
1912		
Oct. 5	Indiana University	13-0
Oct. 12	Open	
Oct. 19	University of Iowa	34-14
Oct. 26	Purdue University	7-0
Nov. 2	University of Wisconsin at Madison	12-30
Nov. 9	Northwestern University	3-0
Nov. 16	University of Illinois at Champaign	10-0
Nov. 23	University of Minnesota	7-0
1913		
Oct. 4	Indiana University	21-7
Oct. 18	University of Iowa	23-6
Oct. 25	Purdue University	6-0
Nov. 1	University of Illinois	28-7

Nov. 8	Northwestern University at Evanston	14-0
Nov. 15	University of Minnesota at Minneapolis	13-7
Nov. 22	University of Wisconsin	19-0

1914
Oct. 3	Indiana University	34-0
Oct. 10	Northwestern University	28-0
Oct. 17	University of Iowa	7-0
Oct. 24	Purdue University	21-0
Oct. 31	University of Wisconsin at Madison	0-0
Nov. 14	University of Illinois at Urbana	7-21
Nov. 21	University of Wisconsin	7-13

1915
Oct. 9	Northwestern University at Evanston	7-0
Oct. 16	Indiana University	13-7
Oct. 23	Purdue University	7-0
Oct. 30	University of Wisconsin	14-13
Nov. 6	Haskell Indians	35-0
Nov. 13	University of Minnesota at Minneapolis	7-20
Nov. 20	University of Illinois	0-10

1916
Oct. 7	Carleton College	0-7
Oct. 14	Indiana University	22-0
Oct. 21	Northwestern University	0-10
Oct. 28	University of Wisconsin at Madison	7-30
Nov. 4	Purdue University	16-7
Nov. 18	University of Illinois at Urbana	20-7
Nov. 25	University of Minnesota	0-49

1917
Oct. 6	Carleton College (cancelled)	
Oct. 13	Vanderbilt University	48-0
Oct. 20	Purdue University	27-0
Oct. 27	Northwestern University	7-0
Nov. 3	University of Illinois	0-0
Nov. 17	University of Minnesota at Minneapolis	0-33
Nov. 24	University of Wisconsin	0-18

1918 (conference play halted; Student Army Training Corps teams
   played the season)
Nov. 2	Purdue University of Lafayette	3-7
Nov. 9	University of Michigan	0-13
Nov. 16	Northwestern University at Evanston	6-21
Nov. 23	University of Illinois	0-29
Nov. 30	University of Minnesota	0-7

Season	University of Chicago vs.	Scores
1919		
Oct. 11	Great Lakes Naval Training Station	123-0
Oct. 18	Purdue University	16-0
Oct. 25	Northwestern University	41-0
Nov. 1	University of Illinois at Urbana	0-10
Nov. 8	University of Michigan	13-0
Nov. 15	University of Iowa	9-6
Nov. 22	University of Wisconsin	3-10
1920		
Oct. 9	Purdue University	20-0
Oct. 16	Wabash College	41-0
Oct. 23	University of Iowa	10-0
Oct. 30	Ohio State University	6-7
Nov. 6	University of Illinois	0-3
Nov. 13	University of Michigan at Ann Arbor	0-14
Nov. 20	University of Wisconsin	0-3
1921		
Oct. 1	Northwestern University	41-0
Oct. 8	Purdue University	9-0
Oct. 22	Princeton at Princeton	9-0
Oct. 29	University of Colorado	35-0
Nov. 5	Ohio State University	0-7
Nov. 12	University of Illinois at Urbana	14-6
Nov. 19	University of Wisconsin	3-0
1922		
Oct. 7	University of Georgia	20-0
Oct. 14	Northwestern University	15-7
Oct. 21	Purdue University	12-0
Oct. 28	Princeton	18-21
Nov. 11	Ohio State University at Columbus	14-9
Nov. 18	University of Illinois	9-0
Nov. 25	University of Wisconsin	0-0
1923		
Sept. 29	Michigan Agricultural College	34-0
Oct. 6	Colorado Agricultural College	10-0
Oct. 20	Northwestern University	13-0
Oct. 27	Purdue University	20-6
Nov. 3	University of Illinois	0-7
Nov. 10	Indiana University	27-0
Nov. 17	Ohio State University	17-3
Nov. 24	University of Wisconsin	13-6

1924

Oct. 4	University of Missouri	0-3
Oct. 11	Brown University	19-7
Oct. 18	Indiana University	23-0
Oct. 25	Ohio State University at Columbus	3-3
Nov. 1	Purdue University	19-6
Nov. 8	University of Illinois	21-21
Nov. 15	Northwestern University	3-0
Nov. 22	University of Wisconsin	0-0

1925

Oct. 3	University of Kentucky	9-0
Oct. 10	Ohio State University	3-3
Oct. 17	Northwestern University	6-0
Oct. 24	University of Pennsylvania at Philadelphia	0-7
Oct. 31	Purdue University	6-0
Nov. 7	University of Illinois at Urbana	6-13
Nov. 14	Dartmouth College	7-33
Nov. 21	University of Wisconsin	7-20

1926

Oct. 2	University of Florida	12-6
Oct. 9	University of Maryland	21-0
Oct. 16	University of Pennsylvania at Philadelphia	0-27
Oct. 23	Purdue University	0-6
Oct. 30	Ohio State University	0-18
Nov. 6	University of Illinois	0-7
Nov. 13	Northwestern University at Evanston	7-38
Nov. 20	University of Wisconsin	7-14

1927

Oct. 1	University of Oklahoma	7-13
Oct. 8	Indiana University	13-0
Oct. 15	Purdue University	7-6
Oct. 22	University of Pennsylvania	13-7
Oct. 29	Ohio State University at Columbus	7-13
Nov. 5	University of Michigan	0-14
Nov. 12	University of Illinois at Urbana	6-15
Nov. 19	University of Wisconsin	12-0

1928

Sept. 29	University of South Carolina	0-6
Oct. 6	University of Wyoming Double-Header	47-0
Oct. 6	Lake Forest College	3-0
Oct. 13	University of Iowa	0-13
Oct. 20	University of Minnesota at Minneapolis	7-33
Oct. 27	Purdue University	0-40
Nov. 3	University of Pennsylvania	13-20

Season	University of Chicago vs.	Scores
Nov. 10	University of Wisconsin at Madison	0-25
Nov. 17	University of Illinois	0-40
1929		
Oct. 5	Beloit College Double-Header	27-0
Oct. 5	Lake Forest College	9-6
Oct. 12	Indiana University	13-7
Oct. 19	Indiana State College Double-Header	18-0
Oct. 19	Ripon College	10-0
Oct. 26	Purdue University	0-26
Nov. 2	Princeton University at Princeton	15-7
Nov. 9	University of Wisconsin	6-20
Nov. 16	University of Illinois at Urbana	6-20
Nov. 23	University of Washington	26-6
1930		
Oct. 4	Ripon College Double-Header	19-0
Oct. 4	Hillsdale College	7-6
Oct. 11	University of Wisconsin at Madison	0-36
Oct. 18	University of Florida	0-19
Oct. 25	University of Mississippi	0-0
Nov. 1	Princeton University	0-0
Nov. 8	Purdue University	7-26
Nov. 15	University of Illinois	0-28
Nov. 22	University of Michigan at Ann Arbor	0-16
1931		
Sept. 26	Cornell College Double-Header	12-0
Sept. 26	Hillsdale College	0-7
Oct. 10	University of Michigan at Ann Arbor	7-13
Oct. 17	Yale University	0-27
Oct. 24	Indiana University	6-32
Oct. 31	Purdue University	6-14
Nov. 7	University of Arkansas	13-13
Nov. 14	University of Illinois at Urbana	13-6
Nov. 21	University of Wisconsin	7-12
1932		
Sept. 24	Monmouth College	41-0
Oct. 8	Yale University at New Haven	7-7
Oct. 15	Knox College	20-0
Oct. 22	Indiana University	13-7
Oct. 29	University of Illinois	7-13
Nov. 5	Purdue University	0-37
Nov. 12	University of Michigan at Ann Arbor	0-12
Nov. 19	University of Wisconsin	7-18

1933

Oct. 7	Cornell College	32-0
Oct. 14	Washington University at St. Louis	40-0
Oct. 21	Purdue University	0-14
Oct. 28	University of Michigan	0-28
Nov. 4	University of Wisconsin	0-0
Nov. 11	Indiana University	7-7
Nov. 18	University of Illinois at Urbana	0-7
Nov. 25	Dartmouth College	39-0

1934

Sept. 29	Carroll College	19-0
Oct. 13	University of Michigan	27-0
Oct. 20	Indiana University	21-0
Oct. 27	University of Missouri	19-6
Nov. 2	Purdue University	20-26
Nov. 10	Ohio State University at Columbus	0-33
Nov. 17	Minnesota at Minneapolis	7-35
Nov. 24	Illinois at Chicago	0-6

1935

Sept. 28	University of Nebraska at Lincoln	7-28
Oct. 5	Carroll College	31-0
Oct. 12	Western State Teachers College	31-6
Oct. 19	Purdue University	0-19
Oct. 26	University of Wisconsin	13-7
Nov. 9	Ohio State University	13-20
Nov. 16	Indiana University	0-24
Nov. 23	University of Illinois at Urbana	7-6

1936

Sept. 26	Lawrence College	34-0
Oct. 3	Vanderbilt University	0-37
Oct. 10	Butler University	6-6
Oct. 17	Purdue University	7-35
Oct. 31	University of Wisconsin at Madison	7-6
Nov. 7	Ohio State University at Columbus	0-44
Nov. 14	Indiana University	7-20
Nov. 21	University of Illinois	7-18

1937

Oct. 2	Vanderbilt University at Nashville	0-18
Oct. 9	University of Wisconsin	0-27
Oct. 16	Princeton University	7-16
Oct. 30	Ohio State University	0-39
Nov. 6	University of Michigan at Ann Arbor	12-13
Nov. 13	Beloit College	26-9
Nov. 20	University of Illinois at Champaign	0-21

1938

Oct. 1	Bradley Polytechnic Institute	0-0
Oct. 8	University of Michigan at Ann Arbor	7-45
Oct. 15	University of Iowa	14-27
Oct. 22	Ohio State University at Columbus	7-42
Oct. 29	De Pauw University	34-14
Nov. 5	Harvard University at Cambridge	13-47
Nov. 12	College of the Pacific at Chicago	0-32
Nov. 19	University of Illinois	0-34

1939

Sept. 30	Beloit College	0-6
Oct. 7	Wabash College	12-2
Oct. 14	Harvard University	0-61
Oct. 21	University of Michigan	0-85
Nov. 4	University of Virginia at Virginia	0-47
Nov. 11	Ohio State University	0-61
Nov. 18	Oberlin College	25-0
Nov. 25	University of Illinois	0-46

Playing of intercollegiate football discontinued on December 21, 1939.

Appendix 2:
Intercollegiate Conference of
Faculty Representatives

Table 1. Intercollegiate Conference University Enrollment Figures

Institution	Academic Year			
	1890–91		1900–1901	
	Male Enrollment	Total	Male Enrollment	Total
Chicago		540 or 594[a]		3,346[b]
Indiana	.	324		600
Illinois	[c]	[c]	[c]	[c]
Iowa	[d]	887	1,198	1,542
Michigan	1,975	2,420	2,992	3,712
Minnesota	[d]	1,002	2,417	3,236
Northwestern	[d]	998	[d]	2,048
Ohio State	[d]	493	[d]	1,465
Purdue	438	530	933	1,012
Wisconsin	500	897	1,369	1,977

a. The two figures are for the academic year, 1892–93, the first year of Chicago's existence. The figures are contradictory and are so recorded in *The President's Report, 1892–
1902:* President Harper's figure was 594 (xxxiii); Dean Judson's figure was 540 (in
his "Report of the Dean of the Faculties of Arts, Literature and Science," 11).
b. Dean Judson's report, 11. This figure includes summer quarter registrants who had
no opportunity to participate in regular intercollegiate athletics. The figure should
be reduced to a three-quarter figure to be usefully comparative with the other institutions' academic year figures. The figure for the 1901–2 academic year, 3,471, was
adjusted to a three-quarter figure of 2,373 in Dean Judson's report, 11–12. Hence a
reasonable and similar adjustment of the 1900–1901 figure might be about 2,250.
c. Data unavailable.
d. Separate sex enrollments unavailable.

Table 2. Intercollegiate Conference University Male Undergraduate Enrollment Figures[a]

Institution	1910–11	1920–21	1930–31	1935–36	1940–41
Chicago	705	1,576	686	523	1,131[b]
Indiana	1,012[c]	[d]	[d]	4,212[c]	2,988
Illinois	4,097	8,743[c]	7,515	6,969	8,264
Iowa	1,296	3,155	4,760	4,568	4,691
Michigan	4,467	7,822	9,765	10,166	11,969
Minnesota	2,642	6,375	9,964	10,676	11,045
Northwestern	3,126[c]	4,425[c]	7,005[c]	6,586[c]	4,276
Ohio State	3,439[c]	6,030	10,225	10,330	12,277
Purdue	1,750	2,753	4,447	4,624	6,568
Wisconsin	2,902	4,594	5,937	6,190	8,107

Sources: Chicago, Office of Al Tannler, University Archives; Illinois, Wendell Barbour (assistant archivist) to author, March 12, July 13, 1971; Indiana, M. D. Scherer (university registrar) to author, July 14, 1971; Iowa, Earl M. Rogers (assistant manuscripts librarian) to author, April 2, 1971; Michigan, Janet F. White (acting head, reference department) to author, March 19, 1971; Minnesota, Maxine B. Clapp (university archivist) to author, March 16, 1971; Northwestern, Devorah Howard (university archivist) to author, April 14, 1971; Ohio State, William J. Vollmar (university archivist) to author, March 29, 1971; Wisconsin, J. Frank Cook (acting director, University Archives) to author, March 16, 1971.

a. The figures in Table 2 are exclusive of noneligible graduate students, where possible. Large numbers were enrolled in professional training, however, which spanned undergraduate and graduate status.
b. Figure for 1939-40.
c. Figure includes female and graduate enrollment.
d. Data unavailable.
e. Figure includes female enrollment.

Table 3. 1895 Presidents' Agreement

1. Each college and university that has not already done so shall appoint a committee on college athletics who shall take general supervision of all athletic matters in their respective colleges or universities, and who shall have all responsibility of enforcing the college or university rules regarding athletics and all intercollegiate sports.
2. No one shall participate in any game or athletic sport unless he be a bona fide student doing full work in a regular or special course as defined in the curriculum of his college and no person who has participated in any match game as a member of any college team shall be permitted to participate in any game as a member of another college team until he has

been a matriculant in such a college, under the above conditions, for a period of six months. This rule shall not apply to students who, having graduated at one college, shall enter another for professional or graduate study.

3. No person shall be admitted to any intercollegiate contest who receives any gift, remuneration, or pay for his services on the college team.

4. Any student of any institution who shall be pursuing a regularly pre-scribed, resident, graduate course without such institution, whether for an advanced degree or in any one of its professional schools, may be per-mitted to play for a minimum number of years required before securing the graduate or professional degree for which he is a candidate.

5. No person who has been employed in training a college team for inter-collegiate contests shall be allowed to participate in any intercollegiate con-test as a member of any team which he has trained, and no professional athlete and no person who has ever been a member of a professional team shall play in any intercollegiate contest.

6. No student shall play in any game under an assumed name.

7. No student shall be permitted to participate in any intercollegiate contest who is found by the faculty to be delinquent in his studies.

8. All games shall be played on grounds either owned or under immediate control of one or both of the colleges participating in the contest, and all games shall be played under student management and not under the con-trol of any corporation or association or private individual.

9. The election of managers and captains of teams in each college shall be subject to the approval of its committee on athletics.

10. College teams shall not engage in games with professional teams, nor with those representing athletic clubs, so called.

11. Before every intercollegiate contest a list of the men proposing to play shall be presented by each team or teams to the other or others certifying that all members are entitled to play under the conditions of the rules adopt-ed, such certificate to be signed by the Registrar or Secretary of the col-lege or university. It shall be the duty of the captain to enforce this rule.

12. We call upon the expert managers of football teams to so revise the rules as to reduce the liability to injury to a minimum.

Source: University of Chicago Faculty of Arts, Literature, and Science, Minutes, October 1892 to February 1896, Minutes of Jan. 19, 1895, as presented to the faculty group by President Harper.

Table 4. Initiation of Physical Education Majors
at Intercollegiate Conference Universities

University	Year of Initiation
Illinois	1919
Indiana	1925
Iowa	about 1920
Michigan	1922
Minnesota	1922
Northwestern	1928
Ohio State	1923
Purdue	1929
Wisconsin	1910

Sources: Illinois, *Transactions of the Board of Trustees, July 17, 1918, to June 15, 1920* (Urbana), 314-16, Record Series 1/0/2, University of Illinois Archives; Indiana, C. E. Richardson (assistant registrar) to author, May 3, 1972; Iowa, Earl M. Rogers (assistant manuscripts librarian) to author, May 1, 1972; Michigan, Virginia B. Passon to author, May 10, 1972; Minnesota, Maxine B. Clapp (university archivist) to author, May 31, 1972; Northwestern, Devorah Howard (university archivist) to author, May 31, 1972; Ohio State, William J. Vollmar (university archivist) to author, May 8, 1972; Purdue, T. N. Gunderson (associate registrar) to author, May 11, 1972; Wisconsin, *University of Wisconsin Catalog* (Madison: University of Wisconsin Press, 1910), 474-81.

Table 5. Comparative Tuition Schedules at Selected Intercollegiate
Conference Universities[a]

	Resident Tuition	Non-Resident Tuition
1920–21		
Wisconsin	none	$154.00
Michigan	$ 80.00 (men)	105.00 (men)
	76.00 (women)	101.00 (women)
Indiana	10.50	30.00
Northwestern (private)	200.00	200.00
Chicago (private)	180.00	180.00
1930–31		
Wisconsin	none	200.00
Michigan	98.00	123.00
Indiana	65.00	100.00
Northwestern	300.00	300.00
Chicago	300.00	300.00
1935–36		
Wisconsin	none	200.00
Michigan	100.00	124.00
Indiana	77.00	112.00
Northwestern	300.00	300.00
Chicago	300.00	300.00

Sources: University of Wisconsin Catalogue, 1920-21, 65, *1930-31,* 15, and *1935-36,* 13-14;
Supplement to University Bulletin, new series, May 21, 1921, 115; *University of Michigan
Catalog, 1930-31,* 24, and *1935-36,* 25; *Indiana University Undergraduate Catalog, 1920-21,*
67, and *1935-36,* 97-98; *Northwestern University Bulletin,* Sept. 4, 1920, 76, Sept. 15, 1930,
20, and March 11, 1935, 29; University of Chicago, *Circular of Information* 20 (April 1920):
8, *Announcement,* March 15, 1930, 3, and March 15, 1935, 10.

a. Undergraduate tuition for one academic year for the colleges of arts and sciences and/
or their equivalents, discounting matriculation and other special fees.

Notes

Abbreviations Used in the Notes

(All in the Department of Special Collections, the University of Chicago Library except as noted.)

Hutchinson Papers	Papers of William T. Hutchinson
Nuveen Papers	Papers of John Nuveen
Stagg Papers	Papers of Amos Alonzo Stagg
Swift Papers	Papers of Harold Higgins Swift
UPP	University Presidents Papers
WRHP	Papers of William Rainey Harper
Minutes, BPC&A	Minutes, Board of Physical Culture and Athletics, Stagg Papers
Minutes, Intercollegiate Conference	Minutes, Intercollegiate Conference of Faculty Representatives, Jan. 11, 1895–June 6, 1913, Office of the Commissioner of the Intercollegiate Conference, Park Ridge, Illinois
Minutes, University Council	Minutes, University Council, 1903–1908
Minutes, University Senate	Minutes, University Senate, Aug. 13, 1902–Oct. 24, 1908

Introduction

1. It is remarkable that relatively few scholars have devoted primary research to intercollegiate football. David Riesman, Reuel Denney, and Frederick Rudolph were the first interpreters of this American institution. Riesman and Denney presented an anthropological-sociological interpretation of the transition of rugby to football, and Rudolph offered a historical description and brief analysis of why the sport became so popular on college campuses. Edwin Cady, John G. Blair, Ronald A. Smith, Michael Oriard, and Murray Sperber have made important published contributions since Rudolph's work in the 1960s, and Allen Guttmann, Donald Mrozek, William J. Baker, and Benjamin G. Rader have included football in their larger historical studies. Guy M. Lewis

and I investigated football directly in our dissertations, Patrick B. Miller, indi-
rectly. There remains, however, a surprising paucity of case studies from all
regions of the country, without which much of our general interpretive work
must remain tentative. And the sheer scale and variety of American high education means that perhaps we shall emerge with case studies of regional and
cultural "types" of intercollegiate football.

See David Riesman and Reuel Denney, "Football in America: A Study in
Culture Diffusion," *American Quarterly* 3 (1951): 309–25; Frederick Rudolph,
The American College and University: A History (New York: Vintage Books, 1962);
Edwin H. Cady, *The Big Game: College Sports and American Life* (Knoxville: Uni-
versity of Tennesssee Press, 1978); John G. Blair, "Football in America," *Mod-
ular America: Cross-Cultural Perspectives on the Emergence of an American Way* (West-
port: Greenwood Press, 1988), 81–94; Ronald A. Smith, *Sports and Freedom: The
Rise of Big-Time College Athletics* (New York: Oxford University Press, 1988);
Michael Oriard, *Reading Football: How the Popular Press Created an American Spectacle* (Chapel Hill: University of North Carolina Press, 1993); Murray Sperber,
Shake Down the Thunder: The Creation of Notre Dame Football (New York: Henry
Holt, 1993); Allen Guttmann, *From Ritual to Record: The Nature of Modern Sports*
(New York: Columbia University Press, 1978), esp. "The Fascination of Football," 117–36; Donald Mrozek, *Sport and American Mentality* (Knoxville: University of Tennessee Press, 1983); William J. Baker, "Varieties of Football," *Sports
in the Western World* (Urbana: University of Illinois Press,1988), 119–37; Benjamin G. Rader, "Intercollegiate Football Spectacles," *American Sports: From the
Age of Folk Games to the Age of Televised Sports,* 2d ed. (Englewood Cliffs: Prentice-Hall, 1990), 172–88; Guy M. Lewis, "The American Intercollegiate Football Spectacle, 1869–1917," Ph.D. diss., University of Maryland, 1965; Robin
Lester, "The Rise, Decline, and Fall of Intercollegiate Football at the University of Chicago, 1890–1940," Ph.D. diss., University of Chicago, 1974; Patrick
B. Miller, "Athletes in Academe: College Sports and American Culture, 1850–
1920," Ph.D. diss., University of California, 1987.

2. Rudolph, *The American College and University,* 349. Thorstein Veblen
coined the "captain of erudition" term after experiencing the early years of the
university as a young instructor, see *The Higher Learning in America: A Memorandum on the Conduct of Universities by Business Men* (New York: B. W. Huebsch,
1918) and David Riesman, "Scientists versus Captains of Erudition," 99–113,
in *Thorstein Veblen: A Critical Interpretation* (New York: Charles Scribner's Sons,
1953, 1960). For the early professorial appointments, see Richard J. Storr,
Harper's University: The Beginnings (Chicago: University of Chicago Press, 1966),
75, 82–83. Harper's recruitment of leading professors and his $7,000 salaries
for his "Head Professors" had the effect of moving the American professoriat
toward a national marketplace. See also James Bryce, *The American Common-
wealth* (New York: Macmillan, 1907), 672.

3. One thinker would perhaps have us reverse the Rockefeller to Harper
causal relationship. Burton Bledstein asserts that President Harper (and some
other leaders of higher education) "introduced businessmen to techniques of
corporate promotion and exploitation unfamiliar even in the commercial

world." The siting of the parties to this cultural lag promotes either admiration or dismay, depending upon one's viewpoint. *The Culture of Professionalism: The Middle Class and the Development of Higher Education in America* (New York: W. W. Norton, 1976), 289.

Prologue

1. Minutes, Board of Trustees, Sept. 18, 1890; Harper to Stagg, Oct. 21, 1890, A. A. Stagg folder, UPP, 1889–1925; Stagg to Harper, Nov. 25, 1890, box 14, folder 38, WRHP.

2. Samuel Harper wrote several lines each day in his annual leather-bound diary for many years, but he offered little information beyond the daytime temperature and a bare note of what he did that day. Two more entries within the fortnight note the infant's near death and recovery: July 25, "I attended store and the babe became overcome with heat—almost expired," and July 26, "I attended store—the babe well." Box 1, Samuel Harper Papers, Department of Special Collections, Joseph Regenstein Library, University of Chicago. In Thomas Wakefield Goodspeed, *William Rainey Harper* (Chicago: University of Chicago Press, 1928), 4–8, a photograph of his brother Samuel and William Rainey follows page 8. See also Francis W. Shepardson, "Biographical Sketch," *Biblical World* 27 (March 1906): 162.

3. Goodspeed, *William Rainey Harper,* 9–14; Shepardson, "Biographical Sketch," 162.

4. Goodspeed, *William Rainey Harper,* 12–23; Shephardson, "Biographical Sketch," 162.

5. Andrews later served as president of Brown University and chancellor of the University of Nebraska. Goodspeed, *William Rainey Harper,* 29–33; Shepardson, "Biographical Sketch," 163; E. Benjamin Andrews, "The Granville Period," *Biblical World* 27 (March 1906): 170 (Andrews's judgment at 168).

6. Andrews, "The Granville Period," 167–69; Goodspeed, *William Rainey Harper,* 35–36.

7. Ibid., 42–45; Eri B. Hulbert, "The Morgan Park Period," *Biblical World* 27 (March 1906): 171.

8. Goodspeed, *William Rainey Harper,* 50–52; Hulbert, "The Morgan Park Period," 173.

9. Goodspeed, *William Rainey Harper,* 173–75, 56–66.

10. Goodspeed, *William Rainey Harper,* 67–72, 88–97; Frank Knight Sanders, "The Yale Period," *Biblical World* 27 (March 1906): 177–81. For a summary of Harper's work at Chautauqua see Theodore Morrison, *Chautauqua* (Chicago: University of Chicago Press, 1974), 76–78, and John H. Vincent, *The Chautauqua Movement* (Boston: Chautauqua Press, 1886), 183–93. Cf. "Dr. Harper Banqueted," *Chautauqua Assembly Herald,* July 25, 1891, 4, as cited in James P. Wind, "The Bible and the University: The Messianic Vision of William Rainey Harper," Ph.D. diss., University of Chicago, 1983. Cf. Harper to Goodspeed, Oct. 13, 1888, box 1, folder 3, Thomas W. Goodspeed Papers, University of Chicago Archives, Joseph Regenstein Library. For a fuller record of President Dwight's unsuccessful attempt to hold Harper at Yale, see Thomas Wakefield Goodspeed,

A History of the University of Chicago (Chicago: University of Chicago Press, 1916), 104–17; on Harper's subsequent aid to Yale, see Arthur T. Hadley to Harper, July 5, 1905, box 36, folder 19, UPP, 1889–1925.

11. See the entire series of letters, Harper to Goodspeed and Rockefeller to Goodspeed, box 1, Thomas W. Goodspeed Papers, University of Chicago Archives, Joseph Regenstein Library, for the rapidly changing Rockefeller philanthropic landscape. Cf. Goodspeed, *William Rainey Harper,* 82–88, and Richard J. Storr, *Harper's University: The Beginnings* (Chicago: University of Chicago Press, 1966), 18–34.

12. Vincent spoke at a Harper memorial conference in 1937; he had served as dean under Harper, as president of the University of Minnesota, and as president of the Rockefeller Foundation. See "The Relationship of Mr. Rockefeller and President Harper," in *The William Rainey Harper Memorial Conference,* ed. Robert N. Montgomery (Chicago: University of Chicago Press, 1938), 129.

13. Storr, *Harper's University,* 57.

14. Elizabeth Wallace, *The Unending Journey* (Minneapolis: University of Minnesota Press, 1952), 82; *Annual Register, 1892–93* (Chicago: University of Chicago Press, 1893), 18, 42, 100.

15. Box 104, folder 2, Stagg Papers.

16. The Midway Plaisance is a wide city parkway located where the midway of the 1893 World's Columbian Exposition was; it has always run through the university's front yard.

17. William Rainey Harper, *Religion and the Higher Life: Talks to Students* (Chicago: University of Chicago Press, 1904), vii–viii.

18. Harper, *Religion and the Higher Life,* 132–36.

19. Ibid., 183–84.

20. Storr, *Harper's University,* 189.

21. William H. McNeill, *Hutchins' University* (Chicago: University of Chicago Press, 1991), 97.

22. Amos Alonzo Stagg, "as told to" Wesley Winans Stout, *Touchdown!* (New York: Longmans, Green and Co., 1927), 45. *Touchdown!* is Stagg's autobiography, and although it is heavily ghostwritten and uncritical, it is invaluable for its history of the development of intercollegiate football.

23. Stagg, *Touchdown!* 47–50.

24. Ibid., 50–51.

25. Ibid., 51.

26. Ibid., 52–53. Exeter and other independent boarding schools have long accepted "post-graduate" students after they have graduated from other, usually public, high schools. Most of the students are extraordinary athletes who compete for the boarding school while they work up their academic skills to prepare, as Stagg did, for college entrance.

27. Ibid., 72.

28. Ibid., 72.

29. Ibid., 77, 105; Skull and Bones Photo Album, Stagg Papers; *University Magazine* 3 (June 1890): 185, gives details of the club's functioning.

30. Stagg, *Touchdown!* 74–75, 79–80, 106–7; Parke H. Davis to Frank S.

Whiting, Dec. 18, 1930, box 54, folder 19, Stagg Papers; *New York Sun, Boston Herald,* June 1, 1890; cf. *Boston Globe,* June 1, 1890. Stagg's grades appear in the Yale College Student Grade Books (10 vols.), and the "Explanation of the Grading System Used in the Volumes," by Judith A. Schiff, indicates the students' comparative rank, Manuscripts and Archives, Yale University Library, Scrapbook, Yale Glee and Banjo Clubs, 1883–90, Stagg Papers, Manuscripts and Archives, Yale University Library; Scrapbook, 1886–1924, Stagg Papers.

31. *Young Men's Journal,* Scrapbook, Jan.–June 1890, Stagg Papers; Stagg quotation from *Touchdown!* 104, in which Kelly's language is no doubt softened. Compare the photographic use of Stagg as the model muscular Christian, much in the style of Thomas Eakins's anatomical studies in Philadelphia, and of his baseball exploits, Scrapbook, June–Dec. 1890, Stagg Papers.

32. Stagg, *Touchdown!* 105–6; box 24, folder 9, Stagg Papers.

33. When Stagg served as secretary, "enthusiasm in personal work and the starting of the Yale Mission were features of his term." See James B. Reynolds, S. H. Fisher, and H. B. Wright, *Two Centuries of Christian Activity at Yale* (New York: G. P. Putnam's Sons, 1901), vi, 233; Scrapbook, 1886–1924, Stagg Papers; Stagg, *Touchdown!* 110; Ralph Gabriel, *Religion and Learning at Yale* (New Haven: Yale University Press, 1958), 202; Lawrence K. Hall, *Doggett of Springfield* (Springfield: Springfield College, 1964), 94; Goodspeed, *William Rainey Harper,* 26, 73, 76; Statement by William Rainey Harper, Nov. 19, 1904, box 74, folder 4, UPP, 1925–45.

34. Caspar W. Whitney, "Amateur Sport," *Harper's Weekly,* Dec. 12, 1891; Stagg, *Touchdown!* 74–75, 110–12. Allison Danzig, *The History of American Football* (Englewood Cliffs: Prentice-Hall, 1956), 121–28, 499; Lewis, "American Intercollegiate Football Spectacle," 26–82; and Smith, *Sports and Freedom,* 84, 112–14, 147–48, put the Yale program in comparative perspective. For the national scene, see Rudolph, *The American College and University,* ch. 18, and Miller, "Athletes in Academe: College Sports and American Culture." The Yale captain was quoted in Walter Camp, *Football Facts and Figures: A Symposium of Expert Opinions on the Game's Place in American Athletics* (New York: Harper & Brothers, 1894), 5.

35. *Brooklyn Eagle,* Oct. 29, 1888 (this citation and many of the newspaper primary sources cited herein come from the Stagg Scrapbooks in the Stagg Papers).

36. Ibid., 114, 130–31; Stagg was listed as a "junior" (a first-year student in the M.Div. program; the second- and third-year students were, and are, referred to as "middlers" and "seniors"), Yale University Divinity School Registrar Detra J. MacDougall to author, undated letter, and interview, Nov. 6, 1992; *Sporting Times,* Nov. 4, 1888.

37. Rudolph, *The American College and University,* chs. 7, 18. Mrozek, *Sport and American Mentality,* and Dominick Cavallo, *Muscles and Morals: Organized Playgrounds and Urban Reform, 1880–1920* (Philadelphia: University of Pennsylvania Press, 1981) provide helpful surveys of American thinking and innovation during this period.

38. The establishment of frontier colleges was an integral part of the Con-

gregational and Presbyterian ideal of their religious enterprise in the West and allowed the faith to follow the moving frontier. Contrarily, Harvard was marked by an "absence of a missionary impulse," Rudolph, *The American College and University,* 131. The western professor's statement is in *Chicago Tribune,* Feb. 25, 1895. Parke H. Davis, *Football: The American Intercollegiate Game* (New York: Charles Scribner's Sons, 1911), 93, notes, "At one time in this period there might have been counted no less than 45 former players of Yale, 35 of Princeton, and 24 of Harvard actively engaged in teaching the science of the game." Unfortunately, Davis provides neither names nor colleges. A later undocumented claim for the period of the 1880s to World War II was that fifty-three Yale graduates became head coaches elsewhere; see John Durant and Les Etter, *Highlights of College Football* (New York: Hastings House, 1970), 72–73. I have found forty-four Princeton graduates, thirty-nine Yale graduates, and sixteen Harvard graduates who coached at other institutions, based upon other sources. See Lester, "The Rise, Decline, and Fall of Intercollegiate Football at the University of Chicago, 1890–1940," Appendix 1; Allen L. Sack, "The Commercialization and Rationalization of Intercollegiate Football: A Comparative Analysis of the Development of Football at Yale and Harvard in the Latter Nineteenth Century," Ph.D. diss., Pennsylvania State University, 1974, 119, 147–48; and John F. Rooney, Jr., *A Geography of American Sport* (Reading: Addison-Wesley, 1974), map 3.3. Yale graduates tended to go west to coach, and Princeton graduates went west and south; see Christy Walsh, ed., *Intercollegiate Football* (New York: Doubleday, Doran, 1934), 245–462.

39. For examples of press coverage of Stagg's work at Chautauqua and Northfield, see Scrapbook, June–Dec. 1890, Stagg Papers. Cf. *Chautauqua Assembly Herald,* July 22, 1892, for the report of another Stagg lecture, see Scrapbook, 1890, Miscellaneous, Stagg Papers. C. O. Gill and V. C. McCormick were among the Yale all-Americans who played and taught with Stagg at Northfield. Stagg, *Touchdown!* 130–31. See Gulick to Stagg, March 8, 1890, Scrapbook, Jan.–June 1890, Stagg Papers, regarding readings for the course work; for press coverage of Stagg's talks and sample posters announcing his lectures, see Scrapbook, 1886–1925, Stagg Papers. It was during one of Stagg's recruitment absences that Naismith invented basketball, ibid., 131; James Naismith, *Basketball: Its Origins and Development* (New York: Association Press, 1941), 27–28; and Bernice Larson Webb, *The Basketball Man: James Naismith* (Lawrence: University Press of Kansas, 1973), 38; See David I. Macleod, *Building Character in the American Boy: The Boy Scouts, YMCA, and Their Forerunners, 1870–1920* (Madison: University of Wisconsin Press, 1983) for a survey of the evolution of these ideas and actions. The Stagg quotation is from the *Chicago Tribune,* Sept. 20, 1893; other press notice of his evangelistic work appeared in the *Toronto Empire,* Dec. 8, 1888, *Minneapolis Times,* Sept. 25, 1892, and *University of Minnesota Daily,* Jan. 27, 1893.

40. The *New York Times,* Dec. 15, 1890, reported the spectators at the YMCA-Yale game "persisted" in calling Stagg's team "the Christians," and the *Times* simply called the YMCA team "Stagg." Tickets for the Amherst-YMCA college game at Springfield in 1890 were imprinted "Football. Stagg's Eleven vs.

Amherst." Scrapbook, June–Dec. 1890, Stagg Papers. Representative media praise for Stagg's coaching included *Harper's Weekly,* Oct. 24 and Nov. 21, 1891, *New Haven News,* Oct. 18, 1891, *Springfield Republican,* Oct. 15, Nov. 1, 1891.

41. Stagg, *Touchdown!* 46. Stagg was not unusual in stating Alger's "creed" without evidence from the author. Alger probably remains, with Harriet Beecher Stowe, the most famous unread author in American history. Luck and coincidence were as crucial to Alger's formula as his basic premise stated in his primary career-making book: "in this free country poverty in early life is no bar to a man's advancement." *Ragged Dick* (New York: Collier Books, 1962), 108. Alger mentions luck often in his explanation of success, for example, "'I was lucky,' said Dick, modestly. 'I found some good friends who helped me along.'" *Mark, the Match Boy* (New York: Collier Books, 1962), 236, and his incredible plot coincidences amount to much the same thing.

Chapter 1: Origins of Intercollegiate Football at the University of Chicago, 1890–94

1. Stagg, *Touchdown!* 143–44.

2. Stagg to Harper, Nov. 28, 1891, box 14, folder 38, WRHP. Stagg saved a newspaper story about his intention to desert Chicago for Yale's "better offer." See box 1, folder 23, Stagg Papers.

3. Ibid.; Harper to Stagg, Nov. 28, 1891, and Dec. 6, 1890, both in Stagg folder, UPP, 1889–1925.

4. Stagg to Harper, April 12, 1892, underscoring Stagg's, box 14, folder 38, WRHP.

5. The authorization to hire Stagg for the positions was granted Harper by action of the board, see Minutes, Board of Trustees, 1890–96, 26. He was also hired to serve as the resident "head of Snell House" and "receive for the service room rent, heat and light," ibid., 112. The authorization and specifics of the perquisites of the positions seem remarkably detailed for board attention, but no doubt the "heat" noted in the board minutes was profoundly appreciated by Stagg. When Stagg married, he was followed in Snell Hall by Robert Morss Lovett, ibid., 254. Stagg's positions are listed in *Annual Register, 1892–93* (Chicago: University of Chicago Press, 1893), 13; Cf. Rudolph, *The American College and University,* 391; Miller, "Athletes in Academe," 318; and Hal A. Lawson and Alan G. Ingham, "Conflicting Ideologies Concerning the University and Intercollegiate Athletics: Harper and Hutchins at Chicago, 1892–1940," *Journal of Sport History* 7 (Winter 1980): 41n22, on the precedential claims of Stagg's dual position.

6. Lewis, "American Intercollegiate Football Spectacle," ch. 6; Miller, "Athletes in Academe," chs. 2, 3; Smith, *Sports and Freedom,* 118–33; Storr, *Harper's University,* 105; Minutes, Board of Trustees, 1890–96, 96; *University Record,* July 3, 1896, 227.

7. The purposes of the Department were outlined in every *Annual Register* from 1892–93 through the first decade, with only a few changes of phrases during those years. On the Women's Department, see *President's Report, 1892–1902* (Chicago: University of Chicago Press, 1903), 336–68. On the larger is-

sue of women at Chicago, see Lynn Gordon, *Gender and Higher Education in the Progressive Era* (New Haven: Yale University Press, 1990), 85–120.

8. Harper to Stagg, Nov. 5, 1901, box 9, folder 4, Stagg Papers.

9. Gordon, *Gender and Higher Education*, 108.

10. Laughlin to Mrs. George Palmer, Aug. 9, 1896, and Laughlin to Herrick, Aug. 1, 1896, box 22, Robert Herrick Collection, Letters, University of Chicago Archives, Joseph Regenstein Library; *Chicago Post*, Oct. 29, 1892. One of Harper's old Baptist comrades in prying money loose from John D. Rockefeller, President Augustus H. Strong of the Rochester Theological Seminary, thought that Harper "was a born propagandist," in Strong's eulogy, *Biblical World* 27 (March 1906): 235. Harper was quoted in the *University of Chicago Weekly* [*UCW*], Jan. 3, 1895, 147.

11. Stagg to his family, Jan. 20, 1891, Stagg folder, UPP, 1889–1925.

12. *University of Chicago Weekly*, Jan. 3, 1895, 141.

13. *University Record*, July 3, 1896, 227.

14. Stagg to his family, Jan. 20, 1891, Stagg folder, UPP, 1889–1925.

15. Stagg to Harper, March 8, 1892, Stagg's emphasis, box 14, folder 38, WRHP.

16. Quoted in *Chicago Morning News Record*, Sept. 19, 1892; cf. the *Chicago Post*, Oct. 29, 1892, which stated the "goal" of the program, and the *Chicago Interocean*, Jan. 23, 1893.

17. Madeleine Wallin, "First Impressions of the University of Chicago," 2–3, Madeleine Wallin Papers, University of Chicago Archives, Joseph Regenstein Library.

18. Marion Talbot, *More than Lore: Reminiscences of Marion Talbot* (Chicago: University of Chicago Press, 1936), 24; Diary of Demia Butler, Oct. 8, 17, and 31, 1892, University of Chicago Archives, Joseph Regenstein Library; Wallace, *Unending Journey*, 81.

19. The description of Robertson is from the biblical scholar Edgar Goodspeed, who recalled Stagg asking him to chaperone a lunch Stagg had in his rooms at Snell Hall with Miss Robertson. Goodspeed, *As I Remember* (New York: Harper, 1953), 81. Stagg to Stella, Aug. 1894, A. A. Stagg Collection, Amos Alonzo Stagg High School, Palos Hills, Ill. The engagement announcement appeared in the *Boston Journal*, June 25, 1894. For a tribute to the remarkable Stella, see Allison Danzig, *Oh, How They Played the Game: The Early Days of Football and the Heroes Who Made It Great!* (New York: Macmillan, 1971), 49–50. At least one other professor, physicist Albert Michelson, married an undergraduate. Gordon, *Gender and Higher Education*, 113.

20. *Chicago Tribune*, Oct. 2, 1892; Wallin, "First Impressions," 2–3; cf. the description of another student who attended the mass meeting, Butler Diary, Oct. 4, 1892.

21. Eli Felsenthal to Stagg, Oct. 24, 1892, Scrapbooks, vol. 1, Stagg Papers; *UCW*, Oct. 8, 1892, 8; Stagg, *Touchdown!* 160–61. Stagg's claim as creator of the "Chica" yell appears to be contradicted by a letter from a Rockford, Illinois, student's parent who suggested the yell, see D. S. Clark to Stagg, Oct. 3, 1892, Scrapbook, vol. 1, Stagg Papers. The choice of maroon as the university color

and nickname was recorded in the minutes of the 1894 meeting conducted by Joseph Raycroft, Stagg's assistant, box 66, folder 16, UPP, 1889–1925; and see *Cap and Gown, 1906,* 285, on the university's C emblem. The final design of the *C* was done in 1898.

22. *UCW,* Oct. 8, 1892, 4; Butler Diary, Oct. 10, 1892; Stagg, *Touchdown!* 154–55. One of Stagg's most dependable players was A. R. E. Wyant, a Bucknell football star for four years. He lettered for Stagg another three years and on vacant Saturdays journeyed out to Coe College in Cedar Rapids, Iowa, to play for that school. Walsh, ed., *Intercollegiate Football,* 189; R. E. Streeter to author, Jan. 5, 1993; Stagg, *Touchdown!* 164. Cf. Harvard's seventy football candidates in 1892, *UCW,* Oct. 8, 1892, 8.

23. Stagg to his family, Oct. 9, 11, 23, 1892, Stagg folder, UPP, 1889–1925. See Appendix 1 for these scores and others. *University News,* Dec. 7, 1892, 2; Thomas Wakefield Goodspeed, *The Story of the University of Chicago, 1890–1925* (Chicago: University of Chicago Press, 1925), 110.

24. *Chicago Times,* Oct. 23, 1892; *Chicago Morning News Record,* Nov. 3, 1892; *Chicago Herald,* Nov. 6, 1892.

25. The game in Toledo paid Chicago $264, and expenses were $217; total receipts for the season of 1892 were $723.92, and the expenditures were $633.33. Athletics 1 folder, UPP, 1889–1925.

26. *Chicago Post,* Oct. 29, 1892.

27. *Chicago Times,* May 5, 1893; Goodspeed quoted in the *Chicago Herald,* Feb. 4, 1893.

28. Field to Harper, April 3, 1893, Scrapbook, vol. 1, Stagg Papers; Stagg, *Touchdown!* 168–69; *Chicago Times,* May 6, 1893; *Chicago Interocean,* May 6, 1893; *UCW,* Oct. 5, 1893, 6.

29. Laurence R. Veysey, *The Emergence of the American University* (Chicago: University of Chicago Press, 1965), 332.

30. *UCW,* Nov. 2, 1893, 5; *Chicago Herald* and *Chicago Interocean,* Oct. 26, 1893; *Chicago Interocean,* Oct. 29, Nov. 9, 12, 1893; *Chicago Tribune,* Oct. 5, 9, 1893; *Chicago Herald,* Nov. 12, 1893; *Chicago Tribune, Chicago Herald,* and *Chicago Record,* all Jan. 2, 1894. See Allan Nevins's critical remarks on the participation of Stagg, *Illinois* (New York: Oxford University Press, 1917), 202.

31. *Chicago Tribune,* Sept. 20, 1893; *UCW,* Dec. 13, 1893, 123.

32. *Chicago Record,* Oct. 9, 1893; *Chicago Interocean, Chicago Herald,* and *Chicago Tribune,* all Oct. 22, 1893; Francis Peabody Magoun, Jr., *History of Football from the Beginnings to 1871* (Bochum-Langendreer, Westphalia: Verlag Heinrich Poppinghaus O.H.-G., 1938), 74.

33. *UCW,* Dec. 13, 1893, 123.

34. Walter Camp, *Walter Camp's Book of College Sports* (New York: Century, 1893), 149; Davis, *Football,* 249–316, 359–443; John Tunis, *$port$: Heroics and Hysterics* (New York: John Day, 1928), 108; Sheldon Welch and Walter Camp, *Yale: Her Campus Classrooms, and Athletics* (Boston: L. C. Page, 1899), 527; Durant and Etter, *Highlights of College Football,* 51. For the rationale and origins of the "big game," see Cady, *The Big Game,* 3–74; Edwin H. Cady, "The Big Game Captures America," *New York Times,* Jan. 14, 1979; Smith, *Sports and Freedom,*

67–82; Steven A. Riess, *City Games: The Evolution of American Urban Society and the Rise of Sports* (Urbana: University of Illinois Press, 1989), 55–57; Oriard, *Reading Football*, 89–101.

35. *Chicago Times* and *Chicago Interocean,* Nov. 26, 1893; *Chicago Interocean,* Nov. 30, 1893.

36. *Chicago Tribune* and *Chicago Herald,* Dec. 1, 1893.

37. Stagg, *Touchdown!* 136–37; *Chicago Herald* and *Chicago Tribune,* Dec. 17, 1893; *Chicago Herald,* Dec. 31, 1893; *Chicago Tribune* and *Chicago Herald,* Jan. 2, 1894.

38. The team came from the 1894 autumn quarter enrollment of one thousand, 495 of whom were undergraduates, *UCW,* Jan. 3, 1895, 141; *Chicago Record* and *Chicago Herald,* Oct. 22, 1894; *Chicago Tribune,* Oct. 21, 1894; *Chicago Record,* Nov. 3, 1894. The team statistics are recorded in A. A. Stagg, handwritten roster, Scrapbook, vol. 1, Stagg Papers, and in *Chicago Times* and *Chicago Record,* Nov. 28, 1894. Comparatively, Northwestern's team weight average was 180 pounds, Michigan was 175 pounds, Stanford was 172 pounds, and the Reliance Athletic Club foe from San Francisco had a line with no one under six feet, and the lightest member weighed 187 pounds. *Chicago Record,* Nov. 24, 1894, *Chicago Journal,* Nov. 28, 1894, *Young Men's Era* and *Chicago Times,* Jan. 9, 1895. The quotation is from the *Salt Lake City Herald,* Jan. 4, 1895.

39. *Chicago Tribune, Chicago Interocean,* and *Chicago Times,* Nov. 4, 1894; *Chicago Herald* and *Chicago Record,* Nov. 5, 1894. See Nevins, *Illinois,* 202–3 for the development of bad blood in the Midwest.

40. *Chicago Times,* Oct. 6, 1894; *Chicago Post,* Oct. 19, 1894; *Chicago Herald* and *Chicago Tribune,* Nov. 25, 1894; *Chicago Tribune,* Oct. 18, Nov. 25, 1894; *Chicago Interocean, Chicago Times,* and *Chicago Herald,* Nov. 30, 1894.

41. For a superb discussion of this long-standing American condition, see Smith, *Sports and Freedom,* 213–18.

42. *Chicago Times* and *Chicago Record,* Dec. 11, 1894; Stagg quotation from *Touchdown!* 191; *UCW,* Dec. 13, 1894, 123; *Chicago Times* and *Chicago Record,* Dec. 11, 1894; *San Francisco Examiner,* Jan. 3, 1895; *UCW,* Dec. 10, 1894, 135.

43. *Chicago Record,* Dec. 19, 1894; *UCW,* Jan. 10, 1895, 159. The telegraphic correspondence is in Scrapbook, vol. 1, Stagg Papers. Cf. *South Bend* [Ind.] *Tribune,* Jan. 8, 1943, and *Time,* Nov. 23, 1931, 13.

44. *Chicago Herald,* December 2, 9, 17, 19, 1894; *Chicago Record,* December 12, 13, 14, 15, and 17, 1894; *Chicago Tribune,* December 16, 1894.

45. *Chicago Times,* Dec. 20, 1894; *Chicago Record,* Dec. 19, 1894. Cf. *Chicago Herald,* Dec. 20, 1894.

46. Stagg, *Touchdown!* 193–94; *Salt Lake City Tribune,* Dec. 24, 1894; *San Francisco Examiner,* Dec. 22, 25, 1894; *San Francisco Chronicle,* Dec. 25, 1894; *UCW,* Jan. 17, 1895, 168–69.

47. *San Francisco Morning Call,* Dec. 26, 1894; *Los Angeles Express,* Dec. 26, 1894; *San Francisco Examiner,* Dec. 25, 1894; *San Francisco Post,* Dec. 26, 1894.

48. *San Francisco Examiner,* Dec. 26, 1894; *San Francisco Chronicle* and *Chicago Interocean,* Dec. 26, 1894; *San Francisco Morning Call,* Dec. 26, 1894. The *Chicago Tribune* did not mention the Chicago player's bellicosity, but the *New York Her-*

ald on Dec. 26, 1894 headlined "Football and Fisticuffs" and termed it a "sensational scene." Curiously, the *Philadelphia Public Ledger* stated, "The game was free from rough play," and the *Washington Post*, Dec. 26, 1894, probably rewriting the same telegraphic report, agreed. On Hering, Notre Dame's first important coach, see Sperber, *Shake Down the Thunder*, 12, and Jerry Brondfield, *Rockne: The Coach, the Man, the Legend* (New York: Random House, 1976), 51.

49. *Los Angeles Herald* and *Los Angeles Times*, Dec. 28, 29, 1894; *Los Angeles Express*, Dec. 27, 28, 1894; *San Francisco Examiner*, Jan. 1, 1895; telegrams, Departmental Correspondence, 1890–1932, California Trip, 1894, Stagg Papers; Camp, *Football Facts*, 39. The conflicting reports were in the *San Francisco Morning Call*, *San Francisco Examiner*, *Chicago Interocean*, and *Chicago Herald*, all Jan. 2, 1895.

50. *Chicago Tribune*, Jan. 5, 1895; *Laramie Daily Boomerang*, Jan. 5, 1895; Scrapbook, vol. 1, Stagg Papers; Memorabilia Section, Stagg Papers.

51. The inter-regional claim occurs in John Tunis, *The American Way in Sport* (New York: Duell, Sloane, and Pearce, 1958), 52; *Quarterly Calendar* 3 (Feb. 1895): 1–3.

52. See "The Future of Football," *The Nation*, Nov. 20, 1890, 395, for a direct application of the values of the business world to football. Mrozek, *Sport and American Mentality*, 246–47. Robert H. Wiebe's *The Search for Order, 1877–1920* (New York: Hill and Wang, 1967) provides a helpful framework for the rise of the modern university and its accoutrements such as intercollegiate football—they developed graphically within Wiebe's "continuity and regularity, functionality and rationality, administration and management."

53. Stagg to Camp, March 14, 1894, also see March 24, 1894, box 23, Correspondence, Walter Camp Papers, Manuscripts and Archives, Yale University Library; also quoted in Camp, *Football Facts*, 26–127.

54. John H. Finley quoted in Elizabeth Donnan and Leo F. Stock, eds., *An Historian's World: Selections from the Correspondence of John Franklin Jameson* (Philadelphia: American Philosophical Society, 1956), 5.

Chapter 2: The Rise of the Spectator, the Coach, and the Player, 1895–1905

1. This chapter demonstrates the factors of modern sport at the collegiate level that Allen Guttmann defined and argued in *From Ritual to Record*. Guttmann posited secularism, equality, specialization, rationalization, bureaucratization, quantification, and the keeping of records as the elements that characterize modern sport. And he applied his proposition to American sport in *A Whole New Ball Game: An Interpretation of American Sports* (Chapel Hill: University of North Carolina Press, 1988). His discussion of the intercollegiate form is especially helpful.

2. On the evolution of a community of participants into a community divided into watchers and the watched, see Daniel J. Boorstin, *The Creators* (New York: Random House, 1992), 206–13, and Allen Guttmann's survey and interpretation of the centuries and the literature, *Sports Spectators* (New York: Columbia University Press, 1986).

3. Stagg, *Touchdown!* 203; also, Stagg to "Dr. Goodspeed," no date, which described (Thomas) Goodspeed's half-time talk to the boys as well as Harper's, box 24, folder 24, Stagg Papers.

4. Frank Luther Mott, *American Journalism: A History of Newspapers in the United States through 250 years, 1690–1940* (New York: Macmillan, 1941), 579, 443; Lewis, "American Intercollegiate Football Spectacle," 117–18, and 124–28, for the expansion of periodicals due to greatly expanded advertising and favorable postal laws; and Oriard, *Reading Football*, 62–85, 274–76.

5. *Chicago Daily News*, Nov. 29, 1902. The program, menus and guest list are affixed to Scrapbook, vol. 28, Stagg Papers. Cf. *Chicago Chronicle* and *Chicago Journal*, Nov. 29, 1902.

6. *Chicago American*, Oct. 16, 1902, Dec. 1, 1902; Stagg, *Touchdown!* 173–74. Edwin Cady delineated the game constituencies in *The Big Game*, 11–12.

7. Milton Mayer, "Portrait of a Dangerous Man," *Harper's Magazine* 193 (July 1946): 60.

8. "Thanksgiving Day Songs and Cheers," Scrapbook, vol. 3, 118, Stagg Papers; Scrapbook, vol. 34, Stagg Papers: loose pamphlet. The additional stanza appeared in *University of Chicago Songs* (Chicago: University of Chicago Press, "Published by the Glee Club," 1897), 4–5.

9. *Minneapolis Tribune*, Oct. 13, Nov. 4, 1900. The Rockefeller song appeared as a leading composition in the university song book until 1920, when it was demoted to appear as the eleventh song. It was finally dropped in 1921.

10. "Thanksgiving Day Songs and Cheers," Scrapbook, vol. 3, Stagg Papers. Cf. the student description of Rockefeller in the yearbook, *Cap and Gown, 1895*, dedicated to him.

11. John J. MacAloon, *The Great Symbol* (Chicago: University of Chicago Press, 1981); "Football Mass Meeting," Scrapbook, vol. 33, between pages 64 and 65, Stagg Papers; *Chicago Tribune, Chicago Interocean*, and *Chicago Record-Herald*, all Nov. 25, 1903.

12. *Chicago Interocean*, Oct. 8, 1902; *Chicago Record-Herald*, Nov. 21, 1902; G. Stanley Hall, "Student Customs," *Proceedings of the American Antiquarian Society* 14 (1900): 119, quoted in Rudolph, *The American College and University*, 393.

13. *Chicago Chronicle*, Nov. 17, 1902; *Chicago Tribune*, Nov. 18, 1902. The persuasive Wayman served as captain of the women's basketball team at Chicago and as assistant instructor in the women's gymnasium at the University Settlement House, where she conducted a gymnasium class for "the children of the stockyards district," *Chicago Chronicle*, Nov. 18, 1902; *Chicago Tribune*, Nov. 24, 1903. The students were segregated by sex at the rallies, with the men in the choicest seats. On the changing and contradictory attitudes toward women as football supporters, see Gordon, *Gender and Higher Education*, 118. Chicago women outperformed their male classmates in the one realm in which they were permitted to compete equally—the classroom. Women made up 56.3 percent of the Phi Beta Kappa chapter, even with a smaller total enrollment. Ibid., 112.

14. *Chicago Chronicle, Chicago Record-Herald*, and *Chicago Record-Herald*, all Nov. 18, 1902.

15. *Chicago Tribune* and *Chicago Interocean,* Nov. 25, 1903; *University Record* 8 (Nov. 1903): 201.

16. *Chicago Times-Herald,* Dec. 4, 1896; *Chicago Record-Herald,* Nov. 3, 1903; Invitation, Scrapbook, vol. 33, Stagg Papers.

17. *Chicago Tribune,* Nov. 28, 1896.

18. *Chicago Times-Herald,* Dec. 2, 1899; Wallace, *Unending Journey,* 93, describes Laughlin; *Chicago Daily News,* Dec. 2, 1899.

19. *Alumni Directory, the University of Chicago, 1861–1910* (Chicago: University of Chicago Press, 1910), ix.

20. *University Record,* Nov. 10, 1899, 191; *Chicago Tribune,* Nov. 20, 1902; *Chicago American,* Nov. 23, 1902; *Chicago Record-Herald,* Nov. 21, 25, 1902.

21. *Minneapolis Tribune,* Oct. 12, 1900; *Chicago Record-Herald,* Nov. 27, 1903; *Chicago Tribune,* Nov. 13, 1904; *Twelfth Census of the United States* (Washington: Census Office, 1901), 1:455. Total football receipts had exceeded expenses by about $41,000 from 1892 to 1902, see *The President's Report, 1892–1902,* 365–66; *Chicago American,* Nov. 26, Dec. 1, 1902; *Chicago Interocean,* Dec. 25, 1902; *Chicago Record-Herald,* Jan. 17, 1904; Financial Statements, box 11, folder 3, and Department Financial Reports, boxes 21 and 22, in Stagg Papers.

22. Harper to Stagg, Nov. 22, Nov. 23, 1897, box 9, folder 2, Stagg Papers.

23. Harper to Stagg, July 27, June 6, June 24, Aug. 1, 1895, and Stagg to Harper, July 11, 1896, box 9, folder 1, Stagg Papers; Harper to Stagg, June 1, June 15, 1897, box 9, folder 2, Stagg Papers. Spencer Dickson, as early as 1896–97, Dismond, and Cecil Lewis ran the 440-yard dash for Stagg, see Arthur R. Ashe, Jr., *A Hard Road to Glory* (New York: Warner Books, 1988), 63–66.

24. Stagg to Harper, March 24, 1896, Athletics folder 1, UPP, 1889–1925, Stagg's emphasis. Contrast Stagg's views and actions here with the following statement: "Because Stagg considered his department similar to the other departments of the University, he believed that all funds received and disbursed by his department should be put in the keeping of the regular business officer of the University." Kooman Boycheff, "Intercollegiate Athletics and Physical Education at the University of Chicago, 1892–1952," Ph.D. diss., University of Michigan, 1954, 22–23. Boycheff cites only a speech Stagg gave in 1923; he cites nothing from Stagg's long administrative career.

25. Harper to Stagg, July 31, 1905, Stagg to Harper, Aug. 8, 1905, A. A. Stagg folder, WRHP.

26. Butterworth to Stagg, July 22, 23, 1895, box 11, Stagg Papers; Stagg to Harper, July 25, 1895, Athletics 1 folder, UPP, 1889–1925.

27. Adams to Harper, July 16, 1898, and accompanying memoranda, Francis W. Shepardson to J. C. Elson, June 15, 1898, Stagg to Harper, Aug. 8, 1898, all in Athletics 5 folder, UPP, 1889–1925.

28. Raymond E. Callahan, *Education and the Cult of Efficiency* (Chicago: University of Chicago Press, 1962); see Rudolph, *The American College and University,* 389–92, for the context of the rise of the coach; and Smith, *Sports and Freedom,* ch. 11. Samuel Haber, *The Quest for Authority and Honor in the American Professions, 1750–1900* (Chicago: University of Chicago Press, 1991), 280, 283–84, indicates the promise of such inquiry for the coach. See also T. J. Jackson

Lears, *No Place of Grace: Antimodernism and the Transformation of American Culture, 1880–1920* (New York: Pantheon, 1981).

29. *Chicago American,* Jan. 4, 1903; Camp quoted in the *Chicago Journal,* Dec. 4, 1903.

30. *Chicago Chronicle,* Dec. 21, 1902; *Chicago Daily News,* Sept. 26, 1900. Research in English-language newspapers published in Chicago when Stagg lived in the city—1892–1933—indicates that his name was noted more often in the news columns during the entire forty-year period than any other.

31. Stagg and H. L. Williams, *A Scientific and Practical Treatise on American Football for Schools and Colleges* (New Haven: Case and Lockwood, 1893; New York: D. Appleton, 1894); Henry L. Williams to Stagg, May 7, 1927, box 7, folder 8, Stagg Papers. The book's publication was announced by *New York World,* Oct. 21, 1894, *New York Times,* Oct. 27, 1894, and *New York Tribune,* Oct. 28, 1894; also, *Hartford Courant,* Nov. 16, 1894, *Philadelphia Press,* Nov. 17, 1894, and *Boston Advertiser,* Nov. 21, 1894; *Chicago Tribune, Chicago Journal, Chicago Post, Chicago Daily News,* and *Chicago Chronicle,* all March 19, 1904; *Touchdown!* 209.

32. Durant and Etter, *Highlights of College Football,* 81, 79–81. Pennsylvania won, 23-11. On Herschberger, see Walsh, ed., *Intercollegiate Football,* 17. Chicago beat Texas, 68-0, *Chicago News, Chicago Interocean,* and *Chicago Record-Herald,* Nov. 6, 1904. Texas had played Kansas in 1901, see Walsh, ed., *Intercollegiate Football,* 463.

33. *Chicago Interocean,* Nov. 13, 1904; *Chicago American,* Oct. 31, 1905; *Chicago Tribune,* Nov. 5, 1905.

34. *Chicago Record-Herald, Chicago Journal, Chicago Tribune,* and *Chicago Chronicle,* all Nov. 3, 1903. Stagg's statement appeared in *Touchdown!* 301–2.

35. *Chicago Times-Herald,* Oct. 15, 1897; *Harper's Weekly,* Dec. 2 1905, 1731.

36. *Chicago Chronicle,* Aug. 19, 1900; *Chicago Tribune,* Aug. 26, 1900; *Literary Digest,* Nov. 30, 1895, 128.

37. *Chicago Tribune,* Dec. 18, 1902; Stagg, *Touchdown!* 290–93.

38. See Appendix 2, Table 1; Stagg, *Touchdown!* 238, 248; *Chicago Chronicle,* Nov. 18, 1896, *Chicago Journal,* Nov. 29, 1905, and *Chicago Tribune,* Nov. 21, 1897, all in box 38, 1898 Football Practice folder, Stagg Papers; *Chicago Times-Herald,* Nov. 29, 1900; *Chicago Record-Herald,* Nov. 27, 1902; *Chicago Interocean,* Nov. 12, 1904; *Chicago Journal,* Nov. 16, 1905; *Chicago Tribune,* Dec. 3, 7, 1902; *Chicago American,* Dec. 4, 5, 1902.

39. Minutes, BPC&A, Nov. 2, 1901; see also May 24, May 30, 1902.

40. Minutes, BPC&A, May 30, 1902; *Annual Register, 1901–1902* 1 (July 1902): 166–77; *Chicago Tribune,* Nov. 26, 1902.

41. Minutes, BPC&A, May 30, 1902; *Chicago Daily News, Chicago Tribune,* June 3, 1902; *Chicago Interocean,* June 2, 1902; *Chicago American,* June 6, 1902; on the meet itself, see *Chicago American* and *Chicago Record-Herald,* June 7, 1902, and *Chicago American, Chicago Record-Herald,* and *Chicago Tribune,* June 8, 1902.

42. *Chicago Record,* Sept. 3, 1900; *Chicago American, Chicago Interocean, Chicago Record-Herald,* and *Chicago Tribune,* Nov. 26, 1902; Stagg, *Touchdown!* 180–81.

43. *Chicago Interocean,* Sept. 27, Oct. 8, 1902; *Chicago Tribune,* Oct. 12, 1902;

Cap and Gown, 1903 8 (1903): 191; *Chicago Tribune* and *Chicago Interocean,* Sept. 22, 1902; *Chicago Record-Herald,* Oct. 1, 1902, Aug. 23, 1903; *Chicago American,* Sept. 29, 1902, July 31, Aug. 17, Aug. 24, 1903; *Chicago Examiner,* Sept. 11, 1903; *Chicago Daily News,* Aug. 31, Sept. 1, 1903, July 9, 1904.

44. *Chicago Post, Chicago Record-Herald, Chicago American, Chicago Interocean,* and *Chicago Examiner,* July 12, 1904; *Chicago Journal, Chicago Interocean,* July 13, 1904.

45. Harper quoted in *Chicago Examiner,* Jan. 30, 1904.

46. *Chicago Examiner, Chicago Tribune,* June 1, 1903; *Chicago Daily News,* June 2, 1903.

47. *Chicago Daily News,* July 21, 1903; *Chicago Chronicle,* July 22, Nov. 26, 1903; *Chicago Daily News, Chicago Post,* Sept. 1, 1903; *Chicago Tribune,* Sept. 13, 1903, Nov. 30, 1905; *Chicago Journal,* Sept. 15, 1903; *Chicago Record-Herald,* Nov. 26, 1903; Robin Lester, "Fielding Harris Yost," *Dictionary of American Biography,* Supplement 4 (New York: Charles Scribner's Sons, 1974), 917–18. Jordan's speech is in *Proceedings of the Eighth Annual Meeting of the North Central Association of Colleges and Secondary Schools* (Ann Arbor, 1903), 150–51.

48. Henry M. Bates in *Chicago Record-Herald,* Dec. 28, 1902. The player drawing idea was in *Chicago Interocean,* Sept. 26, 1902. For a discussion of the problems of eligibility and common standards among schools in Boston, see Stephen Hardy, *How Boston Played: Sport, Recreation, and Community* (Boston: Northeastern University Press, 1982), 113–23; for the national scene, M. K. Gordon, "Reform of School Athletics," *Century* 57 (Jan. 1910): 469–71, and A. E. Stearns, "Athletics and the School," *Atlantic Monthly* 113 (Feb. 1914): 145–48.

49. *Alumni Directory of the University of Chicago, 1861–1906* (Chicago: University of Chicago Press, 1906), 75; Cooley to Harper, May 31, 1901, box 9, folder 5, UPP, 1889–1925. The two met for lunch almost monthly, see Harper to Cooley, Aug. 8, 1902, Sept. 22, 30, 1903, box 9, folder 5, UPP, 1889–1925. Cooley quoted in *Chicago Interocean,* Nov. 19, 1903. Cf. *Chicago Record-Herald,* Nov. 18, 1903.

50. Cooley et al., letter, Nov. 25, 1903, Athletics 6 folder, UPP, 1889–1925; *Chicago Record-Herald,* Nov. 28, 1903. The *Chicago Chronicle, Chicago Examiner, Chicago Tribune,* and *Chicago Daily News* all noted on Nov. 28, 1903, that the faculty representatives admitted privately that the complaints were well founded.

51. Edwin G. Cooley et al. to the President and Faculty, the University of Chicago, Jan. 27, 1904, Athletics 6 folder, UPP, 1889–1925. The letter took note of the "interest taken by the University of Wisconsin, which has sent a committee from its faculty for conference; and the University of Illinois, which has expressed its sympathy with the movement," p. 5. William Rainey Harper to Edwin G. Cooley, April 6, 1904, Athletics 6 folder, UPP, 1889–1925.

52. Charles R. Van Hise to William Rainey Harper, Sept. 27, Oct. 11, 1904, Athletics 6 folder, UPP, 1889–1925; Harper to Van Hise, Oct. 11, 14, 1904, Athletics 2 folder, UPP, 1889–1925.

53. Minutes, BPC&A, Oct. 29, Nov. 23, 1904.

54. *Chicago Tribune, Chicago Daily News,* and *Chicago Record-Herald,* Sept. 18, 1902; *Chicago Interocean, Chicago American, Chicago Record-Herald,* and *Chicago Tribune,* Sept. 22, 1902; *Chicago Interocean,* Sept. 25, 26, 1902; *Chicago Journal, Chicago Tribune,* Sept. 14, 1904; *Chicago American, Chicago Examiner, Chicago Tribune,* and *Chicago Daily News,* Sept. 15, 1904.

55. *Chicago Record-Herald,* Dec. 6, 1903; *Chicago Daily News,* Sept. 13, 1904; *Chicago Journal,* Sept. 26, 1905; *Chicago Chronicle, Chicago Record-Herald,* and *Chicago Interocean,* Oct. 6, 1905. Steffen was named captain of the Maroon freshman team of 1905, *Cap and Gown, 1906* 11 (1906): 249; Steffen's father was quoted in *Chicago Tribune,* Oct. 10, 1905; Steffen and Vanderboom quoted in *Chicago Tribune,* Oct. 11, 1905; *Chicago Record-Herald* and *Chicago Examiner,* Oct. 10, 1905. For the day-by-day account of the "kidnapped Maroon," see *Chicago Chronicle, Chicago Tribune, Chicago Record-Herald, Chicago Daily News,* and *Chicago American,* Oct. 9, 1905; *Chicago Post, Chicago Tribune, Chicago Interocean, Chicago Examiner, Chicago Record-Herald, Chicago Journal,* and *Chicago Chronicle,* Oct. 10, 1905; *Chicago Tribune* and *Chicago Interocean,* Oct. 11, 1905; and *Chicago Record-Herald,* Oct. 12, 1905.

56. For example, ranking by grades alone did not occur at Harvard until 1869; see Rudolph, *The American College and University,* 329–48. David Riesman first suggested to me that the twentieth century's athletic meritocracy was simply the latest in a series of such meritocracies in American higher education history.

57. Goodspeed quoted in *Chicago Record,* Nov. 28, 1896, after a victory over Michigan. Stagg later termed Goodspeed, "perhaps our most enthusiastic rooter." *Touchdown!* 226.

58. *Chicago Record,* July 19, 1900; *Chicago Tribune,* July 29, Sept. 8, 1900; *Chicago Times-Herald,* Aug. 6, 1900; *Chicago Chronicle,* Aug. 13, 30, 1900; *Chicago Record* and *Chicago Tribune,* Sept. 11, 1900. On Thatcher, see Stagg, *Touchdown!* 277; *Annual Register, 1892–1893* (Chicago: University Press of Chicago, 1893), 14, 36, 43; *Chicago Times-Herald,* Sept. 7, 1900. Thatcher's self-congratulatory letter to Stagg, Oct. 29, 1913, is in box 104, folder 2, Stagg Papers.

59. *Chicago Record-Herald,* Nov. 12, 1903; Telegram, George E. Vincent to A. A. Stagg, Nov. 13, 1903, Scrapbook, vol. 33, Stagg Papers.

60. Minutes, BPC&A, Oct. 3, Dec. 5, 1896, Oct. 23, 1902, Oct. 9, 1901; *Chicago Interocean,* Oct. 3, 1902; *Chicago Record-Herald,* Nov. 21, 1902.

61. See the report of James Hayden Tufts, dean of the Senior Colleges, in *The President's Report, 1892–1902,* 75–77; Minutes, BPC&A, Nov. 28, 1903, report attached, 1–2; "Autumn Quarter, 1903; Records of Members of the Football Team," report filed by Alonzo K. Parker, university recorder, ibid., Jan. 21, 1904.

62. Wallace, *Unending Journey,* 83.

63. Stagg to Harper, Jan. 3, 1898, box 9, folder 3, Stagg Papers.

64. Stagg, *Touchdown!* 214–15; the extended quotation is from Stagg to Harper, Nov. 30, 1904, Gifts file, UPP, 1889–1925; cf. Minutes, Board of Trustees, May 18, 1908 and *University Record* 9 (Jan. 1905): 292.

65. The earliest training table hardly stirred the salivary glands of the team:

oatmeal and water were included at every meal, and eggs were eaten twice each day. *UCW,* Oct. 5, 1893, 2; *Chicago Tribune,* Oct. 18, 1894; *Chicago Chronicle,* Sept. 17, 1896, Sept. 5, 1897, Nov. 25, 1902; *Chicago Tribune,* Sept. 6, 1897; *Chicago Record* and *Chicago Times-Herald,* Sept. 10, 1897; *Monthly Maroon* 1 (Nov. 1903): 1–8; *Chicago American,* Sept. 29, 1902; *Chicago Chronicle* and *Chicago Interocean,* Sept. 22, 1902; *Chicago Record-Herald,* Oct. 1, 1902. The Training folder, Department Historical File, Stagg Papers, and the *Chicago Times-Herald* and *Chicago Tribune,* May 31, 1897, tell of Stagg's strict enforcement of the rules banning tobacco.

66. Note the lack of any critical discussion regarding the training quarters in Minutes, BPC&A, Oct. 3, 1896. Advisory Committee of the Men's Commons to the Athletic Department of the University of Chicago and the Faculty Committee on the Men's Commons, Nov. 23, 1904, p. 2, box 15, folder 7, UPP, 1889–1925.

67. *Chicago American,* Sept. 4, 1903; Minutes, BPC&A, Nov. 14, 1901; Harper to Stagg, Oct. 14, 1902, A. A. Stagg folder, WRHP; Harper to "Mr Allen" (Philip S. Allen), Oct. 23, 1902, Athletics 1 folder, UPP, 1889–1925. The emotional diagnosis was headlined by the *Chicago Examiner,* Oct. 24, 1905, and *Chicago Record-Herald,* Oct. 24, 1905. *Chicago Tribune,* Nov. 27, 1905.

68. *Chicago Post,* Dec. 8, 1902; *Chicago American,* Dec. 9, 1902; *Chicago Tribune,* Dec. 10, 1902; *Chicago Record-Herald, Chicago American, Chicago Chronicle, Chicago Tribune,* and *Chicago Interocean,* Dec. 11, 1902; box 38, Football Practice 1898 folder, Stagg Papers. See the *Cap and Gown, 1907,* 229, for the list of captains and the University of Chicago convocation programs, Convocations 19, 29, 34, 38, 51, and 55, University of Chicago Archives. Harper's statement is in Minutes, University Council, 1903–1908.

69. *Chicago Tribune,* Dec. 2, 1902; *Chicago Post,* Dec. 3, 1902. A theater visit by the team in 1905 was responsible for selling out Louis Sullivan's Auditorium Theatre, *Chicago Record-Herald,* Oct. 29, 1905. Professor Thatcher, "Chicago rooter extraordinary," was a frequent chaperone, *Chicago Tribune,* Dec. 1, 1905. *Chicago Record-Herald,* Oct. 29, 1905; *Chicago Tribune* and *Chicago Record-Herald,* Nov. 2, 1905; *Monthly Maroon* 2 (Nov. 1903): 5.

70. *Chicago Interocean,* Feb. 24, 1904; *Chicago Tribune* and *Chicago Record-Herald,* March 8, 1903; *Chicago Interocean* and *Chicago Examiner,* March 9, 1903; *Chicago Tribune,* March 10, 1903; *Chicago Examiner, Chicago Chronicle, Chicago Interocean,* and *Chicago American,* Feb. 27, 1904. President Theodore Roosevelt complained over a similar matter to President Eliot of Harvard on July 10, 1908: "The action of the faculty has convinced the students that it was because a member of the crew committed the misdeed that the punishment was made heavy." In *The Letters of Theodore Roosevelt,* ed. Elting Morison (Cambridge: Harvard University Press, 1951), 5:1, 119.

71. The list of "All-Time All Americans" selected by the Football Writers Association of America in honor of the centennial of American football in 1969 included Eckersall at quarterback. Durant and Etter, *Highlights of College Football,* 207; John McCallum and Charles H. Pearson, *College Football U.S.A.: 1869–1972* (New York: McGraw-Hill, 1972), 539–43.

72. *Chicago American,* Nov. 23, 1906.

73. Walter Eckersall, "My Twenty-Five Years of Football," *Liberty,* Oct. 23, 1926, 59–62; Brondfield, *Rockne,* 40. Cf. the undocumented, unpaginated panegyric by James Peterson, *Eckersall of Chicago* (Chicago: Hinckley and Schmitt, 1957).

74. *Chicago American,* June 3, 1903, Nov. 23, 1906; Eckersall, "My Twenty-Five Years of Football," 59–62. William V. Morgenstern, long-time University of Chicago sports information and public affairs officer, recalled that Stagg admitted literally taking Eckersall from the Englewood station platform in Chicago as he was waiting for the Ann Arbor train. Oral interview, Aug. 3, 1972. Less than three years later the A.A.U. abrogated its suspension of Eckersall without comment, see *Chicago Tribune,* Nov. 21, 1905; also see box 78, folder 1, Stagg Papers, for undated newspaper clippings and a denial by Stagg that Eckersall received tuition, room, board, and a clerical job for choosing Chicago over Michigan. Cf. Stagg to M. W. Sampson, June 30, 1904, and notorized denials by Eckersall and his parents, Walter and Minnie Eckersall, box 78, folder 1, Stagg Papers. An earlier eligibility controversy in 1898 included the use of Pinkerton detectives to check on athletes, see box 78, folder 4, Stagg Papers.

75. *Chicago American,* Aug. 25, 1904.

76. T. W. Linn, "The Football Season of 1904," *Cap and Gown, 1905* 10 (1905): 177. Eckersall's response to the new play is in box 16, folder 10 and box 24, folder 3, Stagg Papers. The 1904 Michigan game was significant for its injuries. Of the starting Chicago backfield, Eckersall alone remained on the field after twenty minutes of play. Stagg, *Touchdown!* 243–44. Vincent quoted in *The Daily Maroon,* Nov. 24, 1906, 4; Stagg's testimony is in Memorandum, March 25, 1930, box 16, folder 10, Stagg Papers.

77. Walsh, ed., *Intercollegiate Football,* 191. Cf. these headlines from Nov. 1, 1903: "Eckersall Wins for Stagg's Men," *Milwaukee Sentinel;* "Eckersall Wins for Stagg," *Chicago Chronicle;* "Eckersall Gives Chicago Victory," *Chicago Record-Herald;* and "Eckersall Kicks Himself into Glory," *Chicago American,* Nov. 1903. And Eckersall continued to haunt Wisconsin; his 105-yard kickoff return against Wisconsin in 1904, as related by teammate Leo DeTray, is in box 24, folder 3, Stagg Papers.

78. *Chicago Tribune,* Dec. 1, 1905.

79. *Collier's,* Nov. 11, 1905. In his first quarter he was given no academic credit for his two courses, both of them introductory: Political Science I (civil government in the United States) and English I (rhetoric and English composition), although the former could be taken over in order to obtain credit. Eckersall tied for the lowest-ranking student and led in absences, with fifteen in his class of thirty students in civil government. *Instructors' Reports* [IR], autumn quarter 1903, University of Chicago Archives, report of Charles E. Merriam, Civil Government, no. 1. Eckersall was the lowest-ranking student of forty-nine and led in absences (twenty) in his class of rhetoric and English composition. Report of Percy H. Boynton, English Composition, no. 1, *Instructors' Reports,* autumn quarter 1903. Cf. the unusual inclusion of the report, "Au-

tumn Quarter, 1903. Records of Members of the Football Team," filed by Alonzo K. Parker, University Recorder, Minutes, BPC&A, Jan. 21, 1904. Merriam quoted in *IR*, winter quarter, 1904, Report of C. E. Merriam, Municipal Government, no. 23. Cf. the course description and course numbers, both of which are ambiguous, in the *Annual Register, 1903–04*, 227; *IR*, winter quarter, 1904, Report of Percy H. Boynton, English Composition, no. 1. Cf. the course description in *Annual Register, 1903–04*, 305. *Chicago Tribune, Chicago Interocean*, Jan. 31, 1904, *Cap and Gown, 1904*, 224, 228, for records of the freshman meet participation; Minutes, BPC&A, Feb. 27, 1904; for the University Council inquiry, Minutes, University Council, 1903–1908, Feb. 6, April 2, 1904.

80. *Annual Register, 1903–04*, 228–30; report of Oliver J. Thatcher, The Renaissance Age, no. 9, *IR*, spring quarter, 1904. Eckersall found it possible, during his years at the university, to take all four of the courses that were taught most frequently by the understanding Professor Thatcher. One is tempted to wonder if the "gentleman's C" at Harvard had been translated into an "athlete's C" at Chicago. Of the eight grades Eckersall received from Thatcher, all were C. Record of College Work, Walter Herbert Eckersall, Registrar's Office, University of Chicago; reports of Oliver J. Thatcher, Medieval Europe, no. 1, and The Dark Ages, no. 7, *IR*, summer quarter, 1905; report of Oliver J. Thatcher, The Feudal Period, no. 8, *IR*, spring quarter, 1906; report of Francis W. Shepardson, History of the U.S., Later Const. Period, no. 18, *IR*, spring quarter, 1904. For the course description and level, see *Annual Register, 1903–04*, 229–32. Shepardson served on the athletic control board as dean of the senior colleges, *Annual Register, 1905–06*, 13, and *Annual Register, 1906–07*, 43. Eckersall took another course from Shepardson in 1906 and, of eighty students, none flunked. Report of Francis W. Shepardson, U.S. History—Colonial Period, no. 83, *IR*, winter quarter, 1906.

81. During the season of 1904, he was absent nine times and received a B minus for class work and a C plus for the final examination in Shepardson's American History: The Colonial Period, report of Francis W. Shepardson, United States—Colonial Period, no. 83, *IR*, autumn quarter, 1904. Cf. *Annual Register, 1904–05*, 200. During the season of 1905 he was absent eleven times and received a B and a C in Principles of Political Economy and was absent eight times and received two Cs in Modern Industries; report of William Hill, Principles of Political Economy, no. 1, and report of Robert Morris, Modern Industries, no. 6, *IR*, autumn quarter, 1905. During the season of 1906, he was absent five times and received a D and a C in Tariffs, Reciprocity, and Shipping and was absent seven times and received a C and a D in Financial History of the United States; report of John Cummings, Tariffs, Reciprocity, and Shipping, no. 23, report of John Cummings, Financial History of the United States, no. 24, *IR*, autumn quarter, 1906. On Eckersall's lower-division status after three and two-thirds years, see *Annual Register, 1903–04*, 532, *Annual Register, 1904–05*, 434, *Annual Register, 1905–06*, 388 (which notes his summer registration), and *Annual Register, 1906–07*, 392; *Annual Register, 1906–07*, 62, 104.

82. *Chicago Post*, Dec. 1, 1905. A Chicago graduate honored "Eckie" with "Eckersall, Eckersall, limber up your leg / . . . Eckie, quick! do the trick! That

was slick! Wow!" Scrapbook, vol. 45, inside front cover, Stagg Papers. The *Chicago Record-Herald,* Nov. 26, 1905, carried "The Man with the Toe."

83. *Chicago Journal,* Nov. 28, 1905; *St. Louis Post-Dispatch,* Nov. 23, 1905; *Collier's,* quoted in *Chicago Interocean,* Jan. 8, 1907; cf. *Chicago Chronicle,* Jan. 8, 1907; *New York Globe,* Nov. 24, 1906. A typical appraisal of Eckersall's place in intercollegiate football history was written during the mid-1930s: "Almost a universal choice for All Time, All-American Quarter. His Skill, tenacity, speed and headwork combined to make of this man a marvel." Walsh, ed., *Intercollegiate Football,* 191. Glenn "Pop" Warner chose Eckersall as his all-time, all-American quarterback in 1931, *Collier's,* Nov. 21, 1931, as did Grantland Rice in 1951 for the football Hall of Fame, see Peterson, *Eckersall of Chicago.*

84. *Daily Maroon,* Nov. 24, 1906, 1, 2, 4. Cf. the offering of an "Eckie postal card," *Daily Maroon,* Nov. 28, 1906, 2.

85. *Daily Maroon,* Nov. 24, 1906, 4; D. A. Robertson (secretary to the president) to Walter H. Eckersall, Dec. 1, 1906, box 15, folder 7, UPP, 1889–1925: Charles T. B. Goodspeed to George W. Taft, Oct. 4, 1928, "Reminiscences of Thomas Wakefield Goodspeed," inside the front cover, University of Chicago Archives; Charles T. B. Goodspeed, *Thomas Wakefield Goodspeed* (Chicago: University of Chicago Press, 1932), 57. Edgar Goodspeed recalled that his father, Thomas Goodspeed, was deeply pleased to be chosen to present the watch to Eckersall. *As I Remember,* 56–59. Eckersall to Judson, Nov. 27, 1906, box 15, folder 7, UPP, 1889–1925.

86. *Annual Register, 1906–07,* 392; *IR,* winter quarter, 1907.

87. *Daily Maroon,* Feb. 1, 1907, 2.

88. Record of College Work, Walter Herbert Eckersall, Registrar's Office, University of Chicago. The emphasis appears on the transcript. The last entry reads, "Died Mar. 24, 1930." No further record was made of Eckersall's expulsion in the records of the junior college faculty, the University Council or Senate, or the Board of Physical Culture and Athletics.

89. George D. Buckley to Judson, March 14, 1907, box 15, folder 7, UPP, 1889–1925. There is no record of the Eckersall letter to Judson.

90. Ibid. Judson to Buckley, March 15, 1907, box 15, folder 7, UPP, 1889–1925. There is no record of such a conference between Judson and Buckley.

91. Sperber, *Shake Down the Thunder,* 44, 128, 259–60.

92. Dean George E. Vincent to Stagg, Nov. 10, 1908, box 10, Stagg Papers; Stagg to Stella Stagg, Jan. 19, 1924, and Stagg memorandum, Aug. 26, 1931, A. A. Stagg Collection, Amos Alonzo Stagg High School, Palos Hills, Ill.; Knute Rockne to A. P. Ames, March 22, 1929, Notre Dame Director of Athletics Records, box 7: folder 85, Notre Dame University Archives; Stagg, "Walter Eckersall at St. Luke's Hospital," undated memorandum, Walter Eckersall folder, Stagg Papers.

93. Adam's column, "Today's Talk," *Richmond Palladium and Sun-Telegram,* Nov. 12, 1921. Football writer Francis J. Powers stated in the 1940s much of what has become accepted biography: "After graduating from Chicago, Eckersall won new fame as a referee and a sports writer for the *Chicago Tribune.*" Francis J. Powers, "Life Story of Amos Alonzo Stagg," *Official Pro Rules* (St. Louis: C. C. Spink and Son, 1946), 19.

94. Poem by Matthew S. Kelley, Eckersall folder, Stagg Papers; also, the tributes by *Tribune* sports section colleague Edward Burns, *Chicago Tribune*, Nov. 24, 1946, and by 1905 team-mate Merrill C. "Babe" Meigs, *American Weekly*, Oct. 26, 1947.

95. See Bledstein, *The Culture of Professionalism*, 289.

Chapter 3: Football's Year of Trial and Triumph, 1905–6

1. William Graham Sumner, *What Social Classes Owe to Each Other* (New York: Harper and Brothers, 1883).

2. The Helms Foundation determined retrospective "national champions" in 1936, *Official 1993 NCAA Football* (Overland Park: National Collegiate Athletic Association, 1993), 87–107.

3. Ibid.; Durant and Etter, *Highlights of College Football*, 74–75. William J. Baker, *Sports in the Western World* (Urbana: University of Illinois Press, 1988), 203, selects Michigan, Chicago, and Harvard as the strongest teams in the two decades preceding World War I. Walsh, ed., *Intercollegiate Football*, 214. On Yost, see Lester, "Fielding Harris Yost."

4. *Harper's Weekly*, Oct. 28 1905, 1556; *Chicago Daily News, Chicago Examiner, Chicago Post*, and *University of Michigan Daily*, Nov. 22, 1905; *Chicago Tribune, Chicago Chronicle*, and *Chicago Journal*, Nov. 23, 1905; *Chicago American*, Nov. 28, 1905.

5. *Chicago Post, Chicago Chronicle*, Oct. 20, 1905; *Chicago Post, Chicago Tribune*, Oct. 22, 1905; *Chicago Journal*, Nov. 23, 1905; *Chicago Record-Herald*, Nov. 22, 1905; *Chicago Journal*, Nov. 23, 1905, *Chicago Record-Herald, Chicago Journal*, Nov. 25, 1905; George Lytton to Harper, Nov. 21, 1905, Athletics 2 folder, UPP, 1889–1925; *Chicago Tribune*, Nov. 29, 1905.

6. George Lytton to Harper, Nov. 21, 1905, Athletics 2 folder, UPP, 1889–1925; H. P. Chandler (Harper's secretary) to George Lytton, Nov. 22, 1905, Athletics 2 folder, UPP, 1889–1925; Anita McCormick Blaine to Harper, Dec. 6, 1905, box 8, folder 21, UPP, 1889–1925. Blaine, daughter of Cyrus McCormick and daughter-in-law of James G. Blaine, made frequent and large contributions, of which Emmons Blaine Hall (in memory of her husband) for the School of Education was the most significant. Goodspeed, *The Story of the University of Chicago, 1890–1925*, 121, 145–46; *Harper's Weekly*, Oct. 28 1905, 1556.

7. *Chicago Record-Herald*, Nov. 30, 1905; Harper to R. N. Chitwood, Nov. 23, 1905, Harper to Wallace Heckman, Nov. 24, 1905, Harper to Stagg, Nov. 24, 1905, Athletics 2 folder, UPP, 1889–1925.

8. *Chicago Journal*, Nov. 23, 1905.

9. *Chicago Chronicle, Chicago Interocean*, and *Chicago Examiner*, Nov. 30, 1905; *Chicago Tribune*, Dec. 1, 1905.

10. *Chicago Record-Herald*, Dec. 2, 1905; *Chicago Post*, Dec. 4, 1905; *Chicago Tribune, Chicago Record-Herald, Chicago Chronicle*, and *Chicago Examiner*, Dec. 1, 1905; Wallace, *Unending Journey*, 98–99.

11. *Chicago Chronicle, Chicago Examiner*, and *Chicago Tribune*, Dec. 1, 1905; the description of the young woman is in the *Chicago Examiner*, Dec. 1, 1905.

12. *Chicago Chronicle*, Nov. 26, 1905; *Chicago Tribune*, Nov. 23, 1905. Cf.

Chicago Record-Herald, Nov. 26, 1905; *Chicago Tribune,* Dec. 1, 1905. See Leo Marx, *The Machine in the Garden: Technology and the Pastoral Ideal in America* (London: Oxford University Press, 1964) to give context to this campus development of the machine in the football garden and compare with the widespread efforts toward efficiency in America. Callahan, *Education and the Cult of Efficiency;* also see Smith, *Sports and Freedom,* for more on the "rationalization" of the sport. Moreover, American football initially presented a means of demonstrating T. J. Jackson Lears's thesis that the "internalized morality of self-control and autonomous achievement" is "the basis of modern culture," but the machines of the twentieth century curdled football's claims after a scant generation. Lears, *No Place of Grace,* 7.

13. *Chicago Tribune, Chicago Chronicle, Chicago Post, Chicago Daily News, Chicago Examiner, Chicago American, New York Daily Tribune,* and *Philadelphia Press,* all Dec. 1, 1905; cf. Stagg, *Touchdown!* 244–45; Eckersall, "My Twenty-Five Years of Football," *Liberty,* Nov. 6, 1926, 67; and Tom Perrin, *Football: A College History* (Jefferson: McFarland, 1987), 51–52. The rules then allowed the tackler to "carry" the ball carrier during the tackle. The game was essentially a punting contest, with Chicago crossing midfield three times in the first half, Michigan but once. Overall, the Maroons gained 139 yards to 128 for the Wolverines.

14. Stagg, *Touchdown!* 252–53. Wallace gave a vivid account of the incident but remembered that despite following the president's instructions to "run all the way. Tell Stagg the men must win. I am working with them!" she did not get to the field until after the team was back on the field. *Unending Journey,* 99.

15. *Chicago Examiner,* Dec. 1, 1905; *Chicago Interocean,* Dec. 2, 1905; *Chicago Record-Herald,* Dec. 2, 1905.

16. Invitation and Announcement Card, Chicago Alumni Club, Scrapbooks, vol. 46, Stagg Papers; *Chicago Tribune,* Dec. 4, 1905; *Chicago Chronicle* and *Chicago Interocean,* Dec. 5, 1905.

17. *University Record,* Jan. 15, 1897, 526. On the place of compulsory chapel at Chicago and in American institutions, see Goodspeed, *A History of the University of Chicago,* 449–50, and Rudolph, *The American College and University,* 75–77.

18. *Chicago Tribune,* Dec. 2, 1905. The lyricist, Leo DeTray, suffered a serious eye injury and possible loss of sight during the game. Even his eye injury was proclaimed "worth while" by the student editors of the *Cap and Gown, 1906,* 245, as they continued to rejoice in the victory months later.

19. *Chicago American,* Dec. 1, 1905. Also see *Chicago Chronicle, Chicago Record-Herald,* and *Chicago Tribune,* Dec. 1, 1905. The second group of quotations appear in *Chicago American* and *Chicago Tribune,* Dec. 3, 1905. One cartoon depicted a dejected Clark, head bowed and hand to face, walking off the field after the game. An arrogant fan pounds his back and says, "Never mind, Clark; it took Michigan to beat Michigan." Scrapbooks, vol. 46, Stagg Papers. Clark's behavior after the game was described in the *Chicago Daily News,* Dec. 1, 1905, and *Chicago Tribune,* Dec. 1, 2, 1905.

20. *Chicago Herald-Examiner,* Dec. 4, 1925. Three children also survived.

Portland Oregonian and *Detroit News,* June 1, 1932; E. Bennett Fox to Stagg, June 9, 1932, box 24, folder 3, Stagg Papers.

21. Anita McCormick Blaine to Harper, Dec. 6, 1905, box 8, folder 21, UPP, 1889–1925. A parallel comment was expressed by the future Amherst and Wisconsin president Alexander Meiklejohn in "The Evils of College Athletics," in which he concluded the solution to his enumerated evils was that "the undergraduates should be given control of their own games." He also argued against alumni control and new "professional coaches," which would have included Coach Stagg. *Harper's Weekly,* Dec. 2, 1905, 1751–52.

22. Thomas Elyot, *The Boke Named the Governour* (London, 1553 edition), First Book, 82.

23. Morris Bishop, *A History of Cornell* (Ithaca: Cornell University Press, 1962), 48. The observer, Professor Charles A Goodenough of the University of Illinois, was quoted in Westbrook Pegler's column, *Chicago Tribune,* Dec. 1, 1932. Unnecessary roughness had sound antecedents: *Yale Daily News,* Dec. 15, 1884, reported an unusual Yale game: "Not a man was warned off the field, and not one was accused of, or reprimanded for any roughness." For examples of especially proficient slugging, see *Chicago Times,* Nov. 17, 1902, where "teeth rattled on the earth like hail"; *San Francisco Morning Call,* Jan. 2, 1895, where a "gentleman" was "conspicuous" for his pugilistic abilities; and *Chicago Tribune,* Sept. 29, 1895, for a pregame discussion of a player's "slugging qualities." For examples of game officials attempting to enforce their decisions, see *San Francisco Examiner, New York Herald, San Francisco Chronicle, San Francisco Morning Call,* and *Chicago Tribune,* Dec. 26, 1894. For examples of wrangling and cessation of play, see *Chicago Chronicle, Chicago Times-Herald,* and *Chicago Interocean,* Sept. 29, 1895. "The game was remarkable for the general clean character of the playing," *Chicago Times,* Nov. 30, 1894; cf. *Chicago Morning News Record,* Nov. 3, 1892, *Chicago Herald* and *Chicago Times,* Nov. 6, 1892, and *Chicago Times,* Nov. 5, 1893. The unveiling of Harvard's "flying wedge" in 1892 against Yale was "a vivid example of the brutality which then ruled the sport." Scott A. McQuilkin and Ronald A. Smith, "The Rise and Fall of the Flying Wedge: Football's Most Controversial Play," *Journal of Sport History* 20 (Spring 1993): 57.

24. Camp, ed., *Football Facts and Figures,* 96, 98, 101, 106, 122. Another set of figures presented by Camp and his correspondent, a "Dr. Loveland" who served as Wesleyan team physician, reported an injury survey of 250 players from Yale, Harvard, Princeton, and Wesleyan who were active during the 1880s. The survey found more than 9 percent serious injuries, an example of which it described as "a loose ligament in the knee joint." A modern physician feels that 9 percent might not constitute "a high incidence for that mass-play game, but it would be an alarmingly high incidence today" (ibid., 40–41; quote from Charles Schetlin, long-time Columbia University team physician, interview, Sept. 26, 1992). Stagg to Camp, Jan. 11, 1896, box 23, Walter Camp Papers, Manuscripts and Archives, Yale University Library. Danzig, *History of American Football,* 22–28, gives eyewitness testimony of the evolution of the mass momentum problem. Lawrence J. Green, "A Chronology of Changes in

Collegiate Football Rules, 1873–1954," Ph.D. diss., University of Iowa, 1955, Table 25. In "American Intercollegiate Football Spectacle," 109–20, Lewis provides a brief overview of the period, with a helpful emphasis upon the importance of the interest shown by the mass media; and Smith, *Sports and Freedom*, 91–98, is invaluable for the 1890s.

25. The *Chicago Times*, Nov. 12, 1894, promised a "bloody contest" but compare the disappointed *Chicago Record*, Nov. 30, 1894, and the *Chicago Herald*, Nov. 21, 1894; Eckersall, "My Twenty-five Years of Football," 65. The rules committeeman was quoted in *UCW*, Sept. 6, 1894, 4. Rockne's description was given in "To Shift or Not to Sift," *Collier's*, Nov. 29, 1930, 27.

26. Princeton player quoted in Henry Beach Needham, "The College Athlete: His Amateur Code, Its Evasion and Administration," *McClure's Magazine* 25 (July 1905): 271–72. Michigan's trainer quoted in *Chicago Record*, Nov. 30, 1896. See *Chicago Record*, Dec. 2, 1896, for a count of the number of teeth Herschberger lost to Michigan elbows, and *Chicago Interocean*, Nov. 30, 1896, for the insouciant note that "Herschberger was used roughly." On Eckersall's danger, see *Chicago Chronicle*, Oct. 18, 1905, and *Chicago Interocean*, Oct. 17, 1905.

27. See Danzig, *History of American Football*, 29, for the 1905 survey by the *Chicago Tribune*; William Henry Harbaugh, *Power and Responsibility: The Life and Times of Theodore Roosevelt* (New York: Farrar, Strauss, and Cudahy, 1961), 12.

28. *McClure's Magazine* 25 (June 1905): 115–28; *Chicago Daily News*, June 14, 1905; the article was reprinted in the *Chicago Tribune*, June 26, 1905. Henry F. Pringle notes that the meat plant inspection bill was "illustrative of the degree to which the innovations for which Roosevelt received credit were suggested by others." *Theodore Roosevelt: A Biography* (New York: Harcourt, Brace, 1931), 301; cf. 258, 300. See G. Wallace Chessman, *Theodore Roosevelt and the Politics of Power* (Boston: Little, Brown and Company, 1969), 139–40, and Harbaugh, *Power and Responsibility: The Life and Times of Theodore Roosevelt*, 260, for explanations of his unappreciative treatment of the muckrakers. Caspar Whitney, an acquaintance of Roosevelt's and editor of *Outing* magazine, had no doubt influenced Theodore Roosevelt's view of the football issue. See Appendix 4 in *The Letters of Theodore Roosevelt*, ed. Morison, 6:1620, 1625–26, for Whitney's luncheons and visits at the White House, and 3:89, 157, for Roosevelt's advice and contributions to the magazine. Theodore Roosevelt's unflattering opinion of Whitney occurs on 486–87.

29. Needham, "The College Athlete," 260–73, Needham's quote, 271. Within the year *McClure's* and Needham rewarded the president for his subsequent response to the football peril with a highly laudatory article, "Theodore Roosevelt, an Outdoor Man," *McClure's* 26 (Jan. 1906): 231–52, in which TR assumed great proficiency in sport and which promoted his gospel of athletic Darwinism.

30. *Chicago Record-Herald*, June 29, 1905; Appendix 2 in *The Letters of Theodore Roosevelt*, ed. Morison, 4:1378. Roosevelt had made no mention of college athletics in earlier June speeches when he appeared at Clark University, the College of the Holy Cross, and Williams College, *New York Daily Tribune*, June 22, 23, 1905.

31. On the abolitions, see *Philadelphia Inquirer,* Nov. 27, 30, 1905, *Chicago Tribune,* Nov. 29, 30, 1905, and *Chicago Chronicle, Chicago American,* and *Chicago Examiner,* Nov. 30, 1905. For a general discussion of reform, see *The Nation,* Dec. 7, 1905, 455. For coverage of the rugby development, see *New York Times,* Oct. 10, 1905, Stagg, *Touchdown!* 255, Orrin Leslie Elliot, *Stanford University: The First Twenty-Five Years* (Palo Alto: Stanford University Press, 1937), 225–48, *World Today* 13 (Oct. 1907): 1049–51, and *Sunset Magazine* 18 (Nov. 1906): 82. See Rudolph, *The American College and University,* 375–77, for the presidential quote and for the suggestion that Roosevelt's criticism was merely the extension of the Square Deal to the gridiron. President Eliot's thinking and actions can be seen in *New York Daily Tribune,* and *Chicago Record-Herald,* Oct. 12, 1905; Eliot to Roosevelt, Dec. 12, 1905, quoted in Henry James, *Charles W. Eliot* (Boston: Houghton Mifflin, 1930), 157.

32. *Chicago Record-Herald,* Nov. 21, 1905.

33. The suggestions for reform outlined by Pennsylvania's board of coaches essentially addressed recruitment and eligibility problems and rejected the criticism of brutal play as "more apparent than real." *Philadelphia Inquirer* and *Chicago Examiner,* Nov. 27, 1905. Walter Camp promoted the athletics of consensus constantly in the public press, see *Chicago American, Chicago Record-Herald, Chicago Tribune,* and *Chicago Daily News,* Nov. 29, 1905, and the *Philadelphia Inquirer,* Nov. 30, 1905. See *Chicago Interocean,* Nov. 5, 1905, for estimated figures (probably too low) of football income at Harvard, Yale, and Chicago and the resultant dependence of the institutions on the source. Cf. Needham's exact accounting in "The College Athlete" of Harvard, West Point, and Yale receipts and expenditures, his especially trenchant criticism of the "significance" of the building of Harvard Stadium, and perhaps the first description of intercollegiate athletics as "a business—and rather a noisome business at that."

34. See Stagg's judicious discussion of this eastern reticence toward effective control and western equality, *Touchdown!* 208–9, 254–56; also James, *Charles W. Eliot,* 157. Paul Stagg, "The Development of the National Collegiate Athletic Association in Relationship to Intercollegiate Athletics in the United States," Ph.D. diss., New York University, 1947, 103–4. The charge regarding the "football trust" was carried by the *Chicago Post,* Dec. 4, 1905. Yale, which had been the most influential single university during the first thirty years of intercollegiate sports, fell well off the pace and found itself considerably behind other universities by 1905. President Hadley continued to delegate the responsibility for athletic matters to alumnus Camp and the student association. "Sport in his opinion, was not a concern of the faculty." Lewis, "American Intercollegiate Football Spectacle," 257. I use the term *disciple* to characterize Stagg's relationship with Camp, but my use is based as much on intuition as on citation. Camp and Stagg had many areas of difference, among them the proper control of each college's intercollegiate athletics and the all-American player selection (Stagg thought it impossible to make informed choices after the game had spread beyond New England and some midatlantic states), but Stagg was unnaturally reticent to criticize Camp or his ideas because he enjoyed the vicarious importance that Camp's attention to Stagg's Chicago en-

terprise provided. See Stagg to Camp, Dec. 1, 1908, Walter Camp Papers, Microform Series 1, reel 16, regarding Stagg's successful nomination of his quarterback, Walter Steffen, for Camp's all-American team. Cf. Stagg's benign use of Camp's congratulating Stagg after the 1924 Illinois game. Ibid., following p. 348. Finally, Stagg's arrangement of a $4,500 gift to the Walter Camp Memorial Fund from the University of Chicago speaks volumes. *President's Report, 1926–1927* (Chicago: University of Chicago Press, 1928), 37.

35. Stagg, *Touchdown!* 184, and Danzig, *History of American Football,* 25, give details of the formation of the Football Rules Committee in the 1890s. The colleges who enjoyed seats on the old Rules Committee—Yale, Harvard, Princeton, Cornell, Pennsylvania, Navy, and Chicago—did not send representatives to McCracken's first or second meetings. Paul Stagg claimed the MacCracken reform group was "bitterly opposed to the old Football Rules Committee," and both the old and new ruled committees quite reluctantly agreed to amalgamate, with a member of the older group as president, the secretarial post held by the new group, and Walter Camp as the editor of the New Rules Book. Stagg, "The Development of the National Collegiate Athletic Association," 105–10; see also, Minutes of the Football Rules Committee, 1905–6, box 50, Football Rules Committee Meetings file, 1906–32, Stagg Papers. Stagg wired Walter Camp on January 11, 1906, before the joint meeting (which Stagg did not attend), that Camp was to use Stagg's vote as he wished, but "Chicago favors amalgamation." Correspondence Series 1, box 23, folders 651–52, Walter Camp Papers, Manuscripts and Archives, Yale University Library. By the end of the next football season, and hearing of Harvard's continuing discussion of abolition, Stagg wired Camp again: "If Harvard doesn't play football, Chicago could take H's place on Yale schedule. confidential." Ibid. The older committee managed to retain effective control of the committee, and in 1920, eleven eastern and three midwestern members were on the "combined" committee. As late as 1926, seven eastern members, two from the Great Plains, and only one each from the South, Midwest, Southwest, and Pacific Coast regions made up the committee. Box 50, Football Rules Committee Meetings file, 1906–32, Stagg Papers.

36. Box 50, Football Rules Committee Meetings file, 1906, 1907, 1908, 1909, and 1910, Stagg Papers; Green, "A Chronology of Changes in Collegiate Football Rules," Tables 1, 5, 15, 22. One of the best statements on the nature of reform under the hands of the Rules Committee was made by new Harvard President A. Lawrence Lowell in a letter to Princeton President Woodrow Wilson: "I should think it would be better to put the emphasis in our submission on the reduction of injuries, and not in the attractive character of the sport, which would be present enough in the minds of the Committee." Jan. 13, 1910, Woodrow Wilson Papers, Seeley G. Mudd Manuscript Library, Princeton University. Used by permission of the Princeton University Libraries.

The prescient observation regarding the forward pass was made by *The World Today* 11 (Nov. 1906): 1135. The two leading universities that tried to do without football, Stanford and the University of California, substituted rugby for football, only to return because the old English game was not as attractive for their constituencies. Roberta Park, "Football to Rugby and Back," *Journal of Sport History* 11 (1984): 15–40. Also see John Hammond Moore, "Football's Ugly Decades, 1893–1913," *Smithsonian Journal of History* 11 (Fall 1967): 49–68, John S. Watterson, "The Football Crisis of 1909–1910: The Response of the Eastern 'Big Three,'" *Journal of Sport History* 8 (Spring 1981): 33–49, and Ronald A. Smith, "Harvard and Columbia and a Reconsideration of the 1905–06 Football Crisis," *Journal of Sport History* 8 (Winter 1981): 5–19.

37. On the earlier group, see Merle Curti and Vernon Carstensen: *The University of Wisconsin: A History, 1848–1925* (Madison: University of Wisconsin Press, 1949), 1:705. The presidents and their institutions who were Intercollegiate Conference charter members in 1895 were: Harper of Chicago, Draper of Illinois, Angell of Michigan, Northrup of Minnesota, Rogers of Northwestern, Smart of Purdue (the convener), and Adams of Wisconsin. See Minutes, Intercollegiate Conference, Jan. 11, 1895, Appendix 2, Table 3. In 1899, Iowa and Indiana were added and, in 1912, Ohio State.

38. Minutes, Intercollegiate Conference, Jan. 11, 1895, Feb. 8, 1896. All representatives of the conference were regular members of their university's faculty (Stagg of Chicago was the only representative who coached or taught physical culture, but he was the only tenured physical culture instructor among the seven schools). See ibid., Nov. 30, 1900, for the formation of an "Eligibility Committee" that passed upon eligibility of contestants from "outside" the conference, and Nov. 29, 1901, for the first conference "Arbitrator's Report," which person was confined to determining the status of those institutions from which Conference athletes had transferred. The Committee on Eligibility was finally empowered to investigate and overrule internal eligibility decisions made by each university's athletic control board, upon complaint filed by another conference member. Ibid., June 2, 1905.

39. See *The Athletic Controversy* (Chicago: n.n., n.d.), a printed four-page pamphlet on Michigan, Wisconsin, and Illinois versus Chicago, Athletics 1 folder, UPP, 1889–1925. Also see the growing criticism of Stagg's eligibility procedures: *Harper's Weekly*, Dec. 3, 1898, *Chicago Tribune*, Dec. 17, 1898, and *Chicago Evening Post*, Dec. 16, 1898.

40. *The Athletic Controversy*; C. K. Adams to Harper, March 12, 1899, Athletics 1 folder, UPP, 1889–1925; for internal criticism of Stagg at Chicago, see the undated, handwritten letter probably to Harper, illegible signature, in Athletics 1 folder, UPP, 1889–1925, which is concerned with the lack of belief by the other conference schools in Chicago's good faith and suggests that someone other than Stagg assure the other members, because Stagg would be incompetent and not believed.

41. *The Athletic Controversy.*

42. Ibid.; C. K. Adams to Harper, Nov. 18, 1899, and C. K. Adams to Harper, Nov. 25, 1899, on the resumption of athletic relations, Athletics 1 folder, UPP, 1889–1925. The *Chicago Chronicle* reported on December 9, 1899, that Wisconsin's unhappy President Adams, "who has been opposed to the playing of the game since the advisability of it was first urged in Chicago, shocked the students at chapel today by ordering them in no case to indulge in a dem-

onstration tomorrow in celebration of a possible victory," and described the student body as "bitter in its criticism of the president for what is called unwarranted interference." Also, see *Chicago Tribune* and *Chicago Times-Herald*, Dec. 9, 1899, *Chicago Times-Herald*, *Chicago Interocean*, and *Chicago Chronicle*, Dec. 10, 1899. The *Philadelphia Times*, Dec. 19, 1899, judged the Chicago team of 1899 "in advance of any other" in the country "save Harvard." Harvard's record was spoiled only by a tie with Yale.

43. Minutes, Intercollegiate Conference, March 10, 1906; Curti and Carstenson, *The University of Wisconsin*, 1:540; Joseph E. Raycroft to A. A. Stagg, March 13, 1906, box 12, Stagg Papers; Stagg, *Touchdown!* 255.

44. See *Chicago News*, *Chicago American*, and *Chicago Post*, Dec. 1, 1905, for the call to ban professional or "paid" coaches. See the *Chicago Post*, Sept. 6, 1900, for Michigan, Wisconsin, Illinois, and Chicago. See the *Chicago Times-Herald*, Sept. 11, 1900, *Chicago Tribune*, Sept. 16, 1900, and *Chicago Times-Herald*, Sept. 17, 1900, for Minnesota, Illinois, and Northwestern. On the earlier start by Chicago, Iowa, Illinois, Minnesota, and Purdue in 1903, see *Chicago Record-Herald*, Sept. 6, 1903. On the growth of preseason training camps and football practices under electric lights, practice sessions of up to five hours, and the pervasive use of the training table, see the *Chicago Chronicle*, Sept. 17, 1905, *Chicago Interocean*, Oct. 18, 1905, *Chicago Examiner*, Oct. 19, 1905, and Stagg, *Touchdown!* 255. Minutes, Intercollegiate Conference, March 10, 1906; *A Digest of the Proceedings of the Intercollegiate Conference of Faculty Representatives, 1895–1913* (n.p.: Intercollegiate Conference, 1913), 23–24.

45. See Appendix 2. Seven of twelve points therein are addressed to the problems of the rise of the player.

46. See Appendix 2, points 2 and 3; Minutes, Intercollegiate Conference, Dec. 1, 1906; and *A Digest of the Proceedings of the Intercollegiate Conference of Faculty Representatives, 1895–1920* (n.p.: Intercollegiate Conference, 1920), 19–20.

47. Minutes, Intercollegiate Conference, March 10, 1906.

48. Wilfred B. Shaw, "Michigan and the Conference: A Ten-year Argument over the University's Athletic Relations," *Michigan Alumnus* 54 (1947): 34–48. The "Big Three," Harvard, Yale, and Princeton, followed the midwestern lead and initiated similar player reforms, Stagg, *Touchdown!* 256.

49. Storr, *Harper's University*, 92; Minutes, University Congregation, April 3, April 6, July 3, 1900, University of Chicago Archives; *University Record*, April 27, 1900, 41–42; Minutes, BPC&A, April 14, May 19, June 16, 1900; Minutes, University Council, June 9, Oct. 13, 1900. Lovett later remembered that the opposition to university athletic policies that he represented was mostly confined to the "small group of Harvard men on the faculty." *All Our Years* (New York: Viking Press, 1948), 64. Carl Buck was not a Harvard man. Robert Herrick, of the group, also remembered their futile efforts in his novel *Chimes* (New York: Macmillan, 1926) as they tried to slow a number of curricular and extracurricular developments, and that they were known as the "Harvard gang," 64.

50. Harper to Stagg, Nov. 14, 104, box 10, folder 9, WRHP; cf. Harper to Stagg, Jan. 11, 1905, "We miss you very much," and April 13, 1905, box 10,

folder 10, WRHP. Stagg to Harper, April 18, 1905, and Harper to Stagg, Oct. 23, 1905, box 10, folder 10, WRHP. For Stagg's appraisal of Harper, see Stagg to Mrs. Harper, undated, probably late January or early February of 1906, a draft of a letter of consolation upon President Harper's death: "He inspired me as no other teacher I have ever had." Box 10, folder 12, WRHP.

51. Herrick, *Chimes,* 152. Clavercin served as Herrick's alter ego. Herrick's biographer, Blake Nevius, suggests, "Herrick never quite forgave the energetic westerner, with his salesmanlike approach to higher education, for violating his Cambridge prejudices." *Robert Herrick: The Development of a Novelist* (Berkeley: University of California Press, 1962), 54, and for the novelist's response to the death of the president, 286. Cf. Storr, *Harper's University,* 363, for Herrick's testimony regarding the "ennobling" end of Harper.

52. *Outing Magazine* 47 (Jan. 1906): 495; Harper to Stagg, Dec. 26, 1905, box 10, folder 11, WRHP, and box 9, folder 12, Stagg Papers. The extended quotation is from Stagg to Harper, hand dated, probably later, and certainly erroneously, "Jan. 5-1905," box 10, WRHP. The proper date would have to be after Harper's December 1905 letter. The letter to Harper is handwritten by lead pencil in Stagg's hand and is possibly a later copy, because Stagg was ill at its writing and claimed "he had the article [i.e., Whitney's] read to me" after receipt of Harper's plea, indicating he was not in suitable condition to draft a two-page letter to Harper, who died on January 10, 1906. Before his death, Harper named Stagg as one of his honorary pallbearers, Judson to Stagg, Jan. 11, 1906, box 9, Stagg Papers.

53. The University Senate was the "supreme legislative body in the realm of academic affairs" and "consisted only of head professors." Storr, *Harper's University,* 89–90; Minutes, University Senate, Dec. 2, 1905.

54. Minutes, University Senate, Dec. 2, 1905; *New York Times,* Nov. 27, 1903.

55. Minutes, University Senate, Dec. 2, 1905.

56. Ibid.

57. Minutes, University Senate, Jan. 6, 1906; *Recorder's Monthly Report,* Jan., Feb., March, 1906, 1–2; Minutes, Intercollegiate Conference, June 1, 1906, Dec. 1, 1906; Minutes, University Senate, Jan. 17, 1906.

58. Minutes, University Senate, Jan. 17, 1906. The records here are inconsistent, cf. *Recorder's Monthly Report,* Jan., Feb., March, 1906, 1–2.

59. *Recorder's Monthly Report,* Jan., Feb., March, 1906, 1–2. No minutes of Michigan President Angell's meeting or that of the faculty representatives on March 9 are included in the official Minutes, Intercollegiate Conference.

60. Chicago Alumni Club to the Senate of the University of Chicago, Feb. 2, 1906, appended to Minutes, University Senate, Feb. 3, 1906.

61. Minutes, University Senate, Feb. 3, 1906.

62. The *Chicago Interocean,* Jan. 30, 1906, carried the headline; *Chicago Tribune,* Jan. 29, 1906; Raycroft to Stagg, April 12, 1906, box 12, Stagg Papers; cf. Raycroft to Stagg, Feb. 10, 1906, March 13, 1906, box 12, Stagg Papers.

63. Minutes, BPC&A, March 14, 1906; Minutes, University Senate, March 17, 1906; Storr, *Harper's University,* 338.

64. The Illinois resolution is filed with Minutes, BPC&A, May 4, 1901. A

note of the Illinois indictment and the Chicago board's response appeared in *University Record,* June 28, 1901.

65. Stagg to Harper, July 6, 1905, Athletics 2 folder, UPP, 1889–1925, and box 10, folder 10, WRHP. The only reason the athletic fund had a positive balance was, of course, the football revenues. Harper to Stagg, July 13, July 19, 1905, box 10, folder 10, WRHP, and Minutes, Board of Trustees, July 18, 1905, box 4, folder 5. Cf. Stagg's response to Harper, July 21, 1905, box 10, folder 10, WRHP. The salary figures appear in Minutes, Board of Trustees, March 12, 1907, box 4, folder 7; ibid., Vol. 3, 1900–1902, "Budget Expenditures"; ibid., Vol. 4, 1902–4, "Budget Expenditures," and ibid., Vol. 5, 1904–6, "Budget Expenditures." Stagg's "athletic fund" remained a mystery because even though the trustee minutes include each year's university operating budget, the fund was not included. Stagg's $2,500 salary continued to be listed as before under the physical culture department's budget. Minutes, Board of Trustees, Vols. 3–6 (1900–1908).

66. Ibid., May 21, 1907, box 5, folder 1; Ronald A. Smith, ed., *Big-Time Football at Harvard, 1905: The Diary of Coach Bill Reid* (Urbana: University of Illinois Press, 1994), 323, 336; John McCallum, *Ivy League Football since 1872* (New York: Stein and Day, 1977), 53. Pittsburgh was one of Warner's many coaching stops (Iowa State, Georgia, Cornell, Carlisle, Pittsburgh, Stanford), and he received increases with each change; see Edwin Pope, *Football's Greatest Coaches* (Atlanta: Tupper and Love, 1955), 291–96. Chicago was not unique in its coaching arrangement: John Heisman was lured from his highly successful Clemson job to Georgia Tech in 1904 with a $2,000 salary plus 30 percent of the net gate receipts for football and baseball games. Wiley Lee Umphlett, *Creating the Big Game: John W. Heisman and the Invention of American Football* (Westport: Greenwood Press, 1992), 69.

67. *Chicago Tribune,* Nov. 20, 1904, and quoted in *University Record* 9 (Dec. 1904): 263. A more complete text appears in the A. A. Stagg folder, UPP, 1925–45. The *Christian Science Monitor,* Jan. 2, 1911, repeated the Harper quotation with approval. The image has proved to be lasting, for example, see Robert B. Considine, *The Unreconstructed Amateur: A Pictorial Biography* (San Francisco: Amos Alonzo Stagg Foundation, 1962), and Allison Danzig, "Amos Alonzo Stagg, Patriarch of Football," in *Oh, How They Played the Game,* 48–58.

68. Stagg to Harper, Nov. 14, 1905, contains the Michigan comparison, box 10, folder 11, WRHP. Harper to Stagg, Nov. 16, 1905; Franklin W. Johnson (the boy's principal) to Harper, Nov. 21, 1905; Frank Miller (university examiner) to Harper, Nov. 22, 1905; and Harper to Johnson, Nov. 22, 1905, all in box 10, folder 11, WRHP.

69. Cf. Castle to Harper, March 8, 1900, emphasis in original; cf. Harper to Castle, n.d., George Goodspeed to D. P. Trude, Jan. 30, 1900, and Castle to Harper, March 7, 1900, all in Athletics 1 folder, UPP, 1889–1905. Castle was a dean in the junior colleges, and the instructor was D. H. Carnahan. *Annual Register,* 1899–1900, 21, 28, 239. Kurt Laves to George E. Vincent, May 15, 1906, contains the complaint regarding Stagg's captains, one of whom, Fred Walker, was later hired by Stagg as an assistant coach. Vincent's note to Stagg, May 16, 1906, and Stagg's

reply to Vincent, May 21, 1906, complete the episode. Box 10, Stagg Papers. Edward Parry, a superb track man and footballer recruited at Stagg's Interscholastic Track Meet, reportedly left because "he does not care to remain at the university if not allowed a place in athletics." *Chicago Record-Herald,* Jan. 13, 1907 (the *Chicago Chronicle,* Feb. 5, 6, 1907, wrote of young Parry's professional wrestling prospects). Harold Iddings, a backfield player, also quit. *Chicago Interocean,* Feb. 7, 1907; *Alumni Directory, the University of Chicago, 1861–1910; Alumni Directory, the University of Chicago, 1913.* Cf. the expulsion of a valuable member of the 1908 national championship basketball team for his "second offense" of cheating, which offense occurred six days before the championship game. The expulsion occurred twelve days after the game. *Discipline Record Book,* Vol. 1 (1908–23), University of Chicago Archives. Strangely, the same young man was hired by Stagg the following season as an assistant coach, at least until Dean Vincent heard of the situation and wrote that it seemed "extremely unfortunate to say the least that a man should be employed in these circumstances." Vincent to Stagg, Nov. 10, 1908, Stagg Papers.

70. Minutes, Intercollegiate Conference, March 10, 1906; Minutes, University Council, Feb. 2, 1907.

71. Stagg to Harper and Harper to Stagg, both Aug. 17, 1904, box 10, folder 9, WRHP.

72. *Collier's,* Nov. 11, 1905; Minutes, University Council, June 30, 1906. "Student Service" was listed as a budget line in a number of departments over the years, such as the information office, recorder's office, and business manager's office. The largest figure was for Harper's own line of "Miscellaneous Administration Expense," followed by the deans' offices and physical culture. Minutes, Board of Trustees, Vol. 3 (1900–1901), 10, 326, Vol. 4 (1902–3), 18, Vol. 5 (1904–5), 73, 234, 35, 250. It is by no means certain, however, that these published figures were used for the athletes' financial aid because there were regular students who labored for their grants; then too, the evanescent "athletic fund" was no doubt readily available to be used for the athletic grants.

73. Vincent to Stagg, June 14, 1906, box 10, Stagg Papers. National surveys of rules reforms were given by *New York Herald,* Feb. 11, 1906, and *Washington Post,* March 4, 1906.

Chapter 4: Stagg's University

1. Storr, *Harper's University,* 75. Minutes, Board of Trustees, March 16, 1907, notes the terms of his employment, including a salary of $10,000. Judson quotation in Storr, *Harper's University,* 369. *Chicago Tribune,* Nov. 21, 1909.

2. Storr, *Harper's University,* 369, 370; Minutes, Board of Trustees, Jan. 25, 1909. Robert Herrick's fictional Judson, the unimpressive Abel Donothing, acceded to the presidential office because he was "a safe man, far safer than Harris [Harper] ever was." Herrick, *Chimes,* 158. Robert Morss Lovett, Herrick's best friend and correspondent, felt that Herrick's "caricatures of President Harper and President Judson are cruel and ungrateful." Lovett to Allen T. Hazen, Feb. 24, 1947, box 28, Robert Herrick Collection, University of Chicago Archives.

3. *Recorder's Monthly Report,* Oct.–Dec. 1905, 2; *Recorder's Monthly Report,* Jan.–March, 1906, 2; Minutes, BPC&A, Feb. 24, 1906.

4. Judson's quarterly statement was delivered March 20, 1906, at convocation, *University Record* 10 (April 1906): 159. Judson to R. M. Strong, Feb. 7, 1906, box 15, folder 7, UPP, 1889–1925.

5. Stagg "To the Members of the Board of Trustees," Jan. 24, 1906, box 15, folder 7, UPP, 1889–1925; cf. Stagg "To the Members of the Board of Trustees," Jan. 23, 1906 (first draft), and Jan. 24, 1906 (copy), box 9, Stagg Papers.

6. Judson to Stagg, March 21, 1906, p. 3, box 15, folder 7, UPP, 1889–1925, and box 9, Stagg Papers. Judson claimed that he had "distinctly won" the point at the Intercollegiate Conference that Stagg was not such a "professional coach." Judson to Stagg, March 21, 1906, box 15, folder 7, UPP, 1889–1925, and box 9, Stagg Papers.

7. Stagg to Judson, handwritten copy, March 27, 1906, box 9, Stagg Papers.

8. Judson to Stagg, March 30, 1906, box 15, folder 7, UPP, 1889–1925, and box 9, Stagg Papers.

9. Ibid.; T. W. Goodspeed to Stagg, April 27, 1906, box 8, Stagg Papers.

10. Minutes, BPC&A, June 5, 1906; Stagg to Judson, Aug. 14, 1906, and Judson to Stagg, Aug. 17, 1906, box 15, folder 7, UPP, 1889–1925, and box 9, Stagg Papers.

11. *President's Report, 1905–6,* 97–98; *President's Report, 1906–07,* 102.

12. The need for some reform was noted by *Chicago Record-Herald, Chicago Tribune, Chicago Examiner,* and *Chicago Daily News,* Nov. 20, 1909, *New York Herald,* Dec. 12, 1909, *Daily Maroon,* Nov. 6, 1909, 2, Dec. 16, 1909, 2; see also Minutes, BPC&A, Nov. 17, 1909, Jan. 29, 1910, at which it was decided to follow Stagg's lead and await the rules committee's changes. *Chicago Tribune,* Nov. 21, 1909; *Collier's,* Dec. 18, 1909, 13, 14, 19.

13. Caspar Whitney (editor) to Judson, Nov. 5, 1909, and Judson to Caspar Whitney, Nov. 8, 1909, box 15, folder 7, UPP, 1889–1925. For the statement on the West Point death, see *Chicago Tribune,* Nov. 1, 1909; a similar report appeared in the *Chicago Record-Herald,* Nov. 21, 1909. Cf. *Chicago Journal,* Nov. 1, 1909, and *Chicago Interocean* and *Chicago Tribune,* Nov. 2, 1909. Also, Judson to Nathan Strauss, Jr. (editor of *Puck*), Nov. 11, 1914, in response to Strauss to Judson, Nov. 6, 1914, box 15, UPP, 1889–1925.

14. *Daily Maroon,* Jan. 26, 1911, 2, Jan. 28, 1911, 2, Jan. 31, 1911, 2, and Feb. 3, 1911, 2; *Chicago Tribune,* Jan. 31, 1911. Stagg's angry response in the *Tribune,* Feb. 1, 1911. Nathaniel Pfeffer (Maroon editor) to Stagg, March 10, 1911, and Vincent to Stagg, March 14, 1911, box 19, folder 2, Stagg Papers; *Daily Maroon,* April 4, 5, 6, 7, 1911; Barry Karl, *Charles E. Merriam and the Study of Politics* (Chicago: University of Chicago Press, 1974), 61–72.

15. David Robertson (secretary to Judson) to Stagg, May 14, 1907, Judson to Stagg, May 13, 1907, Stagg to Judson, May 15, 1907, M. H. MacLean to Judson, June 3, 1907, Judson to Stagg, Nov. 6, 1907, and Stagg to Judson, Nov. 12, 24, 1907; all in Stagg Papers, box 9. The United Faculties of Arts, Literature, and Science, Minutes Nov. 23, 1907, addressed the question of the Minneapolis stayover to the Board of Physical Culture and Athletics.

16. Stagg to Judson and Judson to Stagg, April 2, 1909, box 15, UPP, 1889–1925; Judson to Stagg, Jan. 6, 1910, Stagg to Judson, March 4, 1908, in box 15, UPP, 1889–1925.

17. Judson to Stagg, Nov. 6, 1907, Stagg to Judson, typewritten (possibly first draft), Nov. 24, 1907, box 9, Stagg Papers; Stagg to Judson, Nov. 24, 1907, handwritten, attached to typewritten letter dated Nov. 12, 1907, box 15, UPP, 1889–1925; Judson to Angell, Dec. 5, 1906, box 15, UPP, 1889–1925, and box 9, Stagg Papers; Judson to Angell, Dec. 5, 1906, box 15, UPP, 1889–1925; Judson to Stagg, Nov. 26, 1907, box 15, UPP, 1889–1925; Minutes, Intercollegiate Conference, Jan. 26, 27, 1912. Albion Small became the Chicago representative from that date.

18. *The President's Report, 1913–14,* (Chicago: University of Chicago Press, 1915), 10, 107. Judson's and the Board's early shopping list is in Minutes, Board of Trustees, Dec. 9, 1910. The trustees voted to plan and perhaps build new stands, Minutes, Board of Trustees, vol. 8, Oct. 21, 1913, and by June, 1914, they had spent $255,325 on new seating, ibid., 8, June 23, 1914. See *Chicago Tribune,* Nov. 2, 15, 19, 20, 1913, and *Chicago Examiner,* Nov. 2, 21, 1913 for crowd numbers. The numbered jerseys developed from a campaign of the *Chicago Post,* Oct. 7–Nov. 26, 1913. Chicago's use of numerals was applauded by the *Milwaukee-Sentinel,* Nov. 23, 1913, even if the opposing Wisconsin team refused to wear them; the *Chicago Examiner,* Nov. 23, 1913, termed the experiment "a great success." Cf. *Chicago Tribune,* Nov. 23, 1913, Dec. 5, 1920, and Parke H. Davis, member of the Football Rules Committee, to Frank S. Whiting, Dec. 18, 1930, box 54, folder 19, Stagg Papers.

19. *Chicago Journal,* Oct. 20, 1920. The thirty thousand attendance mark was surpassed in 1920 at the Ohio State game. *Chicago American, Chicago Herald-Examiner,* and *Chicago Tribune,* Oct. 31, 1920. Two years later, Stagg told his brother, "We are in terrific need of larger seating capacity. . . . We have no public sale at all." Stagg to George R. Stagg, Nov. 20, 1922, box 1, folder 23, Stagg Papers. The *Chicago Tribune's* summary of the 1920 season included the claim that "in attendance and gate receipts the Maroon team . . . outdrew any other team that ever played in this section of the country." Nov. 22, 1920, see issue of Dec. 5 for comparative figures for Yale, Harvard, and Princeton. Stagg claimed the new facility was the "largest permanent structure of its kind in the collegiate world" after Harvard's. A. A. Stagg, box 74, folder 1932, Stagg Papers. Stagg must have been unaware of the new Syracuse University stadium built in 1908. Lawrence Perry, "The Stadium and College Athletics," *Scribner's* 56 (Nov. 1914): 571–86. Syracuse was not a major national team at the time, and the Harvard, Chicago, Yale, and Princeton stadiums were more significant. Danzig, *History of American Football,* 70.

20. Wallace Heckman to Stagg, Dec. 20, 1922, box 113, folder 13, Swift Papers; box 104, folder 1, Stagg Papers; Minutes, Board of Trustees, July 13, 1915, Dec. 12, 1922; William Scott Bond to Harold Swift, Jan. 28, 1924, and Stagg to Bond, Jan. 26, 1924, box 113, folder 14, Swift Papers.

21. The students' complaint is filed in Minutes, BPC&A, May 22, 1920; see ibid., June 4, 1921, for the petition of the undergraduate council; for the bet-

tering of the student seat placement, see ibid., Oct. 29, 1921. The 1906 conference reform that protected university members from high ticket prices was eroded at all the schools. The reform was annulled in 1919 when the representatives voted to withdraw the 50 cent rate for visiting students. Minutes, Intercollegiate Conference, June 6, Dec. 6, 1913, Dec. 6, 1919.

22. Stagg to David S. Merriam, Dec. 14, 1913, box 10, Stagg Papers; Minutes, Intercollegiate Conference, Dec. 2, 1922; Minutes, BPC&A, May 19, 1922. Information on ticket prices in 1915, 1916, 1917, 1920, and 1921 can be found in box 113, folders 10 and 11, Swift Papers, and Minutes, BPC&A, June 4, 1921. Stagg to Trevor Arnett, Dec. 26, 1924, box 8, Stagg Papers.

23. B. Lambert to Albion Small, Feb. 24, 1917, Albion Small to B. J. Lambert, Feb. 28, 1917, correspondence and resolution in Minutes, BPC&A, April 14, 1917. The degree to which the conference reform attempts had been unsuccessful can be seen in an agreement between Wisconsin and Chicago authorities in 1919 "that the last football game of the season be played in Chicago" by Wisconsin and Chicago "for a period of five consecutive years." Ibid., Nov. 22, 1919.

24. Boxes 81, 83, Stagg Papers; *Cap and Gown, 1908,* 211.

25. Chicago played 152 conference games (twenty-five more than the nearest rival, Illinois) and had the best record for the eighteen-year period. Chicago's percentage was .756; the nearest rivals were Michigan with .743, and Ohio State with .632. Of the eighteen games (actually, twenty-two, but four games were ties) played with conference opponents during the season of 1921, 1922, 1923, and 1924, Chicago lost but two, producing a record of .889, which easily led the conference for the period, although Chicago won the conference championship but twice during the four seasons because each of the two losses relegated the Maroons to second place. Moreover, during the four seasons, Chicago's conference opponents averaged fewer than four points scored against it each game (the best record in the group), and only Iowa scored more total points than Chicago. Chicago's total record with major opponents during the four seasons was twenty-two games won, four lost, and four tied. If ties are discounted, the record is 84 percent.

26. The quotations are from *Chicago Record-Herald,* Nov. 24, 1913, *Chicago Daily News,* Nov. 25, 1913, *Collier's,* Dec. 13, 1913, 23, and *Chicago Examiner,* Nov. 23, 1913. A sampling of the popular press in 1921: *Rockford Register Gazette, Columbia Daily Tribune, Green Bay* (Wis.) *Press Gazette, Winona* (Minn.) *Republican Herald,* Oct. 21, 1921. These articles were almost identical and probably originated at a wire service; a similar article finally appeared in *The Football World,* Dec. 1921, 34–35.

27. Danzig, *History of American Football,* 173, 17, 22, 25, provides evidence for Stagg's innovations at Yale, Springfield, and Chicago.

28. See the thoughtful commentary, "New Football Rules Bring the Punter into Greater Prominence," *Chicago Daily News,* Nov. 2, 1903, which asserted that the new 1903 rules had encouraged and developed "a more open style of play." It was this trend that Stagg mastered by his new techniques. Cf. *Chicago Journal,* Nov. 3, 1903, which also saw the increasing advance of the kicking game.

29. Knute Rockne, "To Shift or Not to Shift," *Collier's,* Nov. 29, 1930, 27, and Rockne's *New York Telegram* statement quoted in Danzig, *History of American Football,* 61–62. Also, Rockne's similar assertion of Stagg's authorship of the shift, *Scholastic,* Dec. 12, 1930, 351. But see Rockne's somewhat less certain attribution to Stagg in "Western Football vs. Eastern," *Liberty,* Jan. 24, 1925, 43–45, and the claims made by others that Yale graduate Dr. H. L. Williams at Minnesota was at least a co-originator with Stagg, Danzig, *History of American Football,* 60. For a concise overview of the shift principle and its evolution, see Stagg, *Touchdown!* 187–88, Danzig, *History of American Football,* 59–60, and *South Bend* (Ind.) *Tribune,* Sept. 27, 1940. Sperber, *Shake Down the Thunder,* 41, notes "as with so many of his so-called inventions" Rockne "merely repeated or improved upon what Harper had done." Cf. Knute Rockne, *The Autobiography of Knute K. Rockne* (Indianapolis: Bobbs-Merrill, 1931), 119, Gene Schoor, *One Hundred Years of Notre Dame Football* (New York: William Morrow, 1987), 36, Michael R. Steele, *Knute Rockne: A Bio-Bibliography* (Westport: Greenwood Press, 1983), 27–28.

30. Stagg to Joseph E. Raycroft, Aug. 11, 1906, box 12, Stagg Papers. For evidence of Stagg's early experimentation, see the hundreds of pass plays he created in 1906 and later, "Football Plays, 1890–1908," and his original practice field note cards, "Football Plays," boxes 30, 31, Stagg Papers. One former Chicago quarterback and later a Notre Dame coach, Frank Hering, claimed that the pass had clear antecedents at Chicago as early as 1894 (the season Hering led the Maroons on the Pacific Coast tour). *South Bend* (Ind.) *Tribune,* Jan. 8, 1943; cf. *New York Sun,* Dec. 8, 1946. For the rules changes that encouraged the forward pass, see Danzig, *History of American Football,* 39, a listing of Stagg's variant uses of the forward pass is on 373–78. McCornack quoted in *Rochester* (N.Y.) *Democrat and Chronicle,* Nov. 23, 1906.

31. *Collier's,* Oct. 25, 1930, 25. Cf. Rockne's views on the forward pass innovations, *Chicago Times,* Oct. 15, 1931. For a detailed description of the evolution of the forward pass at Chicago and Rockne's fairness in attributing these developments to Stagg, see Stagg, *Touchdown!* 303–12. The comparison with Thomas Edison comes from Durant and Etter, *Highlights of College Football,* 81. Further, Stagg probably originated the run-pass option, the wingback principle, the end-around, the quick-kick, the statue of liberty, the fake punt, short punt formations and plays, faking ball possession by quarterback and other backs, and the innovations of the spiral pass from center and the player huddle in which to call the plays. Danzig, *History of American Football,* 38, 44, 50–51, 102, 57, 99, 96, 85, 87. Stagg was at least one of the originators, if not the creator, of the "old" T formation and of several attendant developments: the man-in-motion, quarterback in standing position to receive pass from center, delayed buck, and the quarterback keeper play. Ibid., 74–77. Stagg shared in the development of the kick from placement instead of the drop-kick and the onside kickoff (termed by Stagg the "fake kick-off"). Ibid., 117–18. For a summary of the comparative place of Stagg among other intercollegiate football coaches, see ibid., 173–76.

32. Ibid., 32–42, Stagg quotation on 37.

33. For example, Chicago's first all-American, Clarence Herschberger, received a joint appointment as coach and instructor at Lake Forest College after he spent three seasons assisting Stagg at Chicago and studying graduate physics. *Chicago Interocean,* Sept. 18, 1902, and *Annual Register, 1900–1901* 1 (July 1901): 416. For other Stagg disciples, see *Chicago American,* Dec. 4, 1902, *Chicago Times-Herald,* Aug. 21, 1900, *Chicago Interocean,* Sept. 18, Oct. 8, 1902, *Chicago Record-Herald,* Oct. 6, 1902, *Chicago Tribune, Chicago Record-Herald, Chicago American, Chicago Post,* and *Chicago Chronicle,* Dec. 24, 1902. A list of coaching alumni is given in the *University Record,* Jan. 19, 1900, 290. See Stagg's listing of alumni who were directors of athletics at other schools, Stagg to Judson, Aug. 14, 1906, box 15, folder 7, UPP, 1889–1925. Cf. *Chicago Journal,* Aug. 25, 1905; *Chicago Chronicle,* Aug. 26, 1905. On the Notre Dame connection, see *Scholastic,* Oct. 7, 1899, 86. *Scholastic,* Nov. 13, 1897, 163, carries the acknowledgment of Stagg's help. See *Scholastic,* Oct. 17, 1896, Nov. 13, 1897, 162, for the Stagg and Hering notes; and on Hering and Harper, see Sperber, *Shake Down the Thunder,* 12, 37–63; Brondfield, *Rockne,* 51–52, 58, 71–81. Sperber charges Stagg, along with Fielding Yost and others, with repeatedly blocking the admission of Notre Dame to the Intercollegiate Conference, at least partially due to anti-Catholic sentiment. I find the charges regarding Stagg as possible but not probable and certainly not persuasive based on the vague evidence that Sperber provides or when weighed against the record I have noted here. Sperber, *Shake Down the Thunder,* 12, 44, 125, 210, 445. For an example of his work with a former assistant, see Stagg to Joseph E. Baycroft (Princeton athletic director), Aug. 11, 1906, box 12, Stagg Papers. For training innovations, see *Chicago Herald-Examiner,* Oct. 14, 1932, *Life,* Nov. 27, 1939, 80. In 1897, Raycroft took Herschberger and his ailing left foot to Professor Michelson's physics lab for the "first clinical x-ray." "First x-Rays" file, Joseph E. Raycroft faculty files, Princeton University Archives, Seeley G. Mudd Manuscript Library. Also see *Chicago Tribune,* Nov. 7, 1897, Stagg, *Touchdown!* 222, box 104, folder 2, Stagg Papers.

34. *Chicago Record-Herald, Chicago Tribune,* Aug. 10, 1913; *Chicago Record-Herald,* Sept. 7, 1913. The dedication date of the new stands was termed, "Stagg Day." *Chicago Tribune, Chicago Record-Herald,* and *Chicago Examiner,* Oct. 5, 1913, and see the special lapel labels for "Stagg Day" in Stagg Scrapbook, Vol. 112. The first suggestion that the field be named "Stagg Field" was in the *Chicago Tribune,* Oct. 26, 1913, in the column of Sports Editor Harvey T. Woodruff. The *Chicago Tribune* began calling the field "Stagg Field" within a fortnight (Nov. 1, 1913), while the other newspapers continued to term it "Marshall Field" (*Chicago Interocean,* Nov. 2, 1913) and "Midway Field" (*Chicago Examiner,* Nov. 2, 1913). The enthusiasm of Ickes and other graduates was carried in the *Chicago Tribune,* Nov. 2, 1913. On the football dinner, see *Chicago Examiner, Chicago Interocean,* and *Chicago Tribune,* Nov. 20, 1913. Finally, seeing that the $100,000 gift goal would have to be put aside, Judson dutifully presented a communication to the trustees from hundreds of university alumni asking for the signal honor for Coach Stagg; the trustees voted the change to "Stagg Field." Minutes, Board of Trustees, Oct. 27, 1914.

35. Minutes, University Council, May 2, 1908, and Joseph E. Raycroft to Stagg, Feb. 22, 1908, box 12, Stagg Papers; Minutes, United Faculties, Nov. 23, 1907, University of Chicago Archives; Minutes, Board of Trustees, July 9, 1918, Nov. 13, 1917.

36. Harry Pratt Judson to Stagg, Nov. 9, 1921, box 10, Stagg Papers; Minutes, Board of Trustees, Nov. 8, 1921, Oct. 10, Nov. 14, 1922.

37. Minutes, BPC&A, May 11, 1922; G. O. Fairweather to Judson, May 17, 1922, Wallace Heckman to Stagg, July 31, 1922, G. O. Fairweather to Judson, Dec. 5, 1922, and Judson to G. O. Fairweather, Dec. 8, 1922, all in box 15, UPP, 1889–1925; Stagg to Judson and Stagg to Swift, Dec. 9, 1922, Stagg to Swift, Jan. 11, 1923, box 113, Swift Papers.

38. Goodspeed, *A History of the University of Chicago*, 462, notes the significance of Swift's appointment as the first alumnus; see also Dorothy V. Jones, *Harold Swift and the Higher Learning* (Chicago: University of Chicago Library, 1985). For an example of Swift's interest in the enrollment of a prospect, see David S. Merriam to Harold H. Swift, Aug. 29, 1919, box 113, Swift Papers.

39. Stagg, self-memorandum, "Our Athletic Fund and Its Poachers," box 22, Stagg Papers; Minutes, Board of Trustees, March 13, Aug. 9, 1923, June 12, 1924; Swift to Messrs. Wallace Heckman and Nathan Plimpton, Dec. 16, 1922, Swift to Trevor Arnett, Aug. 21, 1924 and William Scott Bond to Swift, July 16, 1924, box 113, Swift Papers. Cf. T. W. Goodspeed to President Burton, Aug. 17, 1923, over the change of athletic field management away from Stagg, regarding which the coach had already written Burton: "I feel embarrassed and Humiliated by it," Stagg to Burton, Aug. 14, 1923. All pieces in A. A. Stagg folder, UPP, 1925–45.

40. Stagg to Dudley Reed, May 9, 1913, and Reed to Stagg, May 13, 1913, box 12, Stagg Papers; Minutes, BPC&A, April 24, 1913.

41. Minutes, Board of Trustees, May 20, 1913, July 10, 1917, and ibid., Vol. 9, 1915–16; Swift to Messrs. Wallace Heckman and Nathan Plimpton, Dec. 16, 1922, box 113, Swift Papers. Stagg's salary was moved to $7,000 in 1920, to $7,500 in 1923, and to $8,000 in 1924. Ibid., July 13, 1920, May 8, 1923, Oct. 16, 1924.

42. Howard J. Savage, *American College Athletics*, Bulletin 23 (New York: Carnegie Foundation for the Advancement of Teaching, 1929), 230. See Sperber, *Shake Down the Thunder* 249–50, 305–10, for other examples of the limits of the Carnegie reports.

43. The first quotation from Stagg to C. Harney, March 4, 1899; the latter quotation from Stagg to Claude Dalenburg, July 24, 1902. All of the foregoing letters and many others can be found in box 13, Stagg Papers.

44. Stagg to James Lightbody, Aug. 12, 19, 27, 1903. Lightbody had responded (Aug. 1, 14, 23, 31, 1903) to Stagg's letter of inquiry (July 28, 1903) about his abilities; the Des Moines letter, Stagg to Oley Kintz, March 19, 1903. All in box 13, Stagg Papers.

45. Stagg to E. S. Turner, Sept. 2, 1907. Other examples of this kind of appeal by Stagg were in letters to William Bresnahan, Aug. 28, 1907, and to Leo DeTray, Sept. 6, 1904 ("I shall do my utmost to enable you to develop and make

a great reputation for yourself." This boy made his reputation by losing the sight of one eye in the 1905 Michigan game.) All of the forgoing letters in box 13, Stagg Papers. There is a noticeable decrease in the number of extant letters and records of contacts to prospects in the Stagg Papers about 1904–6.

46. Minutes, BPC&A, Feb. 8, 1908, April 10, 1913.

47. Minutes, Intercollegiate Conference, Nov. 30, 1912. For examples of the continuing problem of enforcement see ibid., Dec. 5, 1914, Dec. 4, 1915, June 2, 1916. Chicago's Board of Physical Culture and Athletics was also uneasy about the adherence to the rule at other schools. Ibid., Nov. 25, 1916.

48. Examples of Stagg reciting the chapter and verse of the rule: Stagg to Fred H. Jacks, Sept. 16, 1915, and Stagg to Leonard Henjum, March 9, 1916. Quotation from Stagg to Henry C. Calhoun, Aug. 7, 1919. Other examples in which Stagg broke the letter or the spirit of the conference rule: Stagg to Daniel Trude, July 29, 1914, Stagg to Charles L. Pyke, March 8, 1917 (Stagg argued that the bigger universities in bigger cities, with an athletic director with "prestige," would be the best place for Pyke's son to attend, and "my position . . . during the past twenty-five years has given me special power in helping place our athletes who wish to coach"), Stagg to Harvey G. Gregerson, Nov. 30, 1928. All in box 13, Stagg Papers.

49. Minutes, BPC&A, May 28, June 6, June 18, Oct. 29, 1910, May 13, 1915, Jan. 24, 1920, May 9, 1924, April 29, May 23, 1925; *Cap and Gown, 1926,* 417.

50. *Special Souvenir Issue, Eighth Annual National Interscholastic Basketball Tournament* (n.p., n.n., n.d.), 23–26.

51. Minutes, BPC&A, Jan. 24, Feb. 2, April 24, 1920, May 28, 1921, March 16, 1922, May 9, 1924, April 29, May 23, 1925; *Cap and Gown, 1925,* 467; *Cap and Gown, 1926,* 417.

52. Stagg to P. F. Neverman, May 6, 1926, box 65, Stagg Papers; Ickes in *University of Chicago Magazine* 31 (Oct. 1928): 2–3. Ickes had earlier helped Stagg quash the efforts of eastern college graduates to initiate student direction of athletics at Chicago. Box 104, folder 2, Stagg Papers; "Stagg's Interscholastic," box 65, Stagg Papers.

53. *Daily Maroon,* June 7, 1910, 2, June 8–11, 1910, 1, 3; "Interscholastic Extra," June 11, 1910; Stagg to "Chicagoan" (form letter mimeographed), May 24, 1922, box 113, Swift Papers. For the promise of fame and other questionable approaches, see box 65, especially folder 1926, Stagg Papers. The Oklahoman was Ira Davenport, who proved a fine runner for Stagg, an Olympian, and, in turn, recruited one of Chicago's finest football players—Jay Berwanger. Interview with John Jay Berwanger, Nov. 7, 1992.

54. Most of the interscholastic tournament materials are in boxes 65, 76, Stagg Papers. On the revenue surpluses that were made by the interscholastic meetings by the 1920s, see Stagg to P. F. Neverman, May 6, 1926, box 65, Stagg Papers.

55. *Annual Register, 1919–1920,* 27; Angell, "Memorandum for the College Deans," dated March 5, 1919, in Minutes, BPC&A, April 18, 1919. Angell became dean of the faculties in 1911. In a limited early-twentieth-century

study of students' comparative academic work at Cornell, football players finished at the bottom, although more anecdotal studies elsewhere showed uncertain results. Miller, "Athletes in Academe," 463n41.

56. Stagg to Dean George E. Vincent, July 31, 1909, box 10, Stagg Papers. Stagg estimated a loss of one-third of his football candidates, even if the rule were not applied retroactively. Minutes, BPC&A, March 16, 1922.

57. Stagg to H. O. Page, Aug. 21, 1911, H. O. Page to Stagg, Aug. 12, Aug. 28, 1911. Other examples of Captain Page's diligent work for the team and Stagg, letters of Page to Stagg, Jan., Feb. 1912, and July 15, 1913. All in box 11, Stagg Papers.

58. Dudley B. Reed to Stagg, Jan. 15, 1915, Stagg to Dudley B. Reed, Jan. 23, 1915, Stagg to Reed, June 5, 1913, and Reed to Stagg, June 7, 1913, box 12, Stagg Papers. Page's plan for Dean Lovett was in Page to Stagg, July 39, 1913, box 11, Stagg Papers.

59. Walter A. Payne to Stagg, Sept. 21, 1920, Stagg to his wife, Stella, Jan. 31, 1919, box 10, Stagg Papers; *IR*, spring quarter, 1920.

60. Minutes, BPC&A, Jan. 28, 1922; Rule 7, paragraph 2, of the "Conference Rules of Eligibility," Nov. 10, 1913, box 77, Stagg Papers.

61. Ibid.; Minutes, BPC&A, Jan. 28, 1922.

62. Ibid.; *Cap and Gown, 1907*, 67.

63. Harold Swift to Harry P. Judson, March 18, 1922, box 15, UPP, 1889–1925, also in box 113, Swift Papers; Judson to Swift, March 20, 1922, box 15, UPP, 1889–1925; Minutes, Intercollegiate Conference, April 1, 1922.

64. Minutes, BPC&A, Jan. 26, 1924.

65. Ibid.; the corrected evidence was noted by the university recorder in the minutes at an unspecified later date; *Cap and Gown, 1925*, 67, and Eckersall's judgment is on p. 40 of the yearbook.

66. *Rochester* (N.Y.) *Democrat and Chronicle*, Nov. 23, 1906. Raycroft had served as Stagg's loyal and invaluable assistant in the department and as the sponsor of the university Y.M.C.A. chapter. *Cap and Gown, 1895*, "Official Organizations," no pagination. Joseph E. Raycroft to Stagg, Nov. 26, 1911, box 12, Stagg Papers. Cf. Joseph E. Raycroft to Stagg, Nov. 21, 1913, box 12, Stagg Papers, for another unfavorable report. The testimony of eastern coaches agreed with Raycroft regarding their sparse use of the new offensive weapon. See Danzig, *History of American Football*, 39.

67. See Walsh, ed., *Intercollegiate Football*, 154, 358, for the Army and Notre Dame schedules. The *Chicago Tribune*'s Walter Eckersall clearly saw the educative significance of the Notre Dame victory over Army, Nov. 9, 1913. Cf. *Chicago Post* and *Chicago Record Herald*, Nov. 24, 1913, for the records of Michigan and Notre Dame over eastern opponents that season—Michigan defeated Cornell, Pennsylvania, and Syracuse. Notre Dame also defeated Penn State. Only Pennsylvania and Cornell could be considered "major" teams in 1913, and both those teams were not especially strong that season. Notre Dame played only three teams of any reputation, and none of the three (Army, Penn State, Texas) played a major schedule. See Grantland Rice, column, *Collier's*, Nov. 29, 1913, 22, and Danzig, *History of American Football*, 38–42. Moore, in "Football's

Ugly Decades, 1893–1913," argues that Notre Dame's victory over Army was the major factor leading to a virtual cultural and economic revolution in football. This argument is greatly exaggerated, and Moore's brief for John Heisman is more a regional plea than argument. Miller, *Athletes in Academe*, 436, repeats the myth, without citations (for such as its acceptance), that forward passing burst on the horizon as an effective tactic with the 1913 Army–Notre Dame game. The Notre Dame contribution to intercollegiate football is large and genuine, and it need not be inflated with fallacious history.

68. The year 1913 was Chicago's last year to enjoy a distinct lead from Stagg's rapid adjustment to, and use of, the post-1905 rules changes, and the Maroons won four of the nine western championships during the period. The *Chicago Examiner*, Nov. 24, 1913, headlined, "Maroons Best Football Team in America"; cf. *Chicago Daily News*, Nov. 25, 1913, and Walter Camp's national comparisons, *Collier's*, Nov. 29, 1913, 22. Harvard played five major opponents, Chicago played seven; they were both undefeated and untied, and Harvard scored 107 points to their opponents' eleven. Chicago managed 124 points to twenty-seven for the opposition. Walsh, ed., *Intercollegiate Football*, 80. Stagg judged his 1913 team the best he had developed under the new code of 1906. *Chicago Interocean*, Nov. 24, 1913. Walter Eckersall made the distinctions between the Harvard and Chicago style of play, and others agreed with him. See *Chicago Tribune*, Dec. 28, 1913, *Chicago Daily News*, Dec. 27, 1913.

69. *Chicago Tribune*, Sept. 20, Dec. 5, 1920.

70. Minutes, BPC&A, April 28, 1920, Dec. 10, 1913.

71. Statement by Amos Alonzo Stagg, dated May 8, 1921, box 42, Stagg Papers; *Chicago Tribune*, Sept. 20, Dec. 5, 1920.

72. Enthusiastic pregame write-ups appeared in the *Chicago Journal, Chicago Daily News, Chicago American*, and *Chicago Herald-Examiner*, Oct. 21, 1921. The *Philadelphia Public Ledger*'s prediction of the game was typical of the eastern press: "Princeton will breeze in" (Oct. 21, 1921). Grantland Rice picked Princeton over Chicago by 14-0, *New York Daily Tribune*, Oct. 22, 1921. Walter Eckersall was the *Chicago Tribune* columnist who admitted the lack of eastern enthusiasm, Oct. 22, 1921. The *New York World*, Oct. 22, 1921, was keenly interested, however; termed the game the "most important contest in years"; and predicted "the wily Stagg is not apt to fool the Tigers with his shifts." An attendance of fifty-five thousand was expected, and 644 tickets were sold in Chicago. *Chicago Herald-Examiner*, Oct. 21, 1921. The special train was run by the Pennsylvania Railroad especially for Princeton and Chicago alumni from Chicago. Box 113, Swift Papers. The politicians and other public figures were noted by the *Chicago Daily News* and *Chicago American*, Oct. 22, 1921. Ring Lardner and a "crowd of former Chicagoans" were very much in evidence, according to the *Chicago Herald-Examiner*, Oct. 23, 1921. Heywood Broun's description, under his byline, was carried by the *New York World* and the *Baltimore Sun*, among others, Oct. 23, 1921; Damon Runyon's column was in the *New York Sun*, Oct. 24, 1921, and the *Boston Globe* and *Boston Herald*, Oct. 23, 1921. However, the *New York Times*, Oct. 23, 1921, described Princeton as "tamed and humbled"; the *Philadelphia Inquirer*, Oct. 23, 1921, spoke of Princeton's "deep humiliation"; and the *New York Herald*, Oct.

23, 1921, headlined, "West Humbling East for First Time in History," and then criticized Stagg's direction of the game, claiming that Chicago should have "rolled up a bigger score."

73. Most eastern columnists predicted a disastrous season for Princeton after the Chicago humiliation, but the Tigers beat Virginia (34-0), Harvard (10-3), and narrowly lost to Yale (7-13). Harvard later beat Yale (10-3). Walsh, ed., *Intercollegiate Football,* 128, 80; *Outing* 79 (Jan. 1922): 156, 162.

74. Danzig, *History of American Football,* 243–54, 356–59; *New York Herald,* Oct. 29, 1922; *New York Evening Post,* Nov. 2, 1928; *Princeton Alumni Weekly,* Jan. 10, 1930, 300, and Oct. 24, 1972, 12–13; *Princeton Herald,* Nov. 15, 1947; Red Smith column, *New York Times,* Oct. 27, 1972. See *Chicago Tribune,* Nov. 4, 1922, for the statistical proof that the Princeton team won faultily.

75. Walsh, ed., *Intercollegiate Football,* 80; Judson to Hibben, Jan. 2, 1923, and Hibben to Judson, Jan. 4, 1923, box 15, UPP, 1889–1925.

76. *Outing* 75 (Jan. 1920): 200, 76 (Jan. 1921): 158; John Durant and Otto Bettman, *Pictorial History of American Sports* (New York: A. S. Barnes, 1952), 158; Danzig, *History of American Football,* 239–42; *Chicago Tribune,* Dec. 12, 1920. Cf. Eckersall's season summary in *Chicago Tribune,* Dec. 26, 1920. *Chicago Herald-Examiner,* Oct. 30, 1920. Walter Camp's views were given in *Collier's,* Dec. 18, 1920, 8–9. Camp said that Ohio State, the Intercollegiate Conference champion, "Took the greatest advantage of the modern rules." Walsh, ed., *Intercollegiate Football,* 246, 273, 396–446; Umphlett, *Creating the Big Game,* 46–47. The tertiary frontier developed in the Southwest and Rocky Mountain states from the 1890s to World War I, see Walsh, ed., *Intercollegiate Football,* 245–463. The Midwest was the primary frontier, and it served the secondary and tertiary frontiers with coaching leaders. Ibid., 211, 425, 217, 281, 186, 448; John F. Rooney, Jr., *A Geography of American Sport* (Reading: Addison-Wesley, 1974), 36–47. For the centennial all-American teams, see Durant and Etter, *Highlights of College Football,* 207.

77. *Chicago Tribune,* Dec. 5, 1922.

78. Ibid., and Nov. 29, 1921; Rockne, "Western Football vs. Eastern," 43; Sperber, *Shake Down the Thunder,* 84–362; Schoor, *One Hundred Years of Notre Dame Football,* 37; Brondfield, *Rockne,* 81. Hardy, *How Boston Played,* 104, notes the appearance, at the turn of the century, on the playgrounds of Boston of the democratizing influence of football (and hockey), which "ignored, to a great extent, the race lines between Irish, Jews, and Italians." Knute Rockne's life ended in 1931 when he became the first famous American to die in a commercial airline crash. His body was identified by Jess Harper, his former coach and mentor, whose ranch was not far from the crash site at Cottonwood Falls, Kansas. Brondfield, *Rockne,* 17.

79. Sperber, *Shake Down the Thunder,* 163–72; *Chicago Herald-Examiner,* Dec. 1, 1924; Walsh, ed., *Intercollegiate Football,* 358. Notre Dame played, and won, ten games, including the Rose Bowl against Stanford; in the East, against Army, Princeton, and Carnegie Tech; in the Midwest, against Wabash, Lombard, Wisconsin, and Northwestern; in the South, against Georgia Tech; in the West, against Stanford; and in the Plains, against Nebraska.

80. See Rader's excellent chapter 9, "The Age of Sports Heroes," *American Sports,* 131–50.

81. The *New York Times, Chicago Tribune,* and *Chicago Herald-Examiner,* Dec. 30, 1924, carried the Camp selections. The *Chicago Tribune* was cognizant of the significance of these changes. A *Tribune* writer (Dec. 16, 1924) remembered the few westerners on Camp's all-American in the early days, noted Eckersall's choice of seven westerners and four easterners for his 1924 team, and continued, "So the tide has set in the other direction. Possibly in a few years the east will be as fortunate to have one or two names in this list as was the west a quarter century ago." The *Chicago Herald-Examiner,* Dec. 25, 1924, reported that eastern representatives on the Football Rules Committee wished to return to the slower, more forcible style of play when that section dominated the game. The paper commented, "The western brand of football is too progressive" for the East. Camp seems to have wanted just such a move away from the speed and deception of the western game. Ibid., Nov. 27, 1924. The trend of the comparative weakness of the Big Three continued. *Literary Digest,* Jan. 15, 1927, 66–71.

82. The *Chicago Tribune* Dec. 3, 1924, listed the teams in order that led the nation in attendance: Michigan, Pennsylvania, California, Harvard, Yale, Notre Dame, Ohio State, Chicago, and Illinois. Michigan had 340,000, Illinois 225,000. "The previous record single game attendance of about 80,000 set and equaled several times in Yale bowl [*sic*], was eclipsed when 90,000 saw Stanford and California in their annual classic at Berkeley, while the Western Conference games were watched by close to 1,500,000, a figure shattering all previous marks." *Chicago Herald-Examiner,* Dec. 1, 1924.

83. Danzig, *History of American Football,* 48–69.

84. The number of non-eastern all-Americans increased in 1920 to six (of thirteen named). There were four to six such players named each year until 1924, when nine non-easterners were selected. This majority was consistently maintained. *Official 1993 NCAA Football* (Overland Park: National Collegiate Athletic Association, 1993), 302–8. A study of the regions represented by the team that attained serious mention as the best in the nation indicates that from 1889 to 1918 the East had thirty-six such teams put forward as worthy of the honor, the non-East nine. The period of cultural equity, 1919–26, shows ten each for the East and non-East, and the period of cultural reversal begins in 1927. The period from 1927 to 1940 shows four eastern teams and thirty-seven non-eastern teams considered as possible national champion. Dan Jenkins, *Saturday's America* (Boston: Little, Brown, 1970), Appendix; also see Miller, "Athletes in Academe," ch. 3.

85. Harold "Red" Grange and Ira Morton, *The Red Grange Story* (1953; repr. Urbana: University of Illinois Press, 1993), Rice's quotation on x, and ch. 6. Grange was taken out for a long period in the Michigan game but returned to score one more touchdown and catch six passes for sixty-four yards toward an offensive total of 402 yards gained, Howard Roberts, *The Big Nine: The Story of Football in the Western Conference* (New York: G. P. Putnam's Sons, 1948), 75–84. Grange's version of the 1924 Michigan game appears in Danzig, *Oh, How*

They Played the Game, 385–89. Sixty-five thousand attended the Michigan game to dedicate the new Memorial Stadium in Urbana, Illinois, a town of twelve thousand then and more than a hundred miles from a city of any size; Lester, "Fielding Harris Yost," 917; Walsh, ed., *Intercollegiate Football,* 210.

86. Grange and Morton, *The Red Grange Story,* ch. 9, 62, ix–xii.

87. Stagg assistant Fritz Crisler, later Minnesota, Princeton, and Michigan coach, scouted Illinois and Grange and devised the Chicago strategy. Powers, "Life Story of Amos Alonzo Stagg," 26–27.

88. Stagg, *Touchdown!* 345; Grange, *The Red Grange Story,* 63.

89. Grange, *The Red Grange Story,* 64; Stagg, *Touchdown!* 346.

90. Grange, *The Red Grange Story,* 65–66; Stagg, *Touchdown!* 348; Camp quoted in Grange, *The Red Grange Story,* 68; Roberts, *The Big Nine,* 34–35. Although Grange referred to this 1924 epic as his "toughest game," he may properly have forgotten what Stagg's men did to him the next year in Urbana. He gained a paltry twelve yeards on sixteen carries against the Maroons for his poorest record ever, and this the week after gaining 363 yards in thirty-six tries in the mud against eastern champion Pennsylvania. He termed the Pennsylvania effort the "best day" of his career. Grange, *The Red Grange Story,* 78–79, 76; Stagg, *Touchdown!* 350; Roberts *The Big Nine,* 34–35, 75–84. Chicago history professor William T. Hutchinson recorded in his diary: "A big day on this campus. Forty thousand attended the football game. To everybody's surprise Chicago tied the University of Illinois, 21 to 21." Daily Journal, Nov. 8, 1924, Hutchinson Papers.

91. Powers, "Life Story of Amos Alonzo Stagg," 28.

Chapter 5: The Decline, 1925–38

1. Minutes, Board of Trustees, March 13, Aug. 9, 1923; Minutes, BPC&A, Nov. 22, 1924, Oct. 31, 1925.

2. Wilkins to "President Mason," Nov. 10, 1925, box 9, folder 10, UPP, 1925–45; Wilkins to Stagg, Nov. 18, 1925, and Swift self-memo, Nov. 20, 1925, Wilkins to Mason, revised version, Nov. 23, 1925, box 113, folder 15, Swift Papers. If Wilkins's call at Chicago for discussion went unheeded, he was more successful with the Committee G Football Report he completed for the American Association of University Professors in 1926. The report prompted discussion elsewhere, but the local AAUP officer, Professor of Political Economy James A. Field, found little encouragement to use the report at Chicago. Field to F. C. Woodward, April 16, 1926, and Woodward to Field, April 22, 1926, box 9, folder 10, UPP, 1925–45. Vice-president Woodward advised Field to await the receipt of a forthcoming Intercollegiate Conference report. There is no further mention of the matter.

3. John G. Hibben to Judson, Jan. 4, 1923, A. Lawrence Lowell to Judson, Jan. 2, 1923, James R. Angell to Judson, Jan. 2, 1923, box 15, UPP, 1889–1925. The data on the ratio of seats to student matriculation is in *Heffelfinger's Football Facts,* ed. "Pudge" Heffelfinder (Minneapolis: Heffelfinger Publications, 1938), 18. Cf. Lawrence Perry, "The Stadium and College Athletics," *Scribners* 56 (Nov. 1914): 571–86.

4. Judson to Swift, Jan. 30, 1923, box 43, UPP, 1889–1925; *Chicago Tribune,* Dec. 23, 1924; Stagg, *Touchdown!* 172–73. An example of the unifying uses of a stadium drive is given in James Gray, *The University of Minnesota, 1851–1951* (Minneapolis: University of Minnesota Press, 1951), 555.

5. Storr, *Harper's University,* 70–71; A. R. E. Wyant to Burton, June 8, 1923, Burton to Wyant, July 21, 1923, Burton to George E. Vincent, Nov. 11, 1924, box 15, UPP, 1889–1925. Burton's youthful classmate quoted in Thomas Wakefield Goodspeed, *Ernest DeWitt Burton: A Biographical Sketch* (Chicago: University of Chicago Press, 1926), 10.

6. "The Program for Athletic Development at the University of Chicago" (n.p.: n.n., 1924), a copy is filed in box 15, UPP, 1889–1925; Minutes, Board of Trustees, Nov. 14, 1922, Sept. 11, 1924, Dec. 10, 1925.

7. Burton to Paul S. Russell, Nov. 6, 1924, Burton to Stagg, Nov. 12, 1924, Stagg to Burton, Nov. 14, 1924, box 15, UPP, 1889–1925.

8. Burton to George E. Vincent, Nov. 11, 1924, George E. Vincent to Burton, Nov. 17, 1924, box 15, UPP, 1889–1925; Minutes, Board of Trustees, Sept. 11, Oct. 16, 1924.

9. Walter Wilson to Stagg, Nov. 13, 1924, Stagg to Walter Wilson, Nov. 17, 1924, Burton to Swift, Nov. 18, 1924, Swift to Burton, Nov. 20, 1924, Burton, memorandum, pp. 1–2. Box 15, UPP, 1889–1925.

10. *Chicago Examiner,* Nov. 22, 1914; *The President's Report, 1922–23* (Chicago: University of Chicago Press, 1924), 25; *The President's Report, 1923–24* (Chicago: University of Chicago Press, 1925), 29; *The President's Report, 1924–25* (Chicago: University of Chicago Press, 1926), 25; *The President's Report, 1925–26* (Chicago: University of Chicago Press, 1927), 30–31. For Stagg's financial predictions, see Stagg to Wallace Heckman (university business manager), Jan. 11, 1923, box 113, Swift Papers, and Minutes, Board of Trustees, March 13, 1923.

11. Swift to M. C. Meigs, April 18, 1929, General Athletics file, UPP, 1925–45. The field house was not completed until 1932, box 104, folder 2, Stagg Papers. The record of trustee action is one of confident predictions by Stagg, trustee action, and subsequent revenue shortfalls followed by rearranged or scaled-down building plans. A sampling: Minutes, Board of Trustees, Sept. 11, 1924, Dec. 10, Sept. 10, Oct. 8, 1925, April 12, 1928.

12. J. F. Steiner, "1921 to 1930 Attendance and Revenue Study for the Presidents' Research Committee," showed attendance at forty-nine major institutions grew 219 percent, and receipts at sixty-five major institutions grew 310 percent over the period. See box 114, folder 5, Swift Papers; Benjamin A. Rader, *American Sports* 2d ed. (Englewood Cliffs: Prentice-Hall, 1990), 182; Arthur A. Fleisher et al.,*The National Collegiate Athletic Association: A Study in Cartel Behaviour* (Chicago: University of Chicago Press, 1992), 43; "Comparative Statement of Net Incomes from Football of the Conference Universities," box 21, Stagg Papers. The budget predictions, increasingly inaccurate, were presented by Stagg and approved by the Board of Physical Culture and Athletics. Minutes, BPC&A, Oct. 30, 1926, Nov. 2, 1927, Oct. 27, 1928. Projections and actual receipts for the seasons of 1928, 1929, and 1930 are in ibid., Oct. 26, 1929, Oct. 25, 1930. Frederic Woodward to Howard J. Savage, Oct. 31, 1930, General Athletics file, UPP, 1925–45.

13. The comparative net revenue figures are given in John Griffith (intercollegiate conference commissioner), Memorandum, Feb. 3, Dec. 15, 1925, to "The Directors of Athletics of the Western Conference," box 84, Stagg Papers; "Statement Showing the Number of Student Coupon Books Sold by Conference Universities during the Years 1926, 1927, 1928, and 1929," Athletic Department file, unprocessed, Walter Dill Scott Papers, Northwestern University Archives; and see the statements of proration of commissioner's office expenses for the Intercollegiate Conference, 1926–29, 1930–33, boxes 85, 86, Stagg Papers, which include the football receipts figures for each conference school.

14. *Chicago Tribune,* Dec. 26, 1931; Grange and Morton, *The Red Grange Story,* 89, 98–107, 112; Walsh, ed., *Intercollegiate Football,* 242; see Riess, *City Games,* 155–56, 143–45, for a survey of municipal stadium building; Harold M. Mayer and Richard C. Wade, *Chicago: Growth of a Metropolis* (Chicago: University of Chicago Press, 1969), 276, 294; Perry Duis and Glen Holt, "The Classic Problem of Soldier Field," *Chicago Magazine* 27 (April 1978): 170–73.

15. *Chicago Herald-Examiner,* Oct. 9, 1928; *Chicago American,* Oct. 13, 1928; *Chicago Tribune* and *Chicago Herald-Examiner,* Oct. 14, 1928; Walsh, ed., *Intercollegiate Football,* 242; *Chicago Tribune,* July 20, 1933. Soldiers Field was supported by civic leaders and newspapers who mounted campaigns to draw Army-Navy and other national matches, *Chicago Herald-Examiner,* Dec. 3, 1925. On declining Chicago ticket prices and rising competitors' prices, see L. R. Steere to Robert M. Hutchins, Aug. 19, 1932, University of Chicago Press Release, and W. B. Harrell to H. H. Swift, Feb. 8, 1933, box 116, folder 7, Swift Papers; W. B. Harrell to L. R. Steere, July 13, 1933, L. R. Steere to H. H. Swift, July 14, 1933, box 114, folder 5, Swift Papers.

16. C. W. Seabury (president, Chicago Association of Commerce) to Knute Rockne, Sept. 30, 1929, Notre Dame Director of Athletics Records, box 18:171, University of Notre Dame Archives. Cf. E. M. Starrett to Knute Rockne, April 26, 1929, Notre Dame Director of Athletics Records, box 20:8, University of Notre Dame Archives, regarding Chicago as Notre Dame's "home town." In 1914 Stagg requested of the trustees, on behalf of Stagg's disciple Jesse Harper, Notre Dame athletic director and coach, that Stagg Field be loaned to Notre Dame for their November football game with the Carlisle Indians. The Chicago trustees resolved that "it is not desirable to permit the use of the Athletic Field for games of this sort," request denied. Minutes, Board of Trustees, Feb. 17, 1914.

17. The headline was in the *Chicago Tribune,* Sept. 17, 1931. Cf. *Chicago American,* Sept. 16, 1931, and *Christian Science Monitor,* Sept. 25, 1931, for other pessimistic predictions. On the Michigan game, see *Detroit Times,* Oct. 11, 1931, *Chicago Herald-Examiner* and *New York Times,* Oct. 18, 1931; on the Indiana game, see *Chicago Tribune,* Oct. 25, 1931, and *Chicago Herald-Examiner,* Oct. 24, 1931; for the Purdue game, see *Chicago Daily News,* Oct. 31, 1931; for the Arkansas game, see *Chicago Tribune* and *Chicago Herald-Examiner,* November 8, 1931; for the Illinois game, see *Chicago Tribune,* Nov. 15, 1931; the homecoming game with Wisconsin is described in *Chicago Tribune,* Nov. 22, 1931. *Chicago Herald-Examiner,* Oct. 24, 1931.

18. Stagg to H. F. Woodcock, Nov. 18, 1931, box 43, Stagg Papers; *Chicago Tribune,* May 20, 1932.

19. The original survey of these studies and changes from Burton to Hutchins is Reuben Frodin, "Very Simple, but Thoroughgoing," in *The Idea and Practice of General Education* (Chicago: University of Chicago Press, 1950), 41–60. "Hutchins' name, of course, was immediately associated with the New Plan for the College, even though he had done little more than give Dean Boucher a green light." McNeill, *Hutchins' University,* 33, 16–71. For an overview of "the so-called Hutchins College," see John J. MacAloon, "Introduction," in John J. MacAloon, ed., *General Education in the Social Sciences: Centennial Reflections on the College of the University of Chicago* (Chicago: University of Chicago Press, 1992), 3–22, and the essay by David E. Orlinsky, "Not Very Simple, but Overflowing: A Historical Perspective on General Education at the University of Chicago," 25–76. Cf. Ernest H. Wilkins, *The Changing College* (Chicago: University of Chicago Press, 1927).

20. Stagg to F. E. Bowser, Aug. 23, 1920, box 13, Stagg Papers; Stagg to Francisco Fernandez, Aug. 25, 1930, box 2, "Department Historical File" (preliminary processing), Stagg Papers; also see Stagg to Charles McClung, Jan. 19, 1927, and Stagg to Harvey G. Gregerson, Nov. 30, 1928, box 15, Stagg Papers; Stagg to Harold S. Ofstie, Sept. 25, 1929, box 2, "Department Historical File," Stagg Papers; Stagg to Christy Walsh, Dec. 23, 1932, box 111, folder 5, Stagg Papers; Minutes, BPC&A, Feb. 24, 1923. The Stanford study was published in their *Faculty Bulletin,* Feb. 6, 1929; the Columbia study was noted in *Report on College Athletics and Scholarship to the Carnegie Foundation for the Advancement of Teaching,* 52–65; the Minnesota study was published in Donald Paterson and Emerick Peterson, *Athletics and Scholarship,* Research Bulletin, no. 1 (Nov. 1928), published by the University of Minnesota. Commissioner John L. Griffith added, "We all know . . . that some persons in the Conference colleges are practicing dishonesty in the matter of giving inducements to athletes." Memoranda from Griffith to Athletic Directors of the Intercollegiate Conference, Aug. 8, 20, 1925; the conference "reaffirmed" in 1927 a formal 1922 statement regarding recruiting because it had not been followed, Minutes, Intercollegiate Conference, May 28, 1927, all in box 85, Stagg Papers. For the Intercollegiate Conference's attempt to increase the rigidity of regulations, see ibid., Jan. 28, 1927, *Chicago Tribune* and *Chicago Herald-Examiner,* Jan. 29, 1927.

21. On comparative tuition levels, Appendix 2, Table 5; David H. Stevens to Stagg, July 17, 1929, box 85, Stagg Papers.

22. Stagg to Frank Crowell, Jr., Dec. 22, 1928, box 13, Stagg Papers; Minutes, Board of Trustees, May 14, 1936.

23. Woodward to Stagg, Feb. 10, 1928, Athletics General file, UPP, 1925–45; Special Souvenir Issue, 8th Annual National Interscholastic Basketball Tournament, 23–26, box 65, Stagg Papers.

24. Box 65, Stagg Papers, contains most of the letters detailing the sorry tale. For an example of Stagg's position, see his encouragement of an Oklahoma school superintendent to transgress his state regulations, Stagg to L. R. Stegall, telegram, May 14, 1930, box 74, Stagg Papers.

25. Woodward to Stagg, Feb. 19, 1930, box 65, Stagg Papers; *Chicago Tribune,*

April 9, 1930. Stagg quoted in *Chicago Journal,* April 27, 1930. See the scores of letters in box 65, Stagg Papers. Support for Stagg by two sportswriters and Knute Rockne appeared in *Chicago American,* May 12, 1930, *Chicago Post,* April 28, 1930, and *Chicago Herald-Examiner,* May 14, 1930. Professor Linn's outburst was written in his regular column, "Round about Chicago," *Chicago Herald-Examiner,* April 9, 1930. Linn took up the mantle of Oliver Thatcher as the leading faculty football backer on campus. Linn, a minister's son and Jane Addams's nephew, had entered Chicago in 1893 as a first-year undergraduate.

26. Minutes, PBC&A, April 26, 1930. The committee's report is found in box 65, Stagg Papers. Woodward to Stagg, May 23, 1930, ibid. (as is the material relating to subsequent local tournaments). The *Hyde Park Herald,* Dec. 21, 1939, reported that thirty-two Chicago public high schools were to compete in the twenty-second annual tournament and noted, "Until 1931, the tournament was national in scope, when it was limited to Chicago area high schools. This year, only Chicago public high schools will be represented." Stagg, Memorandum, "Comments on the Interscholastic Meet Field Held on June 12th and 13th, 1931," box 74, Stagg Papers. James E. Rogers, chair, field service, of the American Physical Education Association, listed "Some High Spots of the Past Year in Physical Education" and included "the abolition of the National High School Basketball Championships held at the University of Chicago," *Journal of Health and Physical Education* 2 (June 1931): 10.

27. *Literary Digest,* Nov. 15, 1930, 28, covered the Big Ten. Examples of schools that began to recruit actively with official approval during the period are: the Naval Academy, *Chicago Tribune,* Dec. 16, 1931, and Carnegie Institute of Technology, Francis Wallace, "Pigskin Preview of 1938," *Saturday Evening Post,* Sept. 24, 1938, 5, 63. The result of the new methods was increased suspicion and ill-will among the schools and conferences. For the Southern Conference, see *Christian Science Monitor,* Dec. 19, 1931; for the Pacific Coast Conference, see *San Francisco Call-Bulletin,* Oct. 31, 1934. Cf. the survey of the difficulties in *Literary Digest,* Jan. 9, 1937, 32–33, and Savage, *American College Athletics.*

28. Stagg to Harold Swift, March 10, 1931, box 10, Stagg Papers, and Stagg to Frederic Woodward, March 10, 1931, box 9, folder 4, UPP, 1925–45. On Northwestern, see Scott to Kenneth L. Wilson, Oct. 6, 1933, Harold H. Anderson (student editor of Northwestern's *Daily* in 1921–22) to Kenneth L. Wilson, Nov. 13, 1931, Athletic Department file, unprocessed, Walter Dill Scott Papers, Northwestern University Archives, and Wilson's explanation to the Intercollegiate Conference, March 6, 1931, box 9, folder 4, UPP, 1925–45. Also, oral interview with Elizabeth Sargent Doughty, former undergraduate tutor at Northwestern, July 15, 1972. On Notre Dame, see A. Schymeinsky to Rockne, June 21, 1929, Notre Dame Director of Athletics Records, box 18:168, Keith L. Roche to Rockne, April 24, 1929, box 18:46, Knute Rockne to H. Dockweiler, March 20, 1929, and W. G. Rich to H. Dockweiler, Feb. 21, 1929, box 18:92; Sperber, *Shake Down the Thunder,* 296–300, 375–77, 451–52.

29. Early physical education courses had been offered in the 1890s, and physical education teacher preparation courses had commenced in at least six-

teen state normal schools by 1902. The major universities followed. C. W. Hackensmith, *History of Physical Education* (New York: Harper and Row, 1966), 375–76; on the initiation of the physical education majors, see Appendix 2, Table 4. A course in cheerleading was included at Purdue. *Chicago Tribune,* Nov. 25, 1931.

30. Stagg to Dudley B. Reed, Sept. 6, 1923, regarding Burton's interest, box 12, Stagg Papers; Hackensmith, *History of Physical Education, 404*–5. *National Collegiate Athletic Association, 50th Anniversary* (n.p.: National Collegiate Athletic Association, 1955), 23, notes that in 1918 the organization recommended that physical education be conducted with full curricular rights and responsibilities and carried under a legitimate academic department structure, just as William Rainey Harper had done at Chicago in the 1890s. Professor Judd's suggestion was noted by Dudley B. Reed to Stagg, Feb. 28, 1912, box 12, Stagg Papers.

31. See Frodin, "Very Simple, but Thoroughgoing," 41–60. Minutes, BPC&A, Feb. 28, April 13, June 21, Oct. 31, Dec. 2, 1931 (final meeting); Minutes, Board of Trustees, Feb. 11, 1932; Minutes, University Senate, Jan. 19, May 28, 1932; Minutes, College Faculty, May 18, 1932.

32. Minutes, BPC&A, Nov. 28, 1914. As an example of the uses of such campus football: "One day Rockne happened to pass when Gipp was doing some kicking. He marveled at the length of Gipp's punts. . . . Thus simply, began the career of George Gipp." Arthur Hope, *Notre Dame: One Hundred Years* (Notre Dame: University Press, 1943), 353.

33. Hackensmith, *History of Physical Education, 399.* For the relation of intercollegiate sports and general athletic activity on the campus, see Forrest Crissey, *The Saturday Evening Post,* March 13, 1926, 14–15, 62, 64, 66, and *Chicago Tribune,* Nov. 11, 1923. Northwestern consistently had more than 80 percent of its male undergraduates participating in intramurals, and in 1929, more than 90 percent were involved. Walter Paulison, ed., *Intramural Athletic Program* (Evanston: Division of Intramural Athletics, 1927), 5; Kenneth L. Wilson to Walter Dill Scott, Dec. 13, 1930, Athletic Department file, unprocessed, Walter Dill Scott Papers, Northwestern University Archives. On the Harvard and Pennsylvania programs, see *Christian Science Monitor,* Oct. 24, 1931.

34. Holden's advice to Swift is included in Athletics file, UPP, 1925–40. A *Chicago Tribune* series on intramurals had come to the same conclusion regarding Chicago's backwardness. It included the following colleges: Illinois, Notre Dame, Michigan, Ohio State, Wisconsin, Iowa, and summary, respectively, Jan. 9, 10, 11, 12, 13, 15, 18, 1923. The 1930 autumn quarter budget appears in Minutes, BPC&A, Oct. 31, 1931. Hutchins claimed erroneously that Chicago had a "pioneer" intramural program, *1930 Carnival Booklet* (sixth annual Intramural Carnival) (n.p.: n.n., 1930), 2.

35. Minutes, BPC&A, April 24, May 22, 1926, Nov. 2, 26, 1927.

36. *Athletic World,* Feb. 1923, 17.

37. *Chicago Tribune,* Nov. 11, 1923; Fielding H. Yost, "Playing the Game," *Chicago Journal,* Nov. 11, 1927. Conference Commissioner Griffith noted in 1925 that all of the institutions but Purdue increased enrollment at a faster

rate than did Chicago from 1914 to 1924. Memorandum, July 29, 1925, box 84, Stagg Papers. See *School and Society,* Dec. 17 1938, 765–86 for the continuation of this enrollment trend; by the late 1930s, however, all other conference institutions surpassed Chicago's growth.

38. Knute Rockne's column in *Chicago Herald-Examiner,* Nov. 30, 1929; Warner quoted in *Chicago Tribune,* Sept. 4, 1932; *Chicago Tribune,* Oct. 27, 1933; figures on the area of origin of the players from a study by Intercollegiate Conference Commissioner's Office, box 86, Stagg Papers, and from *Chicago Times,* Nov. 24, 1931. *University of Chicago Magazine* 19 (Dec. 1926): 85; *Chicago Daily News,* Nov. 5, 1935.

39. The figures on the player reservoirs appear in Stagg to G. J. Sweetland, Oct. 25, 1927, box 2, Stagg Papers. One player and coach during the 1930s remembered that no more than twenty players during any season in the 1930s were near the Big Ten standard. Oral interview, John Jay Berwanger, Nov. 7, 1992. Michigan and Northwestern figures are given in *New York Herald-Tribune,* Oct. 18, 1925, and *Chicago Herald-Examiner,* June 11, 1926. The Chicago figures are in *Chicago Herald-Examiner,* Sept. 23, Oct. 21, 1932, and *University of Chicago Magazine* 3 (Nov. 1937): 23.

40. Fall 1908 statement in Stagg's hand, box 104, file 3, Stagg Papers; Stagg to Burton, Sept. 19, 1923, and Bill Moff to Stagg, Aug. 8, 1923, box 8, Stagg Papers; Stagg to Dudley B. Reed, Aug. 8, 1922, and Dudley B. Reed to Stagg, Aug. 20, 1922, box 12, Stagg Papers. Herrick caricatured Dean Robertson as "Little President," the none-too-talented heir apparent of Judson, see *Chimes,* 197; see also Robert M. Lovett, "Key to *Chimes,"* addendum, box 1, Robert Herrick Collection. A part of Stagg's difficulty was that he persisted in personnel arrangements that might have been appropriate in the early years but seemed impossible in the 1920s. For example, he was the only Big Ten football coach who also coached a second varsity sport, track. Albon Holden to President Max Mason, Nov. 28, 1927, and Mason to Holden, Nov. 29, 1927, box 9, folder 5, UPP, 1925–40,.

41. *The University of Chicago Song Book* (Chicago: Undergraduate Council, 1921, 1927), 16. Other songs in which Stagg was noted or alluded to:

Song	Allusion or Note
"Wave the Flag"	"With the grand old man to lead them,"
"'C' Stands for Cherished Courage"	"O stands for old man the best coach in this land,"
"1893"	"Then Stagg was catcher, pitcher, coach, shortstop, and halfback, too,"
"For the Varsity"	"It must be Stagg's men who have the ball,"
"The Song of the 'C'"	"To 'Old Man' Stagg and his splendid dream,"

Ibid., 9, 10–11, 15, 77, 22.

42. See boxes 19, 110, Stagg Papers, for materials on Stagg's participation

in the university fund drive. For an example of Stagg's fund drive rhetoric, see *Orlando* (Fla.) *Sentinel,* Dec. 20, 1924. On Ickes, see *University of Chicago Magazine* 31 (Oct. 1938): 2–3; cf. Ickes's memories of the Midway are in *Autobiography of a Curmudgeon* (Chicago: Quadrangle Books ed., 1969), 20–26. Richberg, general counsel of the National Recovery Administration under Franklin D. Roosevelt, had been a member of the track team, a football cheerleader, and writer of the school song. *University of Chicago Magazine* 27 (March 1934): 19. Friend, appointed to the Circuit Court of Cook County by Governor Frank Lowden to begin his distinguished judicial career, had been a star trackster under Stagg, *Chicago Tribune,* Sept. 17, 1920.

43. Swift to Judson, Oct. 1, 1915, box 113, Swift Papers; Judson to Stagg, Oct. 1, 1915, Judson to Reed, Oct. 1, 1915, and Stagg to Judson, Oct. 4, 1915, box 10, Stagg Papers; Reed to Judson, Oct. 4, 1915, box 113, Swift Papers. Swift's continued questioning and urging due care during the following season indicates that he was still concerned, Judson to Swift, Sept. 29, 1916, box 113, Swift Papers.

44. For Swift's care and feeding of the Maroons, see Swift to S. Bangs, Nov. 11, 1915, Swift to Stagg, Nov. 18, 1915, Dudley B. Reed to Swift, Nov. 15, 1915, box 113, Swift Papers. On Swift's attendance at team practice, see Swift to Stagg, Sept. 18, 1918, box 10, Stagg Papers. Memories of Swift's concern for the football team and frequent presence at the Deke house, oral interviews: John Jay Berwanger, Nov. 7, 1992, James L. Cate, May 15, 1970, Omar Fareed, Feb. 3, 1993 (by telephone), Keith I. Parsons, Feb. 2, 1993, Edward W. Rosenheim, Nov. 4, 1992.

45. Copy of letter, Frederic Woodward to Reed, undated, attached to memorandum addressed to Stagg and C. O. Molander, Sept. 28, 1932. A similar Woodward note caused Stagg to criticize Reed's response, Stagg to Reed, Oct. 4, 1929, and Reed to Stagg, Oct. 9, 1929, Reed to Stagg, Oct. 24, 1932, and Stagg's disappointing response to Reed, Oct. 25, 1932. All in box 12, Stagg Papers.

46. *Cap and Gown, 1914,* 238–39; *Annual Register, 1929–30,* 62; Stagg to Dudley B. Reed, Oct. 20, 1924, box 12, Stagg Papers; see Intramural Sports folder, 1924–25, box 76, Stagg Papers, for evidence of friction between Stagg and Molander, and folders 1926, 1927, and 1928 for further developments. Molander to Stagg, July 1930, Report, complains of insufficient facilities for intramurals, box 76, 1930–32 folder, Stagg Papers. On the imbroglio over Stagg's reorganization, see (all in box 76, Stagg Papers): Stagg to W. E. Nissla (assistant advisor, intramurals), June 15, 1932, Stagg to R. Howard, July 7, 1932, Stagg to John Lynch, July 7, 1932, Howard to Stagg, July 8, 1932, Lynch to Stagg, July 11, 1932, Stagg to Lynch, July 16, 1932, and Stagg, "Memorandum Regarding the Intramural Athletic Situation at the University of Chicago in 1932," July 13, 1932. Stagg vented his strong feelings in "Disloyalty of the Intra-mural Division," box 104, folder 2, Stagg Papers.

47. *Daily Maroon,* Oct. 29, 30, Nov. 3, 1931; Linn's attack appeared in the *Chicago American,* Nov. 3, 1931. *The Phoenix* 13 (Nov. 1931): 14. Linn saw himself as defender of the gridiron faith, and he loved the opportunity to speak at

the annual football dinner. Oral interviews: Norman Maclean, May 20, 1969, Edward W. Rosenheim, Nov. 4, 1992. Dean of the Colleges Ernest Wilkins complained in 1925 at the tone he thought Linn had set at the football dinner when he excoriated individual players. Wilkins pronounced Linn's speech "the most offensive instance" of such comments. Wilkins to Max Mason, Nov. 23, 1925, box 113, folder 15, Swift Papers. Horwitz's opinion of other students was not shared by other players of the 1930s, many of whom worked with Horwitz when he served later as an assistant coach. Oral interviews: John Jay Berwanger, Nov. 7, 1992, Robert J. Greenebaum, Nov. 5, 1992, Lewis B. Hamity, Nov. 13, 1992, James K. Goldsmith, Nov. 30, 1992, Saul S. Sherman, Jan. 21, 1993.

48. Box 111, folders 1, 4, 5, Stagg Papers. On Christy Walsh, perhaps American sport's first "agent" and founder of the ghost-writers' stable of column writers, see Benjamin G. Rader, *Baseball: A History of America's Game* (Urbana: University of Illinois Press, 1992), 122, and Sperber, *Shake Down the Thunder,* 194–96. *Chicago Herald and Examiner,* Sept. 5, Oct. 31, Nov. 21, 1931.

49. Swift to Stagg, Jan. 17, 1923, Stagg to Swift, Feb. 27, 1929, Swift to Stagg, Aug. 18, 1925, Stagg to Swift, Augu. 19, 1925, box 113, Swift Papers.

50. Stagg to Burton, Aug. 14, 1923, T. W. Goodspeed to Burton, Aug. 17, 1923, box 74, folder 4, UPP, 1925–45; Burton to William Scott Bond, July 12, 1924, box 15, UPP.

51. Burton to A. R. E. Wyant, July 21, 1923, Burton to George E. Vincent, Nov. 11, 1924, Swift to Burton, Aug. 8, 1923, Burton to Paul S. Russell, Nov. 6, 1924, Burton to James A. Pollock, March 25, 1925, Burton to Stagg, Nov. 12, 1924, all in box 15, UPP. For Burton's seeking advice on a new faculty representative to the Intercollegiate Conference to replace Albion Small (Burton suggested Dean Gale, Stagg approved), see Burton to Stagg, Oct. 22, 1923, Stagg to Burton, Oct. 23, 1923, box 8, Stagg Papers.

52. Stagg made his judgment regarding the new president, whom he remembered chiefly as a high-jumper at Wisconsin, in a letter to Dudley B. Reed, Aug. 24, 1925, box 12, Stagg Papers. Swift pointedly left Mason entirely out of his history of university administrations, although Swift had led the trustees when Mason served. Dorothy V. Jones, *Harold Swift and the Higher Learning* (Chicago: University of Chicago Library, 1985), 26.

53. Box 74, folder 4, UPP, 1925–45; *Pulse* 2 (Nov. 1938): 24–25.

54. Survey materials and "Notation" on conversation with H. O. Page are in box 5, folder 1, UPP, 1925–45; box 104, folder 2, Stagg Papers. Another remarkable statement came from K. L. "Tug" Wilson, the athletic director at Northwestern reponsible for the success of that institution's athletics in the late 1920s. Wilson gave evidence that Chicago South Side players who chose Northwestern would not go to Chicago as long as Stagg and his son remained as coaches. Ibid. Professor William T. Hutchinson later wrote after a Chicago defeat: "No doubt Stagg is a 'Grand Old Man,' but I think he should retire." Daily Journal, Oct. 1931, Hutchinson Papers. The materials relating to President Mason's decision to allow Stagg to remain in his position are contained in A. A. Stagg folder, UPP, 1925–45, and indicate President Burton's prior commit-

ment to Stagg, Stagg's clear desire to remain, and Mason's decision. Burton to Stagg, Oct. 17, 1924, Stagg to Mason, May 14, 1926, Mason to Stagg, May 24, 1926; see also, Minutes, Board of Trustees, Jan. 13, 1927. There was a require- ment by university statute of a yearly invitation from the trustees for any person to remain beyond age sixty-five. For an example of such a yearly let- ter see Frederic Woodward to Stagg, Nov. 21, 1927, and see the memorandum, May 21, 1926, regarding the arrangement among Mason, Woodward, and Stagg. Trustee Minutes, Dec. 8, 1927, Dec. 13, 1928, Jan. 9, Dec. 11, 1930, also contain further extensions for Stagg. Those minutes show that a good num- ber of top professors, some of them founding faculty, were granted such ex- tensions. On Mason's unexpected resignation, see McNeill, *Hutchins' Universi- ty*, 171n1.

55. Hutchins's attitude about tennis was recalled in oral interviews with William V. Morgenstern, Aug. 3, 1972, James L. Cate, Oct. 10, 1969, William T. Hutchinson, July 28, 1972, and Jay Berwanger, Nov. 7, 1992. On the Yale game and festivities, see *Chicago Herald-Examiner, Chicago Tribune, Chicago Daily News,* and *Chicago American,* Oct. 17, 1931. For an example of Hutchins obtain- ing football tickets for Yale alumni, see Robert Stevens to Hutchins, Nov. 10, 1924, and Hutchins to Robert Stevens, Nov. 11, 1924, box 3, part 5, Robert Maynard Hutchins Papers, Addenda, University of Chicago Archives.

56. Savage, *American College Athletics,* 298; Rader, *American Sports,* 187.

57. Walter Steffen to Harold Swift, Feb. 14, 1933, box 115, Swift Papers. Will Connolly, *San Francisco Chronicle,* Oct. 6, 1938, characterized the Hutch- ins offer. For other examples of similar interpretations of Stagg's departure see *Chicago Herald and Examiner,* Dec. 19, 1932, and Danzig, *Oh, How They Played the Game,* 49.

58. Stagg to Hutchins, Feb. 14, 1930; see large organization chart in Stagg's hand and notes from a conference, held Feb. 18, 1932, "Preserve carefully" and "Memo. on what Mr. Stagg wanted at one time." The notation is signed "HS," for Hutchins's secretary, Harriet E. Servis; Hutchins to Stagg, April 4, 1932, Football General file and box 74, folder 4, UPP, 1925–45.

59. Hutchins to Stagg, May 26, 1932, box 34, folder 1, Presidents' Papers, Appointments and Budgets, 1925–45, and Hutchins to Stagg, Dec. 6, 1932; Stagg to Hutchins, Dec. 12, 1932, Hutchins to Stagg, Dec. 12, 1932, Football General file, UPP, 1925–45, and box 74, folder 4; Stagg to Naismith, Jan. 27, 1933, box 96, folder 5, Stagg Papers. For one of many letters Hutchins had to write in defense of the manner of Stagg's retirement, see Hutchins to Joseph C. Hazen, Nov. 1, 1932, box 30, folder 9, UPP, 1925–45.

60. Wilder to Hutchins, April 5, 1965, Hutchins Papers, Addenda; Milton Mayer, *Robert Maynard Hutchins: A Memoir* (Berkeley: University of California Press, 1993), 139.

61. Hutchins to Metcalf, Oct. 29, 1932, box 9, folder 9, UPP, 1925–45; Metcalf to Stagg, Nov. 28, 1932, Metcalf to Hutchins, Nov. 28, 1932, Hutch- ins's explanation to Joseph Hazen, Nov. 1, 1932, Football General file, UPP, 1925–45; Minutes, Board of Trustees, Oct. 13, 1932; *Chicago Tribune* and *New York Times,* Oct. 14, 1932. William T. Hutchinson recorded: "In evening an

'extra' was cried by schoolboys in this neighborhood. The paper proclaims that Alonzo Stagg will quit as coach here at the end of this year." Daily Journal, Oct. 13, 1932, Hutchinson Papers. At the Feb. 11, 1932, trustees meeting (Minutes) a list of emeritus professors recommended to continue their year-by-year appointments was presented, including Shailer Mathews, Ernst Freund, Robert Park, John M. Manly, and William A. Craigie; another, mostly older, group, including Stagg and Paul Shorey, was referred to the Board Committee on Instruction and Equipment "with power to act." This procedure no doubt provided trustee cover for the widespread policy of ceasing year-by-year appointments at age seventy for even world-renowned scholars who wished to remain. Board policy on such matters was noted later that year, when it was stated that personnel matters "are handled by the President's Office, and the Board of Trustees seldom, if ever, takes action contrary to recommendations made by that office." Ibid., Dec. 8, 1932.

62. Stagg to Christy Walsh, Dec. 23, 1932, box 111, folder 5, Stagg Papers.

63. On Stagg at Pacific, oral interview: William V. Morgenstern, Aug. 3, 1972; *Stockton* (Calif.) *Record,* Nov. 14, 1938. For adulatory and uncited coverage of Stagg's subsequent career, see Considine, *The Unreconstructed Amateur;* Ellis Lucia, *Mr. Football: Amos Alonzo Stagg* (New York: A. S. Barnes, 1970); Danzig, *Oh, How They Played the Game,* 49–50; and Mervin D. Hyman and Gordon S. White, Jr., *Big Ten Football* (New York: Macmillan, 1977), 89–90. On Stagg's later years, see the Amos Alonzo Stagg Collection, Amos Alonzo Stagg High School, Palos Hills, Ill.

64. The Hutchins family was Presbyterian and Congregational in membership. Mary Ann Dzuback, *Robert M. Hutchins: Portrait of an Educator* (Chicago: University of Chicago Press, 1991), 3–42; Harry S. Ashmore, *Unseasonable Truths: The Life of Robert Maynard Hutchins* (Boston: Little, Brown and Co., 1989), 3–15; McNeill, *Hutchins' University,* 18–25.

65. Ibid.

66. McNeill, *Hutchins' University,* 150–53; Dzuback, *Robert M. Hutchins,* 210.

67. Dzuback, *Robert M. Hutchins,* 67–87; McNeill, *Hutchins' University,* 16–18; Ashmore, *Unseasonable Truths,* 30–35. Hutchins's modest explanation of his election was offered to an alumni group, June 7, 1930, in *The Idea of the University of Chicago,* ed. William Michael Murphy and D. J. R. Bruckner (Chicago: University of Chicago Press, 1976), 277. I am indebted to Richard Storr for the story regarding Swift's early morning telephone call to Dean Hutchins and its effect upon the board president. For Harper's 5 A.M. dictation to a stenographer, see Veysey, *Emergence of the American University,* 367. The similarity of midwestern work habits of the two presidents is noteworthy, just as their intellectual paths and physical profiles were dissimilar.

68. Dzuback, *Robert M. Hutchins,* 67–87; McNeill, *Hutchins' University,* 16–18; Ashmore, *Unseasonable Truths,* 57–62; Carroll Mason Russell, *The University of Chicago and Me* (Chicago: University of Chicago Printing Department, 1982), 43–57.

69. Metcalf's appointment was approved by the board of trustees in Minutes, Oct. 13, 1932; *Chicago Tribune* and *New York Times,* Oct. 14, 1932. The

confidential contacts by Hutchins to Metcalf to replace Stagg as athletic director commence with Hutchins to Metcalf ("Dear Nellie:"), May 25, 1932, and
are in box 34, folder 1, Appointments and Budgets, UPP, 1925–45; for Metcalf's Hutchins clan recollections, see Lawson and Ingham, "Conflicting Ideologies Concerning the University and Intercollegiate Athletics: Harper and
Hutchins at Chicago, 1892–1940," 53, and n115; for Metcalf family history, oral
interview: Harold R. Metcalf, Oct. 24, 1992. Oberlin won 7-6, just five years
after being humiliated by Ohio State 128-0, Walsh, ed., *Intercollegiate Football,*
230, 196.

70. *University of Chicago Magazine* 29 (Nov. 1936): 27–29, and 25 (Midsummer 1933): 406. T. Nelson's nephew, Harold "Geoff" Metcalf, became athletic
director at Chicago during the 1970s after serving many years as dean of students in the Business School.

71. *University of Chicago Magazine* 25 (Midsummer 1933): 409.

72. Ibid. On the administrative changes under Hutchins, see McNeill,
Hutchins' University, 31; on the administrative changes in 1932, which included the abolition of the Board of Physical Culture and Athletics, see John
Moulds, secretary of the board of trustees to Hutchins, Feb. 26, 1932, regarding the board's action of Feb. 11, 1932, box 78, folder 12, UPP, 1925–40, Appointments and Budgets, box 1, folder 4; *Announcements,* April 10, 1934, 30–
32. Metcalf quoted on his department's independence in Press Release, Nov.
5, 1937, University of Chicago Department of Public Relations, box 114, folder 8, Swift Papers; Metcalf to Marvin McCarthy, Jan. 11, 1939, box 2, folder
5, UPP, 1940–46.

73. The golf captain was given three golf balls for each of the four varsity
team members and $25 to cover expenses for the team's trip to an Ohio State
match at Columbus. Oral interview: James K. Goldsmith, Nov. 30, 1992. Student athletes, who should have had the best opportunity to know the athletic
director, knew little of Metcalf or his work. Oral interviews: Robert J.
Greenebaum, Nov. 5, 1992, John Jay Berwanger, Nov. 7, 1992.

74. Danzig, *History of American Football,* 77–80, 362; Walsh, ed., *Intercollegiate Football,* 186; Robert Sherwood, *Roosevelt and Hopkins: An Intimate History*
(New York: Harper, 1948), 40.

75. *University of Chicago Magazine* 25 (June–July, 1933): 423; the 1934 *Cap
and Gown,* 39, reported that the "new athletic regime has been received with
enthusiasm"; oral interviews: William V. Morgenstern, Aug. 3, 1972, John Jay
Berwanger, Nov. 7, 1992, Robert J. Greenebaum, Nov. 5, 1992, Lewis B. Hamity, Nov. 13, 1992, Keith I. Parsons, Feb. 2, 1993.

76. *University of Chicago Magazine* 26 (May 1934): 255, 26 (Nov. 1934): 31,
27 (Dec. 1934): 77–78, and 27 (June 1935): 314–15; oral interviews: William
V. Morgenstern, Aug. 3, 1972, John Jay Berwanger, Nov. 7, 1992, Robert J.
Greenebaum, Nov. 5, 1992, Lewis B. Hamity, Nov. 13, 1992. Northwestern's
poorest season in years (1933) probably helped Maroon attendance in
1934. Walsh, ed., *Intercollegiate Football,* 224.

77. *University of Chicago Magazine* 28 (Nov. 1935): 26, and 28 (Dec. 1935):
25, 27; *Cap and Gown,* 1936; oral interviews: Keith I. Parsons, Feb. 2, 1993,

William V. Morgenstern, Aug. 3, 1972, John Jay Berwanger, Nov. 7, 1992, Robert J. Greenebaum, Nov. 5, 1992, Lewis B. Hamity, Nov. 13, 1992. Only Michigan and Chicago had players selected for the early and late historical-era teams, and the Downtown Athletic Club of New York prize was named the "Heisman" trophy after Berwanger's award year. McCallum and Pearson, *College Football U.S.A.*, 539–51; George Vass, *George Halas and the Chicago Bears* (Chicago: Henry Regnery, 1971), 121; Sheldon S. Cohen, "The Genius of the Gridiron," *Chicago History* (Winter 1986–87): 22–33.

78. *University of Chicago Magazine* 28 (Midsummer 1936): 29, and 29 (Dec. 1936): 25–26; oral interviews: William V. Morgenstern, Aug. 3, 1972, John Jay Berwanger, Nov. 7, 1992, Robert J. Greenebaum, Nov. 5, 1992, Lewis B. Hamity, Nov. 13, 1992, Saul S. Sherman, Jan. 21, 1993, James D. Goldsmith, Nov. 30, 1992, Jane Rinder Coulson and John Coulson, Jan. 7, 1993, Walter J. Blum, Dec. 18, 1992.

79. *University of Chicago Magazine* 29 (Midsummer 1937): 29, 30 (Nov. 1937): 23–24, and 30 (Dec. 1937): 22; oral interviews: William V. Morgenstern, Aug. 3, 1972, James L. Cate, Oct. 10, 1969, William T. Hutchinson, July 28, 1972, John Jay Berwanger, Nov. 7, 1992, Robert J. Greenebaum, Nov. 5, 1992, Lewis B. Hamity, Nov. 13, 1992, Norman Maclean, Oct. 20, 1970, Edward W. Rosenheim, Nov. 4, 1992, Saul S. Sherman, Jan. 21, 1993, Bernard Weinberg, Oct. 3, 1972, Walter J. Blum, Dec. 18, 1992, Jane Rinder Coulson and John Coulson, Jan. 7, 1993; for the record of the "Swift boys," Shaughnessy to H. Swift, Aug. 14, 1938, box 114, folder 8, Swift Papers, and the foregoing oral interviews.

80. *University of Chicago Magazine* 31 (Oct. 1938): 22, 21, and 31 (Nov. 1938): 21; comparative 1931 figures contained in one-page report by Coach A. A. Stagg, Jr., at a meeting of the Department of Physical Culture and Athletics, Oct. 14, 1932; *University of Chicago Magazine* 31 (Jan. 1939): 19; oral interviews: William V. Morgenstern, Aug. 3, 1972, John Jay Berwanger, Nov. 7, 1992, Robert J. Greenebaum, Nov. 5, 1992, Lewis B. Hamity, Nov. 13, 1992, James L. Cate, Oct. 10, 1969, William T. Hutchinson, July 28, 1972, Saul S. Sherman, Jan. 21, 1993.

81. *Chicago Daily News,* Nov. 7, 8, 9, 10, 11, 1938; *Chicago American,* Nov. 8, 1938; *Chicago Tribune* and *Chicago Daily Times,* Nov. 10, 1938; *Chicago Herald and Examiner,* Nov. 10, 1938.

82. *Chicago American,* Nov. 8, 1939; *Chicago Times,* Nov. 9, 1938.

83. *Chicago Times,* Nov. 10, 1938.

84. *Chicago American,* Nov. 12, 15, 1938; *Chicago Tribune,* Nov. 12, 13, 1938; *Chicago Herald and Examiner,* Nov. 13, 1938; oral interviews: William V. Morganstern, Aug. 3, 1972, John Jay Berwanger, Nov. 7, 1992, Robert J. Greenebaum, Nov. 5, 1992, Lewis B. Hamity, Nov. 13, 1992, James K. Goldsmith, Nov. 30, 1992, Saul S. Sherman, Jan. 21, 1993, Walter J. Blum, Dec. 18, 1993, Edward W. Rosenheim, Nov. 4, 1992; *Daily Maroon,* Nov. 15, 1938.

85. *Chicago Evening American,* Nov. 17, 1938; *Chicago Daily Times,* Nov. 23, 1938, carried Chapman's plan, and the quotation was in the Nov. 25, 1938, issue. On November 21, *Chicago Evening American* columnist Leo Fischer nominated the Chicago players as "the gamest bunch of football players of the year."

86. On the complications of the New Plan for Shaughnessy, see the unattributed (but almost certainly written by Shaughnessy) memorandum, "Difficulties," dated "Feb. 1938," box 114, folder 8, Swift Papers; "Time Devoted to Football Practice in 1937," box 30, folder 9, UPP, 1925–45; William B. Benton to Charles W. Nash, Nov. 20, 1937, box 114, folder 8, Swift Papers, and *Chicago Evening American,* Nov. 19, 1938. Dean Leon Smith discussed the problems of preserving eligibility, Development Campaigns, box 10, folder 2, University of Chicago Archives, Joseph Regenstein Library; *University of Chicago Magazine* 29 (Nov. 1936): 27–29. On the failure of the early entrants policy: "But it proved difficult to persuade parents and high school advisers to send sixteen-year-olds off to Chicago." Albert M. Tannler and Robert E. Streeter, *One in Spirit* (Chicago: University of Chicago Library, 1991), 88. In *Robert M. Hutchins,* 149–50, Dzuback notes that only 40 percent of first-year students stayed to graduate in the late 1930s; Charles D. O'Connell (assistant director and director of admissions during the 1950s) recalled that he had to warn President Lawrence Kimpton that the early entrant policy, if it were continued as the college's primary recruiting tool, might lead to a college enrollment below a thousand students, that the graduation rate for first-year students was still about 35–40 percent, and that relations with secondary schools were poor because of the policy. Oral interview, Nov. 20, 1992. On the impact of the New Plan on the players, oral interviews: John Jay Berwanger, Nov. 7, 1992, Robert J. Greenebaum, Nov. 5, 1992, Lewis B. Hamity, Nov. 13, 1992, James K. Goldsmith, Nov. 30, 1992, Saul S. Sherman, Jan. 21, 1993, Omar Fareed, Feb. 3, 1993 (by telephone).

87. The enthusiastic quotation is from McNeill, *Hutchins' University,* 51, and is backed by virtually all alumni from the 1930s who were interviewed for this book. On the lack of enrollment bias, which was certainly a part of most institutions, see ibid., 52–53, but Harold S. Wechsler takes a less benign view. MacAloon, ed., *General Education in the Social Sciences,* 218. Dzuback, *Robert M. Hutchins,* 145–53, provides the best summary of the changing student profile, although Hutchins provided two figures that were significant of the student body in 1939: "over 50% live at home" and "65% working some of way." Hutchins, "Notes on Football," presented to Trustee Committee on Instruction and Research, Nov. 8, 1939, box 21, folder 4, UPP, Appointments and Budgets, 1925–40. Ralph Cannon of the *Chicago Daily News* wrote to Swift, Feb. 17, 1933, box 114, folder 5, Swift Papers.

88. *University of Chicago Magazine* 29 (Nov. 1936): 16; oral interviews: James K. Goldsmith, Nov. 30, 1992, Lewis B. Hamity, Nov. 13, 1992, Edward W. Rosenheim, Nov. 4, 1992, Saul S. Sherman, Jan. 21, 1993, Jane Rinder Coulson and John Coulson, Jan. 7, 1993.

89. *University of Chicago Magazine* 29 (Nov. 1936): 27–29; Metcalf quoted in the *Chicago Evening American,* Nov. 19, 1938; chart on Intercollegiate Conference athletic scholarships, box 30, folder 9, UPP, 1925–45; it should be remembered that Chicago won far more than its share of conference tennis, gymnastics, fencing, swimming and water polo kudos during these years.

90. George A. Works to Hutchins, April 25, 1933, Athletics General file, UPP, 1925–45; Renslow Sherer to John Nuveen, Nov. 21, 1939, stated that Inter-

collegiate Conference game official John Schommer claimed that Chicago's Dean Works was the only dean who "strictly interprets" conference rules, Football General file, UPP, 1925–45; oral interviews with former players: John Jay Berwanger, Nov. 7, 1992, Lewis B. Hamity, Nov. 13, 1992, James K. Goldsmith, Nov. 30, 1992, Saul S. Sherman, Jan. 21, 1993, Keith I. Parsons, Feb. 2, 1993, Omar Fareed, Feb. 3, 1993 (by telephone), Robert E. Fitzgerald, letter to author, Feb. 6, 1993. Neither former faculty member James L. Cate nor administrator William V. Morgenstern knew of any Shaughnessy recruitment initiatives; oral interviews: Cate, May 15, 1970, Morgenstern, Aug. 3, 1972.

91. Faculty oral interviews: Bernard Weinberg, Oct. 3, 1972, James L. Cate, Oct.10, 1969, Norman Maclean, Oct. 20, 1970, William T. Hutchinson, July 28, 1972. Student oral interviews: John Jay Berwanger, Nov. 7, 1992, Saul S. Sherman, Jan. 21, 1993, Robert J. Greenebaum, Nov. 5, 1992, Lewis B. Hamity, Nov. 13, 1992, James K. Goldsmith, Nov. 30, 1992, Edward W. Rosenheim, Nov. 4, 1992, John Coulson, Jan. 7, 1993. Coach Shaughnessy extolled Captain Ellmore Patterson (later to become CEO of a Wall Street banking firm) for "unceasingly" checking "on the class work of the men" which produced "so satisfactory an eligibility record" in 1934. *Touchdown News,* Sept. 1, 1939, 1.

92. Faculty oral interviews: William T. Hutchinson, July 28, 1972, Norman Maclean, Oct. 20, 1970, James L. Cate, May 15, 1970, Bernard Weinberg, Oct. 3, 1971. Student oral interviews: John Jay Berwanger, Nov. 7, 1992, Saul S. Sherman, Jan. 21, 1993, Robert J. Greenebaum, Nov. 5, 1992, Lewis B. Hamity, Nov. 13, 1992, James K. Goldsmith, Nov. 30, 1992.

93. *Chicago Times,* Nov. 16, 1937; *Touchdown News,* Sept. 1, 1934, 1; one of the assistant coaches was Professor Herbert Blumer, an all-American tackle from Missouri (1921) and a Chicago Cardinal (1925–33). Blumer coached while holding an appointment in the sociology department; he later was elected president of the American Sociological Association, 1937 team roster, box 114, folder 8, Swift Papers; Robert K. Merton, Leonard Broom, and Leonard S. Cottrell, Jr., eds., *Sociology Today* (New York: Harper and Row, 1965), 67; oral interviews: John Jay Berwanger, Nov. 7, 1992, Robert J. Greenebaum, Nov. 5, 1992, Lewis B. Hamity, Nov. 13, 1992, James K. Goldsmith, Nov. 30, 1992, Saul S. Sherman, Jan. 21, 1993. The complexity, not to say impossibility, of getting critical Chicago student-athletes to burst out of the locker-room door and vanquish the opponent was elevated to a beloved tradition in the 1950s when the Second City comedy troupe (which originated among College students) created a sketch, "Football Returns to the U of C," in which a teacher-coach vainly introduced the fundamentals of the game to an unlikely cast of would-be players who questioned every concept.

94. The transcribed three-page typed report is in box 117, folder 16, Swift Papers.

95. *Chicago Tribune,* Nov. 23, 1938.

96. John Dewey, *The Social Frontier* 3 (Dec. 1936): 104; also see Dewey, "Rationality in Education," *The Social Frontier* 3 (Jan. 1937): 103–4, and Hutchins's response, "Grammar, Rhetoric, and Mr. Dewey," *The Social Frontier* 3 (Feb. 1937): 137–39.

97. *University of Chicago Magazine* 29 (Nov. 1936): 29.

98. Harper to Stagg, Aug. 17, 1904, box 10, folder 9, WRHP. Hutchins was constantly trying to find ways to separate the Chicago experience from what he termed "big-time, industrial football." Murphy and Bruckner, eds., *The Idea of the University of Chicago,* 225. He was probably looking to show legal rulings on federal taxation held that intercollegiate football was not "educational" because it had the characteristics of a business; at least, he asked for an opinion from young law professor Edward H. Levi in 1938 on a recent U.S. Supreme Court case, *Allen, Collector v. Regents of the University of Georgia.* If so, he was disappointed. Levi concluded, "I should think that the case therefore would be a holding that the conduct of football games and the charging of admission is a business. I don't suppose it decides that the playing of football is non-educational." Levi to Hutchins, June 24, 1938, box 30, folder 9, UPP, 1925–45.

99. Minutes, Board of Trustees, Feb. 13, 1936, is typical of the bad financial news that the board heard of football during the 1930s: football costs were up and revenues were down. Hutchins to Ralph C. Hamill, Oct. 30, 1936, Comments on Football folder, UPP, 1925–45. Hamill was a four-time football letterman, Walsh, ed., *Intercollegiate Football,* 189. The *Rock Island* (Ill.) *Argus,* Oct. 7, 1937 reported rumors "that Chicago is on its way out of the Big Ten." Transcribed in box 117, folder 16, Swift Papers.

100. "Outline of Report on Athletic Situation at Meeting Board on Coordination of Student Interests," Feb. 6, 1937, box 10, Nuveen Papers; Coordination of Student Interests file, UPP, 1925–45.

101. "Gate Receipts and Glory," *Saturday Evening Post,* Dec. 3, 1938, 23ff. Curiously, although many observers thought they knew Hutchins was bent on abolition, Jay Berwanger and perhaps other players believed that some trustees and others took that position but that the president did not. Even after the event, Berwanger averred no knowledge that Hutchins had led the move toward abolition and in fact remembered Hutchins sitting with him in the late 1930s at the annual football dinners and enjoying film of the Berwanger years. Oral interview: John Jay Berwanger, Nov. 7, 1992.

Chapter 6: The Fall, 1939

1. *The Phoenix* 13 (Nov. 1931): 2; William McDermott, "The Greater Cleverness," *This Week Magazine,* Jan. 9, 1938; quotation in Danzig, *Oh, How They Played the Game,* 48–49.

2. Among the players who grew up in the neighborhood and attended games at Stagg Field, oral interviews: quotation from Robert J. Greenebaum, Nov. 5, 1992, Lewis B. Hamity, Nov. 13, 1992, James K. Goldsmith, Nov. 30, 1992; quarterback Saul S. Sherman, Jan. 21, 1993; *Pulse* 2 (Oct. 1938): 4, and 2 (Nov. 1938): 6; Fuqua's essay, ibid., 24–25.

3. *Chicago Daily News,* Nov. 19, 1938; *Pulse* 2 (Nov. 1938): 6. For the origins of the game, Pacific President Tully C. Knoles to Robert Maynard Hutchins, Nov. 8, 1937, and Hutchins to Knoles, Nov. 23, 1937, box 74, folder 4, UPP, 1925–45; *Chicago Herald Examiner,* Nov. 20, 1938.

4. *Pasadena Star News,* Nov. 14, 1938.

5. William Michael Murphy and D. J. R. Bruckner, eds., *The Idea of the University of Chicago* (Chicago: University of Chicago Press, 1976), 211.

6. Murphy and Bruckner, eds., *The Idea of the University of Chicago,* 228–30.

7. Ibid., 232.

8. Sidney Hyman, *The Lives of William Benton* (Chicago: University of Chicago Press, 1969), 179. Benton's *The University of Chicago's Public Relations* (Chicago: University of Chicago Press, 1937) was a pioneer work in American university public relations and fund-raising. Ashmore, *Unseasonable Truths,* 180–83.

9. Swift to Luther W. Tatge, Jan. 23, 1940, 2–3, box 114, folder 9, Swift Papers; Don Birney et al., to Harold Swift, June 7, 1937, Bond to Donald H. Birney, July 15, 1937, and Bond to Harold Swift, July 15, 1937, box 114, folder 8, Swift Papers. Jay Berwanger remembered that Russell was considered to be antifootball by the mid-to-late 1930s. Oral interview, John Jay Berwanger, Nov. 7, 1992.

10. Swift, memorandum, April 22, 1927, Swift to Robert M. Hutchins and Frederic Woodward, Nov. 23, 1932, Swift to Frederic Woodward, Sept. 18, 1933, Woodward to T. Nelson Metcalf, Sept. 20, 1933, Swift to Robert M. Hutchins, Oct. 24, 1933, all in box 114, folder 5, Swift Papers; Swift to Woodward and Woodward to Metcalf also in box 9, folder 4, UPP, 1925–45. The Nov. 23, 1932, letter and Swift to Hutchins and Woodward, Oct. 24, 1932, on the same topic, are in box 9, folder 9, UPP, 1925–45.

11. Swift to Woodward, Nov. 5, 1928, box 9, folder 10, UPP, 1925–45; W. B. Harrell to Swift, Feb. 8, 1933, Swift to William B. Benton, Nov. 9, 1937, William V. Morgenstern to William B. Benton, Nov. 5, 1937, box 116, folder 8, Swift Papers; box 117, folder 16, Swift Papers; also in box 114, folder 8, Swift Papers: Dartmouth President E. M. Hopkins to Swift, Jan. 25, 1937, Swift to E. M. Hopkins, Feb. 5, 1937, Swift to "Messrs. Hutchins and Filbey," Feb. 5, 1937, Swift to Frederic Woodward, Dec. 10, 1937, William V. Morgenstern to H. Swift, March 1, 1938. On Swift's arrangements for the journey to Urbana, which included representatives of several prominent Chicago families (including the Avery, Cushman, Fairbank, Ferriss, Cushman, McNair, Russell, Smith, and Stevens families), see box 117, folder 1, Swift Papers. Other occasions included Chicago at Illinois in 1927, and Chicago at Michigan in 1931—the Hutchinses declined this trip and there appears to be no evidence they ever accepted—both in box 117, folder 1, Swift Papers.

12. William V. Morgenstern, oral interview, Aug. 3, 1972, remembered Swift vividly talking of his recruiting efforts and being "deeply proud" of his players. Oral interviews: John Jay Berwanger, Nov. 7, 1992, James K. Goldsmith, Nov. 30, 1992, Robert J. Greenebaum, Nov. 7, 1992, Lewis B. Hamity, Nov. 13, 1992, Walter J. Blum, Dec. 18, 1992, William T. Hutchinson, July 28, 1972, James L. Cate, May 15, 1970, Saul S. Sherman, Jan. 21, 1993. Swift to Metcalf, Dec. 9, 1933, box 114, folder 5, Swift Papers. Those not from California were from Iowa (two), Michigan (one), Minnesota (one), and Texas (one). The Petersen family from Long Beach must have been pleased with the Chicago connection; three Peterson brothers played as Maroons, box 114, folder

8, Swift Papers. On Parsons: Parsons to Swift, Dec. 3, 1934, box 116, folder 7, Swift Papers, and *University of Chicago Directory, 1934–35*, 101, *University of Chicago Directory, 1935–36*, 103, *University of Chicago Directory, 1936–37*, 109. Parsons, '33, played center for Stagg and always held academic scholarships; he used his job to work his way through the law school, 1932 team roster, box 114, folder 5, Swift Papers. Parsons represented Chicago at school visits and assemblies all over the country; oral interview: Keith I. Parsons, Feb. 2, 1993. One of Parson's "recruits" was Saul S. Sherman, who transferred from Northwestern midway through his first year when the coach was fired. Sherman had the honor of being the first modern T-formation quarterback in college football. The players noted that all of the jobs they held were legitimate; they faithfully carried out the jobs and received about 40 cents an hour. Oral interviews: Omar Fareed, Feb. 3, 1993 (by telephone), Lewis B. Hamity, Nov. 13, 1992, John Jay Berwanger, Nov. 7, 1992, Saul S. Sherman, Jan. 21, 1993.

13. On the players' academic performance, oral interviews: William V. Morgenstern, Aug. 3, 1972, James L. Cate, Oct. 10, 1969, Saul S. Sherman, Jan. 21, 1993 (who remembered one of the "flunk outs" went elsewhere and captained the eleven); and Robert M. Hutchins to Edward H. Levi, Levi to author, Dec. 21, 1992. Hutchins reiterated his witticism tirelessly even after he left the university—"As for me, I am for exercise, as long as I do not have to take any myself." Murphy and Bruckner, *The Idea of the University of Chicago*, 225; Hyman, *The Lives of William Benton*, 179; Swift to William Benton, Sept. 7, 1939, box 114, Swift Papers.

14. Clark Shaughnessy to H. H. Swift, "Monday," box 114, folder 8, Swift Papers. Dean George Works noted that Shaughnessy was "heartily in sympathy with the President with reference to the place of football" at the university. Works to Vice-President Emery T. Filbey, Nov. 16, 1939, box 9, folder 4, UPP, 1925–45.

15. Swift to Clark Shaughnessy, Jan. 26, 1938, box 114, folder 8, Swift Papers; unsigned, unattributed memorandum, "Difficulties" dated "Feb. 1938." The date, substance, and style of the memorandum and the placement with the Shaughnessy-Swift exchange of letters points to Clark Shaughnessy as the author. Shaughnessy's desire for specific majors to enhance his player reservoir is reminiscent of Stagg's judgment at the turn of the century. He felt that law students were the best football prospects for two reasons: "1. The men are older and consequently harder and huskier than the undergraduates of the 'Lit' department. 2. They have more time to give to practice." Walter J. Blum brought this Stagg statement (*University of Chicago Weekly*, Feb. 20, 1902, 446), to my attention.

16. Shaughnessy to H. Swift, Aug. 14, 1938, box 114, folder 8, Swift Papers. Several former faculty and players recalled the large number of promising athletes who failed the Chicago academic work; oral interviews: William T. Hutchinson, July 28, 1972, James L. Cate Oct. 10, 1969, Norman Maclean, Oct. 20, 1970, Bernard Weinberg, Oct. 3, 1972, John Jay Berwanger, Nov. 7, 1992, Saul S. Sherman, Jan. 21, 1993.

17. Robert M. Hutchins to author, Sept. 5, 1973. Swift himself must have

had a premonition about the 1939 season; he wrote the nine-member group with whom he always arranged to sit at football games that he had "somewhat the feeling that some of the group might not subscribe if it were not for the tradition that has been built up of our sitting together" and offered a way out for them. There is no record of how his group responded to his offer. Swift to Vail et al., Sept. 11, 1939, box 116, folder 8, Swift Papers.

18. Heywood Broun column, no date, in letter, illegible signature to "Bob" (Robert M. Hutchins), Nov. 4, 1939, Football General file, UPP, 1925–45. The note suggests the losing football team is excellent publicity; it is likened to the "Walgreen affair," termed a "case of magnificent but dumb luck." The style and intimacy with Hutchins suggests that Thornton Wilder may have been the author. Box 2, UPP, 1925–45. The Walgreen affair concerned some unsubstantiated but widely publicized charges that members of the university were teaching things hurtful to the American republic. When the charges proved false, the accuser, chain drug store owner Charles R. Walgreen, apologized publicly and founded a series of lectures in his name at the university. Hyman, *The Lives of William Benton,* 170–73; McNeill, *Hutchins' University,* 63–65; Dzuback, *Robert M. Hutchins,* 163–66.

19. Oral interviews: William T. Hutchinson, July 28, 1972, William V. Morgenstern, Aug. 3, 1972, Walter J. Blum, Dec. 18, 1992, James K. Goldsmith, Nov. 30, 1992, Mark Ashin, Nov. 23, 1992; *University of Chicago Magazine* 26 (March 1934): 190, 168, and 31 (April 1939): 14; McNeill, *Hutchins' University,* 58–59; Dzuback, *Robert M. Hutchins,* 122.

20. *University of Chicago Magazine* 30 (Jan. 1938): 13–14.

21. *Chicago Tribune,* Nov. 3, 1937; *Daily Maroon,* Oct. 1, 8, 14, 20, 21, 26, 28, 29, Nov. 1, 2, 3, 4, 5, 11, 1937; *University of Chicago Magazine* 30 (Nov. 1937): 17, and 30 (Dec. 1937): 8; *Chicago Daily News,* Oct. 1, 1937; *Daily Maroon,* Dec. 9, 1937; *University of Chicago Magazine* 30 (Jan. 1938): 23; box 114, folder 8, Swift Papers. The following year editor Emmet Deadmon again put *The Daily Maroon* in opposition to football, but with more conditional phrases and subtlety, if less eloquence than McNeill. *Daily Maroon,* Nov. 21, 1938; *Chicago American,* Nov. 22, 1938. The *Chicago Daily News,* Nov. 22, 1938, termed Deadmon's editorial "even-tempered, moderately worded"; *Chicago Herald and Examiner,* Nov. 22, 1938. Deadmon became editor of the *Chicago Sun-Times* in the 1960s.

22. *Pulse* 2 (Dec. 1939): 5.

23. Oral interviews: William T. Hutchinson, Aug. 3, 1972, William V. Morgenstern, Aug. 3, 1972, James L. Cate, Oct. 10, 1969, Norman Maclean, Oct. 20, 1970.

24. *University of Chicago Magazine* 31 (Feb. 1939): 16, 17.

25. *University of Chicago Magazine* 30 (Jan. 1938): 12; Swift to William Benton, Nov. 22, 1937, box 114, folder 8, Swift Papers.

26. *University of Chicago Magazine* 31 (Feb. 1939): 17, and 31 (March, 1939): 2–3; John Howe to William Benton, Aug. 7, 1939, box 114, folder 9, Swift Papers.

27. "Development Campaigns," boxes 1–10, University of Chicago Archives,

Joseph Regenstein Library; *Chicago Alumni Club Year Book and Directory* (Chicago: Chicago Alumni Club 1935), 26–27.

28. "Why Go to College?" *Saturday Evening Post,* Jan. 22, 1938, 16ff. The "football, fraternities, and fun" argument appears on p. 74. This Hutchins article appeared as the third in a series: "We Are Getting No Brighter," Dec. 11, 1937, 5ff., "Why Send Them to School?" Dec. 25, 1937, 10ff., and "What Can We Do about It?" Feb. 19, 1938, 27ff.

29. *Cleveland Plain Dealer,* Jan. 16, 1937; *West Palm Beach Post,* Oct. 23, 1939; *Duluth News Tribune,* Oct. 27, 1939; *Trenton Evening Times,* Nov. 8, 1939; *Worcester Telegram,* Oct. 24, 1939; *Spartanburg* (S.C.) *Journal,* Oct. 28, 1939; *Cleveland Plain Dealer,* Nov. 18, 1939; *Portland Oregonian,* Nov. 12, 1939; *Detroit Free Press,* Nov. 14, 1939.

30. John Tunis, "What Price College Football," *American Mercury* 48 (Oct. 1939): 129–42; Francis Wallace, "Test Case at Pitt—The Facts about College Football Play for Pay," *Saturday Evening Post,* Oct. 28, 1939, 14–15; Francis Wallace, "The Football Laboratory Explodes: The Climax of the Test Case at Pitt," *Saturday Evening Post,* Nov. 4, 1939, 17–18.

31. Robert Maynard Hutchins, *The Higher Learning in America* (New Haven: Yale University Press, 1936), 87; Hutchins to Oswald Knauth, Nov. 1, 1939, Comments on Football folder, UPP, 1925–45.

32. The conversion period lasted about eight weeks according to Harold Swift, Swift to Ernest M. Hopkins, Dec. 22, 1939, and Swift to E. A. E. Palmquist, Jan. 23, 1940, box 114, Swift Papers; Swift to Fred H. Bartlit, Dec. 29, 1939, box 10, Nuveen Papers; *Denver Post,* Feb. 25, 1940; Robert M. Hutchins to author, Sept. 5, 1973.

33. Nuveen to Hutchins, Nov. 15, 1939, box 10, Nuveen Papers. Six days later one of Nuveen's fellow trustees, Max Epstein, wrote that he had come to support the "concise and realistic" views of Nuveen to abolish the game, Epstein to John Moulds, Nov. 21, 1939, box 10, Nuveen Papers.

34. Nuveen to B. H. Cleaver, Feb. 2, 1940, box 10, Nuveen Papers; John Tunis files, box 6, William Benton Papers, University of Chicago Archives, Joseph Regenstein Library; *American Mercury* 48 (Oct. 1939): 129–42. The trustees may have been unaware of the origins of Tunis's stories.

35. Hutchins noted Nuveen's opinion survey, Hutchins to Charles E. McGuire (all-American tackle at Chicago, 1921), Feb. 13, 1940, box 115, Swift Papers; F. H. H. Calhoun to Hutchins, Nov. 11, 1939, and Hutchins to Calhoun, Nov. 18, 1939, Comments on Football folder, UPP, 1925–45.

36. John Nuveen, "Comments of Alumni Council," box 10, Nuveen Papers.

37. Nuveen to Hutchins, Dec. 7, 1939, box 10, Nuveen Papers.

38. Harry Swanson, memorandum, undated, "In Regard to the Football Situation at the University of Chicago," box 10, Nuveen Papers.

39. William V. Morgenstern, oral interview, Aug. 3, 1972. Rosenheim also remembered that *Maroon* editor Emmet Deadmon refused even to give the LaSalle crew a hearing. *Chicago Daily News,* Nov. 23, 1938; oral interview, Edward W. Rosenheim, Nov. 4, 1992.

40. Chapman to Harold Swift, Dec. 29, 1937, Swift to Chapman, Jan. 12,

1938, with blind copy to William Benton and Benton to Swift, Jan. 14, 1938. Benton told Swift, "You are dumping in my lap a problem that I must say I don't feel particularly qualified to handle." Box 117, folder 16, Swift Papers. Chapman quoted in *Chicago Evening American,* Nov. 17, 1938. Sports Editor Edward W. Cochrane of the *Chicago Evening American,* Nov. 14, 1938, issued the challenge to the alumni after the College of the Pacific humiliation and followed it with further advice on Nov. 18: "Chicago owes it to its students to fan into life the dying embers of that OLD FIGHTING SPIRIT." For other newspaper reports of agitation over the Pacific game, see: *Chicago Daily News,* Nov. 17, 1938, *Chicago Daily Times* and *Chicago Daily News,* Nov. 18, 1938, *Chicago Evening American,* Nov. 19, 1938.

41. Harold Swift's self-memorandum, Nov. 16, 1938, indicates he received protest calls from alumni and sports editors alike. Among them, Alumni Club officer Lawrence Whiting reported much opinion that Shaughnessy produce winning teams or leave. Box 117, folder 16, Swift Papers. Also in box 114, folder 8, Swift Papers: John William Chapman to 1938 Football Banquet Committee, Nov. 25, 1938, Dec. 13, 1938; 1938 Football Banquet Program; Russell to Swift, telegram, Dec. 7, 1938; John J. McDonough to H. Swift, Dec. 7, 1938; Swift to John W. Chapman, Dec. 15, 1938; Paul S. Russell to John W. Chapman, Dec. 7, 1938. Hutchins to Rob Roy MacGregor, March 24, 1939, Comments on Football folder, UPP, 1925–45.

42. Chapman to Nuveen, Dec. 12, 1939, Nuveen to Chapman, Dec. 13, 1939, Comments on Football folder, UPP, 1925–45. Stagg's former secretary at Chicago wrote him during the difficult season: "Everyone is up in arms and wants to subsidize and everything else." Helen Seymour to Stagg, Nov. 18, 1939, box 6, Stagg Papers. None of the former Maroon players could remember ever having heard of John Chapman. Oral interviews: Lewis B. Hamity, Nov. 13, 1992, Robert J. Greenebaum, Nov. 5, 1992, John Jay Berwanger, Nov. 7, 1992, James K. Goldsmith, Nov. 30, 1992, Saul S. Sherman, Jan. 21, 1993.

43. The players' teachers' concerns were expressed by Edward Shils, letter to author, May 27, Nov. 2, 1992; oral interviews: Norman Maclean, Oct. 20, 1970, James L. Cate, Oct. 10, 1969, Bernard Weinberg, Oct. 3, 1971. The alumni reactions were: Beatrice Richards to Hutchins, Oct. 23, 1939, Albert Wehling to Hutchins, Oct. 23, 1939, Comments on Football folder, UPP, 1925–45. William V. Morgenstern was the alumnus who ceased attending from fear, oral interview, Aug. 3, 1972. Francis Wallace, "Pigskin Preview of 1939," *Saturday Evening Post,* Sept. 23, 1939, 35. Cf. *Life* magazine's judgment on Nov. 27: "Worst big time football team this year is Chicago." *Time*'s appraisal (Nov. 6) was that the Big Ten Conference was the strongest football group in the country, and Chicago's "teams play like scrubs."

44. Paul S. Russell to George S. Lyman, Oct. 1, 1939; D. E. Challacombe to Hutchins, handwritten letter, no date, Comments on Football folder, UPP, 1925–45.

45. *Look,* Jan. 2, 1940, 42; cf. the *New Yorker*'s hope in its Nov. 12, 1938, issue that Chicago would continue to stand against the professional football programs (82).

46. Unsigned memorandum, "The Coaching Situation, November 8, 1939" (probably by Dean George A. Works as handwritten note orders), Athletics-General folder, "File-Works," UPP, 1925–45, and box 114, Swift Papers, lists alternatives under "Football Policy"; Hutchins to Swift, Oct. 13, 1939, Comments on Football folder, UPP, 1925–45. Dean Works informed Vice-president Emery T. Filbey (Nov. 16, 1939, box 9, folder 4, UPP, 1925–45) that Coach Shaughnessy had been offered numerous head coaching jobs since he came to Chicago in 1933, including Ohio State, Harvard, Wisconsin, and the University of Southern California. The November Works memorandum listed football experts—including Fielding Yost of Michigan, athletic director William J. Bingham of Harvard, and George Halas of the Chicago Bears—who felt that Shaughnessy was one of the finest coaches in the country. Shaughnessy's subsequent career after leaving Chicago for a five-year contract at Stanford, where he took that almost winless 1939 team to an undefeated 1940 season and victory in the Rose Bowl against Nebraska, indicated that the experts were correct. *Chicago Daily News*, Jan. 12, Oct. 30, 1940; Danzig, *History of American Football*, 78, 360–61. Cf. George Halas, with Gwen Morgan and Arthur Veysey, *Halas by Halas* (New York: McGraw-Hill, 1979), 136–45, 199–200, on Shaughnessy's worth.

47. *Chicago Daily News*, Jan. 25, 1940; Memorandum of Dean George A. Works and Athletic Director T. Nelson Metcalf to the Intercollegiate Conference, May 18, 1939, box 115, Swift Papers; *Chicago Tribune*, May 21, 1939. Hutchins's report to the trustees noted, regarding adequate players, that 309 of the 750 eligible undergraduate men were transfers; hence, they were eligible only for a year or two and not one of them transferred to Chicago in order to play football. The 441 "eligibles" constituted by far the smallest player reservoir; the next-lowest number of eligibles at a conference university was 1,800 men.

48. The *Daily Maroon*, Nov. 21, 1938; *Chicago Daily News, Chicago American*, Nov. 22, 1938; and *Chicago Herald and Examiner*, Nov. 22, 1938, carried the opinions of Shaughnessy, Works, and Metcalf. Hutchins's admission is in his "Notes on Football," presented to Trustee Committee on Instruction and Research, Nov. 8, 1939, in box 21, folder 4, UPP, Appointments and Budgets, 1925–40. The alternative of lessened competition was discussed by many, including Franklin Gowdy (football captain, 1924) to Swift, Nov. 5, 1939, who recommended football be continued with smaller schools for two years and if there was no improvement in the record, "We should drop football." John Davenport, 1939 football team captain, also favored this alternative. Mitchell Menachof to Hutchins, Nov. 3, 1939, invited Chicago to enter a new athletic conference "in the making" with Centre College, Michigan State, Toledo, Xavier, and Dayton, among others. Dean Works advised that "some of the institutions" mentioned "are fully as bad if not worse than the members of the Big Ten." Works to Hutchins, Nov. 17, 1939. All of the foregoing except Davenport in Comments on Football folder, UPP, 1925–45; Davenport to author, Nov. 14, 1992. The fourth alternative had been reported by John Nuveen to Hutchins, Nov. 15, 1939, box 10, Nuveen Papers.

49. "Notes on Football," Nov. 8, 1939, box 114, Swift Papers. Bell was a leading partner in a top Chicago law firm and a long-time trustee president at Carleton College. With regard to Laird Bell that autumn, Hutchins remembered that he was "always helpful." Letter to author, Sept. 5, 1973.

50. *Chicago Daily News,* Dec. 23, 1939. The *Rockford Star,* Dec. 23, 1939, also noted the alumni were proselyting; for the football dinner, see *Chicago Daily News,* Dec. 22, 1939. Chapman invited Swift to attend, Nov. 21, 1939, and Swift begged off, Nov. 24, 1939. This correspondence and the dinner program are in box 114, Swift Papers.

51. *Chicago Daily Times,* Feb. 14, 1940.

52. Nuveen to Swift, Dec. 13, 1939, copy to Hutchins, Comments on Football folder, UPP, 1925–45.

53. President Hutchins's memorandum recommending the abolition of football, Board of Trustees, Minutes, Dec. 21, 1939, and box 114, Swift Papers.

54. Ibid.

55. Ibid.

56. Ibid.; Swift to Luther W. Tatge, Jan. 23, 1940, box 114, Swift Papers. Swift also admitted that the trustees felt their action would cause "tremendous disturbance"; Swift to Fred H. Bartlit, Dec. 29, 1939, and Nuveen to B. H. Cleaver, Feb. 2, 1940, box 10, Nuveen Papers. Hutchins recalled that "Harold Swift voted against the resolution to abolish football, but as always, supported the decision of the majority." Letter to author, Sept. 5, 1973.

Epilogue

1. "University of Chicago Press Release, December 21, 1939," box 10, Nuveen Papers. The statement was written by William V. Morgenstern. William V. Morgenstern, oral interview, Aug. 3, 1972.

2. *Daily Maroon,* Jan. 3, 1940, 1–3; *University of Chicago Magazine* 32 (Jan. 1940): 24.

3. H. S. Floyd to Hutchins, Dec. 30, 1939, and J. Frank Lindsey to Hutchins, Jan. 12, 1940, box 10, Nuveen Papers.

4. *Chicago Daily News,* Feb. 5, 1940.

5. Boxes 114, 115, 116, Swift Papers; box 10, Nuveen Papers; Nuveen to B. H. Cleaver, Feb. 2, 1940, box 10, Nuveen Papers.

6. *Milwaukee Journal,* Jan. 15, 1940.

7. Rice's column in the *New Orleans Tribune,* Jan. 5, 1940; *Philadelphia Inquirer,* Dec. 23, 1939; Swift to Elwood G. Ratcliff, Jan. 24, 1940, in response to Ratcliff to Swift, Dec. 23, 1939, box 114, folder 11, Swift Papers. Among the newspapers approving the Chicago action: *Marietta Times,* Jan. 4, 1940, *Bogalusa News,* Jan. 5, 1940, *Asbury Park Evening Press,* Jan. 2, 1940, *Decatur* (Ill.) *Herald,* Jan. 3, 1940, and *Temple City* (Calif.) *Times,* Jan. 3, 1940. These and other local and regional newspaper comments are in box 114, folder 11, Swift Papers. If America's greater and lesser daily newspapers found the topic tempting and the university's action worthy of commendation, one little-known weekly published scant blocks from Stagg Field blasted the president and university. The *Hyde Park Herald*'s editorial asked pointedly on Dec. 29, "Did the

raucous epithets of the athletic fields at last disturb the supercilious peace of Dr. Hutchins' sanctum?" The neighborhood weekly termed the abolishment an "easy solution" that demonstrates "that it is better not to strive than to strive and lose. When applied to athletics, this attitude defines the intellectual snob." The local paper was no doubt economically dependent upon the 55th Street Business Men's Association, whose recruitment efforts were noted.

8. *Chicago Tribune*, Dec. 23, 1939.

9. Ibid. Colonel McCormick's need of President Hutchins in his isolationist campaign was noted by William T. Hutchinson, history department head at the time and biographer of Cyrus McCormick, oral interview, July 28, 1972, and collaborated by university public relations director William V. Morgenstern (whose brother was a *Tribune* executive), oral interview, Aug. 3, 1972.

10. *Chicago Tribune,* March 10, April 19, 22, 26, 27, May 19, 1940; *Chicago Herald-Examiner,* Dec. 22, 1939, April 22, 1940; *Chicago Daily News,* Dec. 22, 23, 1939, Feb. 23, April 27, 1940. Arch Ward named Hutchins as the anonymous source of the "crooked" statement and claimed it was made "at a cocktail party in the Blackstone Hotel." *Chicago Tribune,* March 12, 1940.

11. Joseph E. Raycroft to John Nuveen, Feb. 2, 1940, Nuveen to Raycroft, Feb. 19, 1940, box 10, Nuveen Papers.

12. Box 114 Swift Papers; box 10 Nuveen Papers; Swift to Homer Guck, Dec. 29, 1939, and Swift to Robert B. McKnight, Dec. 28, 1939, box 114, Swift Papers; Joseph L. Eaton to Swift, Dec. 24, 1939, box 10, Nuveen Papers.

13. William A. Comerford to Hutchins, Jan. 12, 1940, box 10, Nuveen Papers.

14. W. E. Gwatkin, Jr., to Hutchins, Jan. 15, 1940, Margery Rohan Parks to Nuveen, Jan. 17, 1940, Constance Weinberger Altshuler to Nuveen, Jan. 24, 1940, box 10, Nuveen Papers.

15. Nuveen to Walter L. Lingle, Feb. 2, 1940, and *Kansas City Star,* March 8, 1940, both citations in box 10, Nuveen Papers.

16. On Swift's misgivings over the abolishment see Swift to Luther W. Tatge, Jan. 23, 1940, discussed Hutchins, "It is true, in my opinion, that he cares less for what you and I got out of the University by way of activities, than we do.... I believe very definitely that Mr. Hutchins is so anxious to prove that it can be dispensed with improvement to our college that he will make serious effort along other athletic and activity lines to prove his point"; and Swift to Frank S. Whiting, Dec. 22, 1939, in which Swift writes the trustees' decision was "one more important experiment wherein we shall see what we shall see." Both in box 114, Swift Papers. Swift's disclaimers to the charges that the trustees were "railroaded" by Hutchins appear in Swift to Fred H. Bartlit, Dec. 28, 1939, box 10, Nuveen Papers, Swift to Henry F. Otto, Jr., Jan. 23, 1940, box 114, Swift Papers, and box 115, Swift Papers.

17. Nuveen to L. C. Wheeler, Jan. 24, 1940, a letter that has much Hutchins phraseology, box 10, Nuveen Papers.

18. Nuveen to Chapman, June 4, 1940, box 10, Nuveen Papers.

19. Dzuback, *Robert Maynard Hutchins,* 210; McNeill, *Hutchins' University,* 101; Hutchins to C. C. Williams, Nov. 29, 1941, Comments on Football folder, UPP,

1925–45; *University of Chicago Magazine* 34 (Oct. 1941): 13, and 34 (Nov. 1941): 1, 4–5, have enthusiastic reports of the Fiftieth Anniversary Drive; see John Tunis, *Survey Graphic* 30 (Oct. 1941): 504–5. For reports submitted during the campaign, some of which indicate the Alumni Foundation drive was poorly handled at the beginning, see box 10, Development Campaigns, 50th Anniversary. For a commendatory view of Hutchins as fund-raiser, see Ashmore, *Unseasonable Truths*, 200–204; for a view that Hutchins was not, on balance, a successful fund-raiser, see Dzuback, *Robert Maynard Hutchins*, 208–10; for a cautious view that "Hutchins may not have been satisfied by his success as a fundraiser," see McNeill, *Hutchins' University*, 101.

20. William T. Hutchinson, oral interview, July 28, 1972. The possibility of abolishment had been discussed regularly by faculty members at the Quadrangle Club, according to Hutchinson, and the "great majority" favored the decision. Hutchinson, honored at the time for excellence in undergraduate teaching, remembered little student unhappiness with the abrogation. William V. Morganstern, oral interview, Aug. 3, 1972, noted little student upheaval over the decision. In oral interviews James L. Cate (May 15, 1970), Norman Maclean (Oct. 20, 1970), and Bernard Weinberg (Oct. 3, 1972) recalled widespread but cautious support among faculty who worried about the financial impact on the institution. Box 114, folder 11, Swift Papers, provide the 1940 enrollment. Lloyd Lewis of the *Chicago Daily News*, Dec. 23, 1939, gave the consensus view of campus opinion. The player who wrote Hutchins his support was David M. Durkee, Jan. 15, 1940, box 10, Nuveen Papers. John Davenport, captain in 1939, was quoted by a reporter as critical of the action, newspaper clipping, unidentified, in Bill McGuire to Nuveen, Dec. 23, 1939, box 10, Nuveen Papers. Davenport later stated that "at no time have I regretted having been to our beloved school. . . . I was always proud that we were truly amateurs when even in those days there was lots of proselyting at the major schools." Davenport letter to author, Nov. 14, 1992. The *Daily Maroon*, Jan. 3, 1940, gave the results of Metcalf's poll of the players and admitted the decision took away one of the paper's "traditional issues."

21. In oral interviews James L. Cate (Oct. 10, 1969), William T. Hutchinson (Aug. 3, 1972), Edward W. Rosenheim (Nov. 4, 1992), and William V. Morgenstern (Aug. 3, 1972) all noted the small importance attached by Hutchins to student opinion over football or over anything else. Morgenstern, who prepared the draft for Hutchins's January speech, reminded Hutchins that although newspapers were claiming that the president had not addressed the students for four years, he had spoken at one student dinner during that period, Morgenstern to Hutchins, Jan. 5, 1940, box 30. Reports on the Hutchins's speech were carried in the *Chicago Daily Times, Chicago Daily News,* and *Chicago Tribune*, Jan. 13, 14, 1940. In oral interviews Saul S. Sherman (Jan. 21, 1993), Robert J. Greenebaum (Nov. 5, 1992), John Jay Berwanger (Nov. 7, 1992), Lewis B. Hamity (Nov. 13, 1992), and James K. Goldsmith (Nov. 30, 1992) noted the campus invisibility of Hutchins. Other students, who were selected to be in the Adler-Hutchins Great Books Seminar, saw him regularly; oral interviews, Jane Rinder Coulson and John Coulson, Jan. 7, 1993, Mark

Ashin, Nov. 23, 1992, Walter J. Blum, Dec. 18, 1992. The *Chicago Maroon,* Oct. 4, 1963, 10, carried the student quotation. Hutchins was asked to comment on the controversy over the institution of a football "class" in 1963, which had prompted the student to write of football and symbolism. Hutchins refused: "My mind is fixed on higher things." *Chicago Maroon,* Nov. 12, 1963, 12.

22. In 1955, the Council of the University Senate opposed the return of intercollegiate football when Chancellor Lawrence Kimpton inquired. The *Chicago Maroon* covered that story and the continuing drama in the issues of Oct. 22, Nov. 1, 5, 12, 1963. Dean Simpson's quote was in the Nov. 12 issue.

23. The Wick and Simpson quotations appeared in the *Chicago Maroon,* Feb. 21, 1964.

24. *Topeka State Journal,* clipping, no date, box 10, Nuveen Papers.

25. The advice of Notre Dame president Father John O'Hara appeared in *Chicago Daily Times,* Jan. 18, 1940.

26. On the erosion of Chicago's academic rank, see Ashmore, *Unseasonable Truths,* 77, and MacNeill, *Hutchins' University,* 43, 168–69.

27. McNeill, *Hutchins' University,* 97. After his undergraduate years at Chicago, McNeill completed his M.A. in history there and then did his doctoral work with Carl Becker at Cornell, returning to Chicago as an assistant professor in 1947 after war service. When McNeill turned to practical alternatives to the problem Hutchins faced in 1939, one wonders if the college editor of the 1930s may not have advised better than the distinguished professor of the 1990s on this issue. McNeill asserted that the university should have linked up with the Chicago Bears to form a "graduate football team for a graduate university." Never mind that the Bears and professional football constituted a pariah in proper collegiate circles then, or that intercollegiate football was and is an undergraduate enterprise, or that no group of proficient professional players would agree to enroll for the graduate school course load, much less emerge from such a muddled endeavor with sanity intact, McNeill concluded that the absence of such an arrangement "was a missed opportunity of monumental proportions" and, as such, "represents the greatest lost opportunity of Hutchins' regime." Ibid. Chicago Law Professor Walter J. Blum recalled the time when Chicago's South Side professional football team, the Cardinals, was undergoing some financial difficulties and he was authorized in the late 1940s to inquire of the team's owners if they would be interested in selling to the university. The idea was that Stagg Field was empty and that the purchase would be a prudent financial move; the professionals would continue as they were unencumbered with any academic relationship, purely business. Blum met with a Cardinal intermediary and quickly learned that the deal was deemed unwise on several counts, principally that Stagg Field and supporting athletic facilities would lose their tax-free status. In addition, some of the Cardinal players had gotten wind of the possible deal, and they had revolted. They were concerned that their play at Stagg Field (the site of the first self-sustaining atomic reaction in 1942) would lead to their sterility. Oral interview: Walter J. Blum, Dec. 18, 1992.

28. McNeill, *Hutchins' University,* 97, 98.

Index

O'Connell, Charles D., *272*
Office of Physical Education, 153
officials. *See* referees
Ofstie, Harold S., *262*
O'Hara, Father John, *284*
Ohio State University, 139, 172
Olander, Milt, 124
Olympic Games, 36, 101
Onwentsia Golf Club (Lake Forest), 54
open game, idea of, 103, 116
Order of the C, 46, 157, 159, 161, 166,
    175–76, 179
Oriard, Michael, *217–18, 226, 228*
Orlinsky, David E., *262*
Otto, Henry F., Jr., *282*

Pacific Alumni Club, 150
Pacific Athletic Revolving Loan Fund,
    150
Page, H. O. "Pat," 113, 147, *255, 267*
Palmer, Alice Freeman (Mrs. George),
    224
Palmer House, 67
Palmer Stadium (Princeton), 99
Palmquist, E. A. E., *278*
parity, between eastern and western
    teams, 117–19, 121
Park, Robert, 269n. 61
Park, Roberta, *243*
Parker, Alonzo K., 232n. 61, *235*
Parks, Margery Rohan, *282*
parochial schools, universities' relations
    with, 120–21
Parry, Edward, 247n. 69
Parsons, Keith I., 170, *266, 270, 273,*
    276n. 12
Paterson, Donald, *262*
Pattengill, Albert H., 42
Pattengill, Henry, 78
Patterson, Ellmore, *273*
Paul, David, 2
Paulison, Walter, *264*
Payne, Walter A., 113, *255*
Peabody, Endicott, 73
Pearson, Charles H., *233, 271*
Pegler, Westbrook, *239*
Perrin, Tom, *238*
Perry, Lawrence, *249, 259*
Petersen family, 275n. 12
Peterson, Emerick, *262*

Peterson, James, *234, 236*
Pfeffer, Nathaniel, *248*
Phi Beta Kappa, 170, 228n. 13
philanthropy, and football success, 33
Phillips-Exeter Academy, 8
Physical Culture and Athletics, Depart-
    ment of: autonomy of, 42, 105, 139;
    facilities for, 23; faculty of, 138–39;
    and financial aid for students, 89–90;
    football's origins in, 167; funding for,
    40; procedures of, 97–98; purpose of,
    17–18; reorganization of, 144, 153;
    reputation of, 17, 137, 142
physical education: and higher educa-
    tion, 17; as major, 137–38, 161–62,
    263–64nn. 29–30; rationale for, 6, 12;
    and recruitment of players, 20; and re-
    quirements, 17–18, 20, 37
Pinchot, Gifford, 11
Pinkerton detectives, 234n. 74
players: academic status of, 52, 89, 126,
    134, 155, 160–62, 171–72, 232n. 56;
    characteristics of, 22–24, 26–27, 46,
    140, 158, 226n. 38; coaches as, 22, 24;
    diet of, 53, 80, 89, 233n. 65, 244n. 44;
    financial aid for, 89–90, 108, 137, 162,
    174, 184–85, 190; health of, 139, 142–
    43; housing for, 53–54, 80, 89; majors
    for, 137–38, 161–62, 171, 263–64nn.
    29–30; payment for, 80–81, 178–79;
    recreation for, 54–55, 233n. 69; reten-
    tion of, 51–55, 137–40; rewards for,
    169; roles of, 46; scholarships for, 89–
    90, 108–9, 190; training of, 53–54, 80,
    157, 244n. 44. *See also* alumni; eligibil-
    ity; recruitment; uniforms
plays: forward pass, 77, 102–4, 116; in-
    novations in, 102, 122, 251n. 31; mass
    momentum, 73; Notre Dame shift,
    103; open game idea, 103, 116; shift
    formations, 102–3; T formation, 155,
    157, 276n. 12
Plimpton, Nathan, *253*
politics, and ticket scalping, 67–68
Pollock, James A., *267*
Pope, Edwin, *246*
Porter, Noah, 8
Powers, Francis J., *236, 259*
Preliminary Statement (Harper), 84
Presbyterianism, 2, 7, 11, 151

Books in the Series Sport and Society

A Sporting Time: New York City and the Rise of Modern
Athletics, 1820-70
Melvin L. Adelman

Sandlot Seasons: Sport in Black Pittsburgh
Rob Ruck

West Ham United: The Making of a Football Club
Charles Korr

Beyond the Ring: The Role of Boxing in American Society
Jeffrey T. Sammons

John L. Sullivan and His America
Michael T. Isenberg

Television and National Sport: The United States and Brit-
ain
Joan M. Chandler

The Creation of American Team Sports: Baseball and
Cricket, 1838-72
George B. Kirsch

City Games: The Evolution of American Urban Society
and the Rise of Sports
Steven A. Riess

The Brawn Drain: Foreign Student-Athletes in American
Universities
John Bale

The Business of Professional Sports
Edited by Paul D. Staudohar and James A. Mangan

Fritz Pollard: Pioneer in Racial Advancement
John M. Carroll

Go Big Red! The Story of a Nebraska Football Player
George Mills

Sport and Exercise Science: Essays in the History of Sports
Medicine
Edited by Jack W. Berryman and Roberta J. Park

Minor League Baseball and Local Economic Development
Arthur T. Johnson

Harry Hooper: An American Baseball Life
Paul J. Zingg

Cowgirls of the Rodeo: Pioneer Professional Athletes
Mary Lou LeCompte

Sandow the Magnificent: Eugen Sandow and the Beginnings of Bodybuilding
David Chapman

Big-Time Football at Harvard, 1905: The Diary of Coach
Bill Reid
Ronald A. Smith

Leftist Theories of Sport: A Critique and Reconstruction
William J. Morgan

The Babe: The Life and Legend of Babe Didrikson Zaharias
Susan E. Cayleff

Stagg's University: The Rise, Decline, and Fall of Big-Time
Football at Chicago
Robin Lester

REPRINT EDITIONS

The Nazi Olympics
Richard D. Mandell

Sports in the Western World
Second Edition
William J. Baker